The Palestinian National Movement in Lebanon

SOAS Palestine Studies

This book series aims at promoting innovative research in the study of Palestine, Palestinians, and the Israel-Palestine conflict as a crucial component of Middle Eastern and world politics. The first-ever Western academic series entirely dedicated to this topic, *SOAS Palestine Studies* draws from a variety of disciplinary fields, including history, politics, media, visual arts, social anthropology, and development studies. The series is published under the academic direction of the Centre for Palestine Studies (CPS) at the London Middle East Institute (LMEI) of SOAS, University of London.

Series Editor:
Dina Matar, PhD, Chair, Centre for Palestine Studies, and Reader in Political Communication, Centre for Global Media and Communications, SOAS
Adam Hanieh, PhD, Reader in Development Studies and Advisory Committee Member for Centre for Palestine Studies, SOAS
Board Advisor:
Hassan Hakimian, Director of the London Middle East Institute at SOAS

Current and Forthcoming Titles:

Palestine Ltd.: Neoliberalism and Nationalism in the Occupied Territory, Toufic Haddad

Palestinian Literature in Exile: Gender, Aesthetics and Resistance in the Short Story, Joseph R. Farag

Palestinian Citizens of Israel: Power, Resistance and the Struggle for Space, Sharri Plonski

Representing Palestine Media and Journalism in Australia since World War I, Peter Manning

Folktales of Palestine: Cultural Identity, Memory and the Politics of Storytelling, Farah Aboubakr

Dialogue in Palestine: The People-to-People Diplomacy Programme and the Israeli-Palestinian Conflict, Nadia Naser-Najjab

Palestinian Youth Activism in the Internet Age: Social Media and Networks after the Arab Spring, Albana Dwonch

The Palestinian National Movement in Lebanon: A Political History of the 'Ayn al-Hilwe Camp, Erling Lorentzen Sogge

The Palestinian National Movement in Lebanon

A Political History of the ʿAyn al-Hilwe Camp

Erling Lorentzen Sogge

I.B.TAURIS
LONDON • NEW YORK • OXFORD • NEW DELHI • SYDNEY

I.B. Tauris
Bloomsbury Publishing Plc
50 Bedford Square, London, WC1B 3DP, UK
1385 Broadway, New York, NY 10018, USA
29 Earlsfort Terrace, Dublin 2, Ireland

BLOOMSBURY, I.B. TAURIS and the I.B. Tauris logo
are trademarks of Bloomsbury Publishing Plc

First published in Great Britain 2021
This paperback edition published 2023

Cover design: Adriana Brioso
Cover image: Palestinian refugee camp, Ein El-Hilweh, in Lebanon. (© In Pictures
Ltd./Corbis via Getty Images)

A catalogue record for this book is available from the British Library.

A catalog record for this book is available from the Library of Congress.

ISBN: HB: 978-0-7556-0283-4
PB: 978-0-7556-4234-2
ePDF: 978-0-7556-0284-1
eBook: 978-0-7556-0285-8

Series: SOAS Palestine Studies

Typeset by Integra Software Services Pvt. Ltd.

To find out more about our authors and books visit www.bloomsbury.com
and sign up for our newsletters.

To Viljar, Laura and Hammude.

Contents

List of Illustrations

Maps

Figures

Acknowledgments

Throughout the work with this book, I have been privileged to learn from the best of mentors and colleagues. I would like to begin by thanking Brynjar Lia, Professor in Middle East studies at the University of Oslo (UiO), for taking me under his wing as a PhD candidate and for his guidance, enthusiasm, patience, and unrelenting support in every capacity imaginable. Likewise, I would like to thank my second advisor Dag Tuastad, Associate Professor in Middle East studies at UiO, for sharing his expertise and competence in the topic, and for always making himself available. I would also like to extend special gratitude to my examiners Julie Peteet and Rex Brynen for offering invaluable comments and advice along the way.

Thanks to everyone at the Department of Culture Studies and Oriental Languages (IKOS) at UiO for being fantastic colleagues. I am incredibly grateful to both IKOS and the Faculty of Humanities for funding my work and for believing in my project, and I would like to thank head of department Bjørn Olav Utvik for his continuous support and encouragements. I am greatly indebted to Einar Wigen, Berit Thorbjørnsrud, Jon Nordenson, Jacob Høigilt, Jørgen Jensehaugen, and Kari Anderson for offering extensive moral support and practical advice throughout the years.

I am very honored to extend my gratitude to Professor Hilal Khashan for hosting me as a guest researcher at the Department of Political Studies and Public Administration at the American University of Beirut for nearly a year and for introducing me to his wonderful staff and colleagues.

I would like to express my deepest appreciation to Martin Yttervik and his team of colleagues for offering to assist me on a number of occasions. I am eternally indebted to activist and researcher Manal Kortam for her help in facilitating my fieldwork, for her endless support and genuine interest in my project from an early stage. I am still not sure why she offered to assist me when I, as a virtual stranger, came asking for help an evening in Beirut in the fall of 2013, but I am certainly happy that she did. I hope she will take this book as a testament to my gratitude for all she has done. The same could be said for Dr. Qassem El Saad and Yasser Dawoud, without whose support I would likely not have been able to conduct my fieldwork in ʿAyn al-Hilwe. I hope having me around was not too much of a burden, knowing that the work you do is infinitely more important than mine. Furthermore, I would like to thank Hachem Hachem and ʿAli Salam for their support in the field. This also extends to Zaliha, Iyad, Tareq, Nader, Souad, and Hibba.

I am forever grateful to Nidal Hamad for taking me on my first trip to ʿAyn al-Hilwe and who, as an experienced and well-revered author in Lebanon, has inspired me to do my best. Whether we will meet at "ʿAbd al-Sultan" or "Carmel," the next round of coffee is on me. Many thanks to my good friend Nizar Laz for providing invaluable comments and advice throughout the years. I would like to extend my sincere gratitude to Zafer Khateeb and his team for their kind assistance and sharing their expertise and knowledge with me. Thanks to every friend and stranger who took the time to sit down with me and share their experiences, whether the streets of the camps were filling up with water during the winter months or the sun was burning during summer. Every meeting has been a truly humbling experience, and I am committed to relaying your stories as accurately as I am capable of.

I am greatly indebted to the Institute for Palestine Studies in Beirut for granting me access to its archives. I would also like to thank Ahmad Salman and the staff at the *Safir* newspaper for letting me rummage through their archives on more than one occasion. Apologies for filling your desks and floors with hundreds of scattered photocopies!

Many thanks to the talented architect (and graphic designer) Bjørnar Skaar Haveland for creating the maps in this book. Thanks to Bjørnar, Magnus Dølerud, Maja Janmyr, ʿAli Salman, and Ole Denstad for every moment shared in Beirut and elsewhere. Thanks to Marwan, Abu Khalid, and Abu ʿAli for always greeting me with a smile in the Shatila camp. My kindest regards goes out to the Hassan family for their hospitality, kindness, and accepting me as a guest in their home even though they were going through one of the most troubled periods of their lives. I hope you are doing well back in Damascus.

Thanks to everyone who took the time to read my material and provide me with invaluable advice on how to improve it. It is my pleasant duty to thank Tine Gade, Ismael Sheikh Hassan, and Kjersti Berg for lending their expertise and for selflessly sharing their material with me. My warm gratitude goes out to Professor Bernard Rougier who commented on a very early draft of one of the chapters of this study. I hope he will appreciate the book, although we differ in our conclusions regarding the Islamist movements in the Palestinian camps. Huge thanks go out to comrades Mathilde Becker Aarseth, Charlotte Lysa, Erik Skare, Olav Gjersten Ørum, and Laila Makboul for their feedback on various chapters and for their company. Thanks to Are Knudsen and Marie Kortam for every inspiring conversation over the years. I owe special gratitude to Sophie Rudland, Yasmin Garcha, and the editors of this book, for their kind assistance and for believing in my work.

Thanks to mom and dad for their enduring support. Above all, I would like to thank the one and only Veslemøy Oma and the treasure of my life, my son Viljar, for their kindness, patience, and, not the least, for reminding me to get a grip once in a while.

Note on Transliteration

In the course of this study, the reader will be introduced to many Arabic names and phrases. When spelling these, I follow a set of principles loosely based on the transliteration guidelines provided by the *International Journal of Middle East Studies (IJMES)*. They are as following:

1. In the main text, personal names, names of organizations, groups, movements, political parties, and newspapers are spelled without diacritics. The letters ʿAyn (ʿ) and Hamza (ʾ) are always spelled out, with the exception of the initial Hamza (Hamzat al-Wasl).
2. In the endnotes and the bibliography, names of all Arabic-language publications are spelled in full transliteration with diacritics for the benefit of experts and Arabic-speakers.
3. Arabic words or names that have been absorbed into the English language are written according to their established spelling. For example, I write "Yasser Arafat" instead of "Yasir ʿArafat." Names of living people may vary according to their preferred English spelling. Otherwise, point 1 applies.

Some groups, movements, and organizations have established names in the English language. In these cases, I use these rather than their original Arabic name. For example, I write the Palestine Liberation Organization rather than *Munazzamat al-Tahrir al-Filastiniyya*. When the Arabic version of a group's name is more known than the English translation, however, I use the former. For example, *ʿUsbat al-Ansar* (League of Partisans).

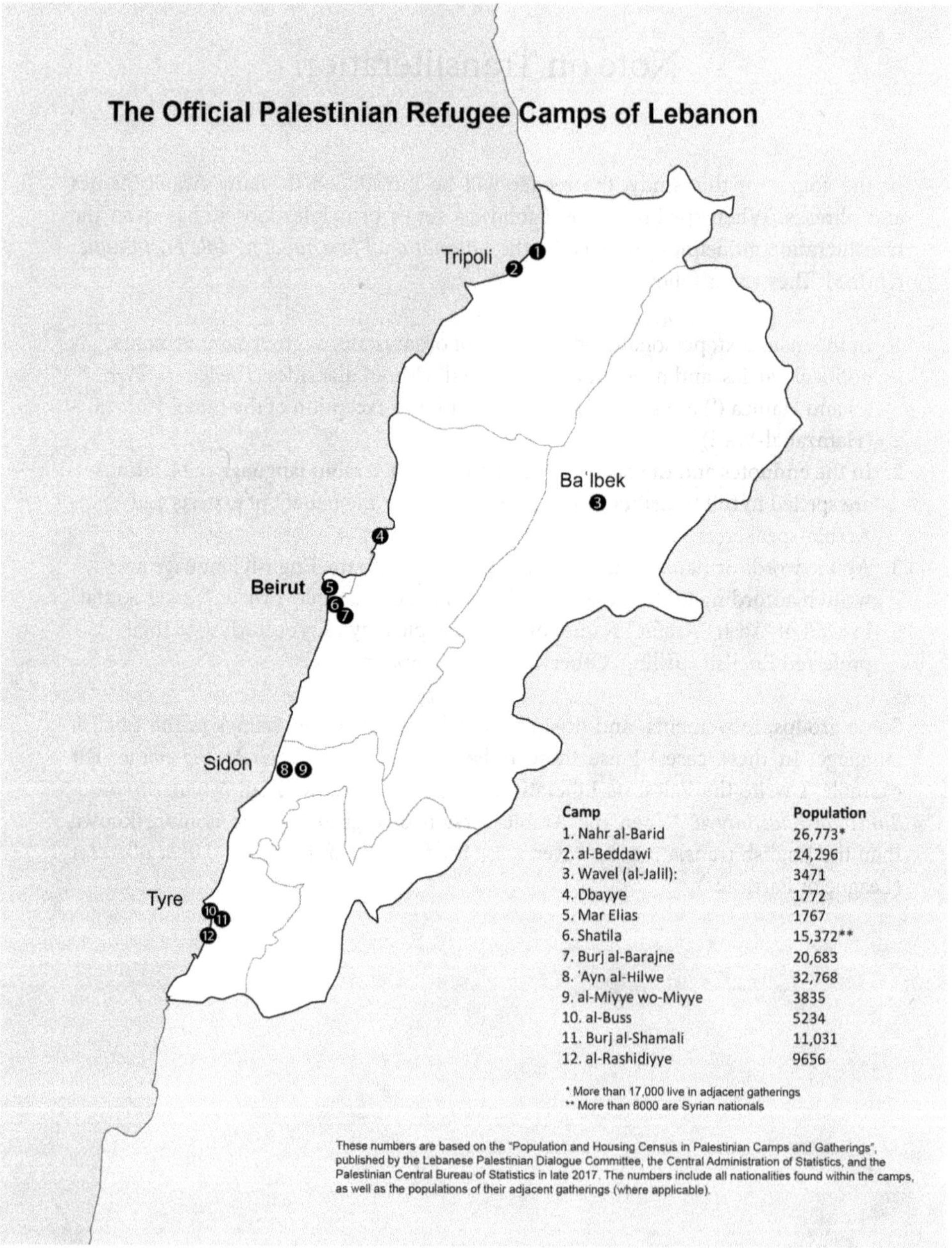

Map 1 The Official Palestinian Refugee Camps of Lebanon. Created for this book by architect Bjørnar Skaar Haveland.

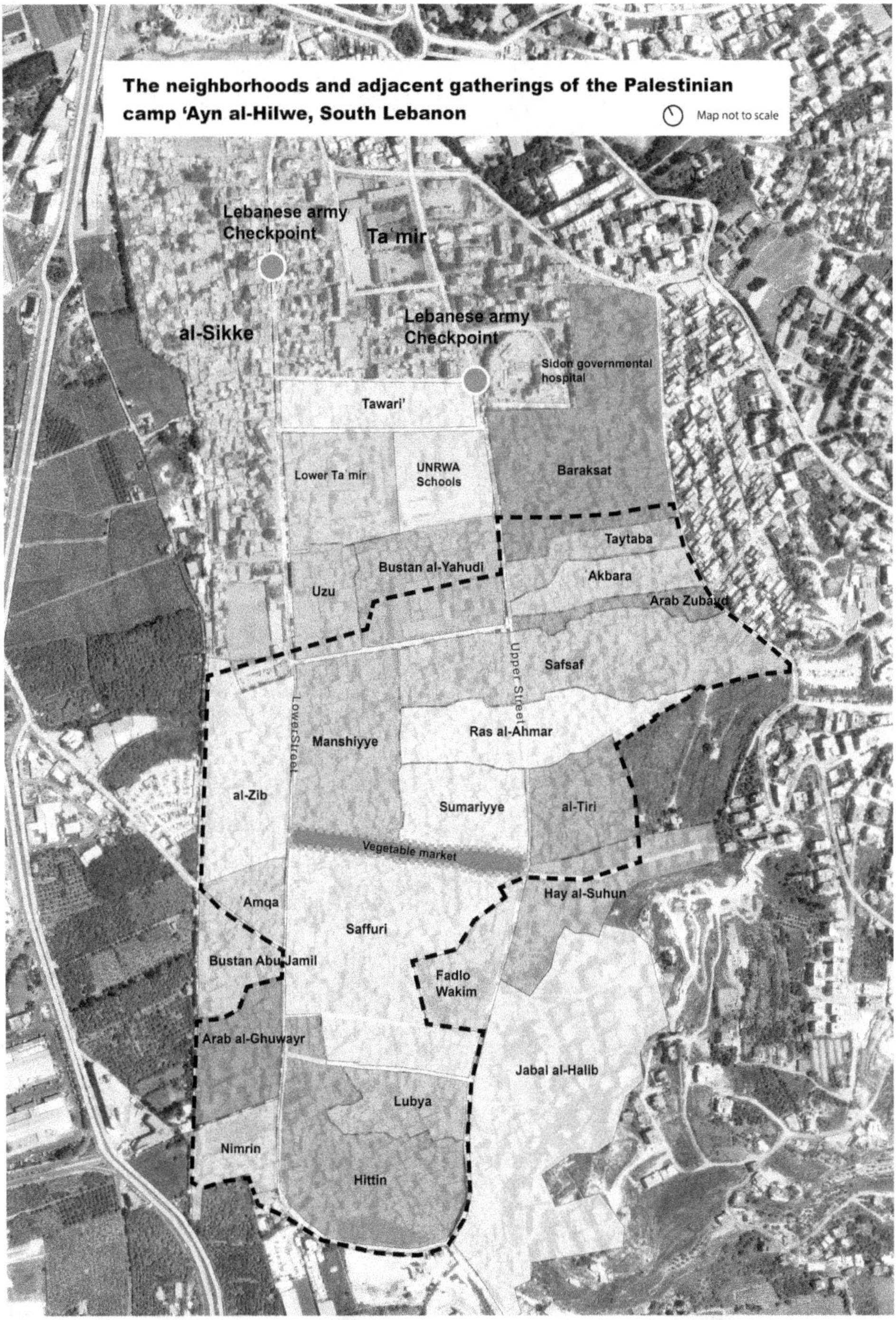

Map 2 A suggested map of the neighborhoods of 'Ayn al-Hilwe and its adjacent gatherings. Based on two maps issued by UNRWA (1997 and 2015), and testimonies of locals. The striped line depicts the "official borders" of the camp, as UNRWA define them. Created for this book by Skaar Haveland in cooperation with the author.

1

ʿAyn al-Hilwe and the National Movement

In May 2014, the media reported that the Fatah movement was in the process of conducting a large-scale military exercise in Lebanon's southernmost Palestinian refugee camp, al-Rashidiyye.[1] Head of the PLO's National Security Forces in Lebanon, Subhi Abu ʿArab, informed the press that the drills were the first of their kind since 1991 and came as a part of a larger effort the organization was undertaking to bolster its presence in the country's Palestinian camps.[2] To assist him, Palestinian officers with military training from universities in Russia, Germany, and Pakistan flew in from Ramallah to oversee the process. While the new recruits, 150 in total, would be stationed in the Beirut area and the Biqaʿ Valley, the lion's share were to participate in a joint police effort in the country's most populous and notoriously turbulent camp, ʿAyn al-Hilwe.

The events took place at a critical point in time. Recurring clashes between Fatah's armed forces and Islamist militants had caused widespread fears among inhabitants that ʿAyn al-Hilwe would implode into violence and be dragged into a war against the Lebanese army—a scenario all too familiar for Palestinians in Lebanon. In 2007, the Nahr al-Barid camp near the northern city Tripoli was completely destroyed in a battle pitting the military against a jihadi group that had infiltrated the place coming from Syria. More recently, the devastating war that had laid waste to al-Yarmouk—the once-vibrant Palestinian majority district of the Syrian capital—had been a harsh reminder of how vulnerable the refugees were in the face of regional turmoil and how easily their political leaderships seemed to become entangled in the domestic conflicts of their host nations. In Lebanon, these events and others had rekindled contentious debates regarding a long-standing arrangement of Palestinian self-rule in the country's refugee camps. Maybe the time had come, as the Ministry of Interior suggested, for the Lebanese army to reclaim these spaces and disarm the Palestinian militia groups within them.

After much deliberation, this plan was scrapped in favor of another. In the spring of 2014, Palestinian and Lebanese stakeholders announced that they had agreed on the formation of a *Joint Palestinian Security Force* in ʿAyn al-Hilwe.[3] Gathering factions across political blocs, the aim was to build an internal military police consisting of militia groups that had otherwise spent decades competing for the control over various streets, neighborhoods, and checkpoints within the refugee camp. Now, a wide selection of ʿAyn al-Hilwe's political movements, ranging from Marxist-Leninist militias to Islamist militants, would patrol the streets together, with the hope of filling the prevailing vacuum of authority, all the while defining an established security provider for the Lebanese state with which to coordinate.

At the time, I was meeting an array of Palestinian leaders in conjunction with a research project, and would frequently hear mention of these new arrangements. As an outsider, there were many things I struggled to understand, such as why political groups that owe their very existence to the national struggle for Palestine were spending substantial resources to safeguard an impoverished refugee camp miles away from the homeland. This especially decades after their armed campaigns across the Lebanese border toward Israel had come to a halt, and the center of national politics having shifted from the countries of exile to the Palestinian Territories with the signing of the 1993 Oslo peace accords. What was so important about ʿAyn al-Hilwe? My interlocutors, on the other hand, scoffed at these questions, deeming them naïve. For them, the situation was painstakingly obvious. When their new police force deployed in the camp known among inhabitants as the *Capital of the Diaspora*[4] (ʿAsimat al-Shattat) the following summer, what was at stake was nothing less than the survival of what many regarded as the last bastion of Palestinian self-determination outside of the homeland. It was a matter of existence for the national movement in exile.

The Palestinian refugee camps in Lebanon have been widely studied and are continuously subject to academic inquiry. Yet, there are many aspects of their internal lives that remain poorly understood. That particularly pertains to the activities of the Palestinian political factions, many of whom cut their teeth in Lebanon during past days of armed struggle and retain a significant presence here. In the current period, however, little attention has been paid to their organizations, their internal dynamics, their goals, and their relationships with the camp populations they govern, Palestinian leaderships elsewhere, or other regional patrons. This book, in turn, provides an ethnographically rich study of political life in ʿAyn al-Hilwe and other refugee camps in Lebanon, as it has evolved since the early 1990s until the present day, where I seek answers to the following questions:

1. *How should we understand the political struggles fought in ʿAyn al-Hilwe in the post-Oslo era?*
2. *Which actors seek to control the camp? How do they do it, and for what reasons?*
3. *What role do the Palestinian faction leaderships in Lebanon currently play in the politics of the region, if any?*

Ultimately, I seek to understand why a poverty-stricken camp in the margins of society remains so contested by so many actors in the present. In order to find an answer to these questions, we need to start from the beginning.

The Capital of the Diaspora

Found on the outskirts of the southern coastal city of Sidon, and hosting some 33,000 inhabitants on an area not exceeding one square kilometer, ʿAyn al-Hilwe is the most populous of twelve official refugee camps in Lebanon.[5] Although the camp has over the years come to host a number of other Arab and non-Arab nationalities, the vast majority of its inhabitants hail from villages of the Galilee region of historical Palestine that were destroyed and occupied by Jewish paramilitary groups in 1947–8. The violence that bereft the Palestinians of their lands and which ended in the creation of the state of Israel signifies, in the words of anthropologist Julie Peteet, a rapture in both time and space.[6] The *nakba*, meaning the calamity or catastrophe, marks a fundamental before and after in Palestinian history. It condemned the over 700,000 who fled and abandoned their homes to a future of dispossession and a life in exile (*ghurba*), while "violently crafted and maintained borders" became a defining feature of the lives for those unable to return.[7] Over seventy years later, the Palestinian camps, found in Lebanon, Syria, Jordan, and in the Palestinian Territories, are indicative of the unresolvedness of the refugee question and the failure of the international society to provide any lasting solutions for the refugees. The word "camp," just like its Arabic equivalent *mukhayyam* (derived from *khayma*, or tent), alludes to a preliminary measure. It describes something that will be removed or taken down when the crisis is over. In Lebanon, the makeshift tent villages that were originally set up by the Red Cross in the months to follow the *nakba* have over the years been replaced by urban landscapes embodying an aura of permanence. Renowned for its long winding shopping streets and its lush vegetable market that daily draws customers from outside, ʿAyn al-Hilwe has become a part of Sidon's urban fabric. At the same time, there are both physical and social barriers that clearly demarcate the camp from its urban surroundings.

The concrete walls which in part run along its ledges, and its heavily guarded entrances, where Lebanese soldiers routinely check the papers of those leaving or entering, are telling of the Palestinians' place, or rather lack thereof, in the Lebanese republic. In a country where political power is distributed based on the assumed proportion of eighteen ethno-religious groups, otherwise known as sects, the Palestinian refugees have often been accused of constituting a threat to the sectarian power-sharing system that has defined the modern state of Lebanon since its formation in 1943. When at least 100,000 Palestinians fled across the Lebanese border a few years later, fears were that the refugees would alter the demographic make-up of the state and tip the balance in favor of the Muslims, who at the time were demanding greater political representation. To date, we find across the Lebanese political spectrum, albeit most explicitly expressed among the Christian right parties, an axiomatic aversion to granting the Palestinians basic civil rights. The aversion is based on the perception that such a process would be the first step into a slippery slope resulting in collective naturalization (tawtin), which the constitution clearly forbids.[8] Whereas a high number of Christian Palestinians were able to obtain citizenships in the first few decades to follow the *nakba*, this is an option no longer available to Lebanon's current population of roughly 200,000 Palestinian refugees, who after nearly four generations in exile enjoy fewer rights than most visiting tourists do.[9] Because they are legally treated like stateless foreigners, the Palestinians cannot naturalize, are prevented from owning or inheriting property, and are locked out of at least thirty-six syndicated professions.[10] Obtaining work permits remains an arduous task, and those who do not work for an NGO or a foreign company typically have to settle for a life of day labor or unemployment. Under these circumstances, it is perhaps not surprising that most of Lebanon's Palestinians find themselves living inside of the overpopulated and impoverished urban slums that constitute the refugee camps (or nearby gatherings) where many rely on the ever-declining services provided by the UN Work and Relief Agency for Palestinians in the Near East (UNRWA).

As refugees are caught up in the day-to-day struggles of surviving in hostile surroundings, it is perhaps easy to assume that their circumstances are hardly conducive to political activity. That is not always the case. In ʿAyn al-Hilwe, we find a complex patchwork of faction headquarters, offices of political parties, armed groups, and para-military forces that are telling of the degrees of political and territorial autonomy that the Palestinian refugees in Lebanon, despite everything, continue to enjoy. Understanding this paradoxical duality of dispossession and rightlessness, on the one hand, and political agency, on the other, lies at the core of this study.

The Politics of Exile

To date, no Lebanese state institutions exist within ʿAyn al-Hilwe, and members of the army or the Internal Security Forces refrain from entering, unless in agreement with the Palestinian leaderships. This arrangement of Palestinian self-governance in the camps dates back to the late 1960s.

Unlike its neighboring states, Lebanon lacked the internal cohesion to control the burgeoning Palestinian guerilla groups that gained enormous popularity following the 1967 six-day war against Israel. Rocked by domestic strife and subject to frequent Israeli punitive attacks, the Lebanese government sought to solve a brewing crisis by formally granting the Palestine Liberation Organization (PLO) the freedom to commence its "Palestinian revolution" from Lebanese soil, as long as it did not challenge the sovereignty of the state.[11] At a time when the Israeli occupation made political life impossible in the Palestinian Territories, the 1969 Cairo Agreement—to be discussed in greater detail in the next chapter—offered the PLO, its leader Yasser Arafat, and the camp populations at large an autonomy unparalleled by any other state.

Scholars have argued that this situation of self-rule allowed the refugees to construct a new self-image for themselves, where they went from being "peasants to revolutionaries,"[12] from *fellahin* (farmers) to *fidaʾiyyin* (guerillas),[13] and from "pawns to political actors."[14] Out of the plentiful scholarly accounts of the PLO's days of revolution in Lebanon (1969–82), the works of Yezid Sayigh and Rex Brynen are of particular relevance, as they explore the transformative effect that the armed struggle had on the Palestinian national movement.[15] Armed struggle became a "political arena," Sayigh argues, as it provided channels through which mass participation in national politics could take place, serving as "the most effective means of mobilizing the scattered diaspora."[16] Moreover, the Cairo Accords allowed the PLO to pursue its ambitions of asserting itself as a state power intending to take charge of the homeland. The refugee camps soon witnessed the rapid formation of elaborate state-like institutions, ranging from schools and clinics to political administrations and paramilitary forces. While the Popular Committees (al-Lijan al-Shaʿbiyya) would mediate between the camp populations, the guerilla leaders, and Lebanese authorities, the Armed Struggle Command (Qiyadat al-Kifah al-Musallah) took the role as the camps' military police. By the mid-1970s, the camps were no longer impoverished urban slums but resembled Palestinian states in the waiting.

Although the PLO aimed to mobilize a broad Arab front to join its armed campaigns against Israel, its militant activities in Lebanon were instead a catalyst for the outbreak of a fifteen-year-long civil war (1975–90),[17] where an increasingly complex host of armed actors, including Lebanese militias and Syrian military forces, turned their weapons against the organization. The final blow came in the summer of 1982, when Israel invaded the country and forced the PLO to capitulate and abandon Lebanon through the ports of Beirut. Whereas the organization's leadership relocated to Tunis, Palestinian guerillas immediately began slipping back into the refugee camps, and Yasser Arafat did everything he could to rebuild his organization in Lebanon throughout the mid-1980s. These efforts, however, were made irrelevant by what was taking place in the Palestinian Territories. In December 1987, collective frustrations with the Israeli occupation erupted in the popular mass revolt we know as the First Intifada. With the birth of the Hamas movement in the Gaza Strip, and the emergence of a new generation of Fatah leaders to take charge of the national movement in the Territories, the uprising set in motion a chain of events that ultimately paved the way for direct peace negotiations between Israel and the PLO.

The Post-Oslo Landscape

The Oslo peace accords, signed on the White House lawn in Washington in September 1993 by Israeli Prime Minister Yitzhak Rabin and Yasser Arafat, marked the preliminary end of armed struggle for the PLO. It allowed the organization's leadership to return from Tunisia and lay the groundwork for the creation of a quasi-state power known as the Palestinian National Authority (PA). The PLO became subsumed into this new authority, effectively subordinating its liberation agenda to the PA's government responsibilities, which included coordinating security measures with Israel. Meanwhile, the leading faction within the PLO, Fatah, embarked on the difficult transition from guerilla movement to a state-supporting political party. Few events in the history of the Palestinian national movement have been as divisive as the Oslo accords. Critics condemned the asymmetric nature of the agreement, in which the most prominent Palestinian leader had vowed to recognize the state of Israel without receiving in exchange a mutual recognition, let alone any guarantee of Palestinian self-determination. Bogged down by the realities of the Israeli occupation and fraught with internal strife, the PA not only lacked geographical contiguity, territorial sovereignty, or economic autonomy, but internal bickering of whether or not to draft a constitution before full emancipation could be realized left the Palestinians without a functioning legal order (at least until the present-day *Basic Law* was introduced in 2002). With little opportunity to usher into an independent Palestinian nation, the PA instead emerged as a one-man system and a textbook example of what scholars have called *neopatrimonial rule.*[18]

The concept draws on Max Weber's theories of *patrimonial authority*, which the German sociologist developed in his seminal writings on early European state formation. In short, patrimonial administrations featured no distinction between private and public good but were built around the personal power of the ruler, who would exchange services and benefits for political loyalty.[19] The concept of *neopatrimonialism*, on the other hand, belongs to the discussion of modern statehood and has often been associated with the study of postcolonial administrations, whose leaders introduce patrimonial methods of power to manage political schisms and mitigate growing crises that arise in the post-independence period.[20] Neopatrimonial systems feature the emblems and exteriors of independent and democratically organized administrations, such as elections, legal systems, and parliaments. Yet personal ties to the center of power continue to determine the degree of influence that a political actor holds, because the ostensibly neutral state apparatus in reality finds itself monopolized by a ruling elite.[21] Typically, offices, ministries, and public jobs will be doled out with the aim of creating or maintaining informal networks of loyalty and dependency, while public resources are captured and used for private rent-seeking. Although neopatrimonial administrations come in many different forms and shapes, from decentralized orders with many competing centers of power (Lebanon, Iraq) to one-party states (pre-war Syria), they invariably feature bloated bureaucracies of public servants and other intermediaries, whose main function is to maintain the flow of patronage between the ruler and the ruled. Ultimately, neopatrimonial elites do not offer their people a well-functioning or accessible political system. Rather, they entrench their rule and build coalitions through the tactical distribution of scarce resources among their clients.[22]

That is not to say that those presiding at the top of such hierarchies are not troubled by political competition. As noted earlier, the incentive to resort to neopatrimonial leadership is often a response against political fragmentation. As the head of the PLO, Yasser Arafat came to rely on patronage to build consensus and retain cohesion within a geographically dispersed organization characterized by a myriad of competing leaderships each pursuing their own agendas. This involved basing his rule on a type of "bureaucratic chaos and tactical maneuvering," Menachem Klein writes, which only intensified with his election as the head of the would-be Palestinian state.[23] In office, Arafat would disrupt the communication between PA branches, constantly duplicate and disperse authorities, and promote a sense of competition between his subordinates, be they ministers or security branches.[24] Meanwhile, he silenced critics by integrating them into government positions or by marginalizing them from the political scene completely.[25] This tendency became clear in the first Palestinian general elections in 1996, Amal Jamal notes, whereafter Arafat immediately dropped a number of young and critically minded electees, and replaced them with older loyalists with less popular support[26]—a process which would inevitably set the "young guard" of the Fatah movement on collision course with its aging leadership.[27] It is no coincidence that the political culture fostered by the PLO/PA also has been referred to as *neopatriarchal*, which is similar to the concept of neopatrimonialism, but places extra emphasis on the leadership's tendency to exclude the younger generations from power, along with the bid to impose its control over familial institutions as a part of the political economy.[28]

Notably, research on Palestinian politics has following the Oslo process gradually gone from being a study of a diasporic mass movement to one of bureaucracies, governments, and elites vying to maintain political control in geographically defined areas. This is particularly true for the PLO's current rule in the West Bank,[29] but is increasingly also the case with Hamas, which following its 2007 takeover of the Gaza strip has emerged as a proto-state in its own right, faced with maintaining internal security, paying salaries, and cracking down on dissent.[30] It should be mentioned that the Palestinian leaderships do by no means represent an anomaly in the context of the Middle East, seeing as neopatrimonial rule is understood to be a dominant feature among many of the political administrations of the region.[31] This also extends to the internal administrations of the Palestinian refugee camps in Lebanon, which I will argue remain deeply enmeshed in the volatile political economies of competing Palestinian leaderships, as well as that of their host state. Yet this notion is perhaps not as intuitive as it sounds. As the study of Palestinian politics has increasingly become focused on the West Bank and the Gaza Strip, the refugee camps of the countries of exile have instead found themselves subsumed by scholarly debates far removed from the realm of the national movement.

Island of Insecurity or Mirocosm of Palestinian Politics?

Unlike the body of research dealing with the PLO's early period in Lebanon, current studies of the Palestinian camps have devoted significantly less space to concepts such as national ambitions and political strategy. As I will elaborate later, scholars inspired by the seminal works of Italian philosopher Giorgio Agamben have tended to view the present-day camps through the prism of exception and emergency, where all ordinary life is suspended and human agency is made impossible, due to the totalitarian policies implemented by the state and humanitarian relief organizations. Others have concluded that the camps plunged into a state of chaos after the 1982 Israeli invasion, allowing them, eventually, to become breeding grounds for international terrorists. In particular, research on 'Ayn al-Hilwe has been permeated by discussions of violence and radical Islamism. On this note, the surge of Salafism among Palestinians in Lebanon in the mid-1990s, the most anti-nationalist strain of political Islam, has largely been equated with the death knell of the Palestinian national project in exile.

Security concerns and the increasingly complex bureaucratic process it takes to obtain the Lebanese army's permission to enter a camp like 'Ayn al-Hilwe are perhaps among the factors that have discouraged larger scholarly studies of the place in recent years. As follows, we are left with the impression that the Palestinian camps of Lebanon have lost their historical role, becoming instead "ungovernable zones of poverty and delinquency," disconnected from Palestine and cut off from "Middle East political history."[32] What, then, does this exploration of 'Ayn al-Hilwe offer by contrast?

Main Arguments and Outline of the Study

The national movement's era in exile is far from over. In the pages to follow, I will show that the Palestinian refugee camps in Lebanon in general, and 'Ayn al-Hilwe in particular, have, due to their relative territorial autonomy and their absence of any specific state authority, remained important hubs for dissident exiles and opposition leaders of various affiliations to forge alliances and strengthen their influence within the broader Palestinian political scene. On this note, the book opens with an up-close investigation of the socio-spatial organization of ʿAyn al-Hilwe to get a better sense of the place in which these exiles operate. Rather than constituting secluded or dangerous islands cut off from the outside world, I argue that the present-day camps can more readily be conceptualized as *Palestinian states in exile*, or brokered spaces hosting a number of overlapping indigenous, religious, and factional authorities which all offer important glimpses of Middle East history **(Chapter 2).**

In addition to inviting the reader to reconsider scholarly axioms prevalent in the study of refugee camps, my hope is that this book will also cast new light on leadership structures in Palestinian faction politics, where far more takes place outside of the established centers of power than what has been accounted for in the literature. As the reader will understand by now, this is not primarily a story about presidents and national leaders. It is one of disgruntled exiles, restless neighborhood militias, and anonymous bureaucrats, many of whom have continued to wield disproportionate amounts of political capital, due in no small part to the fact that the main Palestinian leaderships have found themselves vying to reimpose their control of the refugee camps of Lebanon in the post-Oslo era. In this regard, the book calls attention to a critical juncture that occurs at the turn of the millennium, when the PLO leadership (and Hamas) embarks on a grand-scale return to Lebanon. As the peace process derails and the hopes for a viable two-state solution start to wane, we see President Yasser Arafat attempt to strengthen his bargaining hand vis-à-vis Israel by rebuilding the PLO's political and military institutions in the refugee camps **(Chapter 3)**. The PLO's diplomatic standing in Lebanon improves greatly when Syrian military troops abandon the country following the 2005 popular uprising known as the Cedar Revolution. However, the establishment of a foreign mission to Beirut unleashes new and intense rivalries between Palestinian elites jostling for position, some of whom resort to funding private militia forces in ʿAyn al-Hilwe and other camps as to pressure their superiors. Tracing the fallout of these events, the book shows that Palestinian politics is not exclusively a top-down hierarchy. More precisely, it illuminates a phenomenon often mentioned but seldom explored in the context of neopatrimonial rule, namely, how otherwise disposable intermediaries make themselves indispensable by manipulating and breaking chains of patronage, by siding with rival elites, and by capturing resources to build their own micro-constituencies within their respective (faction) administrations. In our case, this not only extends to unruly Fatah camp commanders in exile locked in feuds with their own leaders in the homeland but also disenchanted jihadi militants who, having grown weary of their image as Lebanon's primary public enemies, go on to strike unorthodox alliances with both Lebanese and Palestinian elites to improve their standing **(Chapters 4 and 5)**. In other words, the case of ʿAyn al-Hilwe is a primary example of the how mid-ranking officials are more than capable of creating their own "bureaucratic chaos."

The story of ʿAyn al-Hilwe is also a story about Lebanon. We will experience how the Palestinian camp finds itself immersed in the power struggles of Lebanese leaders eager to stake their claim for the city of Sidon, and who rely on the support of both regional allies and local camp-based militia groups to achieve their goals. Ultimately, this exacerbates a dynamic in which internal actors use external sponsors to buttress their position in the camp, while external actors use resources to influence camp politics for broader Palestinian, Lebanese, and regional purposes. To this end, the stakes are raised considerably when Lebanon is rocked by the breakout of war in Syria, and various armed actors connected to the conflict begin enlisting paperless and marginalized Palestinian youth to counter the influence of their rivals. Exploring these dynamics up close, **Chapter 5** provides a detailed account of the camp's expanding militia economy, how factions recruit followers, and how regional conflicts are reinterpreted according to local fault lines. From here, the book goes on to investigate the calls for Palestinian unity as referenced in this chapter's introduction. While the Palestinian majority areas in Syria find themselves engulfed by war, the Palestinian factions in Lebanon make arrangements to launch a new Unified Political Leadership in Beirut, as well as a joint military police force in ʿAyn al-Hilwe—a project seen as a primary vehicle for safeguarding what is left of Palestinian autonomy in exile. **Chapter 6** sees guerilla fighters from various factional affiliations struggle to adapt to their newfound role as police officers, all the while managing the expectations of both Palestinian and Lebanese authorities who engage in numerous public and internal altercations regarding the mandate and the purpose of these new institutions.

As I take the reader through the socio-political geography of the Capital of the Diaspora, it is my hope that the people we will encounter, the streets we will walk in, and neighborhoods we will visit along the way will tell a story that is larger than the camp itself. Despite being an impoverished society in the margins, ʿAyn al-Hilwe finds itself a scene of the most central struggles of the region, where concepts such as autonomy, self-determination, and sovereignty are negotiated by a range of informal actors through a constant re-shaping of alliances and power balances. That being said, this is not exclusively a story about armed factions. The book ends by investigating the emergence of a new generation of Palestinian activists who challenge the hegemony of the camp-based leaderships and who see themselves as a part of a broader, youthful protest movement in national politics **(Chapter 7)**.

A Note on Sources and Methods

The story I tell in this book is largely presented through piecing together biographies of both spaces and people that are not necessarily well known in the context of Palestinian political history. First of all, the study builds on fieldwork conducted intermittently in five Palestinian camps in Lebanon (and various faction offices outside the camps) between September 2013 and June 2017. Throughout this period, I conducted roughly 200 interviews of which 80 might be said to constitute elite-interviews. By this, I mean formal conversations with representatives of political factions, neighborhood militias, NGOs, Lebanese leaders, or other types of organizations. In the field, I was also able to observe a number of conferences, meetings, or other gatherings held in various Popular Committees, party offices, or religious institutions. A round of additional interviews was conducted with ex-members of the al-Aqsa Martyrs' Brigades in the Balata refugee camp in the West Bank in the fall of 2019, which allowed me to verify claims made about the strong ties between Fatah militants in Lebanon and the Palestinian Territories during the Second Intifada.

The above-mentioned ethnographic material has been supplemented with written primary sources such as Arabic language newspapers accessed at a number of public and private archives in Beirut, in addition to magazines, pamphlets, videos of Friday sermons, and other types of media published by the Palestinian factions.

The reader will note that the people we meet in this book are mostly men. I attribute this, at least to some degree, to the political marginalization that the women of the Palestinian national movement have experienced from the 1980s and onwards, but it is undoubtedly also a result of my position as a male researcher operating in a society influenced by patriarchal culture. In general, I experienced many difficulties when reaching out to the rank and file of the different Palestinian factions, which I rarely encountered with their top leaderships. Typically, mid-management or casual members were often afraid to "speak out of line" or in one way or another misrepresent their own movements. Agreeing to meet for formal interviews often involved building trust over time, and I seldom had the opportunity to do that with the women. In the few instances that I was able to meet female party members, the latter insisted that we would do so under the supervision of male/senior party fellows, and the conversations tended to become contrived and unnatural. By contrast, the activist collectives that we meet in the last chapter of this book took great pride in having high degrees of female representation and fostering progressive ideals. At the same time, their affiliates were among the most hesitant to share their stories with me. Because they were continuously accused of conspiring with foreign powers, the act of meeting with a Western researcher like myself was not without risk. Again, it was the male activists who were willing to take this risk. That does not mean that the women of the Palestinian camps did not take part in shaping this study, as interlocutors, friends, or colleagues who have given me valuable feedback on parts of my manuscript.

2

The Anatomy of a Palestinian State in Exile

Entering ʿAyn al-Hilwe is reminiscent of crossing a border between nations. When passing through the camp's main entrance near the Governmental Hospital of Sidon, the several layers of Lebanese soldiers checking passports,[1] the lines of cars waiting to pass inspections, and the main gate, shaped like the al-Aqsa mosque and displaying the words "Our nation is Palestine, and its capital is Jerusalem," all contribute to the impression that one is indeed crossing into a new country. The world that unfolds only reinforces this feeling. As one is greeted by Palestinian flags, murals, posters, and drawings of Yasser Arafat and other national heroes on nearly every street corner, and is exposed to dialects and accents tracing their origins to the Galilee region, there are few reminders that one is still in Lebanon.

The fact that the Palestinian camp is fenced in by checkpoints, cement walls, and military watchtowers speaks miles of the security regimes that define the everyday lives of its inhabitants. Moreover, the clusters of concrete apartments and mazes of narrow alleyways—many of which are plastered with posters commemorating "martyrs" who fell in past revolutions or in recent clashes—are indicative of the harsh realities of life in exile. The same goes for the poverty, overcrowding, and unsanitary conditions that abound. Nonetheless, one would be remiss not to mention that ʿAyn al-Hilwe is also a living, breathing community that features colorful neighborhoods and sprawling markets. It is a place where people have carved out their lives and put down their roots, and that they feel a deep sense of connection to. It is where families have clung on and scraped by for generations, often against near-impossible odds, all the while living in neighborhoods named after the towns and villages that their families hail from. Many will claim that the camp is both their home and a symbol of the homeland that was lost. The more ideologically committed residents might even describe their living in the camp as an act of *sumud* (steadfastness) or *muqawama* (resistance), where staying put and refusing to integrate into their host state are a way of affirming Palestinian identity and demanding the right to return. Furthermore, certain political leaders view its ground as an extension of their respective state-building projects in the Palestinian Territories. These sentiments will likely be shared by many of the armed guards of the Palestinian Authority's *National Security Forces* who are stationed in great numbers along the streets of *Baraksat*—the first neighborhood to appear beyond the main entrance—and whose presence is indicative of a strong Palestinian incentive to maintain degrees of territorial control in exile.

These few meters are a journey of many contradictions, and offer a glimpse into why it might be such a bewildering and humbling experience to conduct a study of the history of a refugee camp. Michel Foucault famously stated that "space is fundamental in any form of communal life; space is fundamental in any exercise of power."[2] This is a notion to which most scholars who have studied refugee camps and their inhabitants can attest. However, researchers across academic disciplines have not always agreed on who wields power within these spaces. As follows, they have sought to define and conceptualize refugee camps in widely different ways. Are they temporary shelters or permanent homes? Are they constructed in order to "warehouse" the undesired, or to offer protection for the persecuted? Are they international zones governed by humanitarian law, or non-state spaces prone to conflict and insecurity? Are they ghettos, squats, or slums? And what about the Palestinian camps that have a history of militancy and political activism—who exercises power within these spaces?

In this chapter, I will take the reader on a tour of ʿAyn al-Hilwe's socio-political geography and spatial setting, while I dwell on the questions sketched out above. My goal is twofold. First, I aim to provide the reader with the necessary background to understand how the camp came into being, and how it fits into Palestinian and Lebanese history. Second, I will engage the reader in a discussion about how different scholarly frameworks have shaped our understanding of camp politics in the present, while I explain how I both depart from and build on this body of knowledge. As a point of departure, I heed the call of anthropologist Dag Tuastad who argues that internal actors should be given more consideration in discussions about power and authority in the Palestinian camps. Rather than settling on the notion that the camps have become *states of exception*, he argues, there are compelling reasons to reimagine these spaces as *Palestinian states in exile*.[3]

Beyond the State of Exception

The hardship, persecution, and legal repression that refugees and encamped populations often are subjected to are reasons why many researchers have turned to the seminal works of the Italian philosopher Giorgio Agamben, as foreshadowed in the introduction to this book. In his writing, Agamben draws upon the ideas of Hannah Arendt who wrote extensively about the plights of non-citizens and stateless people throughout the World Wars. For Arendt, the concentration camps of the Nazi regime were the ultimate expression of totalitarianism and domination, a space where the juridical person was eliminated.[4] Agamben brings with him these perspectives from wartime Europe in his investigations of modern-day refugee politics. In similar spirits, he views the encamped refugee as an individual completely subordinate to sovereign power, such as the nation-state or humanitarian agencies, which in turn governs and regulates the lives of the stateless in a permanent "state of exception."[5] Because these actors strip the refugee of their political rights and commit only to maintaining their biological existence, Agamben claims, encamped people are moved from the political sphere to a biological realm.[6] Deprived of their legal status, the refugee becomes *homo sacer* (a sacred man), a person who according to Roman law could be killed by anyone without consequence, not unlike those eliminated in the Nazi concentration camps.[7]

Agamben's theories and the emergence of what we might refer to as *critical camp studies* mark a radical shift in terms of moving the discourse from one of the efficiencies of humanitarian relief to the elusive yet oppressive regimes of power that detain, isolate, and regulate the life of encamped people. These ideas have also left a significant imprint on the study of Palestinian camps. Researchers inspired by Agamben have likened the refugee camps of Lebanon to "spaces of exception,"[8] arguing that their inhabitants have been condemned to a state of "bare life," living at the mercy of a sovereign Lebanese state and its security regimes which take part in suspending "all authority over the camp."[9] In recent years, nonetheless, scholars have increasingly come to rethink the applicability of Agamben's treatises on sovereignty on modern-day refugee camps, particularly as his ideas do little to establish the camp dweller as a person capable of exerting human agency.[10] Taken to their logical conclusion, Agamben's theories seem to suggest that encamped refugees are incapable of acting as political beings; after all, they can only inhabit biological life. Nonetheless, the Palestinian refugees in Lebanon have throughout decades in exile demonstrated that being stripped of their most basic rights has not bereft them of their agency, collectively or individually. Moreover, we are hard-pressed to find one single sovereign state power or authority dictating life within their camps. Rather, these spaces feature a diverse "assemblage of political actors, organizations, agencies, religious leaders and the built environment fill the void abandoned by the state", Adam Ramadan writes,

> producing particular Palestinian values, knowledges, rationalities and practices, shaping Palestinian subjectivities, contributing to the suspension of the law, controlling its conditions, sharing in practices of sovereignty and governance.[11]

This is not to say that Agamben's theories are obsolete. At a time when European governments are countering the world's largest refugee crisis by building more barriers, fences, and detention centers, new spaces of exception are, arguably, created every day.

Nonetheless, in the study of refugee camps where several layers of overlapping authorities compete for hegemony, we should not be content with viewing their internal order exclusively as a product of external lawmaking.

The Camp as a Community of Villages

Rather than being constructed with the intent of entrapping and eliminating the unwanted, many refugee camps start out as clusters of improvised shelters that are often shaped by their inhabitants' own needs for protection in times of hardship. In protracted refugee crises, where the chances of returning or moving on are low, these spaces tend to evolve into something more than places of transit. Camps do not only consist of walls and fences, Diken and Lausten remind us, they also have "doors and windows."[12] This is certainly the case with the Palestinian camps, which are among the oldest continuously inhabited refugee camps in history, where residents have continued to stack their apartments on top of each other, layer by layer, in the decades to follow the loss of their homeland.

Although the ʿAyn al-Hilwe camp was originally set up on an abandoned military base (see below), most of the buildings presently found there were constructed after Israel's devastating invasion of Lebanon in 1982, which laid waste to much of its infrastructure. The story of how the camp was rebuilt—which is recounted in filmmaker Dahna Abourahme's documentary "Kingdom of Women"—is in and of itself a powerful story of human agency in the face of rightlessness and dispossession.[13] After the Israeli Defense Forces (IDF) had bulldozed the camp to pieces, Israel inadvertently found itself obligated to provide shelter for the homeless Palestinians under its occupation of Sidon, which lasted until 1985. A lengthy process of negotiation ensued between the Israeli and Lebanese governments; the former wanted to move the refugees further north and as far away from the frontline as possible, while the latter was adamant to keep the Palestinians in the South and out of sight. In her film, Abourahme tells the fascinating story of how Palestinian women, defying the wishes of both governments, began rebuilding ʿAyn al-Hilwe, brick by brick, at a time when many of the camp's men found themselves incarcerated in Israeli detention centers. They refused to accept the simple tents that the IDF had offered them and began rebuilding the shelters and houses they had previously lived in. Against Israel's orders, UNRWA proceeded to tacitly supply the refugees with building materials, while the act of tent-burning became a widespread ritual of protest in solidarity with the displaced people of ʿAyn al-Hilwe.

The ways in which the refugees have (re)constructed their homes are also indicative of how many have an acute understanding of their origins, although the vast majority have never seen Palestine. Immediately after their arrival in Lebanon, Rosemary Sayigh writes, the Palestinians began reproducing social structures from the villages and cities they had left behind.[14] As a response to dispossession and displacement, the homeland's indigenous class structure was reconstructed within the new settlements, while simultaneously becoming crisscrossed by other social relations, such as political affiliations, kinship ties, and locality (between people of the same village or city neighborhood).[15] As can be observed in the map on page *xiii*, this also translates to the physical geography of the camp. In ʿAyn al-Hilwe, most neighborhoods have been named after historical villages of the Galilee region where extended families have remained in the "same" village that their predecessors fled from.[16] Members of the older generation will be quick to point out that these appellations originated from a practical need to navigate between clusters of families and their tents in the early days of exile, rather than being a deliberate attempt to revive the homeland within the camps. However, this does not take away from the fact that village or city of origin continues to serve as the primary identity marker between Palestinian refugees, in Lebanon and elsewhere. When inhabitants of ʿAyn al-Hilwe introduce themselves as coming from Safsaf, al-Zib, Taytaba, or other places, they are referring to the birthplace of their ancestors—although these spaces might also correspond with their present "village" or neighborhood within the camp. After over seventy years in exile, perceptions of status and social arrangements as they occurred in the old country are vividly present in the imagination of the current generations. Even children are quick to distinguish between fellow camp dwellers who speak like "city folk" and those with a "peasant dialect," the latter typically substituting the letter *Qaf* with *Kaf*, rather than the glottal stop (*Hamza*), which is common in the capitals of the Levant. It is no exaggeration when anthropologist Julie Peteet claims that inhabitants of ʿAyn al-Hilwe carry with them a cognitive map of a Galilean landscape transposed.[17]

This is a map, we might add, that is frequently updated and reconfigured according to how political history continues to unfold in the refugees' settlements in exile. In Lebanon's largest Palestinian camp, we find an array of (mostly faction-connected) *Neighborhood Committees* and (ostensibly independent) *Village Unions* that act as representatives of their respective communities or geographical areas (Chapter 7). In similar spirits, a few of the larger extended families have banded together and formed clan-based cooperatives, which are based on kinship-ties more than locality (as is the case with the al-Maqdah and Hajjir clans in ʿAyn al-Hilwe). Whether operating based on the principle of locality or kinship, many of these indigenous institutions will arrange annual collects among relatives in the homeland and the vast diaspora, in order to fund local relief-work, sports clubs or provide basic services to members of their neighborhoods (renovation of houses, provision of water, etc.) Although the phenomenon is far more prevalent among refugee communities in the West Bank and the Gaza Strip, some of these might also organize improvised *Conciliation Committees (lijan sulhiyya)* where clan or village elders take it upon themselves to mediate between feuding neighbors, families, and even political groups.

The perseverance of these forms of social organization should not necessarily be interpreted as nostalgia or attempts to preserve the past, but rather as a means of maintaining a sense of community in the face of dispossession, legal discrimination, and not at least the fragmentation of political power that the camps have experienced in recent decades. As has been the case in history, the Palestinian revolutionary groups tend to view these types of indigenous institutions with great suspicion and have tried their utmost to curtail and coopt the most influential actors. They have not always been successful. In the final parts of this book, we will experience how indigenous camp committees challenge the authority of the political factions through contentious acts, ranging from sheltering fugitives from the law to siding with youth activists in their bid to implement elections in the camp space.

An Urban Landscape in Lebanon

Along ʿAyn al-Hilwe's borders, we find a string of *adjacent gatherings*. These are squats and other informal structures that originally did not form part of the refugee camp but with time have become interwoven in its physical and political geography. Neighborhoods such as al-Sikke (The Railroad), Hayy al-Suhun (The Pottery neighborhood), Bustan al-Yahudi (The Jewish Orchard), and Baraksat (Barracks) are not names of Palestinian villages as such but belong to Lebanese urban history, having been named after the landmarks (and populations) of historical Sidon.[18] The name ʿAyn al-Hilwe itself, meaning "the sweet spring," refers to the many natural springs that are thought to have previously existed in the area.

Despite the physical and social fences that might separate a refugee camp from its surroundings, urban connections have a way of overcoming such barriers. Over time, anthropologist Are Knudsen reminds us, refugee camps go through "socio-spatial changes leading to novel urban forms."[19] In terms of the Palestinian camps, these have not only been urbanized, Michel Agier explains,

> they have also become attractive urban hubs. Migrants and refugees of other origins come and settle in or on the edge of these camps. These places become the core of new urban configurations that are both poor and cosmopolitan, so that some of them now illustrate a new "centrality of the margins."[20]

It is worth noting that the present-day Palestinian camps in Lebanon are not found alongside the border with Israel, as one perhaps would expect, but rather within working-class districts of the country's largest cities, from Tyre in the South to Tripoli in the North. With the exception of the three southernmost camps, their placement is not so much indicative of the places where the Palestinians first arrived, but rather where the refugees went to find work following their displacement. Having received its formal independence from the French mandate power in 1943, Lebanon was at the time in the process of becoming an important financial intermediary between Western markets and the Gulf states, and the refugees filled an emerging need for cheap labor, particularly in the agricultural sector. Whereas the Lebanese government first responded to the influx of refugees by attempting, unsuccessfully, to dump them across the Syrian border, business owners made a case for settling the Palestinians in camps near the citrus plantations of the coastal plain and in the industrial zones of the capital.[21]

In a well-researched piece of urban history, urban planner Ismael Sheikh Hassan and architect Lyne Jabri tell the story of how ʿAyn al-Hilwe initially was constructed on a piece of farmland a few miles from the city.[22] This land had during Ottoman times been bought by the American Missionary Academy of Sidon but was in the early 1940s rented by the British military in Mandatory Palestine, which hired the Lebanese contractor and former student of the Missionary Academy, Emile al-Bustani, to construct a military base on the premises.[23] It was this infrastructure, Hassan and Jabri write, with its characteristic parallel "Upper" and "Lower Street" running alongside its flanks that laid the ground for the current shape of the Palestinian camp.[24] At the time, Britain was locked in a regional conflict with the Vichy Regime of France, and in the summer of 1941 the Allied Forces of World War II proceeded to bombard a group of French troops who had taken control of a former orphanage on the al-Miyye wo-Miyye hilltop overlooking the ʿAyn al-Hilwe military base.[25] By late 1945, a US-brokered compromise was reached in the United Nations to evacuate all French and British troops from Lebanon (and Syria), forcing the parts to abandon their respective military compounds in Sidon.[26] It is doubtful that either party could foresee that both the ʿAyn al-Hilwe and al-Miyye wo-Miyye bases would be taken over by thousands of Palestinian refugees seeking shelter a few years later.

With time, the city of Sidon grew and gradually crept up to its Palestinian newcomers. Following a devastating earthquake in 1956, an elaborate reconstruction plan penned by a French architect called Michel Ecochard paved the way for "the largest public housing project in Lebanon," Marwan Ghandour writes, "which would include middle to low income Lebanese families housed in proximity to" the Palestinian camp.[27] This large collection of apartments is today known as Taʿmir (construction) and blends more or less seamlessly with the *Tawari'* and *Lower Ta'mir* neighborhoods found along ʿAyn al-Hilwe's northern parts. However, unlike the latter, Taʿmir proper is not among the many "adjacent gatherings" that are governed by Palestinian parties, and is not connected to the camp's sewage and water networks. If we are to borrow from Victor Turner, we might say that Taʿmir has been cursed with the fate of being "neither here, nor there." Curiously, Lebanese inhabitants of this "gray area"[28] often lament that they are worse off than their refugee neighbors, neglected by their own state and not benefitting from the NGOs or indigenous networks of support found within the Palestinian camp. In this book, we will make several visits to the Taʿmir district. Particularly because the place provides an interesting view with which to explore how Lebanese elites—the same ones who openly or tacitly support the sectarian policies that have left the refugees unable to own property or access the formal job market—are in reality deeply invested in the political economy of ʿAyn al-Hilwe and its Lebanese surroundings. In order to make this point as clear as possible, it might help us to draw parallels between what so often has been referred to as the sectarian nature of Lebanese politics, and our discussion on neopatrimonial rule from the previous chapter.

Since Ottoman times, the principle of consensus has been central for maintaining stability and for distributing political representation in Lebanon. The sectarian power-sharing formula dictates that positions of power are distributed proportionally according to the assumed size of eighteen officially recognized sects, and that political decisions are based on consensus where as many actors as possible take part in the process. This model was important for securing a modicum of stability at the eve of independence, when Christian and Muslim leaders through an informal "National Pact" laid the foundations for a modern Lebanese state,[29] and in 1989 when the Saudi-brokered Ta'if agreement ended the Lebanese civil war and allowed the country to return to parliamentary life. In the name of "mutual coexistence," Ta'if redistributed legislative powers between the president of the republic and the prime minister's office, reserved for the Christian Maronite and the Sunni Muslim sects respectively, all the while seeking to meet the rising demands for representation as fronted by Lebanon's de-facto largest community, the Shiʿa, the latter having organized itself in powerful (and armed) social movements such as Hizballah and Amal in the interim. Although Lebanon's political system has allowed for state consolidation during tense times, it has done little to amend underlying conflicts. Rather, it has paved the way for a sectarian social order where ethno-religious identity and political interests have become woven together in a mutually self-reinforcing relationship that hampers national unity and arguably has bereft the Lebanese of a shared history.[30] This sectarian order is not only present in the parliament but also reproduced in informal ways in fundamental aspects of everyday life. It defines the hierarchies of state agencies and private companies, and runs deep within the urban infrastructure of Lebanon, manifesting itself in the most mundane aspects of life, such as the distribution of electricity and parking lots.[31]

These systems do not thrive because sectarian divisions constitute the natural order of all things. Rather, maintaining and reproducing the sectarian narrative has been in the interest of an otherwise discordant alliance of political elites, business cartels, and communal/religious leaders as a *strategy* for derailing any national debate regarding socio-economic disparities,[32] and as a *compromise* when dividing the spoils of state resources which these actors rely on to build their respective fiefdoms. By contrast, the central state remains dysfunctional and inaccessible for most citizens. In areas where state institutions are virtually absent, inhabitants might rely completely on their local *zaʿim (pl. zuʿama')*, the self-proclaimed communal leader who takes it upon themselves to act like an intermediary between the citizen and the state, and who might be willing to connect their constituents with a host of private or public benefits, ranging from medical treatment to jobs in the public sector, in return for political loyalty. Those who lack the resources to resist the pull of such clientelistic networks often find themselves, whether they wish to or not, immersed in the ideological universe espoused by the communal leaders they depend on. In other words, the complex dynamics embedded in the catch-all phrase *sectarianism (al-ta'ifiyya)* cannot merely be reduced to a matter of ethno-religious belonging. Just as much, sectarian politics revolve around notions of class, socio-economic issues, and politics of patronage.

Insofar as Lebanon might be categorized as a neopatrimonial state, it is not governed by one ruling elite, but features several centers of power none of whom have been able to dominate the other. This is part of the reason why Lebanese politicians traditionally have looked to outside backers in order to gain the upper hand over domestic rivals. Similarly, foreign powers have teamed up with their respective Lebanese partners in order to "gain greater leverage against their own rivals in a geo-strategically significant" area on the eastern Mediterranean.[33] Presently, the United States, France, and Saudi Arabia support the March 14th electoral alliance, led by the Sunni-oriented *Future Movement (Tayyar al-Mustaqbal)*, with Iran and Syria supporting the March 8th alliance led by the Shiʿi movement Hizballah and which also includes the country's most influential Christian party, the *Free Patriotic Movement (al-Tayyar al-Watani al-Hurr)*. As for Sidon, the city emerged in the latter half of the 1980s as a stronghold for the capitalist and future prime minister Rafiq al-Hariri, who was able to win over both militia groups and political competitors by relying on patronage and his exponential access to resources as a Gulf-based contractor with ties to the Saudi Arabian royal family.[34] More than fifteen years after his death, the Hariri Foundation, currently headed by the late prime minister's sister, Bahia, remains a dominant social and political force in Sidon. Based in the upper-scale neighborhood of Majdalun, Bahia al-Hariri operates a robust network of educational, religious, and health institutions, and controls much of the development money that comes into the city.[35] Meanwhile, the closely linked Future Movement, in which she also represents as a Member of Parliament, remains uncontested in local elections.

Yet power balances are not always as settled as they might appear. This becomes particularly clear when looking at the gray areas and informal gatherings of the city. The aforementioned Taʿmir district, for example, has remained an important base for the leftist *Popular Nasserite Organization* since the mid-1960s. Amidst a mounting economic crisis, the head of the party, Maʿruf Saʿd, instructed the city's poor to move in and squat the area's roughly 3,000 newly constructed housing units, promising that the municipality of Sidon would later be forced to grant them the property rights.[36] This has yet to materialize. Neglected by the post-war reconstruction process of the 1990s, the district instead became a makeshift city of improvised architecture, albeit deeply enmeshed in the private economical networks of politicians who have continued to promise to grant residents the rights to their homes at every election. In essence, Sidon's political class regards Taʿmir to be important for at least two different reasons: politically, because the neighborhood is inhabited by marginalized Sunni (and Shiʿ) constituencies, and materially, because it, in the words of the Hariri Foundation itself, hosts the city's main "labor pool," including construction workers, carpenters, and electricians.[37] Forgotten and passed by as it may appear, this part of the city has frequently been subject to turbulent, and often violent, power struggles erupting between a host of political elites, sectarian leaders, and informal militia movements vying to extend their influence beyond the formal reaches of the state and, in the process, pass themselves off as the true guardians of their followers, if not the working classes (Chapter 5).

As we will see in this book, these dynamics do in part also translate to the Palestinian camps. Many of Sidon's political forces enjoy longstanding relations with the Palestinian factions, and assert themselves as champions of their national cause. To date, nearly every party or social movement in the city, regardless of sect, has special representatives tasked with handling the "Palestinian file" (*al-milaff al-filastini*). Usually, this means establishing a rapport with a wide range of Palestinian actors in order to confer in matters relating to anything from security provision to camp infrastructure (see below.) Yet local relief organizations are quick to point out that these relations are not always to the benefit of the Palestinian refugees. In fact, many blame Lebanese stakeholders for intervening in their affairs purely for their own political or economic gains. ʿAyn al-Hilwe not only offers cheap and informal labor, as the leader of a local NGO put it, but certain actors have come to "view the place as an unregulated free market" ideal for arms trafficking, drug trade, and the illicit sale of electricity among other resources.[38] Such claims are far from unsubstantiated. Interestingly, while Lebanese politicians along the right wing/Christian axis have gone on to blame the refugees for stealing state electricity that ostensibly runs unregulated into the self-governed camps,[39] news reports from the summer of 2019 showed that inhabitants of ʿAyn al-Hilwe, in fact, were paying higher electricity bills than those living in Sidon proper.[40] In the camp, many attribute this development to the policies implemented by a cobweb of informal generator owners who, presumably acting with the tacit approval of both Palestinian and Lebanese factions ("the generator mafia"), have been known to appropriate powerlines and resell state electricity to the refugees at above the market price. This business model seems to be based on the expectation shared among many generator owners that the camp's international relief agencies will intervene and cover their client's costs.[41] We will return to both Taʿmir and these networks of power later in this book. For now, we will go on to shed light on the role of international aid in the camp: both as a lifeline for those living in abject poverty and as a contested resource among many.

A Humanitarian Government

It has often been noted that humanitarian relief agencies come to fill the role of a state. In this regard, we are hard pressed to find a better example than the United Nations Work Agency for Palestinians in the Near East (UNRWA). In ʿAyn al-Hilwe, UNRWA presently runs eight schools, which between them host at least 6000 students on the elementary, preparatory, and secondary levels. The agency's local employees also perform a wide range of other tasks, from providing waste management and maintaining sewage networks, to operating shelter rehabilitation services and (two) healthcare centers. Moreover, UNRWA provides secondary and tertiary healthcare through a network of contracted hospitals in Sidon and its suburbs, such as the nearby Hamshari hospital, run by the Palestinian Red Crescent Society.

As a transnational relief agency operating in six different geographical areas, UNRWA's responsibilities and tasks were never meant to become so vast and extensive, nor did anyone intend for the agency to remain operational for decades after the *nakba*. When UNRWA was created in December 1949, its aim was to provide the Palestinian refugees with primary health care, economic relief, and basic social services in a short interim period. In addition, the Western nations that dominated the UN lobbied for using the organization to reintegrate the refugees in their host states through various development projects—hence the "W" in its name.[42] Another body, the UN Conciliation Committee for Palestine (UNCCP), was supposed to facilitate a negotiated solution to the conflict, and deal with contentious political issues such as repatriation, resettlement, compensation, and rehabilitation.[43] This committee, however, failed to reach any solution, largely due to the pressure exerted by the United States, and was left superfluous when Israel sealed off its borders with its Arab neighbors throughout 1949. For its part, UNRWA was unable to implement its work projects because the host nations were reluctant to integrate the Palestinians into their labor forces. As a result, the refugees were left with an ostensibly politically powerless agency intended to provide humanitarian aid in a short interim period, but whose mandate has since been renewed every three years by the United Nations General Assembly because a "just resolution of the question of the Palestine refugees" has yet to be found.[44]

Claims of apolicity notwithstanding, UNRWA has never remained detached from the politics of humanitarian aid, not in terms of navigating the expectations of its donors, nor in its presence among the refugees. When UNRWA in the 1950s (and '60s) begun replacing the refugee's original tent landscapes with huts, temporary shelters, and eventually, semi-permanent modes of housing, the agency found itself forced to seek a firmer definition of the spaces in which it was present. Consequently, it became a key actor in defining which "concentrations of refugees and displaced persons" were to be regarded by both its beneficiaries and their host states as an "official camp," featuring UNRWA's service provisions and a defined leadership.[45] Inadvertently, this also meant deciding which camps and gatherings were to remain "unofficial," whose populations were left in squalor or began moving into the official "UNRWA camps" to access the agency's relief programs. These deliberations overlapped with another contentious discussion about how to determine which camp dwellers were eligible for aid. This question had far-reaching political ramifications because it was intrinsically connected to a process of also defining who constituted a "Palestine refugee"—an appellation that many of UNRWA's beneficiaries understood as a verification of their right to repatriation.[46]

It is in the context of this power to define and administrate people's lives within a set of systems that anthropologist Ilana Feldman notes that humanitarianism, over time, "necessarily becomes something like a government."[47] The allusions to UNRWA as a state or a government are plentiful in the scholarly literature whether these accounts explore the systems of control and coercion allegedly embedded in the concept of humanitarianism,[48] or view the agency as a non-territorial "quasi-state" which lacks coercive power, and "has to achieve its objectives mainly through mediation."[49] We would be remiss, however, if we did not acknowledge the degrees to which this humanitarian government also has promoted human capital. By the 1970s, the agency had emerged as a main provider of another service, which arguably remains its most important: education. In cooperation with UNESCO, UNRWA took charge of the schools in (or near) the camps, and would go on to produce generations of literary refugees with substantial vocational training.[50] The agency's schools were often more robust than those found in the receiving countries, and the Palestinian camp dwellers emerged, in many cases, as better educated and more skilled than their urban working-class neighbors. UNRWA's critics, on the other hand, came to deem the provision of education among its most controversial aspects. This especially because the rise of the agency's education programs coincided with a mass politicization of the Palestinian diaspora. On this note, historian Kjersti Berg explains how the proliferation of armed groups in the camps toward the end of the 1960s made the UN agency uneasy about its unintended role in providing aid for a mounting rebellion, especially after the PLO went on to assume the de facto control of the camps in Lebanon.[51] In 1970, the agency rebranded its "UNRWA camps" "refugee camps" and disclaimed its responsibilities for these spaces altogether. Although it recommenced its services shortly after, it was only to play a limited role, and would no longer profess to be in charge of the camps or their infrastructure.[52] This strategic ambiguity regarding its mandate has allowed UNRWA to carry on and provide for the Palestinian refugees, while avoiding the issue of taking sides in regional conflicts. Yet for the same reason, the question of who is responsible for the camps and their inhabitants has only become more contentious over the years.[53]

Despite having long taken pride in employing a local staff of roughly 30,000, the vast majority of whom are Palestinians working as teachers or medical staff, the refugees feel little ownership of the agency, which they tend to regard as a representative of the Western world powers first. Having been created by UN General Assembly Resolution 302, which underlines the need for preliminary aid until more durable solutions can be found, the Palestinians and their political representatives commonly interpret the agency's perseverance as a promise that the international society remains committed to the more crucial Resolution 194, which guarantees their right of return.[54] Interestingly, the politicized view of refugee aid is largely shared by the agency's staunchest critics. In the fall of 2018, UNRWA's biggest and most important sponsor for decades, the United States, cut its annual donation of $300 million, thereby removing near a quarter of the funding of the agency which was already running with a deficit. The decision seems to have been based on the assertions made by the administration of the US President Donald Trump that UNRWA is unnaturally sustaining "the refugee question" and dragging out the Palestinian-Israeli conflict.[55] This idea builds on the doubtful premise that the protracted nature of Palestinian refugee-hood, and thus the claim to repatriation and return to a Palestinian homeland, solely hinges on UNRWA's existence. By attempting to force UNRWA to close down, the Trump administration was perhaps hoping that the refugees' host states would see no other choice than to assume their responsibility and naturalize them permanently where they are. This would be a crucial step in the American-proposed peace plan for the Palestinians and the Israelis known as the "Deal of the Century." Currently, there is no consensus in the UN to shut UNRWA down or transfer the Palestinian refugees to any other organization. Rather, an array of other donor nations have stepped in and increased their funding, while the chronically cash-strapped agency has attempted to mitigate this existential threat by cutting jobs and reducing some of its services.[56]

Although the Trump administration's cuts did not compel UNRWA to shut down its operations in September 2018, the agency's schools in ʿAyn al-Hilwe were at the time forced to close their classrooms for different reasons. According to the media, tensions were swelling after a conflict had erupted between affiliates of opposing armed Islamist groups in the South Lebanon camp.[57] Reportedly, parents refused to let their children go to class even after the schools had re-opened, because they feared the situation would escalate. Meanwhile, UNRWA staff was unable to go through with its waste collection, causing garbage to pile up in the streets.[58] As these events illustrate, the humanitarian agency does not only face political pressure at the international level. Insofar as UNRWA's operations in the refugee camps might be said to constitute a humanitarian government, scholarly research has perhaps had a tendency to under-communicate the degrees to which its authority is also challenged locally, by the camp-based leaderships.

In the camps, UNRWA officials often report that they find themselves having to assume the role as mediators, because any type of service provision needs to be coordinated with a host of stakeholders with opposing interests. This might range from the Lebanese municipalities where the camps are based to the factional Popular Committees that act as the internal Palestinian administrations.[59] The fact that most camps have two or more parallel factional leaderships only adds to the complexity of the matter, especially as any party that feels left out of the loop might be compelled to respond against the agency with harsh measures.[60] Moreover, the various political groups will often pre-empt any criticism directed at their own shortcomings in governing the camps, by capitalizing on the refugees' legitimate frustrations with UNRWA's reductions in services, urging them to turn their anger toward the agency (Chapter 7). Indeed, hosting demonstrations against UNRWA is a measure that allows the political groups to assert themselves as the true protectors of the refugees while appearing unified in their opposition to the hegemony of the Western world powers. As one Palestinian leader ceded, "Putting pressure on UNRWA" is one of the few things the factions are able to agree on.[61] The camps' relief organizations also find their legitimacy contested in more elusive ways. As mentioned earlier, internal actors might see resources coming into the camp as an opportunity to extend their own line of patronage, and some will go far in their attempts to redirect water, electricity, or even foreign aid to their own neighborhood, kin, political group, etc.[62] In August 2020, sources close to the agency reported with dismay that a representative from one of the camp's competing Popular Committees had appropriated and taken over a load of diesel that UNRWA had provided to fuel generators hooked up to ʿAyn al-Hilwe's electric wells. Although the camp was in the midst of a water scarcity crisis, the former had allegedly gone on to resell the diesel privately on the market.[63] To conclude for now, when we cross paths with UNRWA and its employees in this book, we will not see an omnipresent sovereign dictating the lives of the refugees from above, but a challenged authority countered by mass protests, lockdowns, and factional strife.

A State in Exile

Some scholars have argued that refugee camps, rather than merely warehousing and entrapping marginalized populations, might under certain circumstances become ideal shelters and recruitment grounds for revolutionary groups or other violent forms of political activism. In the monograph "Dangerous Sanctuaries," political scientist Sarah Lischer investigates the role of humanitarian aid in exacerbating armed conflicts through providing insurgent refugees with the means of sustaining their rebellions.[64] She argues, among other things, that refugee groups with strong political cohesion and established leaderships prior to their expulsion—or *state-in-exile* refugees—are the most violent-prone and likely to spread conflicts across borders. "In exile, militants improve their security situation vis-à-vis the sending state," Lischer writes. "They also have greater freedom to raise funds and to develop alliances," and to attain popular support.[65] As the reader will know by now, these dynamics correspond greatly with the trajectory of the Palestinian national movement toward the end of the 1960s.

Not only did Palestinian militia groups find shelter and resources within the camps—in Lebanon, they were able to build a rebel bureaucracy so complex that it in and of itself came to resemble a Palestinian *state in exile*. Since this historical backdrop is so central to the story told in this book, it will be worth our time to explore these events up close.

It should be noted that the crystallization of Palestinian nationalist activism in Lebanon was not initially confined to the refugee camps. At a time when these spaces found themselves patrolled by Lebanese security forces who kept inhabitants under harsh surveillance,[66] the university campuses and their leftist political circles offered more fruitful arenas to organize and seek allies. In the early 1950s, the Arab National Movement (ANM) was built around a core of Palestinian and Lebanese students at the American University of Beirut, among them the future leader of the *Popular Front for the Liberation of Palestine (PFLP)* George Habash. The movement quickly absorbed like-minded circles of young leftists and Arab nationalists based in Syria and Jordan, and eventually Egypt.[67] United by ideals of anti-colonialism, pan-Arabism, and a bid to end the Zionist occupation of Palestine, the ANM diligently recruited supporters at the region's university campuses, while clandestine militant cells coordinated closely with Syrian and Egyptian intelligence. However, after power struggles resulted in the disintegration of the prominent Syrian-Egyptian union in 1961, and following Egyptian president Gamal Abdel Nasser's warnings against a military confrontation with Israel, the Palestinian core within the ANM began losing faith that the promised pan-Arab revolution would bear fruits, and opted instead for a Palestinian solution.

As the ANM gradually broke into different factions, it by and large ceded its position to other organizations, the most important of which was the *Palestinian National Liberation Movement,* otherwise known as Fatah.[68] Founded in Kuwait in 1959 by Yasser Arafat, Mahmoud Abbas, and seven other future leaders of the Palestinian national movement, Fatah rallied around the principles of self-reliance and armed struggle as the primary vehicles of achieving national liberation. As frequently espoused in its periodical *Filastinuna* (Our Palestine), the group envisioned that the liberation of the homeland hinged on the ability to mobilize the masses through military action. Its founders had little patience with Nasser and other Arab leaders, and did not intend to wait for their approval to go to war. On January 2, 1965, the relatively unknown Fatah movement took the center stage of the national struggle when its newly formed military wings, *Quwwat al-ʿAsifa* (The Storm Forces), based in border towns of Jordan, Syria, and Lebanon, announced that they had launched an attack against Israel.[69] The offensive, an unsuccessful attempt at blowing up Israel's National Water Carrier, was in and of itself a military failure. The thirty-four subsequent guerilla raids against Israel that would follow in the same year, most of them carried out from Jordan, were also negligible. Yet they had large political ramifications. The attacks had a tremendous psychological impact on the Israeli population. Moreover, they were a means for Fatah to set the agenda and claim ownership of the armed struggle before any rival entity could do so. This also extended to the recently established Palestine Liberation Organization (PLO), which had been created with the help of the Arab League in 1964, and which came about as a result of the Arab governments' thinly veiled ambitions of monopolizing the Palestinian national struggle for their own geopolitical gains. Unimpressed by the arrogant demeanor of the PLO's leader, Ahmad Shuqairy, who they feared would act as a puppet in the hands of the Arab states, but excited by the structure of his robust organization which was shaped much like a Palestinian shadow government, Fatah sought to "revolutionize" the PLO from within by seeking influence in its highest authority, the Palestinian National Council (PNC), and more importantly, by attempting to drag the PLO and its Arab backers into a war against Israel on the premise of the militia groups.[70] The PLO, which for its part was struggling to live up to its ambition of constituting the sole representative of the Palestinian people, found itself forced to respond to the mounting pressure. At the third Arab League Summit held in Casa Blanca in September 1965, the organization's leader, Shuqayri, went on to suggest the mandatory conscription of all Palestinians in Jordan and Lebanon in the military wings of the PLO, as well as the military fortification of all border villages to Israel.[71] The appeal fell on deaf ears. However, those who deemed the initiation of armed struggle premature at the time would soon come around to the idea.

The embarrassing loss of the Arab armies against Israel in the fateful six-day war in 1967 was a wake-up call that saw the Palestinian diaspora flock to guerilla groups such as Fatah. A year later, Palestinian guerillas claimed their first victory, as they, assisted by the Jordanian army, drove the IDF out of the Jordanian border town of Karame. Having shocked the enemy by recklessly throwing themselves at Israeli tanks and artillery with explosives in their hands, Palestinian fighters gave birth to the image of the *fida'i*—the self-sacrificer—a potent cultural phenomenon that contributed to thousands of refugees and other sympathizers enlisting in the Palestinian guerilla groups.[72] By the end of 1969, Fatah leader Yasser Arafat had replaced Shuqayri as chairperson of the PLO, and the various militias that he had invited to join the organization gradually came to outnumber the troops of its own official military, the Palestinian Liberation Army (PLA). The fact that a generation of revolutionary Palestinians had claimed ownership of the PLO came at a cost. The Arab "confrontation states" were not eager to host an organization they could no longer control. Syria had become anxious about open confrontations with Israel following the six-day war, and Jordan violently drove the PLO out of its territories after guerillas had called for the overthrow of the Hashemite monarchy in 1971. In their search for a guerilla sanctuary, the PLO and Fatah found a more fertile ground in Lebanon.

Hard on the heels of the 1958 insurrection, in which armed Muslim and leftist groups had tried to overthrow the American-backed rule of President Camille Chamoun, Lebanon was already ridden with domestic turmoil when the country's most important financial institution, the *Inra Bank*, run by the Palestinian capitalist Yousef Beidas, collapsed in 1966, causing irreparable damage to the economy.[73] Initially, both events led Lebanon to harden its policies toward the Palestinians. The reviled military intelligence, the *Deuxième Bureau (al-markaz al-thani)*, intensified its surveillance of the refugees, controlling their every movement and subjecting them to arbitrary and hard-handed arrests on the basis of constituting a fifth column. Meanwhile the government used the Intra Bank crisis as a pretext to crack down on Palestinian labor, effectively driving the Palestinian middle classes back into the refugee camps and causing new slum areas to expand around them.[74] None of these measures, however, could prevent the inevitable. As Palestinian *fida'iyin* began pouring in from the neighbor states after the six-day war, South Lebanon was essentially rendered a military zone locked in conflict with Israel.

Tensions along the border accelerated waves of migration from impoverished and marginalized townships in South Lebanon to the suburbs of Beirut, leading to substantial demographic changes in the capital and the country at large. Those who felt alienated by the political class or exploited by the wealthy landowners of the South tended to look to the PLO as an ally able to challenge both parties, as was the case with opposition leaders who did their utmost to capitalize on these dynamics. Inspired by the pan-Arabist winds of the time, and desperately seeking a partner to break the hegemony of the Maronite nationalist side of politics, popular figures along an emerging leftist-Muslim axis, such as the influential Muslim leader Kamal Jumblatt, threw their support behind the Palestinian guerillas and vouched for their armed struggle, as did a substantial portion of the Lebanese public.[75] Lebanon was split, and so was the government. In December 1968, the latter was thrown into a deep crisis after Israeli commandoes bombed the Beirut International Airport in reprisal for the PFLP's terrorist attack on an Israeli airliner in Athens, setting the country on course for a widening political vacuum. Meanwhile, the Lebanese army found itself unable to disarm the PLO. A string of clashes which pitted the army against Palestinian guerillas in the spring of 1969 prompted Egypt's Gamal Abdel Nasser to intervene and mediate between the parties, which ultimately resulted in the signing of the aforementioned Cairo Accords. The agreement, which was initially kept secret from the public, guaranteed the free movement of Palestinian guerillas in Lebanon, and left the refugee camps under the control of the PLO's revolutionary forces, the Palestinian Armed Struggle Command (PASC).[76] Ironically, the Lebanese army commander to sign the agreement was none other than Emile al-Bustani, the same man who had built the ʿAyn al-Hilwe military base decades earlier.

At the height of their power, the PLO's forces counted, according to some reports, as many as 25,000 fighters equipped with "tanks, artillery and rockets", while the size of the Lebanese army, in comparison, did not exceed 17,000 soldiers.[77] That being said, the statist structures of the PLO were perhaps more impressive than its military prowess. Backed by petrodollars from the Gulf States and other sympathizers, the organization became a $1 billion-a-year enterprise and Lebanon's largest employer after the state itself.[78] The heart of the PLO's organization was concentrated in an autonomous enclave in the Fakhani district of West Beirut, which due to its size and ever-growing bureaucratic complexity was jokingly referred to as the "Fakhani republic."

Despite its impressive institutions, the national movement suffered from lack of political cohesion. Political scientist Rex Brynen notes how the internal life of the PLO was characterized by an unhinged competition between the various factions (referred to in Arabic as *fasa'il* or *tanzimat*).[79] Unlike the Palestinian left (or the Islamist groups that later would emerge), Arafat did not have a strong ideological foundation, nor was he a particularly charismatic leader. What he lacked in these capacities, he made up for through meticulous coalition and consensus-building. Similar to the case of Lebanon's Rafiq al-Hariri, Arafat was not in the habit of facing off against competing factions. He roped them in through patronage while he worked scrupulously to establish himself as the center of every relation and asserting himself as a "bridge between different views, including from the PLO itself and the Palestinian diaspora."[80] Like with al-Hariri, Arafat's turn to neopatrimonial leadership was motivated by his wish to ward off competitors and was facilitated by his access to exponential external resources coming in to the PLO's control areas. In the latter half of the 1970s, he would attempt to impose his control of all aspects of the Fatah movement and the PLO state in exile by creating a number of parallel structures within these organizations with the sole aim of redistributing funds from, and thus politically undermining, pre-existing agencies run by fellow Palestinian leaders.[81] As a result, the PLO became cluttered with agencies with no real purpose but which continued to hire camp dwellers en masse. For the faction leaders who were sidelined by Arafat, seeking support from other Arab states such as Iraq, Syria, Libya, Egypt, or Saudi Arabia became a way of attaining influence within the PLO. For his part, Arafat largely overlooked such behavior and even encouraged competition among the armed groups, as long as they did not directly pose a threat to him. Although this tactical maneuvering seemed to keep the PLO intact, the ability to agree on a unified strategy became nearly impossible.[82] The fact that each guerilla leader was, in the self-scrutinizing words of Fatah co-founder Abu Jihad al-Wazir, "free to do whatever they could"[83] resulted in a widespread culture of corruption and clientelism where mid-ranking personnel were able to build their own personal empires of influence within the PLO's control areas.

The Arab League went on to recognize the PLO as the "sole legitimate representative of the Palestinian people," in October 1974, and granted it full membership. A month later, Arafat became the first non-state leader to address the United Nations General Assembly. This diplomatic effort came right after the PLO's adaptation of a "Ten-Point Program," which showed a willingness for compromise and hinted at a possible two-state solution with Israel, albeit affirming its commitment to liberating Palestinian soil through armed struggle. The PLO's hopes for mobilizing a wider Arab military front against Israel, however, began to wane as Lebanon in the spring of 1975 collapsed into civil war, pitting anti-Palestinian and pro-Palestinian militia groups against each other. As conflict engulfed Lebanon, President Suleiman Frangieh, along with a collection of Christian Maronite militias known as the *Lebanese Front*, turned to Syria in hopes that it would intervene on their behalf. As did their bitter enemy Kamal Jumblatt, leader of the PLO-friendly *Lebanese National Movement (LMN)* whom Arafat had persuaded to meet with Syrian President Hafiz al-Assad in similar spirits. Fearing that the PLO would trigger an Israeli intervention and thus hamper his regional ambitions of a *Pax Syriana*,[84] al-Assad sided with Frangieh, who in turn ensured that his geopolitical backers, Israel and the United States, greenlit a Syrian military intervention of Lebanon. In 1976, Syria entered the Lebanese war under the guise of a broader *Arab Deterrence Force* with the tacit (and later public) blessing of its cold war archrivals in order to crack down on its own allies such as the LMN and the PLO.

After a diplomatic line was reestablished between Arafat and al-Assad, Damascus came to ease its campaigns against the PLO. Arafat's "Fakhani republic" kept expanding rapidly in the mid-1970s, but Syria's invasion of Lebanon sent shockwaves into the PLO. Many of the guerilla factions had deep ties to Damascus, not at least because Syria had sought to capitalize on a growing discontent with Arafat after his adoption of the controversial Ten-Point Program. In 1976, al-Assad's invasion of Lebanon created confusion among the pro-Syrian axis of the guerilla factions, which were uncertain how to respond to the military offensive. The PFLP called for the ouster of Syria's own Palestinian army, *al-Sa'iqa*, from the PLO after the group overran its positions in Tripoli in May 1976. Meanwhile, the Syria-backed *PFLP-General Command* was rocked by several defections, with leading figures such as Muhammad Zaidan and Tala't Ya'qub leaving the organization, opting instead (with the help of the Iraqi B'ath party) to revive the former *Palestinian Liberation Front (PLF)*, which ultimately split into a pro-Syrian *Ya'qub wing*, and a pro-Arafat and Iraqi-backed *Zaidan wing* in the early 1980s. In summation, Syria's entry into the Lebanese conflict resulted in paralysis and splits within the Palestinian national movement in exile that it would never fully recover from, and the process laid the foundation of a trend that would only escalate in the decade to follow with nearly every guerilla group splintering into a pro-Syrian and a pro-Arafat branch.

At the time, Arafat's biggest concern, nonetheless, was the fact that the public support for the PLO was plummeting. The popular foundation that the Palestinian guerillas initially had built evaporated as Israel responded with increasingly harsh retaliatory attacks against Lebanon: several raids by air and sea in 1977, a minor invasion of South Lebanon in 1978, and a full-scale invasion in the summer of 1982. When the IDF launched "Operation Peace for Galilee" and an estimated 80,000 soldiers pushed through South Lebanon and began the process of encircling Beirut, Lebanese parties across political divides were pleading for the PLO to pull out of the capital and spare its population from the awaited onslaught. When the war began, Arafat begrudgingly accepted the offer extended by Ronald Reagan's envoy to Lebanon, Philip Habib, to let the PLO evacuate the country peacefully in September with guarantees that the civilian populations of the refugee camps would remain unharmed. These assurances would prove to be hollow. Acting on false information provided by Israeli Defense Minister Ariel Sharon, suggesting that Palestinians had been involved in the recent assassination of President-elect Bashir Gemayel, Maronite militias (guided by Israeli flares fired into the air) entered the Sabra and Shatila camps of Beirut on September 15, and spent more than two whole days slaughtering at least 1,000 Palestinian civilians.[85] The evacuation of guerillas from the ports of Beirut and the harrowing massacre at Sabra and Shatila were watershed events that marked the end of an era for the Palestinians in Lebanon, foreboding a future of both persecution and lack of sound political representation. The PLO, for its part, was forced to give up its near autonomous presence along the frontlines of the national struggle in exchange for a refuge in Tunis, subject to tight governmental scrutiny. It wouldn't take long, however, until Yasser Arafat was back in Lebanon.

By September 1983, the press reported that hundreds of PLO fighters who had originally been evacuated to eight different Arab countries were trickling back into the Palestinian camps of Tripoli and Beirut, while ammunitions and arms were coming in by sea.[86] Nonetheless, Arafat's ambitions of reclaiming his Palestinian state in exile were hampered by two fundamental factors:

1. a brewing rebellion in Fatah's own ranks, and
2. Syria's bid to prevent the PLO from resettling in Lebanon.

Having grown tired of Arafat's autocratic leadership and deeply disapproving of his newfound diplomatic aspirations to become a part of Ronal Reagan's peace plan for the Middle East, a body of distinguished Fatah leaders stationed in the Biqaʿ Valley, headed by Said Muragha (Abu Musa), broke ties with the Fatah mainstream in the spring of 1983 and established a new faction, *Fatah al-Intifada*.[87] Not surprisingly, the group's bid to serve as a corrective movement and set Fatah back on the "path to revolution" was supported materially by Syria (and Libya) along with the other pro-Syrian Palestinian factions.[88] In return, Abu Musa took it upon himself to lead a major Syrian-backed offensive against Fatah in the Biqaʿ Valley and the camps of Tripoli, ending with the expulsion of Arafat's forces from North Lebanon in 1984. The schisms that had manifested themselves in the PLO a decade earlier had now torn the Fatah movement into two.

The situation in Beirut was not much better. Having long outgrown its patience with the PLO's hapless military adventures and their negative impact on the country's Shiʿi population, the Amal movement, acting on Syria's orders, went on to besiege, starve, and shell the Shatila and Burj al-Barajne camps during the years 1985–7.[89] Because of the fierce resistance of their inhabitants, the camps never fell to Amal, although the Fatah movement was expelled from the area when Abu Musa's forces arrived in late 1987.

Arafat fared better in the South. As Syria had been careful not to cross Israel's "red lines" or security zones, the southern parts of the country had ironically become a refuge for Arafat loyalists seeking to evade al-Assad's campaigns in Tripoli and the Biqaʿ. With the Fakhani republic of West Beirut having been lost, Fatah was finding a new foothold in the cities of Sidon and Tyre. Although pro-Syrian and pro-Iranian militias quickly took control of Sidon following Israel's withdrawal from the city in the spring of 1985, the *Democratic Front for the Liberation of Palestine (DFLP)* along with Jumblatt's *Progressive Socialist Party (PSP)*, both friends of Syria, disobeyed orders from Damascus and provided a safe passage for Arafat's forces into ʿAyn al-Hilwe, allowing Fatah to fortify its position in the country's largest camp.[90] Amal, for its part, widened its offensive against the Palestinian camps of Sidon in 1986 but was unable to challenge Arafat's forces that proceeded to surround and destroy the local Amal headquarters at Maghdushe, a strategic hilltop overlooking ʿAyn al-Hilwe.[91]

The war-ending Ta'if accords of 1989 and a subsequent Amnesty Law in 1991 gave Lebanese militia leaders a chance to reshape their movements back into political parties.[92] Unable to stand on its own legs, however, the war-torn Lebanese state was put under the surrogate rule of the Syrian Baʿth party, which asserted itself as a guarantor for peace, and would control the country until 2005. The Cairo accords, which originally paved the way for the PLO's state in exile, were formally deleted as early as 1987. However, this did not do much to change the de facto relationship between the Lebanese state and the Palestinian camp leaderships as said accords were not replaced by any other treaty or understanding. Although the militias of the war were banned, Syria let its nascent ally, the Iranian-backed Hizballah, retain an armed presence by virtue of constituting "the resistance"—a useful deterrent to Israel. For the same reason, Syria did not make a priority out of disarming the Palestinian camps.[93] Although the Palestinians' heavy weapons were mostly handed over to the Lebanese army in the summer of 1991, clashes erupting between Arafat's Fatah and another pro-Syrian splinter group called *Fatah—Revolutionary Council*, near ʿAyn al-Hilwe, escalated into a battle between the camp and the army, which derailed the handover process completely.[94] It has yet to be assumed.

The fault lines of the Lebanese war would continue to dictate the political geography of the Palestinian camps in the years to follow. Arafat's Fatah movement was able to retain a severely reduced *state in exile* within the southern city of Tyre and its three Palestinian camps. Meanwhile, the camps of the northern half of Lebanon, including Beirut as well as the Biqa' in the East, were placed under the rule of the *Alliance of Palestinian Forces* (APF). Headed by an array of Damascus-based factions and also including the Gaza-based Islamists of Hamas and Palestinian Islamic Jihad (PIJ), this heterogeneous collection of Palestinian factions has since the announcement of the Oslo accords been united in their shared rejection of the peace process, their opposition to the PLO, and the insistence to continue on a path of armed struggle.[95] Because of their strong connections to Syria and Iran, leading groups within this framework, like the PLFP-General Command and Fatah al-Intifada, retain to date a range of armories and military bases in the Biqaʿ and Naʿme valleys, and have on rare occasions demonstrated the capacity to fire sporadic rockets into northern Israel.[96] That being said, the armed struggle across the southern border has, as of the late 1980s, largely been taken over by the militarily superior Hizballah, which very rarely has called upon its Palestinian partners to take part. There seems to be consensus among the armed Palestinian groups not to challenge the hegemony of "The Islamic Resistance" in this regard. "We long for the day to strike the Zionist enemy, but it would take a collective Arab effort," Lebanon's leader of the PFLP-General Command, Abu Iyad Ramiz Mustafa, noted during a meeting at the group's offices in Beirut. "In Lebanon, we are merely guests, and it is not up to us to lead the country to war. The memories of '82 are still very painful."[97]

Given such testimonies which in Lebanon are heard across the Palestinian spectrum, one might wonder why each bloc has spent substantial resources to retain a sense of territorial control and widen their influence within the present-day camps. This especially goes for ʿAyn al-Hilwe, which following the peace at Ta'if in 1989 has emerged as one of the most contested spaces in post-war Lebanon. As foreshadowed in the introduction to this book, finding an answer to such questions requires a close reading of how regional dynamics interact with the local reality, as well as a careful analysis of leadership structures within the Palestinian national movement. As far as scholarly accounts go, the present literature on ʿAyn al-Hilwe has given much more space to a type of social movement that ostensibly has little to do with Palestinian politics.

From State in Exile to Islamic State?

Scholars and the international media alike rediscovered the Palestinian refugee camps in Lebanon in the mid-2000s, albeit under very different circumstances. The 2001 terror attacks in New York and Washington, D.C., spurred a number of studies seeking to map out the reserve bases of "al-Qaida's armies" in the Middle East, and ʿAyn al-Hilwe was found to be used as a shelter and a recruitment ground for radical Islamists engaged in the region's wars.[98] Out of the plentiful studies to emerge, political scientist Bernard Rougier's *Everyday Jihad* provides by far the most detailed account of the dynamics at play. In his seminal monograph, Rougier sees clerics and guerilla movements within the camp originally backed by Iran come to trade their Hizballah-inspired "resistance" approach for a Salafi outlook in the run of the 1990s.[99] The author suggests that Hizballah's monopolization of the armed struggle against Israel has helped push Palestinians toward an ideology favoring an inward war against the unbelievers in defense of an imagined global *Umma* (Islamic Nation), over the national struggle for an out-of-reach homeland. Dwelling on concepts such as ideology and identity,

Rougier argues that ʿAyn al-Hilwe, and presumably its population, has gone through an "ideological transplant," from the universe of Palestinian nationalism to the realm of the former jihadi hub of Peshawar in Pakistan.[100] It is in this context that the author makes the claim that the Palestinian refugee camps of Lebanon are no longer a part of Middle East history, as cited earlier.

It would be neglectful, however, not to mention that Rougier takes a different approach in a subsequent monograph dealing with North Lebanon (and its Palestinian camps). In *The Sunni Tragedy of the Middle East*, the author finds that marginal jihadi groups have gained significant popularity among young and disenfranchised men of the area, because the moderate Sunni leaderships have failed to provide for them, materially and spiritually.[101] In this account, the poverty belts of the northern ʿAkkar district or the slums of the city of Tripoli are not seen through the lens of exceptionality but are treated as a microcosm of the struggles of the Arab world. This perspective is more akin to what the reader will find in this book about a refugee camp in South Lebanon. In this monograph, we will encounter some of the same militants and ideologues Rougier and others have covered in their works. However, we meet them at a different point in their militant careers; they are no longer the young revolutionaries they once were. Reeling from decades of turmoil with few victories to show for, some have fallen from grace with the global jihadi movement and have instead asserted themselves as full-fledged Palestinian factions enjoying diplomatic relations with both the mainstream nationalist leaderships and Sidon's political forces. Others have remained on a path of militancy but are no less prone to political opportunism. In all cases, their biographies present us with an important piece of the puzzle for understanding the trajectory of the Palestinian national movement in Lebanon, and the ways ʿAyn al-Hilwe connects to the everyday geopolitics of the region.

A Brokered Space

In these pages, we have seen ʿAyn al-Hilwe go from being a tent landscape set up around an abandoned British military base to emerge as a hub for nationalist activism and Palestinian militancy from the late 1960s throughout the 1980s. What, then, should we make of the place in the present period?

On the surface, the camp resembles a prison structure, where the stateless and unwanted have been relegated to the margins of society. At the same time, it has remained largely self-governed, not because the refugees are militarily superior to their host nation, but because a number of overlapping political deadlocks have prevented the finding of another solution. Although the refugees suffer at the hands of the security regimes of the Lebanese state, and enjoy next to no civil rights, they do not presently live in a "space of exception," devoid of human agency or political expressions. In ways, the socio-spatial organization of a place like ʿAyn al-Hilwe appears more complex than before, as political life in the camp is now shaped by a plethora of actors pursuing their separate ideas of statehood, ranging from Palestinian kinship organizations to Lebanese *zuʿama'* seeking to dominate urban politics in Sidon. The turbulent state of the camp cannot easily be traced backed to one sovereign suspending all law and order, but to the relentless competition between different types of authorities.

When I in this book refer to ʿAyn al-Hilwe as a Palestinian state in exile, I do not suggest that this is the only correct way to conceptualize or understand the refugee camp. Nor do I mean that the present administrations and rebel bureaucracies found there mirror the scope of the PLO's former "Fakhani republic," in Beirut. I use this label based on the *observation* of how pervasive the volatile political economy of the faction leaderships has remained in the everyday lives of inhabitants, and as an *aspiration* to further investigate how it connects to other networks of power, locally or regionally. More importantly, the expression indicates how the main Palestinian leaderships tend to view ʿAyn al-Hilwe and other camps, as extensions of their respective proto-state structures and as territories embedded in their struggle for self-determination and political hegemony.

Far from being exceptional, the political systems we find in the refugee camp are essentially not very different from what we find in the Palestinian Territories or in Lebanon. As a non-state space, the anatomy of ʿAyn al-Hilwe bears many of the hallmarks of neopatrimonial rule: endemic political fragmentation, parallel administrations and superfluous governance structures, and a seemingly uninterrupted flow of external resources, most of which do not benefit its largely impoverished population. Therefore, there are good reasons to draw parallels between the political order of the camp and the trajectory of the national movement's state-building projects elsewhere, particularly the PLO's Palestinian Authority in the West Bank. However, unlike the latter, there is no dominant party or leader in charge of the "Capital of the diaspora." That is not to say that many have not attempted to claim this role. In the main cases of this monograph, which we will soon explore, we will see a number of governments and external actors attempt to claim their stake to the ʿAyn al-Hilwe camp and speak in the name of the Palestinian refugees, such as the PA/PLO, the Hamas movement, Syria, Iran, and Lebanese elites—none of whom are particularly successful in this regard. In order to get a fuller picture of the dynamics at play, we will be forced to lend more scrutiny to the agency of the intermediaries in these exchanges of power, where the camp-based political groups play a crucial role.

Building on what I alluded to in the opening of this book, I put forward that camp politics in Lebanon, or neopatrimonialism for that sake, is much more than a top-down chain of command. Although it is often noted that neopatrimonial rulers rely on efficient power-brokers to facilitate their authority, the mutual dependency in this relationship is seldom given much consideration. As we move forward with our exploration of ʿAyn al-Hilwe's post-Oslo history, we will witness how local camp commanders and middle-rank faction officials are able to accumulate substantial political capital by latching on to more than one sponsor at once, by hampering the policies of superiors (middle-up), and by building their own pockets of influence (middle-down). In the sense that ʿAyn al-Hilwe has remained a Palestinian state in exile, it is first and foremost governed by a set of intermediaries, power-brokers, or, in Arabic, *wusata'*. As follows, we will perhaps need to revise the thesis that the militia commanders of the Palestinian camps, be they secularist or Islamists, are merely nihilistic warlords devoid of tangible political projects, or delusionary revolutionaries clinging on to past glory. At their core, the protagonists of this book are political pragmatists, who have honed an uncanny ability to force themselves onto the negotiation table at critical junctures in Palestinian and Lebanese history. With that in mind, we will move on to shed light on a largely overlooked historical event that has been crucial in terms of determining the current political culture of ʿAyn al-Hilwe and the other camps: namely, the PLO and the Fatah movement's comeback to Lebanon at the turn of the millennium.

3

The PLO's Return to Lebanon

In May 2000, Israeli forces unilaterally withdrew from South Lebanon, thereby ending their eighteen-year occupation, which began with *Operation Peace for Galilee* in 1982. Despite having disengaged from most parts of the country by the spring of 1985, some 10 percent of Lebanon's territories were left under the control of the Israel Defense Forces (IDF). This southern "Security Zone" was intended to serve as a buffer against "terror attacks,"[1] but as time passed, questions were raised about its efficiency. Rather than preventing violence, it seemed to give the Lebanese Hizballah movement and its allies an excuse to mobilize militarily against the occupying power. By the late 1990s, recurring clashes along the border had resulted in casualties on both sides, and had left more than a hundred Lebanese civilians dead.[2] The occupation of South Lebanon was becoming increasingly unpopular in Israel, and Minister of Defense Ehud Barak made the implementation of UN resolution 425, which called for the complete withdrawal of Israeli troops from Lebanon, a pivotal part of his electoral campaign for the prime minister's post, which he eventually won in 1999.

Israel's withdrawal set in motion a chain of events. While civilians in the South rejoiced in the streets and former residents of the "Security Zone" began returning to their homes, the Israeli-backed South Lebanon Army (SLA) collapsed and thousands of its affiliates fled across the border in fear of domestic reprisals.[3] Lebanon's Palestinians celebrated the withdrawal as a victory, and some took it as a sign that a decisive military confrontation against Israel was imminent. In October, Hizballah and pro-Syrian Palestinian groups sent busloads of refugees from the Beirut area to the southern border in order to stage anti-Israel rallies.[4] The demonstrations escalated into armed altercations with Israeli border patrols, resulting in the death of two Palestinian teens. This happened at the same time as Hizballah was able to sucessfully abduct three Israeli soldiers in the Shibaʿ Farms district. Lebanon was on the verge of war. Amidst it all, intelligence reports noted that the PLO had begun a "massive campaign" to bolster its military apparatus in the country's Palestinian refugee camps, particularly in ʿAyn al-Hilwe.[5]

At this point in time, the PLO's organizational presence in Lebanon hardly extended beyond a few scattered offices in the city of Tyre. This was now about to change. Reports were emerging that the head of the Palestinian Authority (PA), Yasser Arafat, was funneling substantial funds into Lebanon in an attempt to rebuild the PLO's infrastructure within the camps (see below). "The Resistance will continue," Munir al-Maqdah, a Fatah commander stationed in ʿAyn al-Hilwe and one among many recipients of these funds eagerly announced to the press: "even if all the armies on earth are massed on the frontier between Lebanon and the Zionist entity."[6] Nonetheless, Fatah's official leader in Lebanon, Sultan Abu al-ʿAynayn, assured the Lebanese media that his movement was far from about to declare a war against Israel, stating that "[t]he position of Munir al-Maqdah does not represent the position of the PLO, and these are not our instructions."[7] This sentiment was echoed by PLO officials based at the PA's head offices in the Gaza Strip, who went on to blame al-Maqdah for acting on behalf of Syria.[8]

Patterns of Contention

As we know, the PLO's initial era in Lebanon (1969–82) was characterized by the rallying cry for armed struggle and the liberation of Palestine. It is therefore timely to ask what prompted the organization's comeback to Lebanon at a point in time when it had renounced all armed activity and was instead pursuing the management of its quasi-state authority in the homeland. What has the PLO and the Fatah movement's political project revolved around in their second phase in Lebanon? In seeking an answer to these questions, we are faced with a challenge. As illustrated above, the leaders of the PLO, generally, and Fatah, particularly, do not always speak with a unison voice. It is not necessarily a straightforward task to identify who represents these organizations in any given matter. As political scientist Amal Jamal reminds us in his study of elite formation in Palestinian politics, the current national movement consists of a "heterogeneous mix of leaders" who seek influence by integrating into the emerging power structures or by disrupting them.[9] In this investigation of the PLO's and Fatah's post-Oslo legacy in Lebanon, I will identify four types of leadership structures that have remained at a near-constant tug of war since the early 2000s: (1) local camp commanders, (2) the homeland leadership in the Palestinian Territories, (3) the PLO's representational office (and Palestinian embassy) in Beirut, and (4) popular countercurrents found within the broader Fatah movement in exile or in the homeland. With this in mind, we will begin our exploration by paying a visit to a camp commander who is a likely candidate to go down in history as one of the most controversial personalities within Lebanon's Fatah branch.

A Portrait of a Camp Commander

The seminal Palestinian scholar Edward Said described living in exile as a continuous state of deprivation, loneliness, and paranoia.[10] These sentiments will likely be shared by many refugees currently living in a place like ʿAyn al-Hilwe. That is not to say that exile is equal to a state of impotence or helplessness. The legacy of Munir al-Maqdah, one of the camp's long-time Fatah commanders, is proof of this.

In September 2015, a friend brought me along for an unannounced visit to one of al-Maqdah's three houses. As we passed through the Bustan al-Yahudi district, we walked alongside a wide asphalted road found in the northern half of ʿAyn al-Hilwe featuring a number of taller cement-like compounds, some of which functioned as both military watchtowers and *dukakin* (shops) where armed guards were selling coffee during work hours. Like many other neighborhoods in this part of the camp, Bustan al-Yahudi was embellished by several large yellow Fatah banners flying from the rooftops. Nonetheless, locals were quick to point out that the armed men in this neighborhood did not necessarily belong to Palestinian President Mahmoud Abbas, whose forces were stationed a few meters further north in the bunker-like landscape of the Baraksat neighborhood. "This is not the Fatah of Abu Mazin," a local resident explained, referring to the nickname of the president. "This is the Fatah of Munir."[11]

In the middle of the Bustan al-Yahudi street, we made a cut through one of the narrow back-alleyways. We found ourselves entering through an anonymous steel door which, to my surprise, led us into a spacious and calm fruit garden lying next to a white mansion. Needless to say, it was an unexpected sight in a camp where more than 30,000 inhabitants compete for space. Here, we found al-Maqdah, sitting on the mansion's front stairs wearing beige pajamas, cutting his toenails while smoking a cigarette. "He calls it the White House," my friend whispered in my ear as the Major-General went inside to get dressed.

The View from the White House

Al-Maqdah returned in his characteristic camouflage uniform and invited us inside to sit in his office, while his servants brought us coffee. His spacious office, complete with a mahogany table, expensive leather couches, and the walls adorned with rare collectables, such as mid-century radios and old hunting rifles, was a far cry from Fatah's rather spartan offices in other neighborhoods of the camp. On the surface, his arrangement seemed to give credence to the often-heard saying that the "Sulta" (the PA) pays its rivals higher salaries than those directly loyal to it. However, there was hardly a soul in the camp that believed that President Mahmoud Abbas was his only employer.

Al-Maqdah has been known to nurture close relationships with regional partners who are not necessarily friends of the PLO/PA leadership. During our meeting, I had intended to inquire about the private hospital he built with the help of a $5 million donation from Sheikh Khalifa, Emir of the United Arab Emirates, and Saudi prince al-Walid bin Talal in 2007, as well as his militia forces who are commonly believed to be funded by Iran and Hizballah.[12] Al-Maqdah, however, was in no mood to discuss these matters. Evidently annoyed by my unannounced visit, he instead spent most of our time addressing the Syrian war and the refugees fleeing for Europe—a major conspiracy orchestrated by Western governments to attain cheap labor, he thought. Although al-Maqdah seemed in no mood to discuss regional allies nor his relationship with the PA, his biography speaks volumes about Fatah's turbulent post-Oslo trajectory in Lebanon.

A Dossier of Dissent

Tracing his origins back to the Galilean villages al-Ghabsiyye and al-Manshiyye, Munir Hassan al-Maqdah was born in ʿAyn al-Hilwe in 1960. Having left school to join the ranks of the PLO at an age of ten, al-Maqdah initially received military training by the DFLP in Syria, before returning to his camp of origin and rising to prominence as a member of Fatah over the next decade. Al-Maqdah became Yasser Arafat's bodyguard in his infamous Force 17 and joined his ship for Tunis following the defeat in Beirut in 1982. However, when Israel withdrew from the Sidon area three years later, al-Maqdah pleaded Arafat for funding in order to return to ʿAyn al-Hilwe with a group of militiamen.[13] Granting him his wish, Arafat sent al-Maqdah back to South Lebanon where he became a key person in rebuilding Fatah's military wings. At a time when Arafat's forces had come under attack by pro-Syrian militia groups in the northern half of the country, Fatah contingents in the South would fortify the organization's position in ʿAyn al-Hilwe by bringing in artillery through the ports of Sidon.[14]

However, when Arafat, in 1988, announced that he had accepted a two-state solution with Israel, his relationship with the cadres in Lebanon began to turn sour. The fact that the PLO, after siding with Saddam Hussein during the Gulf crisis in 1990–1, had lost a significant portion of its Arab funding and could hardly pay the salaries of its military wings did little to improve the situation. When Arafat indirectly (via fax machine) took part in the peace talks at the Madrid Conference in 1991, al-Maqdah led a bloodless coup, seizing all of Fatah's offices in ʿAyn al-Hilwe with his personal force consisting of some 300 men. Arafat sought to quell the mounting tension by pursuing a policy of cooptation which included an official offer to let al-Maqdah assume leadership of Fatah's military wings in Lebanon. Although al-Maqdah reluctantly came back to Arafat's fold, the events cast doubts over who was calling the shots in South Lebanon. Was ʿAyn al-Hilwe run by the PLO's central leadership in Tunis, or a gang of local dissidents?

In the summer of 1993, the tensions resurfaced when al-Maqdah accused the PLO leadership for neglecting the Palestinians in Lebanon. The claims were not baseless. As Brynjar Lia notes, the PLO had begun to sell off the properties and assets of the Fatah movement in the southern parts of the country, "including apartments, land, factories and shares in commercial companies" in preparation to fund the building of a Palestinian police force in the Gaza Strip and the West Bank.[15] At a time when prominent PLO officials chose to resign due to Arafat's "moderate policy toward Israel," al-Maqdah joined their plea for his resignation, citing the grievances of his fighters who had gone unpaid for months.[16] Upon the public revelation of the Oslo accords in September, al-Maqdah urged Palestinians to disregard the peace process, insisting that "We will not lay down our weapons until complete liberation … Sooner or later we will throw the Zionists into the sea."[17]

Following a series of failed attempts at reaching an understanding with him, the PLO gave up on al-Maqdah in October and went on to appoint a new leadership in ʿAyn al-Hilwe, consisting of Lt. Col. Badiʿ Kuraym and Majors Mahir al-Shbayta, Khaild al-Shayib, and Mansur ʿAzzam.[18] Nonetheless, al-Maqdah caught Arafat by surprise when he in a lengthy phone conversation informed the latter that the new Fatah contingents refused to replace him and had instead turned their offices over to him. Within a few weeks, thirty-two leading Fatah officials in the camp had thrown their support behind al-Maqdah, who according to the media carried on under the organization's emblems, logos, and charters.[19]

A Struggle on Two Fronts

As the head of a military organization outside of his homeland, al-Maqdah resembles what political scientist Yossi Shain has dubbed a revolutionary exile. According to Shain, these revolutionaries fall within three different categories based on how they operate and the aims they pursue.

1. First, there are those who struggle from abroad to overthrow a native homeland regime.
2. Then, there are those who fight from outside a claimed national territory to gain independent political status in the international order.
3. Finally, there are those who fight from outside their country's borders against an alien conqueror to regain independence or territory lost in a war.[20]

While the PLO's initial period in Lebanon falls within the third category, the activities of al-Maqdah and other camp commanders like him are indicative of a change of dynamics.

Following the creation of the PA in 1994, these came to wage a struggle on two fronts: both against the Israeli occupation, as well as the native homeland regime engaged in peace negotiations with the former. More concretely, their efforts would revolve around attempting to force the Fatah movement back on a path of militancy and revolutionary violence and in the process challenge the homeland government's legitimacy by sowing doubt about its credibility as a partner in peace. To pursue this strategy, they would go on to team up with resourceful partners sharing their bid to derail the peace process.

Aligning with Syria, Iran

Following the Madrid talks, both Syria and Iran had intensified their funding of a number of Palestinian rejectionist militias in Lebanon. Whereas the logistic support mostly went to fringe groups with little or no public support among the Palestinian people, the mutiny within Fatah in 1993 provided both states with an opportunity to widen their influence within the Palestinian national scene. In June 1994, the Lebanese daily al-Safir claimed that "all of the Palestinian institutions" in ʿAyn al-Hilwe had been seized by Arafat's opponents, and were now fully funded by Iran, including educational, cultural, and health institutions.[21] Iran even took it upon itself to fund Arafat's "Martyr's Institution," a foundation for supporting the families of fallen Fatah fighters, regarded by some as a major vehicle for patronage.[22] Moreover, both Iranian-funded and pro-Syrian militia groups in the camp proceeded to offer al-Maqdah protection against Arafat-backed forces. This became evident when Arafat, in November, mobilized 200 fighters in an effort to reclaim his position in ʿAyn al-Hilwe by ambushing six offices belonging to al-Maqdah and his right-hand commander Khalid al-Shayib.[23] Meanwhile, the militias of Damascus-based groups like the DFLP and the PLFP interfered on al-Maqdah's side. The clashes, which resulted in ten dead and twenty-five wounded, produced no military victory for Arafat. Rather, the violence seemed to turn the camp population against him, as anti-Oslo demonstrations erupted in the streets.[24] Another string of clashes, which rocked the camp for two days in the summer of 1995, saw Arafat further lose ground. This time al-Maqdah's forces seized all of Fatah's checkpoints around the camp, while Fatah's Arafat bloc blamed pro-Syrian forces for assisting them.[25] Syria also assisted al-Maqdah in setting up his own revolutionary force, The Black September 13th Brigades—a reference both to the date when the Declaration of Principles of the Oslo accords was signed and the former Black September Organization formed by Fatah militants in Jordan in the 1970s. When the unit went on to lobby rockets into the Galilee region,[26] this was not only a battle cry against Israel but also a clear message, to whoever was listening, that Yasser Arafat did not fully control Palestinian decision-making—let alone his own Fatah movement.

A Rebel without a Cause?

While Arafat was widely regarded as a secular leader and a political moderate by Western stakeholders, al-Maqdah positioned himself as the polar opposite. In the mid-1990s, he came to adopt an outwardly religious image, taking cues from Islamic resistance groups such as Hamas and Hizballah. In 1998, he was able to obtain Iranian funding to create an Islamic para-military group that he called the Popular Combatant Army (al-Jaysh al-Sha'bi al-Mujahid).[27] In September of that year, al-Maqdah invited the press to observe the graduation of some 200 militants in his new army, where fighters dressed in green and black colors paraded with machine guns and B7 rocket launchers in the soccer field of ʿAyn al-Hilwe, chanting slogans from the Qur'an. "Of course this graduation is the third of its kind in the Popular Combatant Army," al-Maqdah told the press.

> And it is an affirmation of our commitment to [carry] weapons and the option of resistance until the end of the Israeli occupation of all Palestinian land and the liberation of the al-Aqsa mosque. And it is a response to the American arrogance toward our Islamic and Arabic Nation, and the attacks against it in Afghanistan and Sudan, as well as a response to the hostile alliances against our *Umma* (nation) and recently the Turkey-Israeli alliance [...] The pressure on the Palestinian people increases every day, and therefore heroes and *mujahidin* emerge among this people, committed to armed struggle.[28]

Because of his militant outlook, his newfound closeness to Hizballah, and a pending death sentence issued by Jordanian authorities in the spring of 2000 for allegedly having assisted a local al-Qaida cell in plotting to kill both American and Israeli targets, a number of security reports came to identify Munir al-Maqdah as some kind of jihadi militant.[29] Other accounts suspected that he was not much of an ideologue but instead an opportunist ready to "work under a new flag" for a little bit of money.[30] Nonetheless, al-Maqdah had his eyes firmly fixed on Palestine, and his choice of regional partners clearly reflected his ambitions to this end. Although he firmly denied the al-Qaida link, the Fatah commander—never the one to shy away from a media controversy—announced that he would have no moral quandaries about cooperating with Osama bin Laden himself, should the latter seek to "liberate the holy city of Jerusalem."[31]

In the end, al-Maqdah's Popular Combatant Army (and his many claims of having trained a new generation of Palestinian suicide bombers) amounted to little more than Iranian-sponsored psychological warfare. However, the Iranian connection would prove crucial at the breakout of the Second Intifada, the rebellion in which Palestinians rose up against the Israeli occupation through violent means and where the refugee camps of the West Bank and Gaza Strip became bases for the al-Aqsa Martyrs' Brigades (AMB) and other militias.

The al-Aqsa Martyrs' Brigades

In the late 1980s, a group of student activists hailing from the city of Nablus and the Balata refugee camp made ʿAyn al-Hilwe their stomping ground after Israeli authorities deported them to South Lebanon due to their engagement in the insurrection known as the First Intifada (Chapter 1). As strong ties existed between the Fatah grassroots in the northern parts of the West Bank and South Lebanon, it was perhaps not surprising that a close affiliate of the deportees from the Balata camp, Nasir ʿUways, reached out to Munir al-Maqdah years later when a second large-scale rebellion had erupted in the Palestinian Territories.[32] Asserting himself as a vital intermediary between Iran/Hizballah and militants in the West Bank, al-Maqdah would use a Lebanese bank account to funnel substantial sums of money to ʿUways and others like him, who in turn redistributed the funds among AMB cells in the West Bank's refugee camps such as Balata, Jenin, and al-Jalazon. Allegedly, ʿUways would receive approximately $5,000 from Lebanon a week intended to cover living expenses, arms purchases, acquisition of high explosives, and renting apartments.[33] By the time he was captured during Israel's Operation Defensive Shield in the spring of 2002, he had emerged as the military leader of the AMB in the West Bank, and had been involved with arranging suicide attacks and shootings that had claimed the lives of tens of Israeli civilians. Meanwhile, rumors circulating in Israeli media claimed that the police had foiled a four-man cell in East Jerusalem that al-Maqdah had tasked with assassinating none other than Prime Minister Ariel Sharon.[34]

In the midst of the turmoil of the Second Intifada, the PA/PLO assumed a double stance by both attempting to pass itself off as a part of a diplomatic solution while it continued, in many cases, to support militant cells materially. The AMB's links to Fatah were evident from the start, although often-heard claims of Yasser Arafat being in direct and full control of these militants should be taken with a large grain of salt. Not unlike al-Maqdah in Lebanon, various political figures in the West Bank, some of them working for the PA, would compete in extending their own networks within these militia cells, presumably with a view to gain a more important position in the aftermath of the rebellion. This dynamic occasionally resulted in splits and the emergence of parallel AMB leaderships whose agendas, in the words of one of ʿUways' former combatants in the Balata camp, "were not about the nation … their goal [was all about] personal interests and money."[35]

Ultimately, we would be remiss to neglect how susceptible the moderate core of the Palestinian leadership was to the pressure coming from radical elements within its own ranks, who were doing their utmost to push their peers and leaders to respond to the call for arms. In this picture, we should not underestimate the pressure coming from Lebanon and ʿAyn al-Hilwe. No longer merely operating from the sideline, al-Maqdah had managed to inject his influence into the heart of Fatah's organization in the Palestinian Territories. That being said, Hizballah and Iran decided to cut al-Maqdah out of the equation at an early point, either due to the arrest of Nasir ʿUways in 2002 or—as some accounts claim—because he was pocketing too much of the funds for himself. In any case, the dissident camp commander had proved to be a force to be reckoned with and a potential problem for the PA/PLO leadership in the long-term. Back in Lebanon, Arafat's allies had given up trying to purge al-Maqdah's forces from ʿAyn al-Hilwe, and were instead opting for a new strategy: cooptation.

Arafat's Comeback: The Homeland Responds

In late November 1996, Arafat's Tunisia-based envoy to Lebanon, Faruq al-Qaddumi, flew to Beirut in order to initiate reconciliation talks with Munir al-Maqdah.[36] The talks came after al-Maqdah had accused Lebanon's official PLO leader Sultan Abu al-ʿAynayn of ordering his assassination on behalf of Arafat and Mossad a year prior.[37] After months of negotiations, Abu al-ʿAynayn felt reassured enough to leave his offices in the southern Rashidiyye camp to pay al-Maqdah a formal visit in ʿAyn al-Hilwe.[38] Interestingly, sources within the PLO/PA claimed that al-Maqdah, despite his insubordination, had never stopped receiving funds from President Arafat.[39] Fatah had officially fired al-Maqdah twice (in 1993 and 1995) but had kept him on its payrolls. In December 1998, Fatah announced al-Maqdah's dismissal for the third time due to his attendance at the Palestinian National Conference hosted by the opposition movements of the Alliance of Palestinian Forces (APF) in Damascus. However, rumors had it that al-Maqdah's strained relations with Arafat had improved, and that the dismissal was merely an act of political theater. As would soon become apparent, the Palestinian president needed him and other defectors back in the fold as to make sure they would not stand in the way of his ambitions to resurrect the PLO as a political and military branch in the camps of Lebanon.

From Wye River to ʿAyn al-Hilwe

Yasser Arafat's "return" to Lebanon left both journalists and fellow Palestinian officials scratching their heads. However, all parts noted that the timing likely was connected to the peace process and an upcoming round of negotiations with the Israeli authorities. Indeed, the Palestinian president's decision to start funneling money back into the camps of Lebanon coincided with his signing of the Wye River Memorandum of

October 23, 1998, which stated that the Palestinian leadership and Israel aimed for a permanent status agreement by May 4, 1999.[40]

The final status talks were supposed to seal the peace negotiations by resolving the most contentious issues that Israel, by virtue of being the stronger party, had demanded would be postponed until the very end. This included seeking permanent agreements regarding the borders of a Palestinian state, the removal of Jewish settlements in the West Bank and the Gaza Strip, the recognition of a Palestinian capital in Jerusalem, Palestinian sovereignty of the Haram al-Sharif (Temple Mount), and last but not least, the resolution of the refugee problem "through some formula recognizing Palestinians' right of return" as stipulated in UNSC resolution 194. It was speculated that it was the latter point that in particular had Arafat hurry his mobilization in Lebanon. "Arafat wants to be the representative of the Palestinians everywhere, especially for the final status negotiations," Shafiq al-Hut, a former member of the PLO's Executive Committee, commented at the time.[41] "But given that most Palestinians in the diaspora are now against his leadership, to regain this status he needs to build a 'coalition of interests' both with the PLO opposition and with Lebanon and Syria," al-Hut contended.[42] This involved finding a solution with dissident militia commanders who had been running the camps with Syrian and Iranian funding during the past six years. Reclaiming the camps security-wise was a matter of ensuring that they did not become "hostage of any of the political parts" the PLO's leader in Lebanon Abu al-ʿAynayn relayed.[43]

While Arafat embarked on a world tour of capitals in order to drum up international support for the final declaration of Palestinian statehood, Abu al-ʿAynayn made his own tour in Lebanon to appease local parties ahead of the reopening of Fatah's offices in ʿAyn al-Hilwe. During a visit to the Maronite Patriarch Sfayr in the northern parts of the country, he relayed that the PLO was in a critical phase due to the final status talks and the upcoming "negotiations of the fate of the refugees."[44] He underlined that Arafat's project in Lebanon had nothing to do with tawtin (settlement) or seeking to establish permanent Palestinian structures on Lebanese soil but was a way of struggling for the right of return for "half of the Palestinian people" living outside of their homeland.[45] Arafat and his allies not only needed to make an arrangement with Lebanese and Palestinian stakeholders but also depended on reaching an understanding with the Syrian regime due to its de facto military control of the country. As it turned out, the latter had incentives for vouching for the comeback of Arafat's forces.

In the early 1990s, a group of Syrian, Israeli, and American diplomats had gathered in secrecy to attempt to negotiate the fate of the Golan Heights, a rocky plateau in South-West Syria which was seized by Israel during the war of 1967 and—much to Syria's frustration—had been annexed in December 1981.[46] The tone had initially been positive, but the negotiations derailed after Benjamin Netanyahu of the Likud Party took over the prime minister post in 1996, and adopted a harder line than his predecessors. When Ehud Barak's Labor coalition replaced Netanyahu's Likud-led government in 1999, the former gave up the Syrian negotiations completely and turned his attention back to the Palestinian track. This cold shoulder from Barak enraged Damascus, which attempted to pressure Israel into changing its mind on pulling out of the negotiations. In 1999, this involved mobilizing Palestinian allies such as Islamic

Jihad to fire rockets across the Lebanese border and into Upper Galilee, while Syria simultaneously softened its approach with Arafat and the PLO.[47] After all, Arafat had a position at the peace negotiation table, and Syria needed to build bridges to any party that might have a say in the final settlements.

In the short term, this reshuffling of cards paved a way for a rapprochement between Syria and Fatah pertaining to ʿAyn al-Hilwe. When Arafat's forces moved in and reclaimed their former checkpoints in the camp on June 22, no pro-Syrian militia group nor Islamist battalion objected, although the Arafat-loyalists were hardly met with fanfares and jubilations. Arafat's comeback was largely supported by the PLFP and the DFLP, which after a formal reconciliation with the former in Cairo in the summer of 1999 were on their way out of the rejectionist alliance (APF) and back into the PLO fold.[48] In July, Arafat also provided for the resettling of smaller PLO factions, such as the Palestinian Popular Struggle Front (PPSF), the Palestinian Liberation Front (PLF), and the Palestinian People's Party (PPP), that had remained absent from the camp since 1993, but now each received $10,000 to re-open their offices and vouch for the presence of his forces.[49]

Fanfares or not, Arafat's Fatah movement was back in the Capital of the Diaspora, and so was the PLO as a political framework.

Influence Measured in Boots on the Ground

In ʿAyn al-Hilwe, Arafat went on to resurrect some of the PLO's former vocational, health, and educational institutions. The main bulk of his funds, however, went to re-establishing his militia forces, the Palestinian Armed Struggle Command (PASC).[50] In the summer of 1999, the camp saw the rapid deployment of 500 armed recruits, only half of whom were Fatah proper. The other half, it turned out, were unemployed young men who were payed $100 a month in order to carry a rifle for Arafat—or in some cases to put their weapons down for him.[51] Equating political influence with boots on the ground, Arafat sought to play down any opposition to his presence through outbidding rival Fatah militias and by arming the camp population. As a part of his strategy of patronage, he proceeded to invite oppositional actors back into his military organization but made sure that his closest allies outranked them. This was the case with Munir al-Maqdah who now was reinstated and put in charge of an armed Fatah battalion but was told to report to the PASC's new leader Ahmad al-Salih, an Arafat-loyalist who had flown in from Libya.[52]

Whereas Arafat's envoy to Lebanon, al-Qaddumi, claimed that the PASC's weapons were light and would bring a sense of order and stability to ʿAyn al-Hilwe,[53] critics lamented that Fatah's organization had been reduced to an instrument for Arafat to impose his control. One of the critics was the former PLO-veteran and Sidon resident Shafiq al-Hut, who asked why Arafat didn't instead prioritize the building of a robust civil society, warning that the policy of arming the camps would only harm the relationship between the refugees and the Lebanese state.[54] This warning, as we will see next, was not unfounded.

Countered by Sanctions

While Sultan Abu al-ʿAynayn in October 1999 was in the process of adding fifty new recruits to the ranks of the PASC, he was dealt a death sentence by a Beirut court. The PLO chief stood accused of "forming armed bands with the intention of committing crimes against civilians and attacking the Lebanese state."[55] The fact that the judiciary informed him that the sentence would be abrogated in favor of a fair trial should he turn himself in to the authorities only added to the PLO's suspicions that the charges were politically motivated and aimed to hamper Arafat's mobilization.[56] While Abu al-ʿAynayn refused to turn himself in, claiming that certain influential parties were after him, the convictions against him continued to pile up. In late 2000, he was indicted for weapon trafficking and plotting terrorist attacks against Lebanon, adding fifteen years of prison to his pending death sentence. Meanwhile, the Lebanese military would continue to round up Fatah officials on charges of murder, some of them dating back to the 1980s and the days of the Lebanese war.

It was not immediately clear whether these arrests were ordered by Damascus or if Lebanon's security agencies were acting on their own. For his part, Abu al-ʿAynayn claimed that he had been given the green light by Beirut and President Émile Lahud, a friend of Syria's Hafiz al-Assad, to take control of ʿAyn al-Hilwe.[57] However, he now found himself stranded and unable to leave his office in the al-Rashidiyye camp in Tyre. The fact that Arafat had phoned in from Gaza in order to promote him to the rank of Brigadier General and welcomed him as a member of Fatah's Revolutionary Council did little to remedy his predicament.[58] A month later, the Lebanese military tightened its control around the entrances of ʿAyn al-Hilwe and imposed a strict embargo on all building materials into the camp.[59] While Arafat pleaded the Arab League to assist in lifting the embargo, Fatah militiamen in the camp staged an armed demonstration against the Lebanese army and fired their guns in the air. The pro-Syrian opposition factions, for their part, scoffed at the demonstrations and told the press that Arafat enjoyed so little support in the camp that he had been forced to bribe taxi drivers into joining his protests.[60]

Fatah Reclaims North Lebanon

Whereas Arafat's closest allies in Lebanon found themselves imprisoned or hampered by pending death sentences, the former was presented with a window of opportunity at the summit for Arab leaders in Amman in 2001. In a private meeting with Syria's new president, the young and charismatic Bashar al-Assad, the parties made promises to work more closely and to "forget past enmity."[61] This rapprochement allowed Arafat to fly to Beirut in order to discuss the prospects of establishing a PLO presence in the Palestinian camps in the northern half of the country with Lebanese President Émile Lahud. The impact of these talks should not be underestimated. In the years to follow, Fatah members who since the end of the war had lived a sheltered life in the southern camps were finally able to move back to their families in Beirut and Tripoli, where they began the process of resurrecting the movement's offices.[62] Although the pro-Syrian Palestinian militia groups of the APF did not prevent Arafat's Fatah from resettling, the parties could not seem to agree where the movement's new headquarters should be placed.[63] In al-Beddawi, the Fatah leadership had to make private arrangements to rent a piece of land on the outskirts of the official camp. The same scenario was echoed in ʿAyn al-Hilwe, where Arafat's official Fatah wing remained confined to Baraksat, an adjacent gathering north of the "official borders" of the camp. Meanwhile, the heartlands of the Capital of the Diaspora remained under the control of a multiplicity of Fatah militias only partially loyal to the main organization.

Overall, Arafat's bid to reassert his control of the camps of Lebanon had resulted in some rather peculiar arrangements. Although the PLO's guerilla headquarters and Popular Committees were reconstructed in nearly every camp, and Fatah's Armed Struggle Command had resurfaced as the most well-funded Palestinian militia organization in the country, these institutions had no war to fight. There was no armed struggle to coordinate. In reality, they were mere shells and symbols of Arafat's neopatrimonial ambitions to reimpose his control of the Palestinian diaspora and sideline all competition. However, as the final status talks stalled, and ultimately collapsed shortly after the breakout of the Second Intifada in September 2000, and any discussion regarding the refugee question was put on hold indefinitely, the gains of reviving the PLO's state in exile seemed dubious at best. Adding insult to injury, Arafat's diplomatic track with Presidents al-Assad and Lahud did not prevent the Lebanese parliament from, mere weeks after their meetings, passing amendments to the real estate acquisition law for foreigners (1969), which now stated that only citizens of a "recognized state" could own property in Lebanon; another collective punishment of the Palestinian refugees for the PLO's return.[64] As we will see next, some of the tensions between the PLO and the Lebanese state would be eased after both entities went through a change of leaderships in the mid-2000s.

Abbas' Quest for a Palestinian Embassy in Beirut

Following Yasser Arafat's death on November 11, 2004, Mahmud Abbas was within hours appointed the new head of the PLO by the organization's Executive Committee. Having assumed his role four years into the harrowing Second Intifada, Abbas was in dire need for international assistance to rebuild the PA's ravaged infrastructure and collapsed governance institutions. In order to improve the PLO's standing in the region, he quickly initiated steps to heal rifts between his organization and a number of Arab states as well as the Palestinian opposition. This included a rare visit to Syria, where he was received on red carpets and referred to as "Mr. President" although he had not yet been elected President of the PA.[65]

As before, Syria's hospitality did not come without expectations. This time, it was evidently related to the UN's recent issue of Security Council Resolution 1559, which called for a disarmament of all Lebanese and non-Lebanese militias, thereby threatening to demobilize Hizballah and loosen Syria's military dominance in the country. By extension of having a direct line to the Americans, Abbas was now President Bashar al-Assad's only lifeline to Lebanon. These dynamics also brought Abbas to Syria's man in Lebanon, President Émile Lahud. In December, Abbas landed in Beirut, where he met with the latter in order to discuss the prospects of fulfilling one of his primary objectives in Lebanon—normalizing the PLO's relationship with the government and opening a Palestinian embassy in the capital.[66]

The talks about an embassy were interrupted, however, by the 2005 Cedar Revolution, which led to Syria's sudden and unexpected withdrawal from Lebanon. Following the victory of the pro-Saudi and Western-friendly March 14th Alliance, Abbas instead continued his diplomatic effort with the new Lebanese leadership. Prime Minister Fu'ad Siniora, who now also assumed the leadership of al-Hariri's Future Movement, seemed to take greater interest in the plight of the Palestinian refugees than the previous regime.[67] Of course, this solidarity was not unconditional. Seniora was searching for allies to oppose Hizballah's weapons and vouch for a disarmament process.

Rather than lobbying against UNSC Resolution 1559, Abbas threw his support behind the renewed calls for Lebanese sovereignty and disarmament. In contrast to his predecessor, Abbas announced to the media that the Palestinian weapons in Lebanon—although he did not directly oppose them—did not have a political function and were not a sole guarantee for the right of return of the refugees.[68] The same year, the Lebanese-Palestinian Dialogue Committee (LPDC) was established to negotiate a solution to contentious issues like the Palestinian refugees' lack of civil rights, on the one hand, and the proliferation of illegal arms in and outside of the refugee camps, on the other. Much to the dismay of the Damascus-based opposition factions of the APF, Abbas stressed that any dialogue about Palestinian weapons did not rely on the parties' ability to first find a solution regarding civil rights. After all, Abbas' arena of struggle was the international diplomatic scene, and he had little interest in the guerilla factions holed up in the camps. As a token of trust, the Lebanese government granted the PLO a representational office in the western part of the Lebanese capital in 2006, which in 2011 would officially gain the status as the Palestinian embassy to Beirut. For the first time since 1982, the PLO enjoyed official representation in Lebanon.

Calls for disarmament not withstanding, it would soon emerge that the Future Movement and its March 14th alliance lacked the momentum to force Hizballah to disarm, and calls for UNSC 1559 eventually fell by the wayside. As for Abbas, the Palestinian president also found himself at an impasse. Because his diplomatic standing in Lebanon seemed to hinge on his ability to get Palestinian weapons under control, he was simply unable to ignore the camps. It was clear that he had to find a solution with militia commanders in ʿAyn al-Hilwe and elsewhere. This would prove to be a tall order.

Abbas vs. 'Ayn al-Hilwe

The PA's ceasefire agreement with Israel halted the Second Intifada in February 2005 and was regarded as an unpopular move among certain Palestinian leaders. The same month, Abbas sent a delegation to Lebanon in order to map out the political terrain in the camps. In ʿAyn al-Hilwe, Abbas' delegation met with Munir al-Maqdah, who at this point had reclaimed a prominent role within the PASC in Lebanon and still referred to himself as the leader of the al-Aqsa Martyrs' Brigades. Following the visit, al-Maqdah told the press that he had accepted the ceasefire and relayed that he remained in constant communication with Abbas on the situation in the camps.[69] However, a few months later he came to have second thoughts about his relations with the Palestinian president. It appeared that al-Maqdah had his eyes on the new PLO leadership in Lebanon, and when it became clear that Abbas was planning to appoint his close ally ʿAbbas Zaki as the head of the organization's soon-to-open representational office in Beirut, al-Maqdah reacted with dismay. For his part, Zaki would completely ignore al-Maqdah on his own publicity tours, and when one of his delegations failed to visit the camp commander on a round trip in November, the latter resigned from his position in Fatah and blasted President Abbas for neglecting the camps.[70]

While efforts were made to bring him back into the fold, al-Maqdah continued to hamper Fatah's efforts to gain control over the ʿAyn al-Hilwe camp. As early as the summer of 2004, he had created a controversy when he refused to comply with a Fatah-initiated military campaign to move against a troublesome band of jihadis calling themselves Jund al-Sham. Al-Maqdah halted the PASC's momentum by threatening to resign if the military campaigns were to persist, insisting instead on finding a negotiated solution which included pro-Syrian factions, Hamas, and other local Islamist groups.[71] Al-Maqdah's strategic insubordination was tried and tested. Through building alliances with various opposition groups hostile to the PLO, he had essentially made himself indispensable by virtue of being able to obstruct any political process that the PA wanted to carry out in Lebanon. This became particularly problematic following the crisis at Nahr al-Barid in 2007. Weeks of fighting between the Lebanese army and a jihadi group called Fatah al-Islam had resulted in the shelling of the camp, which subsequently was placed under the control of the former. In the aftermath of the crisis, Fatah achieved a diplomatic victory of sorts through its outspoken support of the army. Yet, as the Seniora government was pushing the PLO to secure ʿAyn al-Hilwe, it was becoming painfully evident that the organization's new leadership in Beirut was not calling the shots in Lebanon's most important Palestinian camp.

Particularly worrying was the close relationship Munir al-Maqdah had nurtured with the Palestinian Salafi militia ʿUsbat al-Ansar, held to be the staunchest rivals of Fatah in the camp. "Munir [al-Maqdah] has always had good relations with these guys," a Hizballah official told the press in 2010, adding that "we're afraid that now he will join them and kick Fatah out of the camp."[72] It was perhaps for these reasons that Abbas had begun the process of looking for someone to replace al-Maqdah as the head of PASC in Lebanon. In other words, he needed a new intermediary to maintain his relationship with the various Fatah branches and to make sure that his orders were carried out. This was no easy task. As a retired Fatah official in Sidon put it: "It is almost impossible for al-Sulta [the PA] to find anyone willing to lead Fatah's military institutions in ʿAyn al-Hilwe. Most officials don't even dare to set their own foot inside the camp."[73] These words were no exaggeration. Kamal Madhat, a senior Fatah leader who in September 2008 had been tasked with getting the security situation in ʿAyn al-Hilwe under control and who had stated he would do anything in his power to fulfil his mission—even if he had to open up an office and live in the camp himself—was killed by a roadside bomb only a few months later.[74] The choice eventually fell upon a young Fatah commander hailing from the Saffuri neighborhood of ʿAyn al-Hilwe. Mahmud ʿIsa, better known by his nickname "Lino," was deemed both loyal and fearless, and had already made a name for himself through his heavy-handed campaigns against irregular Islamist militia groups. ʿAzzam al-Ahmad, a member of the Palestinian Legislative Council and Abbas' envoy to Lebanon, had reportedly begun grooming Lino for the PASC leadership in 2009. In al-Ahmad's own accounts, this involved personally paying for Lino's military rank to be bumped up three notches, from captain to colonel.[75] Foreseeing the implications of this move, al-Maqdah had pulled strings in order to have Lino re-stationed in the southern Rashidiyye camp, but his efforts were to no avail. Following the elections of Fatah's Central Committee in July 2009, Lino was appointed as the new leader of the PASC branch in the camps of Lebanon, while al-Maqdah was relieved from his duties—once again.

Cleaning Up the House of Fatah

Al-Maqdah's dismissal came as a part of a larger house cleaning process that Mahmoud Abbas was undertaking. It was not only in the refugee camps that the head of the PA found himself challenged by his own. It had become clear that the widening of the Palestinian diplomatic mission to Lebanon, and the reopening of the PLO's offices in Beirut, had provided new channels of influence that were highly sought after within both Fatah and the PA's Ministry of Foreign Affairs. In preparing for the inauguration of a Palestinian embassy in 2011, President Abbas had decided to purge the local Fatah leadership of competitors and troublesome elements. This had involved removing former PLO chief in Lebanon Sultan Abu al-ʿAynayn, who was forced to resign, only to be re-hired for the position as Abbas' personal advisor in the West Bank, "before the ink of his resignation had time to dry." [76]

Tensions between Abu al-ʿAynayn and President Abbas had been present from the beginning. The former would openly criticize Abbas' support of UN Security Council Resolution 1559, which he referred to as an American-Israeli invention.[77] However, his dismissal and transfer seemed to have more to do with his proximity to Abbas' security chief in Gaza, Muhammad Dahlan.[78] Reportedly, Abbas had received intelligence reports that Abu al-ʿAynayn was "implementing an ulterior agenda" in ʿAyn al-Hilwe—presumably on behalf of Dahlan.[79] Some, in fact, believed that it was this alliance between Abu al-ʿAynayn and Dahlan that had resulted in the assassination of Kamal Madhat, one of Abbas' strongest cards in Lebanon, two years prior. In an interview with the London-based newspaper al-Sharq al-Awsat, Jibril al-Rajub, a member of Fatah's Central Committee, implied that Madhat's assassination was likely connected to his intentions of returning to Gaza after his tenure in Lebanon, where Abbas needed him in order to counter the growing influence of Dahlan, who in turn was rumored to have his eyes on the Palestinian presidency. Promoting Abu al-ʿAynayn to a position in the West Bank was thus a way of keeping him under control and away from both Gaza and Dahlan.

While Lebanon was increasingly becoming an arena of contention for different layers of the Fatah movement, Abbas made sure to fill up the new positions with loyalists. The appointment of Fathi Abu al-ʿAradat as the PLO and Fatah's new leader in Lebanon and Ashraf Dabbur as the ambassador of the Palestinian embassy was in line with this policy.[80] Nonetheless, the PASC in ʿAyn al-Hilwe was still vulnerable to external influence. During my fieldwork, interlocutors from different Palestinian factions claimed that some of Abbas' political rivals within the Fatah framework, whether they were based at the embassy in Beirut or in the Palestinian Territories, had made a practice of grooming their respective militia leaders in ʿAyn al-Hilwe, thereby extending their own line of influence in decision-making processes regarding camp security.[81] Whatever the case, it was clear that Lino had not been able to gain full control of the PASC bureau. To President Abbas' dismay, he had instead become caught up in an unhinged power struggle with Munir al-Maqdah, who despite his demotion, retained his personal militia battalion and did everything he could to hamper the efforts of his opponents to take over the camp. When an investigation revealed that a Fatah combatant had received money from an undisclosed source in order to assassinate Lino (he had by mistake killed his bodyguard instead) suspicions immediately fell upon al-Maqdah.[82] Soon after this debacle, President Abbas made the decision to shut down the PASC for good.

From Armed Struggle to National Security

Abbas appeared to had lost interest in any talks about handing over Palestinian weapons to the Lebanese army after he, for symbolic measure, had gone on to close a few Fatah militia bases near the southern camps in 2006. According to a high-ranking source in Lebanon's *General Directorate of General Security* (henceforth General Security), it was unlikely that the Lebanese army would even make the request to take over the camps due to the number of political deadlocks that would have to be solved in order to ensure an exit plan for the cobweb of rival militia groups outside of the PLO framework.[83] For Abbas' part, not only would a full withdrawal leave the camps in the hands of Hamas and other rivals, but his own Fatah branches had made it clear that they would fiercely resist, should he attempt to disarm them.[84] He was in no hurry to provoke them. However, the fact that a number of camp commanders in ʿAyn al-Hilwe were approaching their retirement age provided the PLO's new leadership in Lebanon with an opportunity to go through with a thorough reform of their militia branches.

In the spring of 2012, The PASC branch was shut down in its entirety and replaced by the new Palestinian National Security Forces (PNSF). The introduction of an ostensibly apolitical agency like the PNSF came in the aftermath of a broader donor-backed effort to rebuild the Palestinian security sector and help the PA re-establish a rule of law in the West Bank. By exporting the PNSF model to Lebanon, Abbas was able to signal his commitment to both improving the security situation in the camps, and bringing in new donor funds to keep unruly camp commanders in line and at peace with the new arrangements. In March, both al-Maqdah and Lino agreed to give up their checkpoints and militia offices and hand them over to an older Fatah veteran and Abbas-loyalist called Subhi Abu ʿArab, who now assumed the leadership of the PNSF in Lebanon.[85] In ʿAyn al-Hilwe, Abu ʿArab proceeded to successfully gather five or six larger Fatah militia wings under his command that had operated more or less independently of the main movement since the early 1990s. This included the Shatila Martyrs' Brigade led by Talal "The Jordanian" Balawne based near the Darb al-Sim checkpoint, the Abu Jihad al-Wazir Brigade led by Shadi al-Sabarbari, the Defense Brigade and the ʿAyn al-Hilwe Martyrs' Brigade, both found in the Baraksat district led by Bilal Aqraʿ and Qutayba Tamim, respectively. Meanwhile, Munir al-Maqdah's brother, Ibrahim "The Peacock" al-Maqdah, handed his al-Aqsa Martyrs' Brigade in the Bustan al-Yahudi district over to one of the largest single battalions in the camp, the Abu Hassan Salame Brigade, headed by the revered Fatah leader Muhammad al-ʿArmushi.

After all was said and done, Abbas' efforts seemed to have payed off. He had improved the PA/PLO's standing in Lebanon to the degree that he had been awarded a Palestinian embassy in the capital, and following the re-organization of Fatah's militia wings in ʿAyn al-Hilwe, even leaders of the pro-Syrian opposition factions admitted that Fatah's organization seemed to function more soundly than it had done in decades.[86] Whereas Fatah's house in Lebanon, for once, appeared to be in order, this was far from the case in the homeland. Not only were the Palestinian Territories ravaged by war and the economy in shards following the Second Intifada, but President Abbas' way of leading the PA was increasingly becoming challenged by a vocal opposition within the Fatah movement. Naturally, it would not take long for these tensions to reverberate in Lebanon.

Countercurrents

In 2013, a number of high-standing cadres and officials of Lebanon's Fatah movement issued a public letter to the Palestinian president and the PA in Ramallah. The letter's signatories aimed to alert their superiors about a "culture of corruption" and "favoritism" present at the Palestinian embassy in Beirut, and in the Fatah movement in general. They made a list of demands: they urged the president to reverse every decision made by the ambassador to Lebanon, Ashraf Dabbur, to separate the Palestinian embassy from the PLO framework, to form a financial investigation committee—and for those guilty of corruption—to be put under investigation by an "anti-corruption authority."[87] Moreover, the statement urged the PA to investigate "all organizational and administrational irregularities in the camps," and demanded the removal of Abbas' envoy to Lebanon, 'Azzam al-Ahmad, from his position.[88] "The leadership in Lebanon and 'Azzam al-Ahmad are a part of the reason why the Fatah movement finds itself in a perpetual state of collapse," Edward Kattoura said in early 2014.[89] As a co-author of the letter, he was at the time a prominent member of Fatah in Lebanon and worked as an advisor at the Palestinian embassy in Beirut. For Kattoura, the evidence of Fatah's decay was found in the inadequate governance of the Palestinian camps, which he believed to have been left in a state of disarray politically, socially, and security-wise due to widespread corruption and internal power plays within Fatah's organization. Before releasing the statement, the undersigned had discussed the possible outcomes of their course of action. They had envisioned three scenarios. If they were lucky, it could be that the president would consider their demands—but there was a possibility he would ignore them. Alternatively, he could respond with harsh sanctions against the whistleblowers, and possibly expel them from the Fatah movement. "The last scenario was the one that happened," Kattoura shared without batting an eye.[90]

In their statement, the Fatah officials had identified themselves as a corrective current. For the movement's leadership, this type of lingo seemed suspiciously close to that of Muhammad Dahlan. Hailing from the Khan Yunis refugee camp, Dahlan had gained notoriety for leading his violent campaign against Hamas during the hostilities of 2007 which ended with Fatah's expulsion from Gaza. Dahlan himself was forced to flee his Gaza home in late 2010 after being accused by his own party of corruption and for making plans to overthrow President Abbas. In June 2011, he was fired by Fatah's Central Committee for the same reasons, and relocated to the United Arab Emirates (UAE). After his dismissal, Fatah continued to single out and fire members of the organization who were thought to work for him. However, these campaigns also seemed to give Dahlan some momentum. For those critical of the policies of Mahmud Abbas, in terms of both his moderate line with Israel and his consolidation of power within the PA, Dahlan quickly became the favored choice. In 2014, Dahlan proceeded to brand himself the leader of a "Democratic Reform Current" within the Fatah movement, and announced his plans to run as a candidate for the Palestinian presidency.[91]

In addition to his bases of support in Gaza and the West Bank, Dahlan would from his Gulf exile seek to mobilize and build alliances with the Fatah leaderships outside of Palestine. To this end, he tasked his right-hand man, Khalid Ghazzal, a former Palestinian ambassador to both Poland and Hungary, with setting up a number of committees to communicate with the Fatah leaderships of the diaspora.[92] This brought Ghazzal to Lebanon, where Dahlan already enjoyed quite a bit of popular backing, not at least due to his wife Jalila Dahlan's charity work in the camps.[93] President Abbas, for his part, would go on to label Dahlan a traitor and stated that anyone who partook in his activities was committing an act of "national treason."[94] In Lebanon, Edward Kattoura and his companions faced similar allegations. Throughout 2013, they were fired from their positions one by one. While the dismissals at first persisted quietly and systematically behind the scenes, things went from tense to chaotic once the expulsions reached the heart of Fatah's security apparatus in ʿAyn al-Hilwe.

Corrective Current or Dahlan's Cronies?

In ʿAyn al-Hilwe, Jalila Dahlan nurtured a working relationship with former PASC commander Lino, and would rely on his help when conducting her charity work. The Fatah leadership, on the other hand, suspected that Dahlan was funding Lino behind the scenes, and went on to accuse him of embezzling funds from the movement. ʿAzzam al-Ahmad, the man who previously had ensured Lino's promotion to the PASC leadership, was now tasked with flying to Lebanon in order to fire him. While appearing on a talk show on the Lebanese al-Mayadeen TV channel, al-Ahmad told the viewers that Lino from day one had opposed "the decisions, systems and traditions [of Fatah] because it appears he doesn't know them."[95]

Despite his dismissal, Lino had no plans to giving up his security functions and continued to bolster his personal militia force with the support of Dahlan. When I met the father of five at his headquarters in the Saffuri neighborhood of the camp in October 2015, he had largely become the public face of Lebanon's chapter of the Democratic Reform Current. His office had a distinct bamboo hut interior design, and its walls were decorated with pictures of several prominent Fatah leaders such as Abu Jihad al-Wazir and Yasser Arafat. However, unlike the other Fatah compounds in the camp, there was no picture of Mahmud Abbas. Lino revealed that he held the latter personally responsible for ʿAyn al-Hilwe's decaying security situation. "The camps and the refugees are Abu Mazin's least concern," he shared.[96]

As with Kattoura, it was not an outspoken support for Dahlan's candidacy that drove him; his dissent seemed to be informed by other circumstances. Throughout the years, Lino had gained notoriety due to his campaigns to crack down on hostile Islamist militants in the camp. Although he was often outnumbered, he had fearlessly pursued the most dangerous jihadi actors—sometimes to the extent where it was not clear where Fatah's campaigns ended and his blood feuds began. In the process, he had made many enemies, and he had probably survived more assassination attempts than any other Fatah leader in the camp. He had largely accepted his demotion in 2012, when Abbas reintegrated his forces into the PNSF framework, and put him under the command of Subhi Abu ʿArab. What had provoked Lino beyond what he could bear was the fact that Abbas had made Munir al-Maqdah the second-in-command of the organization, a man who, in part, had made a career of making troublesome alliances with Islamists militants. "The PLO, and particularly Fatah, do no longer have an interest in facing the extremists (*al-mutatarrifin*)," Lino claimed.

> I live by the philosophy that anyone who commits a crime must face consequences. There can be no exception. If there is no *hisab* (accountability), there is no solution. [...]. Wherever the extremists go, they cause damage. There have been previous experiences, haven't there? Must I remind Fatah that there is something called Nahr al-Barid or al-Yarmouk? We are seeing a wholesale of the camp's stability and security. The outlaws have become the leaders of the camp, because Fatah is asleep. They want to surrender the camp—I understand them in this way. Subhi Abu ʿArab [leader of the PNSF in Lebanon] is very weak.[97]

If the Abbas-loyalists were not hungering for an armed confrontation against the camp's Islamist militants, Lino's personal forces certainly looked like they were up for the task. In and around his compound in al-Saffuri, I met a number of combatants carrying M16 assault rifles, many of whom appeared to be in their late teens or early twenties and spoke so eagerly about defending their commander that they seemed ready to follow him into the grave.

Reformism or Revivalism?

For an outside observer like myself, it did not immediately seem clear how running a separate security operation in defiance of the main organization was to contribute to a stronger Fatah movement. Did these armed forces have any other purpose than serving as a Dahlan-organized blow to Abbas' military capacities in Lebanon? Lino's militiamen aside, the Democratic Reform Current's ability to inspire any reform from the inside seemed questionable, as most of these officers had been removed from their positions of influence.

Lino, however, begged to differ on all accounts. First of all, he did not view himself as a "Dahlani." His opposition to Abbas was greater than his support of Dahlan. Furthermore, he had no doubts about the Democratic Reform Current's ability to counter Abbas' policies from Lebanon. For Lino, his work was a long-term project. Given the Palestinian president's heavy-handed campaigns against and arrests of Dahlan supporters and other dissidents in the West Bank,[98] the camp commander underscored the need for the Fatah movement of Lebanon to rise up to the challenge and build a robust countercurrent in exile. "For years Mahmud Abbas has treated the PA as his family enterprise," he contended.

> But he doesn't own the camps. He doesn't own ʿAyn al-Hilwe. Through our activities we are living proof that Fatah remains strong, even though Abu Mazin has tried to weaken it. If we build a strong organization here, then our brothers in Gaza and the West Bank will be encouraged to build a strong opposition where they are. [Our people] give our voice strength so that it carries all the way to Ramallah, and we are relaying the message that we are not defectors. On the contrary, we are the real Fatah, and we are the ones who are keeping the torch of revolution lit until Abu Mazin leaves office and goes home. It won't be long. Let's be clear: the old man is at the end of his days. After him, Fatah will return to its former strength. Of this I am sure.

Judging from his words, Lino was not as much a reformist than he was a revivalist. When he on New Year's Eve 2014 rivalled the Abbas-loyalists celebration of Fatah's fiftieth anniversary with his own armed parade, where he was observed carried through the crowds with a machine gun in hand, this was not reform work.[99] Rather, what he was doing was attempting to revive the revolutionary spirit of the Fatah movement, a spirit that arguably had been lost under Abbas' leadership.[100] More importantly, his public dissent was a warning of the countercurrents existing in a state of hibernation within the ranks of President Abbas' own Fatah movement, ready to wake at any moment.[101]

Fatah's Seventh Congress

Leading up to the launch of the Fatah movement's long-awaited seventh congress in 2016, rumors were circulating that President al-Sisi in Egypt had taken upon himself to mediate between Abbas and Dahlan. The congress was the movement's first since 2009, and was hyped as the event that would "usher in a new age for the Palestinian party currently ruling in the West Bank."[102] Analysts speculated to what extent the Abbas wing of Fatah had the strength and courage to host it without the Dahlan wing, especially as powerful forces such as the Arab Quartet, consisting of Saudi Arabia, Egypt, Jordan, and the UAE, had been pushing for the reinstatement of the latter in the Fatah leadership. However, when the congress finally took place in December, it became clear that no reconciliation was to happen, and that Abbas was perfectly capable of hosting the event without the Democratic Reform Current.

During the congress, four delegates from Lebanon—secretary of the Fatah movement, Rif'at al-Shana'; ambassador Ashraf Dabbur; leader of Fatah's unions, Amine Jibril; and PLO/Fatah leader Fathi Abu al-'Aradat—were elected to the Revolutionary Council, the movement's parliamentary body.[103] They were accompanied by a fifty-member delegation from Lebanon who were invited to join the congress in Ramallah.[104] As for the affiliates of Lebanon's Democratic Reform Current (who had been referred to as a "Trojan horse" by the opposing bloc),[105] these proceeded to host their own congress in the 'Ayn al-Hilwe camp.

On November 29, hundreds of camp dwellers gathered in the Saffuri neighborhood where Edward Kattoura and a number of other expelled officials of the Fatah movement lined up on a stage, not entirely dissimilar to the one Abbas would find himself delivering his three-hour speech at the seventh congress a day later. While huge Fatah banners swayed in the wind, the officials took turns at addressing an exhilarated crowd. At one point the speeches stopped, and the mood went from joyful to ecstatic as it became known that Mahmud Lino 'Issa was getting ready to take the stage. As the drums of one of Fatah's revolutionary anthems began playing, the phone cameras recording the event turned to the narrow alleyways of the camp, where the commander made his carefully orchestrated entrance.[106] He was accompanied by a squadron of armed fighters in camouflage clothing, their faces painted black. The crowds cheered and sang along with the song—*fida'i, fida'i, thawra thawra, hatta al-nasr* (fdia'i, fida'i revolution, revolution until victory)—while Lino took the microphone. Lino announced from the podium in his characteristic hoarse yet charismatic voice while grinning sardonically that the event which Mahmoud Abbas was hosting in Ramallah was little more than a conference for employees of the PA who likely had no other choice than to turn up if they wanted to keep their jobs. It was not, in his eyes, a congress for the Fatah movement. This in particular, he went on to claim, because the diaspora leaderships were hardly represented. On this note, he went on to blast the Fatah delegation from Lebanon for giving the Palestinian president a sense of much-needed legitimacy through their presence, because would Abbas dare to hold a congress "without the refugees of Lebanon?" "Silence is no longer permissible, and raising our voice is no longer sufficient," Lino concluded toward the end of his speech. "What is required is for us to unite our ranks to confront this collapse and the consequences of this deterioration. We will remain loyal to the blood of the martyrs, adhering to the principles and ideas that paved the way for Fatah in the first place."

Mahmoud Abbas, for his part, was happy to turn his back on these dissidents and likely had no problem drowning out whatever white noise was coming from the camps of Lebanon with the applause and cheers from the 1,300 cadres who attended the congress in Ramallah. However, in all his showmanship, Lino was highly accurate regarding at least one matter. As recent history has shown, no current or future leader of Fatah, or self-proclaimed representative of the Palestinian people for that matter, will be able to ignore ʿAyn al-Hilwe for very long.

The Struggle Continues

At the beginning of this chapter, I asked what prompted the PLO and the Fatah movement to attempt to reclaim the Palestinian camps of Lebanon in 1999, and what their political project has revolved around since. Although Yasser Arafat's military mobilization ironically was not indicative of any ambition to resume armed struggle, it had much to do with the search for Palestinian statehood. At the end of the millennium, the future of the Middle East was set to be negotiated between a host of actors looking to reach their respective final agreements on borders, statehood, and autonomy. At the time, both Palestinian and Syrian leaders found themselves engaging in talks with Israeli state officials with the United States acting as a broker, and for a brief moment, Iran and its Lebanese ally, Hizballah, were left debating among themselves to what extent "the Islamic Resistance" in Lebanon had any viable future as an armed anti-Israel entity. As the region held its breath regarding these fundamental issues, the PLO's resurrection in Lebanon seems anecdotal in comparison. Nonetheless, the organization's ambition to reestablish its "state in exile" was closely linked to all of the abovementioned geopolitical struggles. Revitalizing the PLO's militia branches and faction headquarters allowed Arafat, as the head of the PA, to create bureaucratic structures with which to reinlist renegade camp commanders, outbid Iran and Syria as the main patrons of the camp populations, and, hopefully, keep any hostile party from interfering in the peace process.

Arafat's successor, Mahmoud Abbas, on the other hand, is reputed to have abandoned any ambition of making headway in the so-called refugee question, and resents any mention of the camps or their weapons playing a "political role."[107] Yet his PNSF remain present in ʿAyn al-Hilwe and elsewhere. We must, in part, attribute his security branch's presence as a response to the pressure exerted opposition groups and countercurrents within Fatah, who have used these spaces to convene, map out supporters, and stage demonstrations, in a way that would be difficult for them to do in the West Bank. By contrast, Abbas has little to offer followers or subordinates in terms of ideology, and much less a way forward for the national movement. In lack of any viable political project apart from seeking international support for a dying two-state solution, he has continued to rely on PA state salaries to keep his fractious Fatah movement together, and in Lebanon, his security branch has emerged as his most important vehicle for patronage.

Although Fatah has reclaimed its position as the most robust Palestinian faction in Lebanon, in terms of size, member-base, and budgets, the organization appears so fragmented and ridden with disunity that it, at times, seems inaccurate to speak of it as a single movement. As a shopkeeper in ʿAyn al-Hilwe put it during one of my visits:

"There is no Fatah in our camp. There are only chieftains (*ru'us*)." Ultimately, the PLO's return to Lebanon has further entrenched an unsound militia-culture in the camps, where quarrelsome guerilla commanders climb the ranks of the various battalions and assert themselves as the leaders of streets, districts, and neighborhoods—sometimes with great measures of autonomy. This especially goes for the actors who have linked themselves to more than one sponsor and seem to feed off of their superiors' collective insecurities as to who is actually in charge. This is a dynamic which we will continue to explore in the following chapter, as we turn our attention to the Islamists of 'Ayn al-Hilwe.

4

ʿAyn al-Hilwe's Islamic Forces

In June 2013, Lebanon was shaken by clashes pitting the entourage of the charismatic Sunni cleric Ahmad al-Asir against the Lebanese army in the ʿAbra district of Sidon. Having led a popular campaign against Hizballah from his small mosque since late 2011, al-Asir and his closest followers had gradually armed themselves. After having hosted a string of antagonistic demonstrations and repeatedly shutting down the city center in protest of Hizballah's armed presence, al-Asir eventually wound up in a forty-eight-hour long violent confrontation against the Lebanese army, resulting in the death of eighteen soldiers, and the defeat of his own militias. After the clashes, many of al-Asir's followers, among them the renowned pop-singer-turned-Islamist, Fadel Shaker, sought refuge in the nearby ʿAyn al-Hilwe camp, where some still remain at the time of writing.

The Battle of ʿAbra coincided with a growing public interest in Lebanon's Salafi movement.[1] Scholars and intelligence bureaus alike found themselves guessing how long it would take for domestic actors to find a common cause with a burgeoning region-wide jihadi-Salafi current that had emerged in tandem with the ongoing conflicts in Syria, Iraq, and elsewhere. Reports of Palestinian youth slipping out of ʿAyn al-Hilwe and making their way to the strongholds of the Islamic State (IS) in Raqqa and Mosul seemed to support the claim that the instability of the Palestinian camp had regional implications.[2]

Those paying close attention would have noticed an interesting parallel development take place. It would soon emerge that Lebanon's General Security bureau was working close with a constellation of the camp's veteran Islamist militants to mitigate the crisis and mediate with the fugitives from al-Asir's group in order to agree on the terms of an extraction. One of these actors was *ʿUsbat al-Ansar al-Islamiyya* (The Islamic League of Partisans), an armed Salafi movement previously known for fighting alongside al-Qaida in Iraq. Not surprisingly, these conflicting dynamics had many analysts scratch their heads. Had ʿAyn al-Hilwe indeed once again become the center of "jihadi mobilization" in Lebanon,[3] or had this "myth of Islamist violence" within the Palestinian camp, been greatly exaggerated, because leading groups seemed to be curtailing rather than creating violence?[4]

I contend that neither of these conclusions is necessarily wrong, although this largely comes down to a question of which actor or group one chooses to analyze. In this chapter and the following, I will assess the trajectory of ʿAyn al-Hilwe's Islamist militants, their organizations, strategies, and goals. I am in particular interested in understanding the nature of their relationship with the Lebanese authorities and their connections to the broader Palestinian national movement. How did these militants, who once were known as Lebanon's primary enemies of the state, come to act as the authorities' local intermediaries? As the reader probably already can guess, this is a story far more complex than any radical movement simply putting down its weapons and "coming to its senses." It is a story of ideological dead ends, of political splits and inter-faction rivalries, and not at least, of a refugee camp becoming sucked into a race for hegemony led by Sidon's political and communal leaders.

Enemies of the State or Tacit Proponents of the Order?

Before we move on, I will briefly explain what lies in the expression global jihadism, and how the term might be understood within a place like ʿAyn al-Hilwe. The label jihadism (or Salafi-jihadism) has commonly been ascribed to a current of militant Islamism which first took shape in the early to mid-1990s, and emerged in earnest of the Gulf war and the fall of the communist regime in Afghanistan. The event coincided with a wave of foreign fighters from the Middle East leaving their respective countries behind in order to fight in Bosnia, Chechnya, Kashmir, Afghanistan, and elsewhere to defend a worldwide *Islamic Nation* (*Umma*) and to topple regimes seen as hostile against the Muslim populations. A second wave took place in the wake of the 9/11 terror attacks in 2001 and was provoked by the US occupation of Iraq two years later. Recently, the Middle East has experienced a third wave of global Jihadism in tandem with the Arab uprisings and the ensuing civil wars in Syria, Iraq, and Libya.

Whereas the actors we will meet in the course of these few chapters have shown an uncanny ability to connect with the elaborate transnational networks of support and recruitment which have sustained the jihadi movement for decades and let it manifest itself across substantial geographical stretches, the geographical reach of their own organizations remains quite limited. Although many of the people I interviewed for this part of the book tended to idolize the image of the restless jihadi knowing no bounds or borders, there was little question that they still found themselves restricted to the confines of a refugee camp in South Lebanon, unable to escape the scrutiny of the local political forces, such as Hizballah or the Lebanese army (externally) or the PLO (internally). They were operating in an unfavorable political landscape, and it was widely acknowledged that retaining an organizational presence meant having some form of arrangement or understanding with the local authorities—directly or through other actors. In other words, there are good reasons to revisit some of the claims made in the post-9/11 literature that militant Islamists have rendered ʿAyn al-Hilwe, or parts of it, a parallel social order more attuned to a world of global Salafism rather than the affairs of the Palestinian diaspora.[5]

Although most of the actors I have investigated espouse some form of pan-Islamist ideals, and in some cases acknowledge following a Salafi doctrine, they rarely express the anti-nationalist sentiments associated with the latter. Even among the Salafis whom I met, I found that the typical calls for restoring a global caliphate were often mixed with Palestinian national liberation narratives.[6] Moreover, some of the movements that publicly prided themselves with constituting the vanguards of their respective Islamic (or nationalist) revolutions appeared not to have been militarily active for decades, rendering their self-ascribed labels as Islamic combatants or jihadis somewhat problematic. In this investigation, I subscribe to the notion that ideology is "contextually variable and flexible rather than fixed,"[7] and that factors like spatial setting, the local balance of power, networks of allies, and access to material resources will often interfere with or take part in shaping any revolutionary group's rationale. As we move on, we will see that these actors' *repertoires of contention*, to borrow an expression from the literature on social movements, extend far beyond the realm of violence. Not unlike the camp commanders and guerilla leaders we met in the previous chapter, the militant Islamists of ʿAyn al-Hilwe seek influence by disrupting and manipulating balances of power, but also by integrating into the established order, whether we are talking about that of the mainstream Palestinian factions or the political class of the city of Sidon. In pages to follow, I will identify three competing Islamist frameworks in ʿAyn al-Hilwe that have adopted widely different strategies in response to the ever-changing political reality in Lebanon: **1.** *The Islamic Forces* **2.** al-*Shabab al-Muslim (The Young Muslim Men)*, and **3.** *Ansar Allah (Gods Partisans)*. We will explore all frameworks in detail. In this chapter, however, I am mostly concerned with the trajectory of the oldest and most fundamental of the three; the Islamic Forces.

A Heterogeneous Alliance

Distinguished by its tall white minaret towering above ʿAyn al-Hilwe's Lower Street, the *Nur Islamic Center* is arguably the camp's most renowned religious institution, and usually fills up with people at every Friday sermon. Interestingly, the same building also hosts the headquarters of a militia movement of a few hundred combatants known as *al-Haraka al-Islamiyya al-Mujahida* (The Islamic Combatant Movement, henceforth HIM). In starch contrast to the rather pristine design of the mosque's exterior, the movement's head office features a wall of screens transmitting surveillance footage from the nearby streets, a fortified metal door, a *diwan* for receiving guests, and a huge banner displaying a picture of the al-Aqsa mosque adorned with a rifle, a Qur'an, and a black flag with the *takbir* laid out in white letters. In this office, I had the chance to meet the mild-mannered Islamic scholar Jamal Khattab, who is both the imam of the Nur mosque and the leader of the militia organization. Enjoying no official presence outside of ʿAyn al-Hilwe, HIM does nonetheless hold a unique place in both Palestinian and Lebanese history, as it was among the first armed Islamist movements to emerge in the country. "In the camps, the idea of jihad (*al-fikr al-jihadi*) was present long before the Salafi doctrine (*al-manhaj al-salafi*)," Khattab said during our conversation. "You might find people, even among us, who since have been inspired by Salafism. But, the struggle for the Palestinian homeland remains at the center of all our activities."[8]

Aspirations of national liberation notwithstanding, Khattab's career is not distinguished by militancy or violence, but by his talent for meticulous alliance building. This is evident when considering his position as the general secretary of the Islamic Forces (al-Quwa al-Islamiyya). Regarded as ʿAyn al-Hilwe's leading Islamist authority, this ideologically heterogeneous alliance includes the local branches of larger Palestinian nationalist movements such as Hamas and Palestinian Islamic Jihad, as well as the pan-Islamist and non-militant Hizb al-Tahrir. More often than not, the label simply refers to the long-standing cooperation between Khattab's group and the armed Salafi movement ʿUsbat al-Ansar. That being said, his diplomatic relations extend far beyond the camp, because a number of Lebanese stakeholders have come to regard the Islamic Forces as key assets in terms of resolving conflicts in urban Sidon. In order to understand this, we need to begin at the start.

Al-Haraka al-Islamiyya al-Mujahida

In 1975, the outbreak of civil war in Lebanon spurred debates among the country's Islamist movements whether or not to take up arms in self-defense. In the decade to follow, Sidon would see the emergence of powerful armed groups such as the *Quwwat al-Fajr* militias of Lebanon's branch of the Muslim Brotherhood *(al-Jamaʿa al-Islamiyya)* and the Hizballah-friendly Islamic Front *(al-Jabha al-Islamiyya)*.[9] However, the first Islamists to arm themselves were a group of Palestinian students hailing from the ʿAyn al-Hilwe camp.

One of those who had been in charge of gathering these young students was the shaykh Ibrahim Ghunaym. Hailing from the village of Saffuriyya in the Nazareth region where he was born in 1924, Ghunaym worked as a teacher at a Quranic school when he was forced to flee Palestine with his family in 1948, after Jewish paramilitary forces had attacked his hometown.[10] When settling down in North Lebanon in the early 1950s, he crossed paths with a Syrian shaykh who introduced him to the Naqshibandiyya Sufi order and took him under his wing as a student. After having spent eight years as his apprentice, Ghunaym relocated from the Nahr al-Barid camp to ʿAyn al-Hilwe in 1962, where he began holding Friday sermons from his home. Establishing himself as a local proponent for said Sufi order, he was one of the first scholars to teach classes in Islamic jurisprudence in the Palestinian camp. He was also known for his conciliation work, where he would frequently be called upon to broker between the different political factions. After having made a name for himself, Ghunaym began leading the prayers at the Nur and Jamayze mosques in the camp, while he also received official certification by the Mufti of Lebanon to hold sermons in some of the congregations of Sidon proper. During his classes in ʿAyn al-Hilwe, Ghunaym found himself surrounded by a dedicated circle of students, including the Palestinians Jamal Khattab and ʿAbdallah Hallaq, who currently serve as HIM's leader and religious advisor, respectively.

Toward Militant Activity

In his classes, Ghunaym would often dwell upon the humiliating defeats of the Palestinian and Arab nationalist elites in the wars of 1967 and 1973, while underscoring the need for the formation of an armed resistance against the Zionist enemy within an Islamic framework.[11] Nonetheless, his network's military aspirations did not materialize until it became acquainted with a Palestinian guerilla from the West Bank called Hamid Abu Nasir, better known as Abu Jihad.[12] Having fought against Israeli forces in the Battle of Karame in the Jordan Valley in 1968, Abu Jihad wound up in ʿAyn al-Hilwe a few years later, where he became closely acquainted with Ghunaym's circle of students.[13] Enjoying strong ties with affiliates of the Muslim Brotherhood based in the Gulf as well as the PLO, Abu Jihad pulled strings in order to establish military training bases within the ʿAyn al-Hilwe and Rashidiyye camps.[14] He was also successful in setting up militant cells in the Sarafand, ʿAdlun, and Majdalun districts of greater Sidon. In its first manifesto from 1975, following the breakout of war in Lebanon, Abu Jihad's militias identified themselves as al-Haraka al-Islamiyya al-Mujahida, the Islamic Combatant Movement, and vowed to wage a war against "the Zionists and their Christian crusader allies in the region."[15] These young Palestinians would go on to cut their teeth by carrying out guerilla attacks against members of Bashir Gemayel's Christian militias known as the Lebanese Forces in South Lebanon, who at the time were among Israel's closest allies.[16] During Israel's minor invasion of South Lebanon in 1978, HIM became complicit in blowing up a bus carrying members of the Israel Defense Forces (IDF) near Sidon's governmental palace, known as the Sarai operation,[17] and subsequently went on to join Fatah's Jarmaq Battalion for a string of military campaigns directed at the IDF.[18]

Unlike Fatah, however, HIM also attracted devout Lebanese Muslim youth who wanted to participate in the armed struggle against Israel. Tensions grew between the Palestinian militants and Lebanese Islamist circles, as the latter did not approve of such behavior. At one point, when it became clear that the Lebanese branch of the Muslim Brotherhood had ordered Abu Jihad to shut down his militia cells and attempted to cut off his funding from Brotherhood affiliates in the Gulf, tens of members left the organization in protest and instead joined HIM.[19] First and foremost, the militia group consisted of Palestinians from Sidon who saw HIM as a viable alternative to the secularist factions associated with the PLO. This metamorphosis became evident during Israel's full-scale invasion of Lebanon in June 1982. When the IDF pushed toward Sidon coming from the South and began encircling the city, the chain of command of the PLO's official militia battalions, among them Fatah's Qastal Forces, broke down completely, as senior officials were either arrested or fled the area for Beirut.[20] Whereas Sidon fell on June 9, the IDF's offensive against ʿAyn al-Hilwe, on the city's eastern outskirts, was repulsed and went on for five more days, causing major setbacks for the Israeli army. Interestingly, the battle of ʿAyn al-Hilwe has gone down in both Palestinian and Israeli history as one of the most substantial acts of resistance against the 1982 Israeli invasion.[21] A subsequent American military report attributed the stiff resistance in no small part to the efforts of a "Sunni fundamentalist group" headed by Shaykh Ibrahim Ghunaym who fought "with suicidal fervor and intent."[22]

Embracing Khomeini

Abu Jihad returned to Jordan in 1983, and HIM's ties to both the PLO and the Muslim Brotherhood withered with his departure. Nonetheless, the movement was already in the process of finding new sponsors. As was the case with many other Islamists at the time, HIM's new leader, ʿAbdallah Hallaq, had been highly inspired by the Iranian revolution of 1979 and Khomeini's doctrine of *Velayat-e Faqih* (rule by jurisconsult), and viewed that the Palestinians had much to learn from the way that the Iranians had organized their state. At a time when Iran was exerting substantial efforts to broaden its imprint among Lebanon's Islamic scholars, Hallaq received help from contacts at the Iranian embassy in Beirut to set up *The Congregation of Muslim Scholars* in 1982. This congregation gathered Sunni and Shi' scholars under one umbrella, and became a main proponent of Iranian influence in the Palestinian camps. "There were perhaps differences in doctrine, but [the Iranian revolution] had a huge impact on the Islamic sphere in general," the group's current leader Jamal Khattab recalled.

> It was proof that, in the way that the Iranians were able to create a state and free themselves of the tyrant regime, we as Palestinians could work towards the liberation of Palestine from an Islamic angle, and establish our state in her.[23]

An ostensibly secularist national leader like Yasser Arafat shared the enthusiasm for the Iranian revolution. "Today Iran, tomorrow Palestine," he announced following a visit to Teheran in 1979, while receiving guarantees from Khomeini that the new regime would "turn the victory of Israel."[24] However, Arafat's recognition of Israel's right to exist in 1988 and his controversial support for Saddam Hussein during the latter's military campaigns against Iran caused the PLO's relations with Khomeini to turn sour.[25] In Lebanon, Iran's closest ally, Hizballah, would increasingly rely on the aforementioned Islamist networks to undermine the influence of Yasser Arafat and the PLO within the camps.

Redefining Jihad through Education

Despite aligning with Hizballah and its "Islamic Resistance" ideology, HIM chose to phase out its military operations after about a decade into its existence. In an interview with the Lebanese daily al-Mustaqbal, 'Abdallah Hallaq explains how he in 1986 allegedly made the decision to terminate "the military order of the movement."[26] With both Israel and the Lebanese Forces having withdrawn from Sidon in the spring of 1985, the focus of the movement's activities "moved towards the realms of education and propagation through the mosques and cultural institutions," Hallaq contends.[27] The choice was likely also influenced by a bid to steer clear of the mounting conflict between Hizballah and the Amal movement, which erupted into a full-scale conflict in the last phases of the Civil War. "We consider that what is required is the use of arms in the right direction, against the Jews, and to liberate the land from the occupation," Hallaq explains in the interview. "Using arms in other places is a great error, for we need to use them only in confronting the Jews."[28]

Although HIM retains a visibly armed presence at its headquarters in 'Ayn al-Hilwe and is reputed to have roughly 400 armed volunteers in the camp, the group has since channeled its "jihad" through social, religious, and educational means. In the late 1980s, Ibrahim Ghunaym used his Iranian contacts to set up an Islamic donor network called *Majlis Ri'ayat al-Shu'un al-Diniyya*, commonly abbreviated as Murshid (guide). Functioning as a sponsorship council for Islamic educational purposes, the

Murshid organization became a key component in funneling funds from both private and institutional sponsors in the region.[29] With funds coming in from a wide array of regional sympathizers, HIM has over the years been able to establish a number of robust institutions in ʿAyn al-Hilwe, such as its media center *al-Risala*, which transmits the Nur Mosque's Friday sermons on YouTube and local TV networks, its *Huda* kindergarten, and its *Muslim Student Union* (*Ittihad al-Talaba al-Muslimin*). The latter has been central in establishing Qur'anic schools in ʿAyn al-Hilwe and developing a curriculum for religious studies from the primary to the university levels, offering scholarships for young Palestinians wishing to pursue studies at Islamic institutions in Lebanon, in addition to forming a missionary council for women.[30] At its outset, the Murshid network provided HIM with a certain degree of financial freedom, allowing it to end its dependency on Iran as a sole sponsor. In fact, since ʿAbdallah Hallaq passed on the leadership to the young Palestinian scholar Jamal Khattab in 1994, the movement's shaykhs and clerics have emerged as vocal critics of both Iran and Syria's role in the region. Although the movement retains a diplomatic relationship with Hizballah, Khattab has repeatedly called out the latter for its military engagement in the Syrian war, and thereby, in his view, abandoning the Palestinian revolution.[31]

The Group's Current Vision and Organization

Because HIM was instrumental in laying the groundwork for the first iterations of organized religious activism and Islamic militancy in ʿAyn al-Hilwe, the group's historical role has among scholars been understood as that of paving the way for more extreme incarnations of Sunni militancy to come, such as jihadi-Salafism.[32] While this assertion is not unfounded, it should be noted that the movement's scholars have themselves not embraced the Salafi doctrine, but instead appear to espouse an ideology mixing militant Palestinian nationalism with sentiments of pan-Islamism. The movement's bi-annual publication *Minbar al-Jihad* (the pulpit of Jihad), along with its extensive online archives of videotaped Friday sermons, is revealing of this trend.[33] An edition of Minbar al-Jihad from April 2015 provides a good example of how HIM views its place in the world. The pamphlet opens up with an analysis of the current state of the *Umma*, where the worldwide suffering of the Sunni sect is explained by offering a comparison to how Palestinians suffer under Israeli rule.

> This labor, toil, pain and injury that the Islamic Umma is subjected to, from its eastern to its western outskirts, reflect the reality of the confrontation between the truth—which is represented by the Islamic movements, their parties and men [...]—and the yoke of the settlers that control Palestine, its holy soil and people.[34]

This is followed by an article written by ʿAbdallah Hallaq, who recounts and praises past *martyr operations* (*ʿamaliyat istishhadiyya*) carried out by Hamas and Islamic Jihad in the homeland.[35] Next, we are introduced to a survey showing a growing acceptance of Islam among Europeans and Americans,[36] before the pamphlet moves on to a text on female combatants in Palestine,[37] and a report from a meeting between the Islamic Forces of ʿAyn al-Hilwe and a delegation from the Hariri family and the

Future Movement.[38] Finally, the pamphlet ends with an expression of support for Hamas, which condemns the movement's recent placing on Egypt's terror list.[39]

Despite ideological similarities with Hamas, there are also obvious differences. For example, Hamas' diplomatic effort to reach out to the international community by easing its violent rhetoric and by rewriting its charters[40] finds no resonance in a movement like HIM, which retains a starch anti-West rhetoric. These differences were evident when Israeli Prime Minister Benjamin Netanyahu in January 2015 drew parallels between Hamas and the French jihadis who carried out the terror attacks against the *Charlie Hebdo* magazine in Paris. While Hamas' politburo responded by condemning the violence in Paris,[41] Jamal Khattab organized a sit-in in the ʿAyn al-Hilwe camp where he in front of numerous Palestinian TV stations condemned the magazine for publishing blasphemous drawings of the Prophet, instead praising the "young believers and combatants" who had killed "those evil-doers."[42] In his speech, Khattab also went on to scorn the Hariri foundation's own daily "al-Mustaqbal" for having printed the slogan "Je suis Charlie" on its front page, likening it to blasphemy.[43]

This type of rhetoric is likely the reason why critics have accused Khattab and his followers of training terrorist cells and foreign fighters in secrecy. The most creative accounts claim his Murshid-funded kindergarten is in reality a training ground for child soldiers.[44] Back at his offices, the shaykh himself scoffed at such rumors. Despite expressing a certain sense of sympathy with the young men who at the time were making their way from ʿAyn al-Hilwe and other places in Lebanon to fight the Baʿth party and its allies in Syria, Khattab underlined that the Islamic Forces of the camp had not approved of this jihad, maintaining that "as Palestinians, our eyes are on our lands. We view that any other type of warfare is a distraction from the cause."[45]

Despite being a staunch opponent of any past or present Palestinian-Israeli peace initiative, Khattab shares the opinion held by the other Palestinian rejectionist groups, that the current regional climate hardly allows for any confrontation against Israel organized from the countries of exile (Chapter 2). "The last thing we want, is to sit idly by and watch our people be killed," he lamented. "However, we can't fight this battle on our own. It is the duty of the Arab states and Islamic communities to assist the Palestinian people in freeing their lands."[46] In the interim, his position is that a strong Islamic opposition is one of the few obstacles keeping the PLO from "solving the refugee file" with Israel, thereby "deleting the right of return" and in essence, selling out the Palestinian diaspora. In line with this thinking, the Islamic Forces of 'Ayn al-Hilwe have attempted to assert themselves as a political authority with the intention of sidelining the PLO as the sole intermediary between the refugees and the Lebanese authorities. This is something we will explore in greater detail as we move on to shed light on Khattab's closest ally, and one of the most controversial Islamist movements to emerge out of the camps of Lebanon.

ʿUsbat al-Ansar al-Islamiyya

Found in the Safsaf neighborhood of 'Ayn al-Hilwe and built on either side of the camp's Upper Street, the Martyr's Mosque (Masjid al-Shuhada') is among the most impressive-looking buildings in the camp. Taking its name from the martyrs who fell during the war of 1982, the building remains an important icon of Palestinian national resistance. However, it has also served as a base for those who left the camp to join al-Qaida in Iraq in the mid-2000s. As we will see, this duality of Palestinian nationalism and global Salafism is deeply embodied in the doctrines of the 'Usbat al-Ansar movement, which more than thirty-five years after its inception still runs its organization from these headquarters.

From Fida'i to shaykh

It was in the Martyr's Mosque that the 28-year-old Palestinian Hisham Shraydi began gathering a small group of followers in 1985. As a former PLFP fighter, Shraydi had ended up in the Israeli Ansar prison after the war of 1982, but returned to the camp two years later after a prisoner swap.[47] Having previously worked odd jobs as a street vendor, Shraydi would go on to make a name for himself due to his physical strength and his self-sacrificing behavior during the Battle of eastern Sidon in 1985, where he fought alongside the Palestinian guerillas that drove the Lebanese Forces out of the city. When the War of the Camps spread from Beirut to the South in 1986, he led a group of Palestinian militants who carried out raids aiming to break the siege the Amal movement had imposed on the neighboring Miyye wo-Miyye camp, sustaining injuries to his leg in the process.

As a religious man, Shraydi was close to the pan-Islamist Hizb al-Tahrir and was otherwise an acquaintance of Ibrahim Ghunaym's Islamic student circle.[48] However, he took offense when Ghunaym's group and others began advocating restraint pertaining to military operations.[49] Disillusioned with the inaction of his peers, Shraydi went on to fashion himself a cleric and began holding sermons in the Martyr's Mosque in the Safsaf neighborhood. Because of his charisma and reputation as a heroic guerilla fighter, he quickly gained a popular following—much to the dismay of the established scholars and authorities in ʿAyn al-Hilwe and Sidon at large, who disapproved of his lack of formal religious education. "Shraydi was of the perception that virtually anyone could be a shaykh and carry out the rulings of *shari'a.* He had no clear understanding of Islamic concepts," Mahir Hammud recalled. The renowned religious scholar and the Imam of Sidon's Quds Mosque was at the time running an Iranian-funded militia force called al-Jabha al-Islamiyya (the Islamic Front) which controlled parts of the city, and would often meet with Shraydi.

> I used to negotiate with him on a number of occasions. He was obsessed with *hudud* [punishments mandated by God under Islamic law] and preferred to deal with problems using his muscles rather than his intellect. I told him, hudud cannot realistically be implemented unless under the rule of a caliph. Are you a caliph!?[50]

Believing that the defeat against Israel in 1982 was God's way of punishing the Palestinians for having abandoned their religion, Shraydi and his followers at the Martyrs' Mosque would actively, and often physically, attempt to re-shape the camp society in accordance with their interpretation of the Islamic sources. Resembling a neighborhood gang as much as a congregation, his entourage would rough up fellow-Palestinians wearing Western-style T-shirts or having modern haircuts, and went on to target alcohol vendors with homemade bombs, thereby effectively putting an end to the (open) sale of alcohol in the camp once and for all.[51] The harshest campaigns were, nonetheless, directed at Fatah's leadership, which Shraydi blamed for having lost the battle against the Zionists due to its rejection of Islam.[52]

It would be a stretch to say that he was solely driven by ideology. Both pro-Iranian networks and Syria-backed militia groups saw that Shraydi could be a useful pawn in undermining Arafat's influence and made sure to support his anti-Fatah campaigns materially. As was the case with the Hizballah-friendly Mahir Hammud who would help him out financially "from time to time," as he put it, and even took it upon himself to shelter the Palestinian when he ran into trouble.[53]

What had initially begun as a popular anti-Fatah current would near the end of the decade escalate into bloody confrontations between the parties. When Fatah leader Yasser Arafat made a complete 180-turn and sided with Amal against Hizballah in a string of clashes occurring in the Iqlim Tuffah region in late 1989, Shraydi joined forces with the renegade Fatah commander Jamal Sulayman and his Hizballah-backed Ansar Allah militia in a bid to purge Fatah's military battalions from ʿAyn al-Hilwe. The two were forced to flee the area, however, following a failed attempt to overthrow Fatah in the summer of 1990, which left twenty-one dead and sixty injured.[54] Shraydi announced his return to ʿAyn al-Hilwe a few months later, at a time when the so-called Damascus agreement appeared to have eased some of the tension between the opposing militia groups in South Lebanon.[55] Nonetheless, it didn't take him long to become entangled in a violent discord pitting Arafat's Fatah movement against the Syrian-sponsored Fatah—Revolutionary Council, which erupted anew in February 1991.[56] The tensions seemed to rekindle a longstanding familial conflict between Shraydi's clan and that of the local Fatah leader and Arafat-loyalist Amin Kayid, both hailing from the Safsaf village of Upper Galilee. Following a series of tit-for-tat assassinations, Shraydi was eventually murdered in December 1991.[57]

Following Shraydi's death, his right-hand man, the young Palestinian Ahmad ʿAbd al-Karim al-Saʿdi, better known as Abu Muhjin, assumed the leadership of the movement which by now had come to be known as ʿUsbat al-Ansar al-Islamiyya (the Islamic League of Partisans). Abu Muhjin would not only intensify the bid to cleanse the camp of everything un-Islamic but also reframe the group's militancy within a Salafi current which was just gaining foothold in Lebanon.

From Neighborhood Bullies to Salafi Soldiers

In the mid-1980s, Syria's harsh persecution of Salafi preachers and other Islamist dissidents in the northern city Tripoli created sharp divisions within the Sunni community. Whereas the Tripoli-based *Harakat al-Tawhid al-Islami* (the Islamic Unification Movement) under the leadership of Saiʿd Shaʿban sided with the Syrians, others fought back against the repression and ultimately had to flee the North.[58] Having had to abandon Tripoli himself, Yasser Arafat made sure to build a strategic alliance with the Salafis who resisted Syrian hegemony and offered to shelter the fugitives in the Palestinian camps and other PLO-controlled areas in the South.[59] Several hundred former Tawhid members came to seek refuge in the Sidon area, where Fatah, according to Rougier, helped the defectors set up their own military battalion, the so-called *February 9th Movement*, in the 'Ayn al-Hilwe camp and the nearby 'Abra district.[60]

After the Civil War ended, Lebanon's Salafis became bolder in their criticism of Syria. By the mid-1990s, Lebanon witnessed harsh public altercations between Salafi congregations, on one hand, and Islamists within the Damascus/Teheran axis, on the other. The pro-Syrian Sufi-oriented Association of Islamic Charitable Projects, commonly referred to as *al-Ahbash* (the Ethopians),[61] launched a campaign against Salafism which it understood to be a growing trend of "extremists" seeping into the mosques of Lebanon.[62] Whereas al-Ahbash would direct harsh verbal attacks against Lebanon's main Sunni institution, Dar al-Fatwa, and physically block theological rivals from entering their mosques, the Salafis would fight back eagerly, a process allowing them, Zoltan Pall notes, to affirm their identity as the true guardians of the Sunni sect.[63] Not surprisingly, these fault lines reverberated heavily within 'Ayn al-Hilwe. Although the media did not devote much attention to the Palestinian refugee camps at the time, this would all change in August 1995, after the leader of al-Ahbash was gunned down in the popular Sunni district Tariq al-Jadide in Beirut.[64]

The perpetrators, five young men of whom three were Lebanese and two were Palestinians, went on to give an interview to a running news camera mere minutes after the murder, bragging about this brave act of defense on behalf of the Sunni sect. Following their arrest, these men went on to confess, under heavy-handed interrogations, that they had undergone training in 'Ayn al-Hilwe by a cell of Salafi militants calling themselves 'Usbat al-Ansar. This news caused journalists from various publications to dispatch to the camp pleading for an interview with the group's mysterious leader Abu Muhjin. Albeit appearing somewhat bemused by the attention, the latter would feed the media's appetite for controversy by laying bare his group's ambitions to fight for a global caliphate and to turn "the polytheists to God's oneness, and the infidels to the faith of the Muslims," although he always denied having anything to do with the Halabi case.[65]

In essence, the events were a gift for Syria's allies in Lebanon, who could now discredit their Salafi adversaries by implicating them with the fanatic militants in the Palestinian camps. In January 1997, the Council of Justice appointed a special tribunal to deal with the case, which, according to court documents, proceeded to swiftly indict the accused men without offering them attorneys. The court ruling ended in four death sentences, two life sentences, and fourteen other convictions. The court also ruled to declare 'Usbat al-Ansar a terror organization aiming to instigate the Lebanese "to take up arms against each other and urging them to engage in killing and subversion with a view to establishing an Islamic state in Lebanon and Greater Syria."[66] While three of the shooters in the Halabi case were hanged in the courtyard of the infamous Rumiyye prison the following March, Abu Muhijn's death sentence was never carried out, as the authorities had no way of getting a hold of him.[67] He went underground shortly after, never to be seen in public again. Although he is still considered the official leader of 'Usbat al-Ansar, he now allegedly lives in a "land far away from Lebanon,"[68] and his movement has since been fronted by his younger brother, Haytham al-Sa'di, better known as Abu Tariq.

For Abu Tariq and his group, their newfound label as Lebanon's most revered terrorist group did not come without certain perks. The enormous hype that came with this title eventually drove ʿUsbat al-Ansar into the hands of the experienced and well-connected jihadi entrepreneur Basim al-Kanj who had relocated from the United States to Lebanon in the late 1990s and was at the time in the process of building an expansive network of jihadi cells in his native Sir al-Dinnye region in the North. Being a veteran from the war in Afghanistan in the 1980s and having ties to al-Qaida's leadership, al-Kanj took the relatively inexperienced movement under his wings, provided it with new equipment and technological know-how, and put the Palestinian Salafis in touch with a broad network of contacts reaching far beyond Lebanon.[69]

By extent of nurturing an image as Lebanon's primary vanguard of militant Salafism, external sponsors were not hard to find. During my time in the camp, Islamists would always joke about how the "dollars began pouring in" to the offices of ʿUsbat al-Ansar following the Halabi case. Its network of support included Salafi congregations in Australia and Denmark, and it was said that one of the movement's Denmark-based affiliates would travel widely to gather funds from a vast host of sympathizers based in the European subcontinent. Moreover, former advisor to the Qatari government ʻAbd al-Rahman bin ʻUmar al-Nuʻaymi was later indicted by US authorities for donating substantial sums of money to the group in 2001.[70] These sources of income were likely only the tip of the iceberg. Having started out as a clandestine neighborhood gang in the Safsaf district of ʿAyn al-Hilwe, the group had by the millennium transformed into a robust military organization keeping a few hundred volunteers, Palestinians and Lebanese nationals, on standby. Interestingly, although ʿUsbat al-Ansar had built its organization through attracting sponsors eager to fund an anti-Syrian and anti-Iranian fighting force, the movement would not attempt to attack either party. Notably, it would instead obtain the approval of the Syrian authorities to send its foreign fighters to Iraq to join the struggle against the American Coalition Forces.

Initially, the Syrian authorities had not viewed the violent networks emerging in Lebanon's largest refugee camp as much of a threat. After all, the militant Islamists seemed to create a certain buffer against a strong PLO. By the early 2000s, however, it was clear that these actors were becoming a liability—especially due to their tendency to shelter fugitives from the law. In late 1999, Damascus had warned Lebanon about Basim al-Kanj's militant cell in North Lebanon. When the Lebanese army moved in and crushed the "Sir al-Dinnye group" around New Year's Eve, killing al-Kanj in the process, many of the remaining members of his group escaped and found refuge in ʿAyn al-Hilwe where they remained at large. Moreover, a case where four Lebanese judges were gunned down by unknown assailants at a Sidon court the preceding summer had already contributed to nation-wide concerns about the Palestinian camps having become "security Islands" hosting dangerous international terrorists.[71]

While tensions were rising both in ʿAyn al-Hilwe and in North Lebanon, the American invasion of Iraq in 2003 conveniently provided the Syrian authorities with an opportunity to get rid of the worst domestic troublemakers by tacitly offering them a route to the Iraqi battlefields, presumably hoping they wouldn't find their way back.[72] It is a well-documented fact how Syria, during the war in Iraq, willingly asserted itself as a hub for the region's foreign fighters who would be transported by bus from the

International Airport of Damascus to the border town of al-Bukamal, before their exit to Iraq.[73] This open-border strategy allowed Syria, which was concerned about the prospects of an American invasion in the region, to gain leverage vis-à-vis Western governments. Consequently, American diplomats made continuous visits to Damascus pleading Bashar al-Assad to seal the Iraqi border.[74]

Ironically, this policy did far from put an end to jihadi mobilization in Lebanon, but offered amateur groups ample opportunities to gain combat experience, and to connect to al-Qaida's Iraqi branch, headed by the revered ideologue and combatant Abu Mus'ab al-Zarqawi. Working from Herat in Afghanistan, al-Zarqawi had since 1999 been in the process of recruiting militant volunteers in the Levant with a view to combat Western and American influence in the region. Following the 9/11 terror attacks, al-Zarqawi traveled extensively between Iran, Syria, Iraqi Kurdistan, and Lebanon. Al-Zarqawi's Syria-based liaison Badran Turki Hisham al-Mazidi, better known as Abu Ghadiyya, was a key person in funding the jihadis of Lebanon, and would train combatants in 'Ayn al-Hilwe in forging documents ahead of their travel. As for 'Usbat al-Ansar, the movement would recruit foreign fighters extensively on its home turf, while a few of its members went on to assist al-Zarqawi himself in establishing training camps in Iraq.[75]

The Gates to Iraq

A manifesto from 2004 offers insight into how 'Usbat al-Ansar would market itself as a guardian of the world's downtrodden Sunnis during its foray into the region's battlefields. The manifesto opens by stressing how the people of 'Ayn al-Hilwe were "drowning in the darkness of sin" until Shaykh Hisham Shraydi and his successor Abu Muhjin emerged "carrying the banner of Islam" and saving the camp population from its own depravity.[76] From there, it moves on to paint a bleak picture of the world which similarly is in dire need of salvation. This "bitter reality" is attributed to the fact that Muslims have allowed the ideas of nationalism as well as "communism and secularism" to seep into their minds, thereby infesting their lands and weakening their *'aqida* (creed). The only viable solution to end all suffering is outlined in the following five-step strategy:

1. *Da'wa* and proselytization made to God the exalted,
2. enjoining good and forbidding evil,
3. preparing and waging Jihad in the path of God,
4. working to recover the abodes of Islam and reclaiming its usurped authority, and
5. appointing a caliph who will rule according to what God has revealed.[77]

While much has been said on the emergence of transnational ideologies in the refugee camps of Lebanon, one might ask to what degree statements such as the one cited above were representative of the sender's beliefs, and to what extent they were aimed to meet the expectations of a growing audience of supporters or sponsors. The guerillas who were abandoning 'Ayn al-Hilwe for Iraq were not necessarily in the process of trading their Palestinian identity in favor of a global Salafi outlook.

For some, joining the war against the American Coalition Forces was a matter of showing commitment to the Palestinian cause. Because Hizballah had since the late 1980s more or less monopolized the armed struggle against Israel across Lebanon's southern border and seldom invited Palestinian groups to take part, some viewed that confronting Israel's most important geopolitical ally, the United States, in Iraq was their only chance at joining the national struggle. Indeed, members of staunchly nationalistic groups such as Islamic Jihad in Palestine and Ansar Allah were among those who left. In a 2003 interview with the *Daily Star*, dissident Fatah commander Munir al-Maqdah also gave his unequivocal blessings to the allegedly "hundreds of youths" who were heading to Iraq, saying "We wish we are all in Iraq fighting the Americans. Why fight Israel, when you can go and fight their boss [the Americans] in Iraq?"[78] In a 2007 interview with the al-Arabiya channel, Shahade Jawhar, a former ʿUsbat al-Ansar member who had served as a military trainer for al-Zarqawi in Iraq, expressed his frustration with these paradoxical regional dynamics:

> The central cause is the Palestinian cause, but the system in Lebanon is messed up. You have to be able to pass a hundred thousand obstacles to get to Palestine in order to fight the Jews, and it's not going to work out. Iraq is closer. Closer, not in terms of distance, but in the sense that you are able to fight there. [...] Everyone opens the gates to Iraq, while they keep the gates to Palestine closed—even though she is more important.[79]

Ostensibly, these sentiments did not differ much from the message that Abu Musʿab al-Zarqawi himself would relay to his constituents in 2006: "We fight in Iraq, but our eyes are on Jerusalem."[80] That is not to say that the Palestinian foreign fighters were cut from the same ideological cloth. Al-Zarqawi's notorious sectarian and hateful war against the Shiʿ Muslims of Iraq found little resonance in ʿUsbat al-Ansar, which had little interest in provoking Lebanon's powerful Shiʿ movements, such as Hizballah and Amal. Moreover, the PLO's seminal return to the camps of Lebanon in 1999 had made it near impossible for the group to sustain its war against the "secularists" (Chapter 3). At a time when ʿUsbat al-Ansar enjoyed a well-established international reputation as Lebanon's vanguard of militant Salafism, it would be an understatement to say that the movement was struggling to live up to this reputation on its home turf.[81]

Coming under Pressure

Following the disappearance of leader Abu Muhjin al-Saʿdi in the late 1990s, ʿUsbat al-Ansar was rocked by a feud over the movement's leadership, which essentially pitted the group's two dominant families, the Shraydis and the al-Saʿdis, against each other. Resenting the fact that Abu Tariq al-Sʿadi had been entrusted with the leadership, the young ʿAbdallah Shraydi—the son of Hisham—defected in 2001 to form a rival group, *ʿUsbat al-Nur* (The League of Light), taking many of his relatives with him in the process.[82] Another controversy shook ʿUsbat al-Ansar in 2002. After intense pressure exerted by the Lebanese army, and following weeks of brokering by Islamist leaders in and outside the camp, the movement decided to detain and hand over a Tripolitanian militant called Badiʿ Hamade to the army. As a jihadi fugitive from Sir al-Dinnye who since had become wanted for the murder of three Lebanese soldiers in Sidon, Hamade had been sheltered by ʿAbdallah Shraydi and his ʿUsbat al-Nur group.[83] While ʿUsbat al-Ansar defended its actions by referring to the Prophet's peacemaking at al-Hudaybiyya in 628,[84] the breakaway group responded by threatening to turn the camp "and the whole of Lebanon into a pool of blood" should more of its allies be handed over to the authorities.[85]

ʿUsbat al-Nur did not last long, and disintegrated after ʿAbdallah Shraydi and his brother Muhammad were assassinated by Fatah militants in 2003 and 2004, respectively.[86] These incidents of violence resulted in new security arrangements in the camp. In order to mitigate the crisis, the PLO and the pro-Syrian factions of the APF made agreements to form a joint Follow-Up Committee (*Lajnat Mutabaʿa*). Headed by longtime Saʿiqa leader in South Lebanon, Abu Bassam al-Maqdah, this committee would essentially function as a reconciliation council for resolving internal strife.[87] Because of their resolute actions during the Badiʿ Hammade-affair, Jamal Khattab's group and ʿUsbat al-Ansar were invited to join this committee, thereby giving these Islamists a sense of political legitimacy. As for the dissidents of the Shraydi family and the Sir al-Dinyye fugitives, however, these new arrangements merely underscored what they long had suspected; the Islamic Forces and ʿUsbat al-Ansar were not to be trusted.

Later in this book, I will come back to this episode and explain how these splits gave birth to the revered Jund al-Sham movement, which established itself as a rival to the main Islamist groups in the camp following the murder of the Shraydi brothers. For now, it suffices to say that these defections left ʿUsbat al-Ansar with a leadership more prone to pragmatism and political opportunity, than what was the case with rival jihadi networks. Although Abu Tariq al-Saʿdi—a person described as "ill-tempered and passive-aggressive, with a militant mindset"[88]—remained the group's leader, ʿUsbat al-Ansar's decisions were from this point on increasingly made by his more level-headed cousin, Abu Sulayman al-Sʿadi and the scholar and imam of the Martyr's Mosque, Abu Sharif ʿAqal, acting as the movement's political advisor and official spokesperson respectively. As we will see next, the collective's knack for mediating conflicts would prove crucial in the time to follow.

New Pacts: From Taʿmir to Nahr al-Barid

Prime Minister Rafiq al-Hariri's assassination on February 14, 2005, sparked harsh international reactions and unleashed a wave of anti-Syria protests in Lebanon, forcing Syria to end its near thirty-year long occupation and pull its troops out of the country a few months later. In his monograph about Sunnism in North Lebanon, Rougier gives an interesting account of how these events provided al-Hariri's political party, the Future Movement, with an opportunity to exert its influence in areas of the country that previously were firmly controlled by Syria.[89] Eager to establish a counterweight to Hizballah and its armed forces, while at the same time affirming its position as the guardian of Lebanon's Sunnis, the Future Movement now reached out to a number of Salafi shaykhs who had found themselves persecuted by Syria and its allies. While the most obvious contenders to the new regime faced violent arrests,[90] others threw their support behind the Future Movement, which in return made sure that the new anti-Syrian majority in the parliament voted in favor of a general amnesty for detained militants from the aforementioned Sir al-Dinnye clashes.[91] In the process, Rougier writes, "Salafi notables became recognized as special intermediaries between the new power and their militant flock."[92] As we will see next, these dynamics also had large implications for the Islamist militants in ʿAyn al-Hilwe at a time when the Future Movement was in the process of amending ties with the Palestinians (Chapter 3).

In the summer of 2006, Lebanon's new Prime Minister Fu'ad Siniora met with the PLO's local representative, ʿAbbas Zaki, in order to discuss matters like lifting the Syrian-imposed embargo on building materials to the country's southern Palestinian camps, in addition to the refugees' lack of the right to inherit and own property. As a token of trust, Siniora announced plans to embark on a first ministerial visit to the ʿAyn al-Hilwe camp in July. Nonetheless, his delegation was forced to postpone its visit, when an ambulance belonging to the Hariri Foundation was hit by a roadside bomb when passing the camp's adjacent Taʿmir district.[93]

A chain of clashes pitting the PLO's military wings against the new Jund al-Sham militia in 2004 had caused the latter to withdraw to the working-class neighborhoods located on the camp's northern outskirts, which were increasingly becoming a shelter for militants seeking to evade both the Palestinian and the Lebanese authorities. At the time, the press was connecting Taʿmir to a number of violent incidents, and issued reports of foreign fighters making their way back to this area following their return from Iraq.[94] For Lebanon's new leadership, bringing a sense of stability to these neighborhoods quickly became a matter of prestige. In the short term, this meant finding an arrangement with local militia groups as to ensure that the Lebanese army could deploy in the area.

One of the politicians to weigh in on the matter was Bahia al-Hariri. Having served as a Member of Parliament for the Future Movement since 1992, the late prime minister's sister had emerged a prominent steward of managing Palestinian affairs in her Sidon constituency,[95] and would attempt to resolve the Taʿmir crisis by sending delegations to negotiate with the militiamen of Jund al-Sham—but to little avail. The first round of negotiations, which took place in late October 2005, came to an abrupt halt when Jund al-Sham's delegates came under attack by other gunmen in the neighborhood who seemingly disapproved of these diplomatic efforts.[96] The fact that al-Hariri had offered a wounded Jund al-Sham fighter treatment at one of her hospitals in Sidon hardly seemed to ease the tensions. Suspecting, for his part, that the gunmen who had attacked him were agents working for the Lebanese authorities, Jund al-Sham's military leader went on to make public threats against the army, warning it against entering the area.[97] It was during these events that the Islamic Forces of ʿAyn al-Hilwe came to assert themselves as valuable assets to the Lebanese authorities. Operating a number of militia bases in the Tawari' neighborhood, just south of Taʿmir, and having a direct line of communication with various militants in the area, ʿUsbat al-Ansar had substantial experience in resolving tensions at the local level. Well aware that they would gain nothing from appearing as mere lackeys for the Hariri family and its allies, however, the Palestinian Islamists would simultaneously engage in dialogues with pro-Syrian *zʿuama'* of the new March 8th electoral alliance, such as Usama Saʿd of the Popular Nasserist Organization and the Hizballah-friendly Sunni scholar Mahir Hammud.

In essence, the 2005 Cedar Revolution had intensified a race for hegemony between politicians and sectarian leaders eager to reaffirm their role as patrons of Lebanon's working class Sunnis, and actors along the Iranian-Syrian axis, who did everything in their power as to not lose ground. In Sidon, elites from both blocs would now openly flaunt their connections to a host of Palestinian militia groups, as to underscore their influence beyond the formal reaches of the state. Nonetheless, in this scramble for control, the actor who was able to build the closest relationship to the Islamists of ʿAyn al-Hilwe was neither a Sunni nor a politician. While Prime Minister Fu'ad Siniora sat on the fence, ʿAbbas Ibrahim, the current head of Lebanon's General Security bureau, would in October 2006 become the first Lebanese state official to enter ʿAyn al-Hilwe in decades. Having recently been put in charge of South Lebanon's Army Intelligence (the so-called G2 Branch), Ibrahim did at the time create somewhat of a legacy for himself through his unorthodox style of negotiation. Even though he was a Shiʿ heading an intelligence branch held to be close to Hizballah, he would make a habit of paying unannounced visits to ʿUsbat al-Ansar's headquarters in the Safsaf neighborhood on foot, unarmed and by himself—at night. Keeping far away from the media's search lights, Ibrahim sought to guarantee the army's deployment in Taʿmir by having ʿUsbat al-Ansar take the lead and find a solution with other militant actors in the area. Curiously, the movement's leaders took a liking to Ibrahim's forward style of negotiating, and would in our conversations often refer to him as a "remarkable person."[98] "They weren't used to seeing anyone from outside of the camp," a former official of Ibrahim's G2 Force shared. "I think our meetings left a positive impression on them. They didn't ask for anything in return. ʿAyn al-Hilwe is a place where a priest will turn into a terrorist in the run of a day. All in all, this was more than what we could have hoped for."[99]

In November, the press reported that ʿUsbat al-Ansar was working toward securing an increased army presence in Taʿmir.[100] The Lebanese army was finally able to move in and set up its checkpoints in these neighborhoods in late January 2007. The events, which were celebrated as a victory in the Hariri-owned newspaper, al-Mustaqbal, hardly received much attention elsewhere.[101] Another crisis was already brewing in Lebanon. In fact, the army's deployment in Taʿmir seemed to have forced many of the militants in these neighborhoods to relocate to North Lebanon, where a new Jihadi group, called Fatah al-Islam, had emerged a few months prior.[102] With tensions mounting in the North, it would not take long before ʿAbbas Ibrahim would again call on the Islamic Forces to act as intermediaries.

The Rift with Fatah al-Islam

At the time of its emergence, Fatah al-Islam created a lot of confusion as to who was behind the movement, or which domestic party stood the most to gain from its presence. As there now is a body of scholarly works and reports dealing with the movement's short-lived existence, we can safely discard any previous theory of Fatah al-Islam having acted solely under the sway of any specific regional force. In very rough terms, we find that the group's emergence can be attributed to three interrelated factors.

First, following al-Zarqawi's death in mid-2006, harsh rounds of Sunni infighting between his successors of the Islamic State in Iraq (ISI), and US-backed counter revolutionary tribal forces were increasingly becoming a source of disillusionment for many foreign fighters engaged in the war against the Coalition Forces in Western Iraq.[103] As a result, these gradually began to turn around and head back to Syria. Unsettled by this flow of returnees, and buckling under US pressure, Syria began to impose tighter border security, making the Iraqi jihad harder to access.

Second, eager to deflect the increasing flow-back of jihadis, the Syrian intelligence services diligently assisted jihadi militants in relocating to the Palestinian camps of Lebanon, hoping they would instead turn their aggression against anti-Syrian targets there.[104] Affiliates of al-Zarqawi's Al-Qaida in Iraq—now having renamed itself the Islamic State of Iraq (ISI) —were thus provided with an opportunity to expand their operations in the Levant. A substantial jihadi emigration to Lebanon took place months before the Hizballah/Israeli war broke out in July 2006.

Third, following Syria's retreat from Lebanon in 2005, Abu Khalid al-ʿUmle, second in command in the Damascus-based Fatah al-Intifada group, had taken upon himself to relocate Syria-based militants to his party's military bases in the Lebanese Biqaʿ Valley.[105] In the process, he was able to rekindle his relationship with a Palestinian guerilla named Shakir al-ʿAbsi, a former veteran from his own militia who since had become a seasoned jihadi fighter in Jordan and a close ally of Abu Musaʾb al-Zarqawi.[106] In early 2006, Rougier finds, al-ʿUmle looks to have assisted al-ʿAbsi and his fifty-strong cell of militants in relocating to the Palestinian camps of Beirut, where they were incorporated into Fatah al-Intifada's military wings, much to the surprise of his own party fellows.[107] Reportedly, Abu Musa, the general secretary of Fatah al-Intifada in Syria, had complained that he had been left in the dark as to what was happening within his organization in Lebanon.[108] For his part, al-ʿUmle informed his cadres that the group had acquired new fighters, saying "We must learn from Hezbollah's military and discipline. They are destined for Gaza."[109] Whatever their purpose, the arrival of these bearded strangers provoked reactions from al-ʿUmle's colleagues in the camps of Beirut. In November 2006, he went on to move his fighters away from the Hizballah-dominated southern parts of the Lebanese capital to the Palestinian camps of Tripoli, perhaps assuming that they would be granted a warmer welcome in Lebanon's "Sunni capital" in the North.[110] Once again, their arrival resulted in controversy. After becoming entangled in clashes against the Palestinian factions in the Beddawi camp, Shakir al-ʿAbsi's militia was eventually able to fortify its position in Nahr al-Barid, seizing three compounds belonging to Fatah al-Intifada, the camp's dominant faction.[111]

Despite the group's clear Syrian links, there are no signs that al-ʿAbsi was acting under orders from Damascus when he suddenly declared his split from Fatah al-Intifada, and announced instead the creation of Fatah al-Islam.[112] In his words, Fatah al-Islam was to be "an Islamic group aiming to fight the Jews and those who support them among Western Zionists."[113] More precisely, al-ʿAbsi was in the process of turning the Nahr al-Barid camp into a regional hub for foreign fighters seeking to train and prepare for the "jihad in Iraq".[114] His plans would not materialize. The group's rapid mobilization among Sunni Shaykhs in Tripoli, its provocative bank heists, and its alleged connection to a bomb exploding in the town of ʿAyn ʿAlaq in March 2007 were among the factors that led the Lebanese authorities to monitor the group's movements closely, while the army proceeded to bolster its presence around the camp.

The war that eventually would destroy Nahr al-Barid broke out on May 20. In retaliation of a police raid made against one of their weapon storages in Tripoli the day before, militiamen from Fatah al-Islam ambushed an army checkpoint near the Palestinian camp, causing the military to respond by shelling the area. After roughly fifteen weeks of fighting, Fatah al-Islam was defeated, and the Nahr al-Barid camp completely destroyed. In the process, at least 169 Lebanese soldiers had been killed, more than 200 militants were dead, and the entire refugee camp population of 30,000 were left homeless and forced to seek shelter elsewhere.

For actors who might have been sympathetic to Shaker al-ʿAbsi's cause, the battle at Nahr al-Barid was a decisive demonstration of power, and proof that the military would not hesitate to respond to any provocation. Following the events, even the most extreme demagogues or unsavory militants who previously were calling for the downfall of the state saw no other choice but to alter their rhetoric and curse the likes of Fatah al-Islam. There are, nonetheless, signs that the Islamist environs in the Palestinian camps were split in their view on the group, long before the fighting broke out. In Islamist web forums, the tense relations between Fatah al-Islam, and ʿAyn al-Hilwe's leading jihadi group, ʿUsbat al-Ansar, was at the time a source of heated debate, where proponents of each movement would engage in harsh verbal altercations. In the writings of a cleric affiliated with Fatah al-Islam, Abu ʿAbdallah al-Maqdisi, who published a thorough account of the movement's rise and fall two years after the battles of Nahr al-Barid, we learn that leaders of Fatah al-Islam met with ʿUsbat al-Ansar on a number of occasions leading up to the events.[115] Although both movements espoused a similar type of hybrid rationale, mixing global Salafism with Palestinian liberation sentiments, their leaderships did not see eye to eye. The fact that the Lebanese national Shihab Khudr Qadur (Abu Hurayra), a former member of ʿUsbat al-Ansar who had lived in ʿAyn al-Hilwe for years, now had been made the leader of Fatah al-Islam's military committee, raised many eyebrows in the South. Regarded as a hothead and a loose cannon, Abu Hurayra's designation to such a prominent position had many question the sincerity of Fatah al-Islam as an organization.[116]

More importantly, the new political dynamics in Lebanon had by and large worked in the favor of ʿUsbat al-Ansar and the Islamic Forces in ʿAyn al-Hilwe. Enjoying an understanding with both the state's security apparatus and a number of Sunni notables in Sidon, the movement had learned the rules of the game—to fight internationally, while making peace locally. However, the erratic behavior of Shakir al-ʿAbsi's armed gang threatened to upset these new pacts. A leader of ʿUsbat al-Ansar revealed how he in late 2006 had advised Fatah al-Islam to leave Lebanon altogether and instead head for Iraq:

> We warned the men of Fatah al-Islam that their group posed a danger to the people of the [Nahr al-Barid] camp. We told them, you have to get out of the camp. All other fronts were open. The front of Iraq was open ....get out of this camp and be on your way![117]

The distrust evidently went both ways. According to al-Maqdisi's notes, affiliates of Fatah al-Islam largely disapproved of ʿUsbat al-Ansar's pragmatic peacemaking with the "near enemy" and had, for example, taken issue with the fact that the group had paid tributes to Yasser Arafat—a man they deemed responsible for both selling out Palestine and collaborating with the "infidel west"—following his death in 2004. Furthermore, we learn that Abu Laith al-Suri, the son-in-law of Fatah al-Islam's leader and who had been put in charge of managing affairs in ʿAyn al-Hilwe, had attempted to ease the mounting tension by assuring the camp's Islamists that Shakir al-ʿAbsi had not come to Lebanon to usurp the leadership of ʿUsbat al-Ansar. Instead, al-ʿAbsi had simply intended to "open the market of a closed Jihad." As a token of trust, their fighters were offered access to Fatah al-Islam's military training facilities in Nahr al-Barid—all they had to do was to carry a written note from the leadership to gain entry, or else they would be turned back to their camp. Regardless of these arrangements, al-Maqdisi goes on to lament that when the battles finally broke out in the North, ʿUsbat al-Ansar had not only remained absent from the war but had also began addressing the "errors of the Jihadi movements in facing the regimes," in its Friday sermons, and urged its supporters to "rationalize" their Jihad.

It was likely an easy decision for ʿUsbat al-Ansar not to become entangled in Fatah al-Islam's aggressions against the Lebanese army. Especially when it became clear that the group was fighting a losing war. Remaining in communication with ʿAbbas Ibrahim throughout the crisis, ʿUsbat al-Ansar would continue to guard its areas in ʿAyn al-Hilwe with diligence. This also involved apprehending jihadi dissidents in Taʿmir, who in mid-July 2007 began throwing hand grenades at the neighborhood's new army checkpoints,[118] likely preventing the violence from spreading to the southern parts of the country.[119] Two days later, the group announced that it had "dissolved" the Jund al-Sham faction, where certain former members were allowed to come back to the Islamic Forces.

It was not only Lebanon's new leadership and military intelligence who saw the value of keeping the Islamic Forces within their circle of affiliates. The PLO and Fatah also viewed that the time was ripe to engage in dialogue.

Fatah's Peace Offering

During the days of Abu Muhjin, an informal dialogue was established between ʿUsbat al-Ansar's second leader and the prominent Fatah official Khaled ʿArif. The two were neighbors in the ʿAyn al-Hilwe camp, and had taken a liking to each other despite factional differences.[120] These connections eventually led to a more concerted effort to bury the hatchet between the two movements, but whatever progress was made was lost when Fatah militants gunned down ʿAbdallah Shraydi, the son of ʿUsbat al-Ansar's founder, in 2003.

After the events of Nahr al-Barid, Fatah's leadership in Lebanon made an effort to to revamp the peace talks. On August 16, 2008, the Palestinian embassy in Beirut sent two delegates, among them Edward Kattoura, a renowned Christian Fatah official, to ʿAyn al-Hilwe where they met with ʿUsbat al-Ansar's central leadership, represented by Abu Tariq al-Sʿadi, Abu Sharif ʿAqal, Abu Sulayman al-Saʿdi, and the group's local military leader in the Tawari' neighborhood, Abu ʿUbayda al-Mustafa. In August, a seven-hour long meeting resulted in a five-step plan, a "Charter of understanding" (*mithaq tafahum*), which both parties signed, and that among other things stipulated that ʿUsbat al-Ansar was to accept Fatah's Palestinian Armed Struggle Command (PASC) as the camp's de-facto police, and abide by its authority.[121] When I asked Kattoura about the Islamists' motives for accepting such an arrangement, the former employee of the Palestinian embassy recalled there being a sixth point, which was left out of the official charter. It stated that if ʿUsbat al-Ansar was able to hand over seven outlaws, mainly affiliates of Fatah al-Islam, the PLO was to return the favor by providing the group with a substantial economic compensation. The hope was that by alleviating the movement of some of its organizational expenses, it would become less dependent on troublesome sponsors, Kattoura explained, without specifying whether he was talking about regional actors or local political rivals within the Fatah movement. "I called them every day to make sure the operation was carried out," he continued. "In the beginning they were very hesitant, but after some time they decided to go through with it. [...] Some of these are now in Turkey, while others are in Lebanese prisons."[122]

Many of my sources confirmed that the arrangements between ʿUsbat al-Ansar and Fatah are standing, although they did not always agree on which part of the organization was providing the funding. As we remember from the last chapter, the Fatah movement in Lebanon is made up of a multiplicity of competing leaders, many of whom have sought to make private arrangements with various armed groups within the Palestinian camps in order to bolster their own influence in political processes. "In ʿAyn al-Hilwe, everything begins and ends with Fatah," Kattoura said ambiguously, while peering over his glasses.

Burning Bridges with al-Qaida, Mending Ties with Hizballah

The camp would witness the effects of these new arrangements in the months to follow. When the Fatah movement proceeded to crack down on militia cells beholden to Fatah al-Islam throughout 2008, ʿUsbat al-Ansar stayed out of the way (Chapter 5). Adding insult to injury, the group's spokesperson, Abu Sharif, turned many heads when he in December went on to proclaim that *Shariʿa* forbade violence against the Lebanese military.[123] Speaking at a sit-in arranged by Hamas in support of the Gaza Strip, he urged fellow Islamists in the camp to turn their attention to Palestine instead:

> We, on behalf of the Islamic Forces, say that we should not be distracted by the streets of the camp or the streets of Lebanon. All efforts and energies must be united. Whoever wants God and the Hereafter, will go all his way to Palestine. It is not permissible to use our forces against the Lebanese army, nor against any other army. This is absurd and this is *haram*. We must go against the Zionists. I repeat that

> there are those who intend to distract the people of Palestine, specifically in this camp, from the central Islamic cause, by getting entangled in internal conflicts.[124]

Far from everyone welcomed this new approach. The aforementioned Fatah al-Islam-affiliated cleric Abu ʿAbdallah al-Maqdisi relayed the following report from the camp in March 2009:

> During the four last months, not a single speaker in ʿAyn al-Hilwe has uttered a word of support for Fatah al-Islam, and this also goes for ʿUsbat al-Ansar and their Friday sermons. But when it comes to the war in Gaza, we have seen a dazzling amount of demonstrations, piety, prayer, and euphonious speechescome from al-ʿUsba […]. ʿUsbat al-Ansar speaks with two tongues, and this might pose a danger to its body. It addresses the *mujahidin* in a legitimate Islamic manner, while it at the same time addresses the secularists, the apostates and the nationalist (and Islamist) movements, and these two approaches are in complete contradiction to each other.[125]

This renunciation of violence against the Lebanese army "or any other army" was deemed controversial at a time when al-Qaida's second-in-command, Ayman al-Zawahiri, had urged Lebanon's Muslims to "reject" the UN Security Council Resolution 1701.[126] Having ensured a ceasefire between Hizballah and Israel in August 2006, the resolution provided the multinational United Nations Interim Force's (UNIFIL) with a more muscular mandate and more troops to deploy in the South who were to coordinate their peacekeeping mission with the Lebanese and Israeli governments. Al-Qaida had harshly criticized Hizballah for accepting the presence of such an "international crusader force" and for abandoning the war against the Zionists.[127] While al-Zawahiri had called for strikes against UNIFIL soldiers in Lebanon, ʿUsbat al-Ansar maintained its opposition to such a policy, telling the press that "this [Western] axis is present in Iraq and Afghanistan. If we defeat it there, it won't stay in Lebanon."[128] Rather than "rejecting" Resolution 1701, ʿUsbat al-Ansar would instead go on to receive delegations from the resolution's tacit supporters, Hizballah.

The first official meetings between Hizballah and ʿUsbat al-Ansar took place after the former had ended its short-lived siege of West Beirut in May 2008. A seventeen-month political deadlock had culminated in an open showdown after the government had attempted to shut down Hizballah's communication networks, and the latter moved in to militarily seize positions beholden to the Future Movement for a week, before handing them over to the army. The move caused Lebanese Salafis to accuse Hizballah of using its 2006 victory against Israel as an excuse for imposing its control over Sunni areas in Lebanon, resulting in heightened sectarian antagonism between Sunnis and Shiʿa, and the killing of a dozen civilians in North Lebanon.[129] Acting with Hamas as a broker, Hizballah reached out to ʿUsbat al-Ansar as a part of a broader diplomatic offensive to mitigate the crisis, and extend a hand to Lebanon's Sunni movements.[130] In a subsequent interview conducted by author and Hamas official Ra'fat Morra, ʿUsbat al-Ansar's leadership is asked to relay its position regarding these meetings with Lebanon's most important Shiʿ movement. Here, the group attests to having acknowledged the confessional differences between the two actors, as well as its opposition to Hizballah's geopolitical role as a key-actor in the "Iranian-Syrian project to control Lebanon."[131] Nonetheless, the Palestinian Islamists make it clear that they had no intentions of being distracted by these political divisions, maintaining that their main adversaries were Israel and America. On this note, 'Usbat al-Ansar goes on to commend Hizballah for its recent military efforts and sacrifices in its battles against Israel in 2006, saying "The weapons of al-'Usba [The League] are next to yours, against the Jewish threats" [132] Although the claims are difficult to verify, many of 'Usbat al-Ansar's critics in 'Ayn al-Hilwe seemed to think that Hizballah's arrangements with the group were first and foremost of a financial nature, and had little other political purpose than serving as a blow to the Future Movement's Bahia al-Hariri, who prided herself on being among the Islamic Force's closest interlocutor.[133] Whatever the case, the parties have since met frequently in public, and their diplomatic relationship does not appear to have been disrupted by Hizballah's engagement in the Syrian war.

Following the turbulent years of 2006–8, during which the global jihadi movement attempted to carve out a foothold in Lebanon, 'Usbat al-Ansar remained the only noteworthy actor who had not been broken or dispersed in the process. However, the movement had lost nearly all legitimacy in the eyes of its peers. Its "jihad" against Israel and the United States had become a struggle in which the group was only engaged in theory. While Fatah al-Islam's defeat in North Lebanon saw the remnants of Shakir al-'Absi's group flee back to Syria, causing Damascus to yet again set about "facilitating intensified flows of foreign fighters and supplies into West Iraq,"[134] signs were that 'Usbat al-Ansar's days of global jihad were over.

From Global Jihad to Local Politics

In an article about the Palestinian refugees in Lebanon, anthropologist Nadia Latif cites an older interlocutor who calls out the PLO for abandoning its southern frontlines against Israel during the days of revolution, in favor of building a rebel bureaucracy (or state in exile) in Beirut.[135] Looking at the current organization of 'Usbat al-Ansar, the group might stand accused of having done the same. Remaining conspicuously absent from its hypothesized frontlines, the movement has instead concentrated its efforts on building elaborate political, educational, and security structures in 'Ayn al-Hilwe. In addition to its headquarters in Safsaf, the group runs armed checkpoints in the Jabal al-Ahmar and Tawari' neighborhoods, all manned by middle-aged bearded men in camouflage clothing carrying large walkie-talkies, and greeting passersby with a big smile—even Western visitors like myself.[136] On the surface, there is not much that seems to separate the group from the other militia factions guarding their respective neighborhoods. "They have become a faction (tanzim), almost like Fatah" a local DFLP leader noted. "Except," he added, "they aren't all smoking hashish."[137]

Unlike Fatah, however, 'Usbat al-Ansar does not acknowledge employing any full-time militants, and describes its organization as being largely voluntary. Rather than earning a salary, the movement's affiliates are said to pay *zakat* (religious taxes) to the main organization, and typically have other jobs on the side. For this reason, it is not easy to assess how many people are currently affiliated with ʿUsbat al-Ansar, or what a membership of the movement entails. Armed checkpoints aside, the group's actual military capacities are said to lie in a network of loosely connected supporters who are willing to take up arms to defend its neighborhoods in the case of a crisis. In return, the movement provides basic services in its control areas, and runs a number of religious and social initiatives, including mosques and prayer rooms, and as of 2015, a youth center based in the Tawari' neighborhood which hosts the movement's boy scouts branch called *Futuwwat al-Ansar al-Islami (The Youth of the Islamic Partisans).*[138]

Despite ʿUsbat al-Ansar's disengagement from violence, the movement has not published any revisions of past manifestos or made any concessions regarding its violent history. As a member put it, "We have not changed our view … it is the view on us that has changed!"[139] Although it insists its days of global jihad are not over, the group views that the time is not ripe for such endeavors. Although maintaining that its "long-term strategic goal" is "to establish the rule of God on earth and to restore the Islamic Caliphate,"[140] it has not followed in the steps of the militants affiliated with the Islamic State of Iraq and Syria (ISIS) who sought to realize similar ambitions during the third wave of global jihad. Rather, ʿUsbat al-Ansar has gone on to join the other Palestinian factions in Lebanon in signing a "memorandum of disassociation" pertaining to the conflicts in Syria and Iraq. During a meeting at its headquarters, I witnessed the movement justify its absence from the region's battlefronts by referring to the bitter experiences of the insurgency in Iraq—described as an example of a "pure Jihad" having gone awry. "There is a clear consensus among the world's scholars that if an Islamic country is occupied, the Muslim community needs to work together in order to rid this country of its occupation," spokesperson Abu Sharif said.[141] He had agreed to meet after holding a Friday sermon in the Martyr's Mosque, and met me in his office directly after. Joining the conversation was a group of middle-aged men dressed in gray *jalabiyyat* with huge salt and pepper beards, a few of them carrying Kalashnikovs. "All of our brothers who we sent to Iraq, had a clear purpose and a pure intent. Our mission was to fight the American occupation exclusively!" he continued, addressing his followers as much as the undersigned. "And when we saw that the conflict took a different turn, when the struggle against the occupation instead turned into a bloodbath pitting the Sunnis against the Shiʿa of Iraq, then ʿUsbat al-Ansar pulled out!" His conclusion was followed by affirming grunts of approval by those listening in. "As a Muslim, I want to be able to reap the fruits of my Jihad. In Syria, this is not possible," one of the armed men said sincerely. The leader of the flock, Abu Sharif, weighed in to explain the sentiments more thoroughly:

> We support the struggle to remove Bashar the dictator, the criminal, who tastes the blood of his own people. The revolution began as a righteous cry for freedom and dignity. However, as the revolution gradually became militarized it started to serve the purpose of foreign states within Syria. Just like the Syrian regime is a tool in the hands of foreign powers, Iran, Iraq, Hizballah and Russia, the Syrian opposition, has for the most part, I would say in its entirety, but let's say for the most part, become a tool in the hands of the Arab regimes …. The Gulf States, Turkey and others, which are no better than the regime of Bashar itself.[142]

As for the many reports of youths leaving 'Ayn al-Hilwe for Syria, the movement stressed that the Islamic Forces in the camp had not called for jihad.

> We tell the youth of this camp that Syria has no need for them. The country is already full of youth and men fighting each other, but for whose benefit? As for those who have gone, paradise will accept them, God willing, but this is strictly speaking not a duty (*fard*). However, there is a difference if Syria comes under [American] occupation—we will not hesitate to go.[143]

While 'Usbat al-Ansar, for all practical purposes, remains listed as a terrorist organization by the Lebanese state, efforts have been made to revisit the group's legal file. After taking the office as the head of Lebanon's General Security bureau in 2011, Major-General 'Abbas Ibrahim pulled strings to implement a moratorium on the pending sentences of 'Usbat al-Ansar's troika leadership, Abu Tariq, Abu Sharif, and Abu Sulayman, allowing them to move outside of their native camp for the first time in decades.[144] This arrangement has allowed the three to engage more actively in their role as intermediaries and power brokers, and they have since been observed making frequent diplomatic calls to a host of different actors eager to keep tabs on the situation in 'Ayn al-Hilwe, ranging from Lebanese Sunni parties such as the Future Movement and al-Jama' al-Islamiyya, to Shi' movements such as Hizballah and Amal.[145] In the summer of 2013, the movement's leaders were invited to the PLO's headquarters in Beirut to meet the Palestinian president himself, during his round trip in Lebanon, where the parties reportedly engaged in conversations regarding joint security measures in 'Ayn al-Hilwe (Chapter 6).[146]

It would of course be easy to suspect that 'Usbat al-Ansar's change of behavior is merely an act and that the group has covertly continued to recruit and train foreign fighters, while masking its trail by making friends with the local authorities. There are reasons to believe, however, that the movement's mask has—as the proverb goes—become its face. One indication of this is the near-constant stream of criticism that has followed 'Usbat al-Ansar on its own turf. For example, in January 2015, a statement was shared widely on internet forums calling out 'Usbat al-Ansar for paying its tributes at the funeral of a Hizballah commander, whereas the movement had ignored "the fighters and their leaders in Syria who were killed at the hands of the crusaders and their allies."[147] Ambiguously signed by "The Sunnis of the camp," the statement went on to chronologically describe a number of acts committed by the movement that are meant to show that it has "derailed from the path of Jihad". "We are no longer surprised by the actions of 'Usbat al-Ansar the statement concluded,"

> For it has become a Palestinian Nationalist movement falsely and slanderously wearing the clothes of the Jihadi movements. [...] 'Usbat al-Ansar left the methodology of jihad behind years ago, and has since started to chant the tune of the Palestinian cause, where it brags of its struggle against the Jews, but it has never struck the Jews. Not even with a single missile.

All things considered, these accusations were not unfounded. Wavering between calls for restoring a global caliphate and populist narratives of national liberation, the movement does not only drape itself in the emblems of revolutions it does not take part in, but even as a newfound political force in Lebanon, ʿUsbat al-Ansar's reading of the local reality borders on unabashed opportunism. Along with its allies in the Islamic Forces, it has become its second nature to bet on every horse at once, waiting to see which ally will emerge as the strongest card. This tendency was demonstrated clearly following the 2013 Battle of ʿAbra, which we remember from this chapter's introduction.

Betting on Every Horse

In January 2013, leaders of the Islamic Forces were invited to hold a press conference at the headquarters of the popular Sunni cleric Ahmad al-Asir at his Bilal ibn Rabah Mosque in Sidon. The Palestinian Islamists had taken great interest in the eccentric BMX-riding shaykh, who in the run of a year had gained a wide appeal among Lebanon's Sunnis due to his popular protests against Hizballah's armed presence—a political taboo at the time. The Islamic Forces had met and posed for photo-ops with al-Asair on a number of occasions, and were evidently eager to bask in the brilliance of the Sunni community's rising star and his uphill struggle against Lebanon's most powerful political force. The admiration went both ways. When al-Asir's sit-ins and rallies started to spiral out of control, and his followers found themselves entangled in conflict with proponents of the Islamic Resistance in Sidon, the former turned to his Palestinian colleagues for moral support. At the abovementioned press conference, al-Asir was seen standing next to the general secretary of ʿAyn al-Hilwe's Islamic Forces, Jamal Khattab, with the righteous frown of a child having told on his bully classmates at school. Meanwhile, Khattab addressed running news cameras in a grave tone as he urged all parties to come to their senses and end their "targeting of shaykh Ahmad al-Asir and his supporters," citing him as an important Islamic authority deserving both appreciation and respect.[148]

After the breakout of the disastrous street war between al-Asir and the Lebanese army (supposedly flanked by informal Hizballah battalions) the following June, the Palestinian Islamists rapidly scurried to distance themselves from the unfortunate shaykh. Al-Asir's pleas for military support—allegedly made to both Jamal Khattab and ʿUsbat al-Ansar's leader, Abu Tariq al-Sʿadi—fell on deaf ears in both cases.[149] The leaders of the Islamic Forces instead affirmed their support of the army and reached out to Hizballah, offering instead to broker a solution with the fugitives having sought refuge in ʿAyn al-Hilwe following the clashes. In August 2016, these dialogues resulted in scores of militants from al-Asir's cell handing themselves over to the army on promises of a fair trial, although some of the most wanted fugitives remain at large.[150]

It should be mentioned that the Islamic Forces have not made a habit of forcibly handing over wanted people to the state authorities. Well aware that such behavior could cause their respective neighborhoods in the camp to turn against them, these factions see little or no benefit in persecuting outlaws or wanted terrorists, and have routinely pledged ignorance even in cases when an entire national press corps attests to having traced the movements of suspicious militant cells back to ʿAyn al-Hilwe. There have, nonetheless, been notable exceptions to the rule.

In July 2017, 'Usbat al-Ansar embarked on a joint operation with Hamas, where the parties successfully apprehended the alleged Islamic State-operative and terror suspect, Khalid al-Sayyid, and delivered him to the Lebanese army at the camp's main entrance.[151] Al-Sayyid was believed to be the head of a small network of suicide bombers that, presumably acting on orders from IS in al-Raqqa, had planned a string of terror attacks in Lebanon during Ramadan in 2017.[152] When the cell was exposed in early June, 'Abbas Ibrahim and the Lebanese security agencies made calls to the Palestinian factions in 'Ayn al-Hilwe, asking them to search for al-Sayyid. Reportedly, the latter was lured into a car, before being escorted out of the camp at gunpoint. Following the joint operation, Hamas leader Isma'il Hanniye personally phoned to thank both 'Usbat al-Ansar and his own constituents for their efforts.[153]

We have already covered the informal connections between 'Ayn al-Hilwe's Islamist militants and the Fatah movement. What then are the links between these groups and Fatah's primary Palestinian rival, Hamas? Is it true, as some locals are quick to claim, that these smaller, local groups are in reality merely acting under the orders of their big brethren in the Gaza Strip? We will conclude our investigation of the Islamic Forces by shedding light on how renowned Gaza-based nationalist groups such as Hamas and Islamic Jihad have extended their networks of influence in the camps of Lebanon.

Relations with Hamas and Palestinian Islamic Jihad

The exile leaderships of Hamas and Palestinian Islamic Jihad (PIJ) have since its inception in Damascus in December 1993 taken part in the political constellation known as the Alliance of Palestinian Forces (APF). As we remember, this broad collection of Syria-friendly factions, most often simply referred to as *The Alliance* (al-Tahaluf), was formed as a reaction to the Oslo peace process, and has since strived to assert itself as an alternative to the PLO at a factional level within the refugee camps and at a political level through representing the Palestinians vis-à-vis the region's governments (mainly Syria and Lebanon). As we already know, the APF was dealt a severe blow at the turn of the millennium when founding factions such as the PFLP and the DFLP left the alliance in order to rejoin the PLO framework, and in Lebanon, its influence continued to dwindle when Syria withdrew its troops from the country in 2005. In a southern camp like 'Ayn al-Hilwe, where the APF's activities hardly go beyond releasing the odd statement from the bunker-like offices of local Sa'iqa leader Abu Bassam al-Maqdah, Hamas and PIJ have aligned themselves with political forces that are by no means friends of Syria. In fact, should we believe Hamas' long-time representative in 'Ayn al-Hilwe, Fadl al-Taha, it was he who personally had the idea to enter into an understanding with al-Haraka al-Islamiyya al-Mujahida and 'Usbat al-Ansar, thus laying the groundwork for the Islamic Forces.

"The Islamic Forces, as an official framework, was founded around 1994," he said during a conversation at his office found within the complex of the Khalid bin al-Walid mosque in the Lower Street of the camp.[154] Acknowledging, at least to some extent, the work that had already been laid down by a shaykh like Ibrahim Ghunaym in gathering the camp's Islamists before this, al-Taha viewed that the signing of the

Oslo accords mandated a more concerted effort at opposing the PLO. "Sure, there was a group here and a group there, but there were no joint measures between the Islamic movements," he shared as he recalled sitting down with Jamal Khattab and 'Usbat al-Ansar's second leader, Abu Muhjin, in order to work more closely together.[155] In the early 1990s, they would organize marches and protests where, according to al-Taha, thousands of supporters would chant anti-Arafat slogans in the streets—but they also had political ambitions. "[The] Oslo [agreements] were operational, and the PLO had abandoned its institutions, and closed its offices," al-Taha explained. "In this situation, you don't sit around and wait for help to come; you organize yourself. We saw that a framework like the Islamic Forces could be of service to our people, to guide them and provide for them in the difficult time to come." The fact that 'Usbat al-Ansar became terror-listed by the Lebanese authorities a few short years later was a setback for these ambitions, al-Taha reluctantly acknowledged. "Of course, Abu Muhjin ran into some problems with the authorities, and disappeared from view," he sighed.

> But our cooperation with Shaykh Jamal Khattab and the brothers Abu Tariq, Abu Sharif and Abu 'Ubayda [al-Mustafa, all from 'Usbat a-Ansar] has persisted. Hamas is an essential part of the Islamic Forces.[156]

The fact that Hamas' central role in political life in the Palestinian camps of Lebanon has been largely overlooked in scholarly research is perhaps not so strange. At the time of the formation of the Islamic Forces, al-Taha and other members of Hamas were working in secrecy, and it would take years for them to formally announce their presence.

From Covert Existence to Tanzim

According to an article published in Islamic Jihad's official magazine in Lebanon, *al-Mujahid*, Hamas' origins in the country can be traced back to 1991, when Israel deported four of the movement's leaders from the Gaza Strip, leaving them stranded in the South.[157] After making their way to the Miyye wo-Miyye camp in Sidon, the Islamic scholar Mustafa al-Qan'u, the engineer 'Imad al-'Alami, and the professors Fadl al-Zahar and Mustafa al-Lidawi eventually began the process of scouting for allies. Upon their arrival, it became clear that Hamas already had a small but devout core of followers. In Beirut, a group of refugees calling themselves *The Islamic Media Office for Palestine* were printing pamphlets and eagerly reporting from Hamas' engagement in the ongoing Intifada in the Palestinian Territories. Moreover, the recently established *Islamic League for Palestinian Students* had a presence on the campuses of the American University of Beirut and the Lebanese American University, and made sure to connect the deported leaders with a host of like-minded actors.[158] A year later, when Israel deported 400 additional Palestinians, many of them members of Hamas and PIJ to South Lebanon, leaving them in Marj al-Zuhur, a Lebanese hilltop in the midst of the southern security zone, the first group of deportees had already managed to set up a representational office for Hamas in the southern parts of Beirut, under the leadership of Mustafa al-Qan'u.

Israel had since the 1960s practiced the strategy of deporting troublesome Palestinians to nearby states with the aim to "systematically wipe out" the leaders of a burgeoning national movement, but there is little doubt that these measures in the 1990s ended up strengthening both Hamas and PIJ.[159] As historian Erik Skare notes, the exile in Lebanon provided the deportees with a freedom of movement that had not previously been available to them, allowing them to establish a rapport with both Teheran and Damascus all the while keeping in touch with their own networks in the Palestinian Territories.[160] These connections were important not only for obtaining financial support from external sponsors but also in terms of organizational learning and acquiring military training, not at least through Hizballah's military camps.[161] Indeed, in an older interview with former secretary general of PIJ, Ramadan ʿAbdallah Shallah hints that Hizballah's suicide bombings during days of war in Lebanon were a source of inspiration for the group's own "martyrdom operations," which were adopted as a strategy shortly after the return of the first batch of deportees to the Territories.[162]

Whereas PIJ would rely on Iranian networks when expanding its organization in Lebanon, Hamas initially sought the support of the Lebanese branch of the Muslim Brotherhood, al-Jamaʿa al-Islamiyya, which took the movement under its wings and helped its allies set up a number of offices in the Palestinian camps in the early 1990s, albeit under its own banners and emblems. Anxious to draw attention to their mobilization campaigns in the camps, Hamas' leaders preferred to keep a low profile, and the situation would remain this way until the end of the millennium. Things began to change in 1999, after the king of Jordan went on to jail and expel a number of prominent Hamas' officials accused of "engaging in clandestine paramilitary training" and mingling with various local Islamist groups opposed to the monarchy.[163] Syria, in turn, granted Hamas the opportunity to relocate its politburo from Amman to Damascus. At a point in time when Syria greenlit the PLO's return to Lebanon—an act intended to put pressure on Israel while the fate of the Golan Heights remained undecided—Hamas was similarly able to consolidate its position firmly within the refugee camps of both Lebanon and Syria, where it began to work more openly.[164] Meanwhile, the fellow-Islamists of al-Jamaʿa al-Islamiyya were in the process of reconsidering their alliance with their Palestinian brethren. In the accounts of Bassam Hammud, al-Jamaʿa al-Islamiyya's local representative in Sidon, there was a growing concern that people would conflate the Lebanese political party with the revered Palestinian movement which at the time was making international headlines due to its violent engagement against Israel during the Second Intifada.[165] In May 2001, the parties parted ways on good terms, and all of al-Jamaʿa al-Islamiyya's offices in the refugee camps were turned over to Hamas overnight. "Everything from their sports clubs, to their mosques and health clinics were passed on to us," the leader of Hamas in Lebanon, ʿAli Barake, explained, speaking from his headquarters near the old airport road in Beirut. His premises, a large and well-decorated office adorned with both Palestinian and Lebanese flags, were in and of themselves a testament to the transformation the movement had gone through since its first affiliates arrived in the country a couple of decades earlier. "Finally, Hamas had turned into a faction present in the camps like any other faction," Barake continued. "Before this, we only did political work or media work, but now we were present among our people as a *tanzim* (organization/faction)."[166]

Those who had missed this turn of events at the time would certainly become privy to the changes in December 2001. Coinciding with the celebration of Hamas' anniversary, the movement's then leader in Lebanon, Usama Hamdan, arranged a huge procession for the occasion and chose ʿAyn al-Hilwe as his main stage as he went on to claim the responsibility for the Haifa suicide attack that Hamas' military wings had carried out alongside PIJ's Quds Forces a week earlier.[167] This was a clear signal that the organization was operational in Lebanon. Among the Palestinian refugees, Hamas' popularity would grow exponentially in tandem with its efforts to rebrand itself as a political party and fashion itself a governing actor in the Palestinian Territories. Polls conducted among Palestinian refugees in Lebanon at the eve of Hamas' iconic victory in the Palestinian Legislative Council in 2006 showed that the movement had surpassed Fatah in popular support, if only barely.[168]

Filling an Ideological Gap

We should perhaps provide some nuance to the claims of Hamas having become like "any other faction," because following its formal establishment in Lebanon, the movement seems to have assumed a role opposite of its Palestinian archrival Fatah. First, Hamas (and PIJ) are the only Palestinian factions to openly engage in warfare against Israel from Palestinian soil, and enjoy a substantial amount of legitimacy due to this. Second, Hamas also stands out in that it is not visibly armed within the refugee camps. Although its leaders have been known to arrange collects among refugees to gather funds for building Qassam rockets in Gaza and we should not rule out the possibility of the group operating armories or other military facilities together with its pro-Syrian colleagues or Hizballah, Hamas does, unlike Fatah, not host any official militia branch in Lebanon. Moreover, the movement's tie-wearing officials present themselves in an entirely different way than Fatah's camp commanders who typically parade around in uniforms and military fatigues. Rather than flaunting weapons, Hamas is known for running a robust network of political, educational, and charitable projects, although these are often only loosely tied to the main organization in order to keep these from being afflicted by any economic sanctions that foreign governments have been known to impose on the movement. These institutions range from Qur'an schools, health clinics, Boy Scout clubs, and football teams, to the al-Zaytouna Center for Studies and Consultations—a renowned think-tank found in the ʿAysha Bakkar neighborhood of West Beirut.

In many ways, Hamas and its Islamist colleagues have sought to fill what they perceive as an ideological gap left by the factions associated with the PLO. In this view, the PLO and the Fatah movement function as little more than a "pension bureau" that buys loyalty through salaries and rewards, but has long abandoned its ambitions of recruiting supporters based on ideals or principles, such as the national struggle.[169] Ultimately, these actors have become spiritually and ideologically void. In the Shatila camp, I shared a cup of tea with a younger Hamas official in charge of the movement's charitable projects who was eager to elaborate on the topic. "We have a moral and religious obligation to provide for our people. In our dictionary, there is no such word as rest," Abu Tafish said, speaking from his office, which he simultaneously was running a computer repair business out of.[170] "With Hamas, you don't see any weapons, there is no chaos," he contended.

> Our people know that our arms are in our homeland where they are used for their only legitimate purpose, to fight the enemy [...] There is a sense that Hamas is something exciting, something that attracts people. Fatah can organize a hundred marches, but everybody knows that [they have] surrendered to the Zionists and have nothing to offer other than further concessions.

"As you can see, there is a need for us," Abu Tafish concluded as he scurried around his office attempting to make sense of which visitors had come to register for his movement's welfare programs and who simply wanted to get their computer fixed. "Hamas and al-Jihad [PIJ] are the only honorable people of this camp," an elderly woman concurred while waving a broken laptop over her head.

A Force of Moderation?

Back in ʿAyn al-Hilwe, Hamas official Fadl al-Taha also had much to say about ideology. He expressed a sense of relief when discussing the trajectory of ʿUsbat al-Ansar, whose positive transformation he credited to the countless hours of dialogues the parties have had throughout the years. "We are the ones who made them talk to the world," he boasted. "We took them to the Lebanese authorities. They had 'files' [with the state] all over the place and God knows what else, but we worked hard to find a solution with them."[171] Like many of his party-fellows, he stressed that it was these dialogues that helped ʿUsbat al-Ansar abandon its erratic behavior and "redirect its attention to Palestine." When the movement decided to accept Fatah's peace offering years earlier, the former cited Hamas as its spiritual guide. "We are the same as Hamas, we are the soldiers, the same ideology," leader Abu Tariq al-Saʿdi told anthropologist Dag Tuastad in 2010.[172]

We should of course give such testimonies a substantial amount of weight, although it in many cases would be inaccurate to equate the political pragmatism exerted by militant Islamists in ʿAyn al-Hilwe with ideological moderation. In fact, when the scholar and imam Jamal Khattab organized his aforementioned protest against the Charlie Hebdo magazine in January 2015, essentially praising al-Qaida for its efforts in killing "heretics" in France, he did so in the name of the Islamic Forces and he was flanked by leaders of Hamas and PIJ as he addressed the media.[173] Nor should we accept Hamas' own narrative of being the leading actor within this framework of Palestinian Islamists. On a couple of occasions, I was surprised to find my meetings with high-ranking officials from Hamas turn into them questioning *me* about the organizations of ʿUsbat al-Ansar and Jamal Khattab's HIM, rather than the other way around. Particularly, they seemed concerned about their colleagues' connection to the Fatah movement or other political rivals, and gave the impression that they had been left in the dark on a number of issues. There was obviously a sense of tension within the Islamic Forces, and there is reason to believe that the groups did not cooperate as closely as they sometimes led on to believe. "Don't forget that Jamal Khattab and 'Usbat al-Ansar are stronger than both Fatah and Hamas combined," 'Ali Barake relayed during a meeting at his offices in Beirut.[174] "They are stronger in terms of military capacities," he said. As Hamas' leader in Lebanon, he was perhaps eager to distance his own organization from the militia culture of the Capital of the Diaspora. "As a movement we are found in more than 40 states and have supporters all over the world, but in 'Ayn al-Hilwe, they call the shots."

While these claims should hardly be taken literally—there is, after all, little doubt that Fatah's combatants within the camp by far outnumber those of other factions—these perspectives do perhaps offer some insight into the balance of power within the Islamic Forces. Rather than being an ideological project first, Hamas and PIJ's arrangements in 'Ayn al-Hilwe should primarily be understood as a bid to remain influential in Lebanon's most important Palestinian camp in an era where their own pro-Syrian political framework, the APF, has increasingly become irrelevant.

A Seat in Every Diwan

There is a saying in 'Ayn al-Hilwe that every armed movement in the camp is funded by Fatah—especially the ones that are against Fatah. In another iteration, the proverb makes the same claims about Hizballah. There is likely some truth to both versions. In all probability, we could say this about a host of Palestinian and Lebanese stakeholders, and the saying would still not be entirely false. These observations attest to the commonly held perception that, in the Capital of the Diaspora, pragmatic arrangements tend to defy ideological convictions. Although militant Islamists have with varying measures of success carved out their respective sanctuaries in 'Ayn al-Hilwe and have occasionally managed to latch on to global jihadi networks, they have struggled intensely to transcend the local reality on ground. For the most robust and longest-lasting movements, perseverance has entailed entering into tacit (or not so tacit) understandings with a number of political rivals.

In this chapter, we have seen how these interactions with local political authorities have offered a number of lucrative opportunities. In particular, the Cedar Revolution of 2005 gave the fighters and shaykhs who had found themselves vilified and persecuted under Syria's reign of Lebanon the chance to reframe their purpose and assert themselves as intermediaries of the emerging leadership. Although the Islamist duo of al-Haraka al-Islamiyya al-Mujahida and 'Usbat al-Ansar do not have an organizational reach beyond their native camp, and are ostensibly insignificant in size and popularity compared to other social movements in the country, these groups have been able to retain political relevance by placing themselves at the center of every process, in the middle of every road, and between every political force at junctions in time when power balances between Lebanon's sectarian leaders, the state's security bureaus, and Palestinian stakeholders have been re-negotiated and shaped anew—from the Cedar Revolution to the Battle of 'Abra. By expertly exploiting unresolved tensions between all parties involved, not only have the Islamic Forces have been recognized as full-fledged Palestinian factions expected to engage in meetings at both the PLO's headquarters in West Beirut and Hamas' main office in the southern parts of the city, but they have also cemented their place in the *diwans* of Sidon's most influential Sunni and Shiʿ parties.

This pragmatic reading of the local political reality has led the same actors to abandon their armed struggles, at least for the time being. Despite nurturing an image as jihadi militias poised for war, these self-ascribed revolutionaries have ironically become guarantors of the status quo. Currently, their combatants serve little other function than maintaining a fragile balance of power among the many informal militia groups found between the camp and the city. Naturally, this approach has sparked reactions. Exacerbating internal strife, the abovementioned processes have drawn new lines in the sand between the militants who find themselves protected by legal moratoriums and those who remain simple outlaws or, worse, terrorists. Next, we will turn our attention to the latter and explore how the fringe groups that broke ties with the Islamic Forces during the early 2000s would return to the center of the stage at a point when the Syrian war was threating to spill over into Lebanon.

5

Armies of Outlaws, Sons of the Camp

In January 2014, a PLO official in Beirut expressed concerns about the news he was receiving from ʿAyn al-Hilwe. During a meeting at his offices in the Mar Elias camp, Abu Iyad Shaʿlan said there were clear signs that al-Qaida had gained a foothold in the country's largest Palestinian camp in the course of the last few months.[1]

Having steered clear of the anti-regime revolts of the Arab Spring, and remaining seemingly unfazed by the tensions brewing across its eastern borders, Lebanon had, up until this point, stayed surprisingly peaceful. The year 2013 was a turning point to this end. Hizballah leader Hassan Nasrallah's speech in May, in which he publicly declared his movement's military engagement in Syria on the side of President Bashar al-Assad, caused serious concerns for a spillover of the conflict into Lebanon. When deadly car bombs detonated outside of two large Tripoli mosques in August, killing forty-two, Minister of Justice, Ashraf Rifi, said the events were only "the beginning of the storm."[2] In November, a double suicide blast struck the Iranian embassy in Beirut, claiming the lives of another 22 victims and injuring 140. The latter attacks were claimed by the al-Qaida-linked ʿAbdallah ʿAzzam Brigades, which in a statement said the aggression would continue until Hizballah withdrew from Syria, and "our prisoners are released from the prisons of injustice in Lebanon."[3] The clandestine network's leader, a Saudi national going by the name Majid al-Majid, was originally thought to be working from Syria. However, when he was arrested while attempting to undergo kidney surgery in the southern suburbs of Beirut, it was revealed that he had for some time resided in ʿAyn al-Hilwe.[4] As the Syrian storm was threatening to engulf Lebanon, Abu Iyad and other Palestinian leaders feared that the country's largest Palestinian camp would find itself at the center of it. Despite al-Majid's capture, he was not optimistic. "There are several candidates ready to continue in his path," the veteran PLO official nonchalantly noted while he took a sip of his coffee.[5] He was particularly concerned about a Palestinian called Usama al-Shihabi.

Born in ʿAyn al-Hilwe in 1971 and originally hailing from the ʿArab al-Zubayd village in the Safad district of historical Palestine, al-Shihabi had returned to the camp following a shorter stint in Syria in 2012. Upon his return, he had proceeded to recruit militants to fortify his presence in the areas surrounding his house in his native ʿArab al-Zubayd neighborhood.

He appeared to be accompanied by the Palestinians Bilal Badr and Bilal al-ʿArqub, who were running similar operations out of the nearby Tiri district. Reportedly, militant cells were also emerging in the neighboring Taytaba and Hittin areas. In the midst of it all, al-Shihabi had assumed the role as a spokesperson for these new groups of militants, and was releasing statements under the moniker *Tajammu' al-Shabab al-Muslim (The Gathering of Young Muslim Men).* Not unlike Fatah's Abu Iyad, the US Department of State suspected Syria-linked jihadi networks were expanding within Lebanon's Palestinian camps. In December 2013, it went on to designate al-Shihabi a "global terrorist" presumably having been appointed the leader of the Lebanese branch of the al-Qaida linked Jabhat al-Nusra movement (presently known as Hay'at Tahrir al-Sham).[6]

When I met him in his home three years later, al-Shihabi spoke eagerly about his ambitions to return to Syria and recruit Palestinian youth for the war against Bashar al-Assad. It was clear that he was not without a certain popular following in the camp. However, his supporters did not necessarily consist of the dedicated jihadi warriors one might have expected. Rather, many of them appeared to be people with criminal records who sought protection from the PLO's military wings or feared arrests by the Lebanese army. Up close, the group that was being advertised as Lebanon's new al-Qaida branch, more than anything seemed to resemble a loose patchwork of neighborhood militias whose affiliates were not so much united by a common cause, as their status as outlaws wanted by the authorities.

Ultimately, my pursuit to understand the trajectory of the militants who broke ties with 'Ayn al-Hilwe's main Islamist organizations in the early 2000s had led me to a story about the camp's expanding militia economy during the Syrian war, and how it was supported on the shoulders of outlaws, paperless refugees, and disenfranchized urban youth. In this picture, it was clear that Usama al-Shihabi and his allies were not the only protagonist. In pages to follow, we will see how their sworn enemies from the opposing trench in the Syrian war, namely Hizballah, have similarly appealed to paperless and persecuted youth in Sidon and its Palestinian camps. Before we get to that, we will go back a decade in time, to get a clearer picture of the roots of al-Shabab al-Muslim, which begins with the formation of a movement called Jund al-Sham.

Soldiers of the Levant and Neighborhood Mafias

In 2004, the jihadi movement in 'Ayn al-Hilwe was in a state of disarray. The recent assassinations of the leaders of the offshoot 'Usbat al-Nur group, 'Abdallah and Muhammad Shraydi, were a harsh reminder that Fatah remained the dominant military faction and that the camp was perhaps not the safe haven it had seemed. The fact that the Islamic Forces of 'Ayn al-Hilwe were now in communication with the mainstream Palestinian leaderships regarding security arrangements did not bode well for those who suspected they were also on Fatah's hit list. Fearing a joint effort to apprehend them, a group of militants held a meeting in late May, which ultimately resulted in the formation of *Jund al-Sham (Soldiers of the Levant).*

Its creation was in essence a merger of three different ensembles. First, Jund al-Sham consisted of allies of 'Abdallah Shraydi and 'Usbat al-Nur, as was the case with Usama al-Shihabi, who at this point had already made an enterprise for himself by forging passports for al-Qaida affiliates in Lebanon.[7] This entourage was joined by a group of defectors from ʿUsbat al-Ansar who had followed the movement's military leader ʿImad Yasin when he departed due to an internal dispute in 2003.[8] Finally, Jund al-Sham included several fugitives from North Lebanon who had fled to the camp following the aforementioned clashes of Sir al-Dinnye at the turn of the millennium. Among these was the Lebanese Khalid Sahmarani, better known as "Ghandhi" or Abu Ramiz al-Tarabulsi, who assumed the role as Jund al-Sham's military leader. In terms of funding, a former ʿUsbat al-Ansar operative, Bilal al-ʿArqub, was the movement's key-link to Abu Musab al-Zarqawi's al-Qaida in Iraq and his Syria-based liaison, Abu Ghadiya, and would funnel money into the camp through a bank account registered in the fictitious name Mahmud al-Shamaʿ.[9]

Counting around forty militants, Jund al-Sham was significantly smaller than a movement like ʿUsbat al-Ansar. Nonetheless, its formation suggested that the latter no longer exerted hegemony over the jihadi field in ʿAyn al-Hilwe nor the resources coming into the camp from external sympathizers. Although the two movements both supported the "Iraqi jihad", they differed in their view on the utility of force against the local authorities. Jund al-Sham's affiliates were more reckless in their behavior. For example, Usama al-Shihabi enjoyed an extensive network among Tripoli-based militant cells that had made several headlines through their bombings of American restaurant branches, such as McDonald's and KFC. When the network's main funder, the Yemeni al-Qaida operative known as Ibn al-Shahid (Son of the Martyr) in late 2003, was tried by a military tribunal, he revealed to the court that al-Shihabi had been a key-planner in a recently foiled plot to smuggle a bomb into the U.S. Embassy in Lebanon.[10] Al-Shihabi had gone ahead with the plan, presumably ignoring ʿUsbat al-Ansar's advice that the tight security rendered the embassy an unrealistic target.[11] The plan failed and resulted in several arrests. During his trial, Ibn al-Shahid also revealed that al-Shihabi had become a source of concern for the more levelheaded Islamists in ʿAyn al-Hilwe, due to the way he tended to draw unnecessary attention to the camp. Following one of al-Shihabi's many run-ins with the militia wings of Fatah, ʿUsbat al-Ansar's leader Abu Tariq had reportedly demanded that a-Shihabi abandoned the camp altogether—an idea he vehemently rejected.[12]

Having earned a terrible reputation among inhabitants of ʿAyn al-Hilwe, these militants would attempt to restore their credibility and attain a sense of religious legitimacy by calling on an older and respected Salafi shaykh called Abu Yusif Sharqiyya to lead Jund al-Sham.

The Prince of Shari'a

Born in ʿAmqa in 1944, Muhammad Ahmad Sharqiyya, or Abu Yusif, fled with his father to Lebanon in 1948 where they eventually settled down in the northern Nahr al-Barid camp.[13] He became interested in the doctrines of both the Muslim Brotherhood and Hizb al-Tahrir at an early stage in his life, and began studying religion "in one of the faculties" in Tripoli.[14] Abu Yusif would go on to teach religion himself, despite having had to cut his education short in order to work in construction with his father. During the days of the Palestinian revolution, he was among the many young refugees to receive military training by Fatah—Revolutionary Council (*al-Majlis al-Thawri*) in the Biqaʿ Valley. However, during Syria's crackdown on Tripoli's Salafi movement in the 1980s, Abu Yusif inadvertently found himself on the wrong side of the ideological divide. In his own accounts, a pro-Syrian group like Revolutionary Council took issue with him after he had participated in building a Salafi mosque in the Nahr al-Barid camp. In 1989, he decided to relocate to ʿAyn al-Hilwe after the Revolutionary Council's leader, the notorious Abu Nidal (Sabri al-Banna), allegedly had ordered his assassination. In the southern camp, he used his spare money to buy a compound in the Saffuri neighborhood which he equipped with many additional floors to accommodate his ever-increasing family. Being "married to more than one woman," Abu Yusif had over the years become a father of seventeen. "I am a Muslim man," he told the press: "I get married and divorced according to the laws of Allah."[15]

In ʿAyn al-Hilwe, he continued to work in construction while occasionally teaching classes in religion. Through these classes, he would become acquainted with other Salafis having fled the scrutiny of Syria's forces in the North. In May 2004, some of Abu Yusif's former students approached him about the possibility of leading the Jund al-Sham movement. As an aging shaykh having recently lost his left leg to gangrene and who locally was known as the "Prince of Shariʿa," he provided the group with a façade of piety that it severely lacked. "[W]hen they chose me, they said it was a matter of putting the right man in the right place in terms of religion," Abu Yusif told a journalist.

> ... but I know most of them. We met and discussed many things, and some of them attended my classes. If I had refused to command them, I would have been committing a sin, because the unification of any Muslim group is considered a good deed.[16]

However, it would very quickly become apparent that the parties were a bad match.

Conflicting Mission Statements

From the outset of Jund al-Sham's formation, Abu Yusif would receive journalists at his house, or even arrange press conferences, where he in flawless *fusha* (formal Arabic) relayed the movement's purpose and visions. "After the American aggression on the Muslim people from Afghanistan to Iraq, and with the increase of Jewish terrorism in Palestine, there was no choice [than to create] a resistance movement that relies on the books of Allah and their Jihad against the infidels," he told the press during one of these occasions. "So we began contacting the Mujahid brothers, and we were capable of gathering them all in the highest path of Islam, God's true religion."[17] According to the shaykh, Jund al-Sham had two main goals:

> To carry out "the laws of God based on his scriptures, his tradition, his prophets, the views of previous scholars", and to carry out "jihad in the path of God, where we prepare ourselves to fight the enemies of God: America and Israel and those who commit aggression against us as Muslims."[18]

Abu Yusif acknowledged, nonetheless, that his movement was still "in its infancy" and hardly had the capacities to embark on a war against Israel.[19] Like other jihadi networks in the camp at the time, Jund al-Sham had arranged to send foreign fighters to Iraq, and was found to be sheltering a group of young men from the Gulf, who were undergoing training in ʿAyn al-Hilwe before their dispatch.[20] However, when Jund al-Sham became a national phenomenon in Lebanon it was for widely different reasons.

The movement turned many heads when it released a set of very conflicting statements in the wake of the car bomb that killed Hizballah commander Ghalib ʿAwali on July 19, 2004. In a first statement, Jund al-Sham seemed to claim responsibility for the attack, stating that the group had "carried out the jurisprudence of God against one of the symbols of treachery, the Shiʿ and apostate Ghalib ʿAwali, at the outset of the true struggle to separate blasphemy from Islam."[21] Hours later, the movement's leader, Abu Yusif, reached out to the media to announce that the initial statement had not come from him, but that it appeared to have been forged by Mossad. "We want to clarify that our project in Jund al-Sham is to fight the Zionist enemy and the American enemy," he said, adding that whoever had tried to slander the reputation of his movement was likely to be the very culprit to have carried out "this cowardly crime."[22] Reportedly, Abu Yusif had phoned Hizballah to pay his tributes to ʿAwali and to clarify his position.[23] When the media confronted him about the frequent anti-Shiʿ rants made by some of his companions, the shaykh responded by saying "*la nukaffir illa al-kafirin*—we only commit *takfir* against infidels," and that "the individual has to commit to the ideas of the organization."[24]

In October, only a few months after the group's inception, Abu Yusif announced his resignation from Jund al-Sham, saying that his illness had caught up with him, and that he was unable to go on.[25] His illness aside, rumors were already circulating that he had been threatened to quit by his own followers who did not appreciate his lenient line with Hizballah. "Quit? He was kicked out by those thugs!" a relative of Abu Yusif's currently serving as Fatah's communication officer in the Shatila camp weighed in:

> He was a well-respected shaykh, but those hashish-smoking imbeciles from the Dinnye group [whom he was commanding] couldn't appreciate his knowledge nor his eloquence. Their only concern was doing drugs and creating problems.[26]

Following Abu Yusif's departure, the leadership of Jund al-Sham was passed on to—or in some accounts seized by—the Palestinian Usama al-Shihabi and the Tripolitian Gandhi al-Sahmarani. Under their command, the movement would continue on an increasingly antagonistic path. However, as far as the Lebanese press was concerned, the most controversial aspect of Jund al-Sham was its unusual relationship with Future Movement MP Bahia al-Hariri.

Bahia's Soldiers

In July 2004, the Fatah movement asked all Palestinian leaders, including the Islamic Forces, to help expel Jund al-Sham from ʿAyn al-Hilwe.[27] The request came after Gandhi al-Sahmarani had successfully robbed a weapon armory belonging to a Palestinian Armed Struggle Command (PASC) commander in North Lebanon.[28] Although ʿUsbat al-Ansar managed to reduce some tension by going between the parties and convinced al-Sahmarani to hand back Fatah's weapons, the calm wouldn't last for long. In the months to follow, the camp would be rocked by violent clashes pitting the young Fatah commander Mahmud "Lino" ʿIssa against Jund al-Sham strongman ʿImad Yasin, with both parties competing for the control of the Saffuri neighborhood. Jund al-Sham had perhaps overestimated its ability to take on Fatah's militiamen. During one of these clashes, Lino's forces attacked Yasin's headquarters in Saffuri, burning it to the ground.[29]

It was these confrontations that pushed Jund al-Sham out of the camp itself, forcing the group to relocate to the Taʿmir district on its northern outskirts. As the militants moved into these streets and rented new flats for their families, the movement found a new pool of recruits among Sidon's urban poor and deprived Sunni youth—especially those who had run into problems with the local authorities. Blurring the lines between its image as an al-Qaida inspired movement engaged in global jihad and a neighborhood mafia, Jund al-Sham would specialize in offering protection for any fugitive from the law seeking shelter from the Lebanese authorities or Fatah's militias.[30]

Having laid claim to parts of Taʿmir, Jund al-Sham inevitably became a Lebanese problem as much as a Palestinian one. This explains why the Future Movement's Bahia al-Hariri eventually came to heed Fatah's call for getting rid of these militants. According to anthropologist Are Knudsen, Jund al-Sham had demanded $100,000 to abandon their flats and leave the area behind.[31] At a point where Sidon's politicians were attempting to establish an army presence on the northern outskirts of ʿAyn al-Hilwe, al-Hariri sought to hurry the process along by paying the money out of her own pocket. Hariri's way of dealing with problems, however, only seemed to create new ones. With nowhere else to go, several of the Tripoli-elements within Jund al-Sham went back to the North and became complicit with the emerging Fatah al-Islam movement. As was the case with the aforementioned Shihab Khudr Qadur (Abu Hurayra). Hailing from the Mishmish district of ʿAkkar, he had been made the head of Fatah al-Islam's military committee in September 2006, and made arrangements to transport Jund al-Sham's modest arsenal of C4 explosives to Nahr al-Barid before the army moved into Taʿmir the following January.[32] This was the same Qadur—allegedly acting without the knowledge of Fatah al-Islam's leader Shakir al-ʿAbsi—who in May 2007 had assassinated a dozen or so sleeping Lebanese soldiers at the entry point of Nahr al-Barid, ultimately dragging the movement into its losing war against the Lebanese army.[33]

Whereas an overwhelming majority of Tripoli's Sunni population supported the army during and after its military offensive, this support did not necessarily extend to the Future Movement and the Hariri family who struggled to reclaim face following the farce with Jund al-Sham. All in all, the events spurred a number of enduring conspiracy theories about the Hariris and their Saudi-based financial networks being the main sponsors of a number of regional terror cells, and the pro-Syrian media would jokingly label the militants al-Hariri had bribed as "Jund al-Sitt," meaning "Soldiers of the Madame."[34] Ironically, the jihadi combatants themselves came to resent the Hariris for betraying them, because the latter did not come to their support during the shelling in the North.[35] This little detail did nothing to deter the opposing side. In the fall of 2008, a Syrian TV documentary featuring "confessions" from imprisoned jihadi militants, claimed that Fatah al-Islam had reemerged in ʿAyn al-Hilwe, hinting strongly that the Future Movement and the Hariri family were its funders. Following the airing of the documentary, Future Movement leader Saad al-Hariri blasted the allegations as a gross distortion of the truth, urging the Arab League to establish a truth commission that ultimately would prove that the Syrian regime itself was the guilty party in this matter.[36] Defamation campaigns aside, it was clear that something worrying was taking place in the southern camp. However, there would be no new movement to announce its presence, no new banners, no press conferences or spokesperson to declare their ambitions of rallying the region's Sunnis against the United States or Israel.[37] Rather, ʿAyn al-Hilwe was witnessing the clandestine regrouping of what was left of Lebanon's jihadi movement.

Fatah al-Islam 2.0?

In the fall of 2008, two deadly blasts rocked Tripoli and its suburbs, sending waves of fear through Lebanon. The first of the two tore through a bus carrying Lebanese soldiers on a morning in mid-August, killing fifteen and wounding forty. In late September, a second bomb detonated next to another bus full of army troops, claiming the lives of four soldiers and a civilian, and wounding another twenty.

Although no one claimed responsibility for the operations, there was no shortage of possible culprits. Syria was similarly ridden by domestic turmoil, due in no small part to the presence of hostile jihadi militants who had begun turning their aggression toward the Baʿth regime, and the September bomb in Tripoli coincided with a devastating explosion going off near an office belonging to the secret service on the outskirts of Damascus. Syria's President Bashar al-Assad blamed Lebanon for the regional instability, and lambasted the country's authorities for having lost control of the North, and for lacking the ability to stand up against Saudi sponsored terror networks; another thinly veiled jab at the Hariri family. Others suggested that the Tripoli bombs surely must have been a Syrian-orchestrated effort to let the Baʿth party reassert military control over its neighbor, using counterterrorism as a pretext. "I think Syria is trying to justify why they need to come back to Lebanon," the Tripoli-based parliamentarian Misbah Ahdab told the press at the time.[38] When the Lebanese judiciary, acting under extreme political pressure from several parts, finally reached a verdict and issued its sentences (two years later), these were dealt to a group of militants who appeared to be operating from ʿAyn al-Hilwe.

The state's security agencies had earlier raised concerns about the activities of a Palestinian called ʿAbd al-Rahman ʿAwad (also known as Abu Muhammad Shahrur). Born in the Zib neighborhood of ʿAyn al-Hilwe in 1968, ʿAwad's trajectory was telling of the complicated routes the jihadi movement in Lebanon had taken since its inception. In his youth, he had been a member of Fatah, before jumping ship and becoming a bodyguard for Hisham al-Shraydi and his ʿUsbat al-Ansar movement around 1990.[39] In the mid-2000s, when certain Islamists in the camp came to deem said movement's behavior too pragmatic, he was among those who defected. Furthermore, in 2003 he made his way to Iraq, where he supposedly was entrusted with the leadership of one of-Zarqawi's military battalions, and like many of his peers, he made his way back to Lebanon following al-Zarqawi's death in 2006.[40] Once back in ʿAyn al-Hilwe, his behavior became indicative of yet another trend. His name would now come up in a number of domestic terror-related incidents, and it was believed that he was working alongside former Jund al-Sham leader Usama al-Shihabi.[41]

The two Palestinians were among a group of militants who were dealt death sentences for the Tripoli bombs and now became household names as the Lebanese press took turns guessing which one of them had secretly been crowned the new "emir" of Fatah al-Islam. The theory at the time was that the duo had emerged as a focal point for enraged jihadis eager to avenge the Lebanese army's violent crackdown on Tripoli. Circumstances lent a certain credibility to this claim. For example, one of those who were indicted for the explosions in the North was the young Tripolitanian ʿAbd al-Ghani Jawhar, who was said to have gone to ʿAyn al-Hilwe in order to receive military training from ʿAwad to avenge the murder of both his brothers who had died in the battle of Nahr al-Barid.[42] This network not only did attract Lebanese nationals but also had international backers. ʿAwad and al-Shihabi were likely funded by a Syrian from the city of Hama named Munjid al-Fahham, who had lived in Athens for about a decade and enjoyed extensive contacts in the Salafi communities in Greece and Bulgaria. In the summer of 2009, al-Fahham was thought to have traveled to Lebanon in order to plan the abduction of Western tourists who presumably were to be exchanged for Fatah al-Islam inmates detained in the notorious Rumiyye prison. The plot was foiled, however, with the arrest of al-Shihabi's underage nephew who was detained shortly after he had, on his uncle's orders, brought al-Fahham from the airport in Beirut to ʿAyn al-Hilwe. In his testimonies, the nephew explained how the Syrian national had brought with him several mobile phones and fake passports to the camp, while bags of chemicals and explosive materials were observed at al-Shihabi's flat.[43] Following the episode, a military tribunal dealt both ʿAwad and al-Shihabi a life sentence on top of their pending death sentences.[44]

It was clear that something had to be done about these cells, but fearing the fallout of another camp war, the Lebanese army would make no attempt to enter ʿAyn al-Hilwe. Rather, this time, Palestinian actors were entrusted to deal with the problem.

A War of Attrition

Following the Tripoli bombs, the Army Intelligence met with Fatah commander Mahmud Lino ʿIssa and members of ʿUsbat al-Ansar, requesting the handover of ʿAbd al-Rahman ʿAwad, Usama al-Shihabi, and former Jund al-Sham military commander Gandhi al-Sahmarani.[45] While ʿUsbat al-Ansar, after much deliberation, went on to apprehend a number of less prominent suspects, it was left up to Lino and the PASC to deal with the bigger names.[46] Requests for handovers notwithstanding, the Fatah commander already found himself locked in a guerilla war against several Islamist leaders and was grinding his rivals down clash after clash. In the summer, his forces had fought against several former Jund al-Sham operatives, resulting in the death of

Shahade Jawhar, while leaving his arch-enemy ʿImad Yasin badly injured.[47] However, when he received the request for ʿAwad, the latter had already slipped out of sight and would not be seen for two years.

ʿAwad resurfaced on August 13, 2010, in order to bid his family goodbye. According to his brother, a member of Lino's forces, ʿAwad had been alerted by the recent assassination of one of his closest affiliates and feared that Fatah was closing in on him.[48] Thus, he made the decision to leave the camp. Likely intending to take the Syrian route to Iraq, ʿAwad headed east, but didn't make it further than the Lebanese town of Shtura, where he was ambushed and killed by the Lebanese army.[49]

In ʿAyn al-Hilwe, Fatah's offensive continued, and the following December, Gandhi al-Sahmarani turned up dead. His body was found in a garage adjacent to the camp, his hands and feet bound, with a gunshot wound to his mouth. Whereas Fatah commander Munir al-Maqdah's assurances made to the media that al-Sahmarani had been killed "by his own"[50] seemed speculative at best, there should be no doubt that the underground jihadi networks in the camp were under tremendous pressure at this point. With leaders of the original Jund al-Sham movement being picked off one by one, the noose was now tightening around the neck of Usama al-Shihabi. In the months to follow, Lino and al-Shihabi's militias fought a tit-for-tat war of attrition which included several mutual assassination attempts. In August 2011, the finding of a roadside bomb on Lino's usual route past the Khalid bin al-Walid mosque triggered a full-scale battle between the parts. According to eyewitnesses, shells and rockets "rained over the streets of Sidon" and sent Palestinian families fleeing into the city.[51] The episode caused Sidon's sectarian leaders to intervene and to plea for a ceasefire, while both Lebanese and Palestinian stakeholders were calling for Lino to give up one of his men who stood accused of shooting and wounding one of two perpetrators suspected of rigging the bomb during an interrogation. The Fatah commander stated that the shooter, on the contrary, would be rewarded, adding that he personally would make every effort to drive "Usama al-Shihabi out from his hole."[52]

Fatah's offensive largely came to a halt when Lino was demoted and his PASC militias were dismantled and reintegrated into President Mahmoud Abbas' Palestinian National Security Forces (PNSF) in April 2012 (Chapter 3). Al-Shihabi, for his part, had at this point managed to slip out of the camp, to make his way to Syria along with his closest allies. The few remaining members of his cell, such as the Tripolitan ʿAbd al-Ghani Jawhar and the Hama native Munjid al-Fahham, would go on to die in battle during the war which was now raging in substantial parts of the Syrian mainland. Al-Shihabi, however, returned to ʿAyn al-Hilwe unscathed in August; this time with a new approach.

Al-Shabab al-Muslim and the Syrian Uprising

Usama al-Shihabi invited me to his apartment in February 2016. I had joined a friend of mine on a trip to one of ʿAyn al-Hilwe's markets where he was looking to buy a wedding ring, and al-Shihabi appeared to be on the same errand. The latter hardly acted the way you would expect one of Lebanon's most wanted men to behave, and his movements did not resemble those of a clandestine jihadi living in the shadows. Rather, he was walking around in the streets greeting everyone he saw, including the undersigned. Nor did he think twice about inviting a Western researcher like myself to stop by his flat in the ʿArab al-Zubayd neighborhood a few days later.

Since his return from Syria, he had made a part of his house into a guest lobby, complete with comfortable couches, a large white flag displaying the *shahada*, and huge bookshelves where golden book covers enlaced the *hadith* literature. He also had a stack of TV-monitors displaying footage from security cameras, mirroring the operations of most other faction headquarters in the camp.[53] The image he nurtured, though, was a far cry from that of the other Islamist authorities. For example, he did not wear a traditional *jalabiyya* nor did he have any prayer mark on his forehead. Rather, he wore a black vest, camouflage pants, and a firearm belt carrying a huge, polished revolver. In contrast to the forbearing and even-tempered demeanor of the officials of the Islamic Forces, he would impatiently clutter his sentences with Quranic references, sometimes to the extent that his words were running over one another. Moreover, his long reddish curls and a childlike face gave the forty-something an image of youthful rebellion that his peers lacked. More than anything, his exterior seemed to correspond with the jihadi insurgents fighting against Bashar al-Assad's forces on Syrian soil. In fact, he spoke warmly of Jabhat al-Nusra's battalions stationed in the Syrian border town of al-Qunaytra, whom he remained in touch with via Skype.

Sons of the Camp

With waves of new refugees settling in from the neighboring country, the Syrian war had transformed the Palestinian camps. It had intensified the scramble for scarce resources, with new lines being drawn between the *laji'in*, the refugees who had resided in Lebanon for decades, and the *nazihin*, the displaced families coming from Syria who often found themselves without any social network, let alone a place to sleep. Seemingly, the war had also transformed the likes of al-Shihabi and his allies who now safely emerged from their covers, assuming the image of *qabadayat* or neighborhood strongmen, engaged in a popular struggle supported by many. By virtue of having joined the uprising against the Syrian regime—and perhaps more importantly against its Iranian-backed protector, Hizballah—al-Shihabi now posed as a vindicator of a just cause and as a defender of the displaced refugees from Syria living in tent landscapes along the ledges of a camp like ʿAyn al-Hilwe. This was also the logic applied by the young jihadi militant Bilal Badr when he at one point in 2013 stormed the offices of the Baʿth party's Palestinian arm, al-Saʿiqa with hand grenades in either hand, threatening to turn the offices into a shelter for the refugees having fled the violence of al-Assad's regime.

Nonetheless, al-Shihabi was adamant that his new group, al-Shabab al-Muslim, intended to confine its armed struggle to the Syrian battlefields, thereby echoing the sentiments of Hizballah leader Nasrallah himself, who insisted that his engagement in Syria would not spillover into Lebanon.[54] "The idea [of forming al-Shabab al-Muslim] came to me after Hizballah had entered Syria," al-Shihabi shared:

> There were people from the camp that began thinking, "how Hizballah is striking Syria, I need to strike it in Lebanon." But we have prevented all of our brothers in 'Ayn al-Hilwe from bringing the war to Lebanon, be this in terms of booby-trapped cars, martyr operations or what have you. We view that whoever wants to go fight the party [Hizballah] should do so in Syria. This is our guidance from the Jihadi leadership (*al-qiyada al-jihadiyya*) in Syria—to keep the battle there, while sparing the camps of Lebanon.[55]

That being said, al-Shihabi's role was far from confined to recruiting foreign fighters for Jabhat al-Nusra. Since the formation of his al-Shabab al-Muslim network in late 2013, he was eagerly participating in ʿAyn al-Hilwe's public life. The self-styled shaykh was holding sermons in a smaller mosque near his house, and he had even set up a traditional reconciliation committee where he aspired to mediate conflicts in his control areas. Moreover, he had made a habit of issuing statements about camp affairs, including arrogant decrees stipulating which neighborhoods the different Palestinians security forces were allowed to deploy in or should keep out of (Chapter 6).

Although he obviously set out to provoke the mainstream Palestinian factions, he had a different rapport with the camp's civilians and their institutions. Seemingly having taken to heart the saying of Mao Zedong that a guerilla must move among the people as a fish swims in the sea, al-Shihabi would embark on publicity tours among the Neighborhood Committees in the eastern parts of the camp and pose for photo ops with their members. When I inquired about al-Shihabi's visits to these neighborhoods, community leaders would tell me the same thing: al-Shabab al-Muslim were good people, after all, they were "sons of the camp" (*abna' al-mukhayyam*). The expression was meant to indicate that these actors were not any given fugitives having crept into ʿAyn al-Hilwe; they were a part of the camp's social fabric and lived there with their families.

No One Can Rule Us

There was little doubt that the emergence of al-Shabab al-Muslim had unnerved the preexisting Islamist networks in ʿAyn al-Hilwe. At a time when leaders of the Islamic Forces found themselves swarmed with reporters inquiring about the presence of Jabhat al-Nusra, Usama al-Shihabi's erratic antics made their many assurances that al-Qaida was not found in the camp seem hollow. Not knowing how to react, a group like ʿUsbat al-Ansar wavered between vouching for al-Shabab al-Muslim by insisting that "their rifles are directed towards Palestine, and not Lebanon,"[56] and on other occasions, writing the network off as a group of "armed thugs posing as religious authorities," who worshipped "their guns more than the holy Qur'an!"[57]

The public bickering aside, what was the nature of the relationship between the two Islamist frameworks? In the Safsaf neighborhood, I wound up having dinner with a Salafi cleric with ties to both camps, who helped me illuminate the matter. Jamal Hamad was a former communist and guerilla fighter who had found religion during an extended stay in Bulgaria in the 1980s, and who upon his return to ʿAyn al-Hilwe became a follower of ʿUsbat al-Ansar's founder, Hisham Shraydi. He was adopted as a member of the movement itself for a brief period in 2001, but left quickly due to a personal dispute with the leadership. When I met Hamad, in September 2015, he had become an avid supporter of Jabhat al-Nusra and he would frequently join Usama al-Shihabi on his many publicity tours around the neighborhood. Furthermore, his writings on the conspiracies of the "Western-Zionist alliance" seemed to be shared widely on the Twitter accounts of Syria-based combatants.

Although Hamad still went to ʿUsbat al-Ansar's Martyr's Mosque to pray, and evidently had little reservations about dragging me along for a visit to the group's headquarters, he ultimately believed that his former movement had exhausted its role and betrayed its own principles through its "dialogues with the secularist and the Shiʿa [Hizballah]" as he put it.[58] Eagerly awaiting the fall of Damascus to the rebels in Syria, he was of the perception that the world was at the foothills of a new order—an order where there would be little room for the existing political systems, let alone the Palestinian factions who would soon be made irrelevant. Becoming a part of al-Shabab al-Muslim was not a matter of joining a new faction, the way he saw it. It was more like a *union*, or a *horizontal organization*, Hamad said with a twinkle in his eye, eager to see if I would catch the reference to the Marxist literature he once lived by. Ultimately, supporting al-Shabab al-Muslim was a matter of ensuring that the Palestinian camp was not in the wrong hands once it was Lebanon's turn to become a part of the awaited new world order. Therefore, Hamad was concerned about the new joint security measures in the camp, in which the Islamic Forces now took part (Chapter 6). Surely, he argued, these arrangements would only play into the hands of Fatah. "ʿAyn al-Hilwe is a central reference point for the jihadis," Hamad contended.

> It is unthinkable for us to surrender our neighborhoods to the Palestinian security forces and Fatah. We are for the stability of the camp, but we won't let them encroach on us. It is of vital importance that this camp belongs to us, the Muslims and the jihadis. We are the only ones who are independent, and that is our strength. No one can rule us![59]

Beyond all the rhetoric, Hamad did perhaps have more pressing reasons to be worried about the camp's security forces. While his former colleagues of ʿUsbat al-Ansar had managed to have their legal files cleared and found themselves received in the diwans of Sidon's political elites, pending criminal charges and a litany of bad blood between him and Fatah prevented him from even leaving the Safsaf neighborhood, where he was living under modest conditions with his family. These social factors would prove key in understanding the appeal of a "union" like al-Shabab al-Muslim: although far from all its affiliates were as ideologically invested as Hamad, they were all wanted by the authorities.

A Union of Outlaws

In the neighborhoods where al-Shabab al-Muslim were thought to enjoy a strong popular base, from Safsaf to Taytaba, and from Tiri to Hittin, it would not be uncommon to hear people use the word *matlub* (wanted, or outlaw) as a primary identity marker.

Whereas some of those who described themselves in this way were evidently facing charges of terrorism, others said they were wanted for low-level-offenses that simply had accumulated over the years. It is an open secret that the Lebanese authorities keep many informants within a Palestinian camp like ʿAyn al-Hilwe, who are paid to report suspicious incidents from the inside. In other words, it does not take much for anyone to end up on a wanted list. Often times, having fired a gun in the air at a party or a wedding might be enough. The felony itself seldom amounts to more than a few days in jail and a fine, but when camp inhabitants fail to report themselves to the Lebanese authorities, charges tend to pile up.

Regardless of personal background or the severity of the charges, having become a *matlub* seemed to cause fear and hatred for the outside world. While some reported that they had not moved outside of the camp for decades, others even refrained from moving outside of the street they lived on—at least unarmed. Taking a route by a neighborhood beholden to Fatah was out of the question. With such a limited pattern of movement, arming oneself or joining a neighborhood militia remained one of the few viable means for protection.

On the one hand, al-Shabab al-Muslim appeared to be made up of well-versed jihadis and terrorists, and on the other hand, included civilians with petty "files with the authorities."

To make this argument a bit clearer, al-Shabab al-Muslim attracted career militants such as Bilal al-ʿArqub (Jund al-Sham's former link to al-Zarqawi) who since the Syrian uprising had made a habit of releasing videos of his armed entourage (mostly made up of his own sons and brothers) wearing explosive belts and singing songs about conquering Damascus.[60] However, the network also included people like the father I met in the Taytaba neighborhood, who acknowledged that he didn't know how to pray or read the Qur'an very well but had gone to the step of arming himself, because his teenage son was wanted by the camp's security forces for having hurt a classmate at school. If the "authorities" should show up at his door, he would resist any attempt to hand over his family members. Thus, he remained in communication with the more revered militants of al-Shabab al-Muslim, sharing information about the streets in the neighborhood. "They are trustworthy people," he said. "All of the brothers are *matlubin* like myself, and we lookout for each other."[61]

When examining al-Shabab al-Muslim, it was not easy to see where the civilian defense militias ended, and where the violent jihadi cells begun. What was clear was that this ambiguity provided the perfect cover for the latter. It was no longer possible for Fatah's camp commanders to move in and uproot covert cells wanted by the authorities, without risking dragging entire neighborhoods into violent confrontations.[62] Besides, what Palestinian leader would want to face the accusations of fighting against *abna' al-mukhayyam*, the sons of the camp?

Restless Youth

Insofar as poverty and idleness played into the hands of the camp's extremist networks, the Syrian war and the new waves of refugees arriving in Lebanon only added to their pool of potential recruits. In Downtown Sidon, I found myself in conversation with the leader from an NGO that works with troubled refugee youth who had grown increasingly worried about the situation in ʿAyn al-Hilwe. "There is something that doesn't add up," he said.[63] "Usually there are funerals, there are posters and invitations." The funerals he was referring to were the type of rituals that had noticeably not taken place following a recent six-day turf war that had pitted militants from al-Shabab al-Muslim against members of Fatah (Chapter 6). Six had died, but no one seemed to know their names. The leader of said NGO attributed this to a growing trend: those who were winding up dead in such clashes tended to be paperless strangers or social outcasts. In other words, they were people who no one saw much point in commemorating and were indicative of the Syrian war's impact on the camp's militia economy. Displaced Palestinian refugees or Syrian nationals lacking the means to renew their visas, would often find themselves "trapped" in the refugee camps, he explained, because they feared they would be arrested by the authorities for not carrying legal papers. With nowhere else to turn or seek help, letting themselves be recruited by camp-based militias was a better prospect for many than winding up in prison—or worse—being sent back to their war torn country.

It was particularly the young and the hopeless who were favored targets, my interlocutor told as he shared a disconcerting story. Recently, he had taken a group of around ten minors from ʿAyn al-Hilwe to a clinic in Sidon to treat their drug addictions. The process had been somewhat of an ordeal, not at least because the patients were all wanted by the Lebanese authorities and risked arrests at the camp's entrance. He began pulling some strings hoping to get a guarantee from the Lebanese army that it would let them pass upon their visits to the rehabilitation clinic, but was surprised when the authorities reported back to him that only two of the youths had pending criminal charges. When he inquired into the matter, it turned out that the rest of the minors were merely under the impression that they were wanted because shadowy figures in the camp had reached out to them, informing them that the Lebanese state was after them. The social worker believed this to be a common recruitment tactic used by Islamist militants such as "Jund al-Sham," he said. What he had interrupted was merely the first step of a complex process; to single out the weak and the shunned and gradually lure them in with promises of protection or work.

Back in ʿAyn al-Hilwe, Usama al-Shihabi revealed that he was also deeply concerned about youth, although he had widely different solutions to their problems. "The shabab of this camp are tough (*hami*), some of them tougher than what's good for them," he said.[64] We had moved downstairs, sharing a cup of coffee in a basement across from his flat that he claimed belonged to a youth club that he was running. The place was deep underground, and some of the hallways seemed to lead into narrow tunnel passages presumably stretching across great distances, while a few of the rooms we passed were covered in black jihadi banners. He acknowledged that the camp had seen a surge of young combatants following the influx of new refugees, and lamented that these could serve a better purpose in Syria, fighting against Hizballah and the al-Assad regime. Referring to his recent clashes against Fatah, al-Shihabi was convinced that such bouts of violence would help him persuade both Palestinian and Lebanese stakeholders to assist him in sending his recruits off to Syria. "There is no higher [valor] in Islam than jihad," he said.

> The shabab of this camp know this. They might create many problems in the Lebanese arena, because they will do anything anyone orders them to. So we have two choices: to [have them] stay here and create problems or [let them] go to Syria and have them rid themselves of some tension. After the last clashes, I went to the [Palestinian] political leadership, the ones that meet with [head of the Bureau of General Security in Lebanon] ʿAbbas Ibrahim, and told them: "Tell him the following, inform the *mukhabarat* that we, al-Shabab al-Muslim, are ready to march to Syria—possibly without returning. Put us in Syria in the midst of the battle, far from the Lebanese borders if you must."

"Take us out, will you?" al-Shihabi continued rhetorically while a squeaking ceiling fan spun slowly over our heads. "You will relax. There is no problem, and even the PLO will be pleased."

Insofar as he was hungering to face off against Hizballah's allies, al-Shihabi seemingly did not have to move many meters to find them. As foreshadowed earlier, al-Shabab al-Muslim was far from the only actor to see the potential in enlisting troubled camp youth in their ranks. The network was facing staunch competition from pro-Iranian forces in Sidon who were hastily building their own armies of refugees and urban Lebanese poor. On the last leg of our exploration of ʿAyn al-Hilwe's Islamist militants, we will turn our attention to a group of self-proclaimed jihadis who have emerged as Hizballah's closest Palestinian protégé in Lebanon and who—at the eve of the Syrian war—found themselves the party's most important buffer against the likes of Usama al-Shihabi. Before we get to this, it will be well worth our time to briefly explore the origins of this movement, because very little has been written about these militants previously.

Ansar Allah: Hizballah's Palestinian Allies

In the narrative of its deputy leader, Mahir ʿUwayd, Ansar Allah is an "Islamic jihadi movement" that was launched in 1983, at a time when Sidon was under the siege of the Israel Defense Forces.[65] The group also presents itself as a nationalist militia movement deeply invested in the militant struggle against Israel. "I am, today, not only with the militarization of the uprising," ʿUwayd, told a Palestinian TV channel in early 2016, when the so-called knife-Intifada was raging in parts of Jerusalem:

> I am with the militarization of the Palestinian people in all of the world, and for us to go to the borders and support our people on the inside. [...] We want to take back the lands from the Jews, and face them wherever they are.[66]

On both counts, these are truths with modifications. More accurately, the group's origins can be traced back to a PLO battalion that in the early 1980s was called the ʿAyn al-Hilwe Martyrs' Brigade led by long-time Fatah commander Jamal Sulayman. Having been a close ally of Fatah leader and PLO chairperson Yasser Arafat, Sulayman came to reconsider their relationship during the aforementioned battles of Iqlim al-Tuffah where the Lebanese Shiʿ movements Amal and Hizballah faced off against each other in late 1989 and early 1990. Sulayman had previously fought in the notorious War of the Camps, and was shocked to find that Arafat had made the decision to side with Amal, the same movement which had violently besieged, starved, and shelled a number of Palestinian camps in Beirut and in the South only a couple of years earlier (Chapter 2). He went on to alert Hizballah about Arafat's intentions, allowing the movement to strike first. In the ensuing hostilities, Sulayman's ʿAyn al-Hilwe Martyrs' Brigade joined Hizballah's military campaigns against both Fatah and Amal.[67]

Interestingly, Sulayman found a close ally in the Palestinian guerilla Hisham Shraydi, who at the time was a part of the Iranian-backed offensive against Fatah. In fact, the name Ansar Allah seems to have been the moniker that Shraydi had originally chosen for his group, before changing it into ʿUsbat al-Ansar.[68] As we already know, their efforts to drive Arafat's Fatah out of ʿAyn al-Hilwe failed miserably. In August 1990, Sulayman and Shraydi's forces fled the camp after days of fighting and sought refuge in a nearby Palestinian gathering Wadi al-Zine, where they remained under the protection of Hizballah's affiliates. For his part, Sulayman reappeared at the end of the year, bringing with him some fifty militiamen.[69] Ignoring Fatah's pleas for him to withdraw, he went on to set up bases for his movement in both ʿAyn al-Hilwe and the neighboring al-Miyye wo-Miyye camp, announcing that he had returned to face the "enemies of our people, our cause and our intifada" and "in order for us all to build the bridge of return to our homeland."[70]

Whereas Shraydi's movement would go on to cross paths with the Lebanese Salafi current and violently challenge the Damascus/Teheran axis in Lebanese politics, Sulayman's Ansar Allah would remain firmly under the wings of the latter. "All our financing, in addition to the security and political cover, publicly comes from Hezbollah, and we are not ashamed of this fact," Mahir ʿUwayd told NOW Lebanon in 2007.[71] "Hezbollah is helping us because we took a decision to fight the jihad in 1989 and 1990," he said, "and we had positions in Iqlim al-Touffah, Naqoura and Shebaa. [...] We used to take an active part in the operations launched by Hezbollah, and we always stood in the front rows." In the years to follow the Civil War, however, Hizballah's Palestinian protégés would for the most part find themselves assigned to roles far removed from constituting an anti-Zionist fighting force.

Poison Arrows

While Ansar Allah, as an organization and Palestinian faction, seemed to drop off the map in the early 1990s, the group's name would soon make international headlines. On July 18, 1994, a bomb exploded at the Jewish Center in Buenos Aires, claiming the lives of ninety-five civilians. On the following day, another explosive, carried by a man calling himself Lya Jamal, detonated onboard a commuter flight in Panama, killing twenty-one passengers, among them many Israeli Jewish people. Immediately afterward, a statement signed by Ansar Allah was passed around in the Beirut and Sidon areas, "indirectly" claiming both attacks, as a Lebanese daily put it, by expressing its unequivocal support for the massacres, and claiming to know the name of the perpetrator in Panama.[72] In ʿAyn al-Hilwe, Fatah commander Munir al-Maqdah went on to symbolically round up a few local affiliates of the group that had been seen passing around said pamphlets, but told the media that he believed the statement's real source to be Gaza, implying that his archenemy Yasser Arafat was behind the attacks.[73] However, intelligence agencies more convincingly pointed to Iran and Hizballah as the funders and plotters of the operations, while the existence of an organization called Ansar Allah was doubted.[74]

After nearly ten years of silence, the Ansar Allah name would again appear in the headlines after two rockets were fired at Prime Minister Rafiq al-Hariri's "Future Television" station in Beirut in June 2003. Following the attacks, which resulted in no casualties, an ambiguous statement signed by Ansar Allah was sent out to various media offices, saying that "[O]ur operation aims to make it understood that we will not allow anyone, even if they are powerful or influential, to fire poison arrows at the heart of The Resistance."[75] Although Hizballah itself condemned the events, calling them "a cowardly act" and an attack against freedom of speech, the pro-Hariri press deemed that the operation had the party's fingerprints all over it, and saw it as a response to the prime minister's bid to "clip the wings" of "the Islamic Resistance" politically.[76] Presumably, having Ansar Allah, a marginal Palestinian group, claim the attack, was a way for Hizballah to send a clear and violent message to the Future Movement without formally accepting any responsibility for it.[77] Hizballah would find new uses for its Palestinian militia arm in the period to follow the 2005 Cedar Revolution, allowing Ansar Allah to emerge from the margins and claim a more central role.

A Second Renaissance

After Syria's departure from Lebanon, Hizballah found itself challenged by the Future Movement's political comeback and its calls for disarmament of all irregular militias. In the Palestinian camps, its diplomatic offensive with the PLO was an obvious source of concern.

Initially, Hizballah took it upon itself to keep the pro-Syrian opposition in the camps present by underwriting the budgets of the Alliance of Palestinian Forces (APF).[78] The process saw a clear reduction in the military capacities and political presence of pure Baʿthist-inspired militia groups like al-Saʿiqa in favor of the Iranian-friendly Palestinian Islamic Jihad. It was in the midst of these efforts that Ansar Allah resurfaced in the Sidon area. With new funds, the movement went on to recruit hundreds of new militiamen, and expanded its organizational structure significantly.[79] Ansar Allah now went on to establish a Shura Council, headed by founder Jamal Sulayman and his deputy, al-Hajj Mahmud, a media office ran by Usama ʿAbbas (Abu Ayyub), while Mahir ʿUwayd was put in charge of the movement's military committee.[80]

This metamorphosis became evident in October 2007, when Ansar Allah sought to revive a festivity called "Jerusalem Day"—an Iranian day of protest against Israel in solidarity with the Palestinian people. Riding on a wave of immense popularity that surrounded Hizballah after its "victory" in the 2006 war against Israel, in which the Palestinian group itself had participated, if only modestly so, Ansar Allah launched a large-scale military procession in ʿAyn al-Hilwe.[81] In the accounts of a Lebanese reporter, the procession displayed close to a thousand new fighters and "cubs" who marched in the streets of the camp, where Hizballah's flags and pictures of its leader Hassan Nasrallah were carried next to those of Yasser Arafat.[82] Despite the new recruits and its modest contributions in the 2006 war, it was clear for every observer that Hizballah had not resurrected the Palestinian movement in order for it to join it on the frontlines against Israel. When a reinforced UNIFIL force deployed in South Lebanon after said war, Ansar Allah's few remaining units along the southern border disbanded, and the movement became a phenomenon purely confined to the camps. Nonetheless, within the refugee camps Ansar Allah would continue to expand exponentially. Acting with the Damascus-based Ahmad Jibril and his PFLP-GC movement as a broker, it set up headquarters in the southern al-Rashidiyye camp, as well as in Shatila and Burj al-Barajne in Beirut. As of lately, the movement has also emerged as a dominant faction in the northern Nahr al-Barid camp, despite having been taken over by the Lebanese army in 2007. Naturally, these developments speak volumes of Hizaballah's political power in Lebanon, but they are also telling of how dominant actors rely on brokers or third parties to exert influence in the margins of the state.

A Miniature Resistance Society

In 2007, deputy-leader of Hizballah, Naim Qasim, described his party's goals of creating a "society of resistance."[83] Filling a void left by a neglectful Lebanese state, Hizballah strove to create a culture of dependency that were to bond the country's Shiʿ population to the movement. This society of resistance currently consists of an elaborate network of private schools, robust educational and social institutions, where the movement's notion of the Islamic Resistance and the struggle against Israel are substantiated in all sectors of social life.[84] In the Palestinian camps, Ansar Allah employs similar tools for socialization, albeit on a much smaller scale. Here, the movement runs several youth clubs, boy scouts divisions in addition to a few smaller clinics funded by Hizballah's Islamic Health Commission. Moreover, the Ansar Allah "cubs" (*ashbal*) are preadolescent Palestinians who receive light military training, intended to make them into future members of the armed forces. In the words of Mahir ʿUwayd, the movement has been "opening clubs to absorb the Palestinian youth so they won't just sit around on the streets. [...] Those who participate are trained, qualified and organized."[85]

While there should be little doubt that a movement like Ansar Allah owes its substantial expansion in Lebanon solely to its sponsor's ambitions of dominating urban politics in popular Sunni districts, there is an obvious dissonance between the movement's own nationalist rationale and its de-facto function, which hardly goes beyond constituting a cultural and military counterweight to anti-Iranian groups within the refugee camps. As we will see next, there are signs that this dissonance has become a source of internal tension for Ansar Allah's leadership.

Falling out with the Party of God

In late 2012, Ansar Allah's founder and Secretary-General, Jamal Sulayman, relayed to the media that his movement was severing its ties to its main backer for many years "militarily, security-wise and politically."[86] The statement offered no explanation other than saying that the move was "in the interest of our people and nation" and that Ansar Allah would "continue on the path of jihad and resistance" as an "independent Palestinian Islamist movement no matter how great the sacrifice." In the end, Sulayman's assurances would carry little weight. Before anyone had time to inquire about his cryptic messages, the Sidon-based imam Mahir Hammud had managed to broker an agreement between the parties, who put their differences aside and normalized their relations.

In July 2015, however, Sulayman issued another statement. This time around, he announced his resignation as the movement's Secretary-General, again citing differences with Hizballah. "My resignation is the result of my desire to let the situation run its natural course," Sulayman relayed: "[T]he situation as it is, can no longer stand, as no sane person would ever accept the ... oppression, vexation and hypocrisy that we have been subjected to."[87] What had provoked the movement's leadership to sever ties with its sole sponsor? Analysts suspected at the time that the frictions had something to do with Hizballah's involvement in the Syrian war. More precisely, the quarrel appeared to be connected to the way the Lebanese party was managing the war's fallout in the city of Sidon. Ansar Allah's second-in-command, Mahir ʿUwayd, who now reluctantly assumed the role as the movement's leader, weighed in to explain that the situation that Sulayman cryptically had been referring to had something to do with Hizballah's ties to a separate Sunni militia group that had become a source of much controversy locally.[88]

Sidon's Expanding Militia Economy

Tracing their inception back to 1997, *The Lebanese Resistance Squadrons (al-Saraya al-Muqawama al-Lubnaniyya)* were launched as an initiative by Hizballah leader Hassan Nasrallah in line with his policy to increase his movement's openness toward the Lebanese public. Intending to expand the party's influence beyond the limits of the Shiʿ community, these militia squadrons were in essence Hizballah's way of enlisting citizens from other sectarian backgrounds in its expanding "resistance society." For example, in the 2006 war against Israel, the Squadrons became particularly popular among Christians who with Hizballah's help formed bands of militias with the intention of preventing Israeli helicopters from landing in their towns.

Despite gaining notoriety for their efforts against the Israeli invasion, critics of Hizballah are quick to point out that the same squadrons were used in the party's siege of Sunni neighborhoods in West Beirut in the May 2008 conflict, rendering the efforts to bridge the gap between the Islamic Resistance and Lebanon's non-Shiʿ public dubious at best. Similar accusations have been raised following the recent reinvigoration of the Resistance Squadrons, which took place in tandem with Hizballah's entry into the Syrian war and as the opposition to the party's armed presence in Lebanon grew more vocal. At a time when a popular shaykh like Ahmad al-Assir was building a cult following around his popular rallies against Hizballah in Sidon, the Resistance Squadrons began enlisting jobless and disenfranchised Sunni youth from the area, likely in order to keep any rival social movement from exploiting their feelings of marginalization. In a scoop interview by the Lebanese daily al-Nahar, an officer from the Resistance Squadrons spoke of hundreds of new members having been recruited to face the growing "Sunni jihadi threat," saying "[t]he battle with the *takfiris* cannot be confined to one Lebanese party, but it is a duty for us all."[89]

In terms of preparation and military training, these militias did for all practical purposes lack the stringent discipline of Hizballah's regular forces, and quickly earned a reputation for their rash and careless behavior. In the accounts of the entourage of Ahmad al-Assir, it was the Resistance Squadrons that opened fire upon them in ʿAbra in the summer of 2013, ultimately dragging them into the catastrophic confrontation with the army.[90]

Whereas Hizballah's main Sunni allies in the city appeared to have turned a blind eye to the "Islamic Resistance's" entanglement in the Syrian conflict, the erratic behavior of its reckless militia arms in Sidon seemed more difficult to swallow. In my meeting with Mahir Hammoud, who is widely regarded as a supporter of the party, the shaykh made no attempts at concealing his discontent with Hizballah's unabashed sectarian power politics of arming militarily inexperienced Sunni youth, who he referred to as "armed thugs."[91] As for Ansar Allah, it was difficult to discern to what extent the leadership had come to question its own geopolitical role in the midst of these power plays, or if the movement simply feared being sidelined by other Hizballah-funded militia groups. What was clear was that a local branch of the Resistance Squadrons had emerged in ʿAyn al-Hilwe, and was threatening to upset the extant power balances within Lebanon's largest camp.

Outbidding the Enemy

The local branch of the Resistance Squadrons was predominantly intended to keep the Taʿmir district under control, which is a mixed Lebanese and Palestinian neighborhood, just north of the camp. Reportedly, both Sunni and Shiʿ youth from the area would flock to the organization—not necessarily because they perceived that they were under threat, but because Hizballah was paying its informal militants more than twice than what the mainstream Palestinian factions were offering. For people living in these neighborhoods, earning what at the time amounted to around $400 a month was an outstanding salary and an opportunity they could not pass up. Ultimately, the squadrons' members were left with little other choice than to become a part of this "anti-takfiri force," regardless of the consequences.

The Resistance Squadron's presence in ʿAyn al-Hilwe became a public story when one of their members disappeared under mysterious circumstances in April 2015. Marwan ʿIssa, the nephew of a leader of the Popular Nasserite Organization in Sidon, had been a frequent visitor of the camp where he was known to deal in the illegal arms trade. It was safe to say he knew his way around the place, but this time he had not returned. After a few days of searches, his tortured body was found with a nail gun wound to its head in the trunk of a car parked in the camp's Upper Street.[92] The murder was traced back to a well-known and feared affiliate of al-Shabab al-Muslim called Muhammad Shaʿbi.[93] This news prompted Hizballah (and the Popular Nasserite

Organization) to issue a statement saying that ʿIssa had been martyred by "falseness, treachery and takfirism."[94] Al-Shabab al-Muslim responded with a statement of their own, explaining that the group has had its eyes on the Resistance Squadrons for quite some time.[95] Believing ʿIssa to be a Shiʿ, the statement went on to say that he was not killed for his religion, but because of his alleged habit of insulting the companions of the Prophet (*al-Sahhaba*) and for having made sexual implications about ʿA'isha, one of the Prophet's wives. "This matter may have caused one of the *shabab* to respond by killing him," the statement concluded.[96] After four other affiliates of ʿAyn al-Hilwe's Resistance Squadrons turned up dead in similar fashion in the months to follow, the remaining members had no other choice than to publicly announce that they had disbanded their militias, and promptly vowed to abandon the area. However, this would prove easier said than done.

In the spring of 2014, local members of the Resistance Squadrons had managed to become entangled in a feud with the state's Internal Security Forces (ISF) over a roadblock in the intersection between the Taʿmir and Talaʿt al-Filat neighborhoods. Presuming they enjoyed legal immunity due to their connections to Hizballah, members of the squadrons had become rowdy and loud-mouthed in the face of the Lebanese authorities, and would show off by throwing bottles and stones at the ISF. It didn't take long for armed altercations to erupt between the parties, which would continue sporadically throughout the year. When the call was made to dismantle the militias and to abandon these neighborhoods, many of these militants had found themselves stranded due to their criminal charges, and refused to leave. Ironically, their predicament seemed to mirror that of the outlaws affiliated with al-Shabab al-Muslim, who quite similarly found themselves stuck in their respective neighborhoods of the camp. To their detriment, both groups of outlaws relied on the protection of patrons who were locked in war in the neighboring country, and who, almost feverishly, sought to make sure that the Palestinian camp and its Lebanese outskirts would not come under the control of the opposing party.

A Struggle of Patronage

Finally, in the summer of 2016, coinciding with the joint Lebanese and Palestinian efforts to extradite the camp's outlaws as cited in the previous chapter, Hizballah moved into the Taʿmir district with several black SUVs and swiftly detained eleven members of the Resistance Squadrons, before handing them over to the Lebanese army.[97] Leading up to the events, Ansar Allah's new leader, Mahir ʿUwayd, relayed with confidence his movement's ability to act like an intermediary and go between Lebanese stakeholders and the outlaws of ʿAyn al-Hilwe to find solutions. "We have played a role, and continue to play it, as an internal Palestinian broker (*wasit*)," he told a Palestinian TV channel in a rare hour-long interview.

> We might receive a video clip of [someone calling us] apostates or infidels. We don't have a problem with sitting down with these to explain to them that, today, in this reality, this [behavior] doesn't benefit you as a Palestinian living under this

> ceiling that is the ʿAyn al-Hilwe camp. If somebody wants to make any problems, they will only deprive themselves, or their wife, their children, their parents or the people of their house. All of them, the majority of them, I mean, are sons of the camp. There is a minority that entered the camp from the days of al-Asir, but only a few [....]. All of us, the Islamic Forces, Ansar Allah, the PLO or the APF, we all sit down with them and we all feel at ease through our dialogues with them, because we all share this camp.[98]

However, the calm that was present in ʿAyn al-Hilwe was not of the reassuring kind. Rather, a cold war was brewing. From afar, the fault lines of the Syrian conflict appeared to have been transposed onto the refugee camp, reduced, and configured to its scale. Despite the camp's tendency to absorb the region's conflicts, we would be remiss not to acknowledge the social mechanisms driving these tensions. What was taking place in ʿAyn al-Hilwe and its surrounding neighborhoods was first and foremost a struggle of patronage—a feverish competition between rival patrons, Lebanese or Palestinian, seeking to control the fallout of the Syrian war in Lebanon, or in some cases, capitalize on it. In the process, the camp had become brimful of new militia forces, with veteran jihadi-Salafis and Hizballah-funded militants guarding their specific areas, bound by their respective clientelist networks, and seemingly stranded in their separate ideological universes. Some of the new militia groups to emerge had very little to do with the Syrian war altogether. A few of my interlocutors noted with worry that various Fatah battalions also had begun recruiting displaced Syrian nationals en masse, presumably in order to bolster their own forces vis-à-vis rival camp commanders.

In this light, the brokerage a group like Ansar Allah was undertaking was perhaps of a less noble nature than advertised in the interview cited above. Having mended ties with its main sponsor after the Resistance Squadrons debacle, the movement was at the time relying on Hizballah's funds to add new recruits by the day. These were being payed anywhere between $300–500 a month—nearly the double of Fatah's rank and file—to carry a rifle on a street corner or guard checkpoints in the Palestinian camps.[99] Like most other factions, Ansar Allah appeared to have gained significant political leverage from asserting itself as a diplomatic solution to a problem it undeniably was taking part in creating. These dynamics will be important to keep in mind when we in the following chapter go on to explore the formation of a Unified Political Leadership for the Palestinian Factions, in which the Hizballah-backed movement naturally was invited to take part. Before we move on, we will conclude this story with a few words from one of the young refugees who found himself immersed in the expanding militia economy of ʿAyn al-Hilwe and who was quick to acknowledge the absurdity that he had become a part of.

In a café in Sidon, I had the chance to sit down with two of Ansar Allah's new recruits. They were not outlaws, nor were they paperless, and they were not shy about the fact that economic circumstances rather than ideological convictions had driven them to join the movement. The oldest of the two, who appeared to be in his mid-twenties, revealed that he had recently finished his degree in medicine at a Lebanese university. He had made arrangements to find work in the Gulf, well aware, of course, that he as a Palestinian could never work as a medical doctor in Lebanon. However, his plans fell through when the authorities refused to grant him a visa. "You study medicine at the university [for years], but when you graduate, you have to make a choice. You either leave the country, or remain unemployed," he explained.[100]

> In the camp, they made a party for me after my graduation. But what good is a doctor without a job? My younger brothers had already worked in construction for years and were the breadwinners of our house. As for me, "the doctor", I only had a diploma to show for, no experience. I felt embarrassed, since I am the oldest, but was unable to repay my parents for my education. (...) In the end, I had luck and they recommended me for a job [in the movement]. In all honesty, I cannot say that I feel proud. They say we are a part of The Resistance, but we are not resisting anybody.

"At least send me to Palestine," he said while taking a slow drag from his cigarette, "So that I can go fight for my country."[101]

6

Forming a Palestinian Police Force in Exile

On July 8, 2014, news cameras displayed militiamen emerging from all corners of ʿAyn al-Hilwe, pouring into the main streets of the camp. Normally, such a sight would be grounds for concern, but on this day, the camp's militia forces were heading for a ceremony to be held in the Bustan al-Yahudi street. The occasion was the inauguration of the Joint Palestinian Security Force (JPSF), the camp's new military police.

If we briefly allow ourselves to revisit the opening passages of this book, we will remember how Palestinian leaders announced that ʿAyn al-Hilwe would see its first cross-factional police institution, where members from all political frameworks would participate. The political factions were in dire need to demonstrate that the refugee camps would not become sanctuaries for outlaws or Syria-based jihadi networks, and it was understood that sealing the prevailing power vacuum would take a joint effort. ʿAyn al-Hilwe, a camp that for decades had lived on its nerves due to factional strife and infighting, would now receive a central Palestinian authority to regulate law and order. Instead of every neighborhood being beholden to its own militia movement, members of the factions were now to patrol the streets together.

Whereas Fatah commander Munir al-Maqdah was appointed as the JPSF's leader in Lebanon, and was expected to oversee the force's deployment in the remaining camps, his right-hand man Khalid al-Shayib along with Hamas' Khalid ʿAli Isma'il would lead its local branch in ʿAyn al-Hilwe together. The fact that the Fatah and Hamas leaderships, based in the West Bank and the Gaza Strip respectively, had agreed on a model to fund the joint framework was largely owing to a diplomatic effort exerted by Major-General ʿAbbas Ibrahim, the head of Lebanon's General Security bureau, who had been a driving force behind the project from the beginning. It was rare, if not unheard of, for a Lebanese state agency to publicly vouch for a Palestinian security provider. Thus, when the JPSF launched in July, it was advertised not only as a symbol of Palestinian unity but also as a turning point in the relationship between the Palestinians and the Lebanese state.

With the city of Sidon having become a pressure cooker following the clashes of ʿAbra a year prior, and the threat of war hanging over its Palestinian camps, it would be an understatement to say that much was at stake. The launch of the JPSF appeared to have been hurried to meet its deadline. At the time of their swearing in, the roughly 150 members of the joint force had not yet received their official brassards, an armband depicting branches stretching across either side of a map of Palestine. Meanwhile, the force's new compound in Bustan al-Yahudi and its designated checkpoints throughout the camp were still in the process of being painted in their emblematic red and white colors when Palestinian leaders were taking turns addressing the crowds gathered at the Ziad al-Atrash Martyr's Hall in early July. "Today, you carry a big responsibility," PLO leader Fathi Abu al-ʿAradat declared when he took the podium, turning first to the cadres of the force.

> And we are with you, behind you, and we won't abandon you, for you have the support and the cover [of] the unified Palestinian political decision, as you have a Lebanese cover, politically and security-wise, from our Lebanese brothers whom we thank for their keenness for the force to succeed.[1]

Underscoring that this was the first time the Palestinians enjoyed "political and legal" backing from the Lebanese state, he went on to direct his gratitude to those who would coordinate their efforts with the joint force, such as the army, the military intelligence, and General Security. This new era of trust and cooperation "will serve both Palestine and Lebanon," Abu al-ʿAradat said. Finally, turning to the civilians of the crowd, the PLO leader stressed that the JPSF would not become a "tool of repression." That being said, the joint force would be firm in its response to any misbehavior, he relayed, and deal firmly with any threat to the security of the camp and its people. Abu al-ʿAradat concluded his speech by saying that the deployment of the JPSF in ʿAyn al-Hilwe was only the beginning, promising its spread to the rest of the camps in Lebanon.

***

Nearly three years later, I found myself sitting in the office of the JPSF in ʿAyn al-Hilwe while the force was in the process of deploying in a district of the camp that recently had been razed during a series of hostilities between members of the force and Islamist militants. Much had happened in three years. The JPSF had come under repeated attacks, it had disintegrated and broken down due to internal bickering, resurfaced under a new leadership, while its scheduled deployment in the other Palestinian camps had turned out to be an issue more complex than what had been foreseen. With so much at stake, why had it been such a challenge to keep ʿAyn al-Hilwe's new military police together?

The Dilemmas of Insurgent Policing

Much has been written on rebel groups that assume police functions as a part of their bid to establish territorial control or consolidate statehood. The literature is quite clear that their success in doing so often hinges on their ability to transition from revolutionary units poised for guerilla warfare to law and order agencies able to govern substantial civilian populations. Naturally, there is nothing straightforward about this process, which demands high measures of organizational coherence and experience—not at least to overcome the structural challenges that come with carving out a well-functioning bureaucracy in areas where no central authority exists. In this discussion about the JPSF in ʿAyn al-Hilwe, we will in particular dwell on two challenges that the force has faced in its short existence.

The first has to do with lack of autonomy, and conflicting ideas about mandate. By and large, this has been a result of this non-state military police force being a brokered solution between two asymmetric parties—the Palestinian leaderships and the Lebanese state—who have different perceptions of what security provision entails. As we will see, the JPSF has struggled to navigate between meeting the Lebanese host nation's calls for extraditing dangerous outlaws, while maintaining the internal stability of the camp. Here, there are obvious parallels to the experience of the Palestinian National Security Forces (PNSF) currently operating in the West Bank, which since their creation in 1994 have often stood accused of "running the Israeli occupation's errand" at the expense of the security of the Palestinian civilian populations.[2]

The second challenge has to do with the dilemmas of inter-rebel alliance building. In her monograph about alliance formation in civil war, political scientist Christia Fotini argues that although rebel groups certainly stand much to gain from building strong coalitions in order to maximize their own share of post-war political control, large rebel alliances are inherently faced with commitment problems. With the lack of any "third-party that can credibly enforce the agreed-upon divisions of political control," Fotini writes, the strongest group of any given coalition cannot believably commit "that it will not turn on its weaker partner(s) and capture complete control" once the conflict is over.[3] In other words, the act of backing a robust inter-rebel alliance might pose an existential threat to the less resourceful groups involved. Therefore, the latter will often consider defecting and, thus, prolong the given conflict, even when they appear to be on the winning side. Although ʿAyn al-Hilwe can hardly be likened to a scene of civil war, such inter-rebel deliberations have had large implications for the faction authorities competing to assert their influence over Lebanon's self-governed Palestinian camps. In this chapter, we will see how the joint force's efficiency has suffered from unclear authority structures where competing leaderships have continued to argue over the force's composition, the factional balance between its members, and their placement in politically sensitive neighborhoods in the camp.

Before we move on to these points, we will begin our discussion by exploring the roots of the joint force, and the institution that took part in creating it—a new inter-factional gathering called the Unified Political Leadership for the Palestinian Factions in Lebanon (*al-Qiyada al-Siyasiyya al-Muwahhada li-l-Fasaʾil al-Filastiniyya fi Lubnan*). Our story begins in Damascus.

From Unified Leadership to Joint Force

In early 2012, Hamas leader Khalid Mishʿal made it official. After thirteen years of cooperation, his movement was abandoning its base in Damascus, seeking instead to relocate its politburo elsewhere.[4]

The Arab uprisings of 2010/11 had led to tensions between the Syrian Baʿth party and Hamas. Hamas co-founder Mahmud al-Zahar's support for the popular uprisings that had toppled the regimes of Hosni Mubarak in Egypt, and Tunisia's Ben Ali, where he publicly aired his yearning for "a hot Arab winter" to ripen into spring and bring about the "flowering of Islam," did not sit well with President Bashar al-Assad.[5] The timing for such statements was particularly ill-conceived seeing that al-Assad and his Ba'th Party officials were largely blaming the nascent revolts taking place on Syrian soil on Hamas' sister organization: the Muslim Brotherhood. Hamas, on the other hand, claimed that the Syrian regime had exerted unreasonable pressure on Palestinian groups to take a stand against the uprising—a demand which had been placed in the wake of the anti-regime protests that broke out in al-Yarmouk, the unofficial Palestinian refugee camp of Damascus, in the summer of 2011.[6]

As Hamas went on to relocate its base to Doha in Qatar, its criticism of Syria became more outspoken. In February 2012, Hamas' prime minister in Gaza, Isma'il Hanniye announced his full support of "all the nations of the Arab Spring" and the "heroic people of Syria who are striving for freedom, democracy, and reform."[7] For his part, the Syrian President Bashar al-Assad denied all allegations that he had asked Hamas for any assistance in quelling the protests, and went on to blast the movement for repeatedly having betrayed the hospitality of the Syrian government, contending bitterly that the Palestinian Islamists had "sided against Syria from day one."[8]

After Hamas' departure from Syria, tensions persisted between local proponents of the group and those of the pro-Syrian PFLP-General Command, who allegedly found themselves facing off against each other leading up to the devastating battle of al-Yarmouk in late 2012, where the Free Syrian Army (FSA) and certain Palestinian anti-regime militias clashed with loyalist groups.[9] Although no such hostilities were reported in Lebanon, the Syrian war had pushed the Alliance of Palestinian Forces (APF), where both movements were members, to the brink of collapse. In the Shatila camp, Hamas officials reported that they were no longer welcome to participate in the meetings of the APF's Popular Committee, and that the pro-Syrian groups wanted nothing to do with them.[10] Simultaneously, Hamas' deteriorating relationship with Syria's most important regional partner, Iran, had caused frictions in the southern suburbs of Beirut, where the movement's representational office, at the time, was located close to the headquarters of Hizballah. A frustrated Hamas official living in the Haret Hrayk neighborhood lamented that his party fellows had been placed under Hizballah's scrutiny, and were continuously stopped and harassed at the Lebanese Shi' movement's checkpoints, and struggled to make it to their work places.[11]

The fear of being driven out of yet another Arab state prompted Hamas' leadership in Lebanon to reach out to the PFLP-General Command in the summer of 2013, with a view to overcome the diplomatic crisis and mend fences with the pro-Syrian bloc. "We have agreed to reactivate the Alliance [of Palestinian Forces]," Hamas leader 'Ali Barake relayed between bites as we were sharing a couple of *manaqish* freshly delivered from his office's next-door bakery, the following November. The parties had agreed to put their differences aside, and to strive toward three political goals:

> To support the resistance against the Zionist occupation, to keep rejecting any negotiations with Israel, and to fight for the rights of the Palestinian refugees in Lebanon, politically, socially and juridically.[12]

"This shows that we are capable of overcoming any crisis that has come as a result of our withdrawal from Syria," Barake contended. Although insidious remarks and ill-fated jokes about Hamas being cut from the same cloth as "the jihadi extremists in Syria"[13] continued to be heard in and around the headquarters of pro-Syrian and Iran-supported factions in the camps in the months to follow, the worst tensions eventually subsided, and in Lebanon, the APF framework remained intact with Hamas on board. By contrast, the situation was quite another in the APF's heartlands of Damascus. In 2013, rebel groups proceeded to lay siege to the southern parts of the war-torn Yarmouk district, while the Syrian regime responded by blocking off its northern entrances to starve the insurgents out. What had been a suburb of 160,000 was now reduced to a prison for the remaining 20,000 residents who found themselves entrapped between the warring parties without access to humanitarian aid.[14] One of the most iconic places of Palestinian civilization in exile had been lost.

The truth of the matter was that Hamas was far from the only faction to abandon Damascus. A few weeks after its departure, Palestinian Islamic Jihad (PIJ) followed suit, packed up its politburo, and continued to redistribute its Syria-based leaders between Tehran and Beirut—albeit after consultations with Iran and Hizballah. In the midst of it all, the Lebanese capital was inadvertently becoming the de-facto meeting place for the rejectionist bloc in Palestinian politics. Here, APF officials were also engaging in dialogues with the PLO leadership, which was on good terms with Syria, not at least due to its shared anxieties concerning the Arab spring and popular uprisings.[15] In the Beirut camps, for example, the factions had univocally implemented a non-tolerance policy for any protests or commemorations regarding the Syrian revolution.[16] These circumstances—and perhaps, a shared distaste for Hamas—paved the way for novel forms of cooperation between the PLO factions and the pro-Syrian bloc.

Forming a Unified Political Leadership

In early July 2013, Palestinian President Mahmoud Abbas landed in Beirut for a three-day visit. During his trip, he met a number of prominent Lebanese state officials, among them President Michel Sulayman. Nonetheless, his most important meeting was undeniably held at the Palestinian embassy, where he gave his seal of approval to a Palestinian cross-factional institution that had been in the talks for years.

In the wake of the disastrous events at Nahr al-Barid, the International Crisis Group had urged the Palestinian factions in Lebanon to form a "single representative body" to serve as a unified interlocutor in their dialogues with the Lebanese state.[17] Similar demands were echoed by many Lebanese stakeholders, who viewed that Palestinian political splits had hindered a swift solution to the crisis. To this end, the speaker of the Lebanese parliament Nabih Berri had been the most vocal. By 2012, he had reportedly grown tired of hearing multiple conflicting statements regarding the implementation of security measures in the Palestinian camps in Lebanon, or diverging takes on what was happening in al-Yarmouk. Thus, he put his foot down and announced that he from this point on would refuse to receive any Palestinian group at his ministerial palace in ʿAyn al-Tine, West Beirut, unless they showed up in a unified delegation. "Berri was the one to unify us," Fathi Abu al-ʿAradat said, recounting the events. The PLO's leader in Lebanon explained that Berri's unwavering stance had set important things in motion.

> "It is impossible to understand what the factions are saying," he would tell us, "there are so many of you, what is your decision? When will you be able to speak with one voice?" In the end, he was right about many things. So, we agreed to form a unified Palestinian delegation.[18]

While undoubtedly a step in the right direction, this unified delegation, consisting of both PLO and APF factions, did far from impress all Lebanese leaders. Upon its visits to the offices of ʿAbbas Ibrahim at his General Security bureau, the latter had pointed out that the delegation seemed to be missing crucial actors. After all, how could these officials convincingly assure anyone that the country's most turbulent camp, ʿAyn al-Hilwe, would remain stable, when the Islamists who controlled important neighborhoods within it remained absent from these dialogues? Thus, efforts were made to bring local militia groups like al-Haraka al-Mujahida al-Islamiyya (HIM), ʿUsbat al-Ansar, and the Hizballah-funded Ansar Allah group on board. In fact, during the July meeting at the Palestinian embassy, Major-General Ibrahim had sought to escort a selection of their officials to the PLO's headquarters in Beirut to meet the Palestinian president, Mahmoud Abbas, in person.[19]

At the said meeting, the Palestinian factions laid the groundwork for what a few short months later would be dubbed the Unified Leadership for the Palestinian Factions in Lebanon. The road there, however, had been anything from straightforward.

A Question of Representation

Gathering nineteen faction representatives under one umbrella, the unified leadership's sole purpose was to sign off on statements or decisions that were usually brought forward by the more influential political groups, such as Fatah or Hamas. The latter of the two, which was strenuously trying to reinstate itself at the center stage of Palestinian politics, saw the formation of the unified leadership as a great diplomatic victory, and was among its strongest proponents. However, with more than just a few of the actors involved viewing themselves as the sole representative of their people, gathering the necessary signatures (or votes) in any issue tended to become a slow and laborious process. Moreover, because consensus-building was so central for its mandate, the unified leadership's composition—with one representative fronting each movement—seemed to give fringe groups with no significant popular following or military presence in the camps, a disproportionately large influence over decision-making.

Seeking to amend this problem, representatives of Fatah came up with a suggestion; behind the Unified Political Leadership there should be a Concentrated Political Leadership (*Qiyada Siyasiyya Musaghghara*) that would implement decisions regarding the most pressing matters, and which stripped away some of the smallest factions from the process. Thereafter, the Unified Political Leadership would simply add its signature and "pose for the media," as a faction official put it.[20] Leaders from the pro-Syrian bloc accepted this arrangement and suggested a "3-3-3 formation," the leader of the Palestinian Liberation Front (PLF) in Lebanon, Muhammad Yasin, explained.[21] This involved each political bloc, the PLO, the APF, and the Islamists from ʿAyn al-Hilwe, being represented by three officials each. The PLO, however, had greatly frowned upon the notion of having equal representation to the Islamist bloc, and had instead lobbied for a "5-5-3 formation," raising the amount of seats from the PLO and the APF, while the ʿAyn al-Hilwe-based factions would remain three. "Ultimately, we ended up with two political leaderships that were practically the same," Yasin sighed during our meeting at his office in the Mar Elias camp in Beirut. "The only difference being, that one had thirteen factions, and the other nineteen. How this is supposed to be more efficient, is beyond me," he said, rolling his eyes. "But the PLO preferred it this way, and so it went."

The Unified Political Leadership was announced in October. For the occasion, journalist Haytham Zuʿaytar of the al-Liwaʾ newspaper had gathered Palestinian officials and faction leaders for a celebration at his house in Sidon. At the dinner reception, the spokesperson of ʿUsbat al-Ansar, Abu Sharif—making his first public appearance outside of ʿAyn al-Hilwe—spoke passionately about what he perceived as a new era of cooperation between the Lebanese and the Palestinian peoples. "[We must] open a new page," he said. "The page of fraternal relations based on the principle of cooperation for the security and stability of Lebanon, and in order to fight together in the struggle to liberate Palestine."[22] Some of his newfound colleagues, however, seemed to take these vows of unity with a pinch of salt. Again, members of Fatah seemed particularly pessimistic about sharing political responsibilities with the Islamic Forces of ʿAyn al-Hilwe. "Every political or religious force have their own goals and their projects which can make cooperation difficult," senior PLO leader Abu Iyad al-Shaʿlan said.

> Just look at Egypt. The Muslim Brothers under Morsi made an alliance with al-Sisi and his demons (*Shayatin al-Sisi*), and then they were overturned and the country collapsed. As for the Islamic Forces, they definitely have their agendas, and ways of working to implement their influence, and they are probably just biding their time to overrun the others.[23]

"There is not a complete unity," head of the PLO and the Fatah movement in Lebanon, Fathi Abu al-ʿAradat conceded back at his office at the Palestinian embassy. "But there is coordination," he said, underlining that the Unified Leadership's biggest achievement was forming a Joint Security Force in ʿAyn al-Hilwe.[24]

Toward a Joint Force

It would soon become clear that the decisions signed and issued by Palestinian leaders in Beirut were not enough to alter the reality on the ground—particularly in the South. In the first half of 2014, the refugee camps of Sidon witnessed a string of violent incidents that cast doubts on the Palestinian Leadership's ability to maintain order and resolve internal conflicts.

In early April, a longstanding power struggle between the Hizballah-funded Ansar Allah movement and a Fatah leader in the Miyye wo-Miyye camp, Ahmad Rashid, escalated into a deadly clash that killed Rashid and seven others. Some suspected that Ansar Allah had stormed the Fatah leader's compound due to reports that he was arming unemployed Syrian refugees in order to overthrow his rivals and claim the camp for himself, while others believed the incident had the fingerprints of an internal settlement within the Fatah movement, as Rashid had been a proponent of Muhammad Dahlan. Whatever the case, the killings were not an ideal start for what had been advertised as a new era of Palestinian unity.

Another controversy took place when a leader of the Sufi-oriented Islamist movement al-Ahbash, a mere seventy-two hours after the killing of Rashid, was gunned down by an unknown assailant in ʿAyn al-Hilwe, after having offered his condolences to a family afflicted by the tragedy in the neighbor camp.[25] The fact that the shaykh was killed in the Ra's al-Ahmar district of the camp, beholden to ʿUsbat al-Ansar—the group which had been terror listed for killing the al-Ahbash leader Nizar al-Halabi some nineteen years earlier—made the events appear all the more suspicious. For its part, ʿUsbat al-Ansar was dealing with more pressing issues. Following a series of threats made against the movement's leadership, senior official Taha Shraydi was shot and wounded by rival Islamists from the al-Shabab al-Muslim network, causing the former movement to round up suspects and deploy its gunmen in the streets of the camp.

Suspecting the camp to be on the verge of a full-scale war, Interior Minister Nuhad al-Mashnuq personally traveled to Sidon in order to inquire about the feasibility of deploying the Lebanese army inside of the camp, and setting up Lebanese police stations in certain neighborhoods.[26] For his part, the director of Lebanon's General Security bureau, Abbas Ibrahim, deemed the suggestion unrealistic, and would instead lobby for an internal solution. Demonstrating once again his talent for negotiation, the Major-General was able to convince both Lebanese and Palestinian parties that a multi-factional security force consisting of the camp's political groups would be a more feasible alternative in the short term. After all, the joint framework was already present at the Palestinian embassy. In April 2014, he called the Palestinian factions into a meeting where he proposed his security plan for ʿAyn al-Hilwe.[27] Shortly after, Palestinian leaders notified the press that they were working on a draft for the composition of the force, to be handed over to the Lebanese security agencies for approval.

A Police Force of Revolutionaries

A heavy burden rested on the shoulders of the 150 members of the JPSF at its launch in July 2014. Essentially, not only were these cadres to ensure the unity between rival factions with little history of cooperating, but they were tasked with forming a central authority in a society where no balance of power existed. The very likely fact that the vast majority of them had no previous experience in policing their fellow camp dwellers, let alone having had any time to reflect on what it would entail, only added to the complexity of their mission.

As historian Brynjar Lia demonstrates in his monograph about the history of the Palestinian police, insurgent groups trained for guerilla warfare do simply not turn into policemen and women overnight. Establishing a Palestinian police was crucial in terms of creating a self-governed Palestinian Authority (PA), Lia notes. Yet, as the Oslo peace process faltered, the police cadres struggled to adapt to their new role as a non-political law and order agency, and largely continued to view themselves as a vehicle for national liberation.[28] In ʿAyn al-Hilwe, the JPSF's organization—having been tasked with safeguarding Palestinian statehood in exile—was similarly laden with revolutionary overtones.

The joint security force's ambiguous name, I was told, was chosen in order not to step on the toes or challenge the mandate of any Lebanese police institution. Nonetheless, its leaders were adamant that the JPSF was a military police force (*shurta ʿaskariyya*), and deemed it to be a part of a larger national project of safeguarding Palestinian autonomy, whether in the homeland or in exile. "So you see, the joint force is not only about preventing crime and handing over outlaws," its leader, Munir al-Maqdah, stressed during our meeting at his house in ʿAyn al-Hilwe.[29] "Protecting our camps means protecting the Palestinian cause and the right of return," the longtime Fatah commander said while tapping his fingers rhythmically on his armrest as to underline the point. In essence, he viewed that security provision and armed struggle were two sides of the same coin. These sentiments were echoed in the hundreds of posters that the JPSF's media office had plastered around the camp, and which featured a pictured of al-Maqdah himself superimposed over the rooftops of ʿAyn al-Hilwe, relaying the following message: "The revolution is not only a rifle, but the safety and stability of the sons of our people." Some Palestinian leaders went even further. "In our unity, we will form a solid rock which will break and defeat the Zionist Israeli enemy," the renowned Islamist leader Jamal Khattab expressed at the JPSF's inauguration ceremony, "like we

Figure 6.1 "The revolution is not only a rifle but the safety and stability of the sons of our people."

defeated it in the Battle of Karame [in 1968] and in other battles."[30] As we move on to take a more detailed look at the joint force's composition, training, and equipment, we will see that its revolutionary aspects were more than a matter of rhetoric.

Training and Equipment

In its initial iteration, the JPSF consisted of 150 cadres, where the PLO factions, contributing 75 members, made up its lion's share. The APF groups provided forty members between them, the Islamic Forces designated twenty of their combatants, and Ansar Allah bestowed fifteen of its members for the joint framework. Meanwhile, a hundred more members were kept on reserve as backup.[31] These recruits were spread out between the joint force's three main branches, a civilian, an investigative, and an executive division, with all of them coordinating their efforts with a semi-external institution called the Higher Palestinian Security Committee. As these institutions, in different ways, are indicative of the joint force's aspirations in embarking on its mission, we will explore them individually.

The Civilian Division (*al-qism al-madani*) consisted of what resembled patrol officers. Tasked with governing civilian life, these officers would regulate the flow of traffic in the camp's street, control crowds, prevent crime, and, in essence, "solve the problems of the people" as one faction's official put it.[32] Although the rank and file of ʿAyn al-Hilwe's nascent military police for all practical purposes lacked the means and experience of dealing with civilians, the Joint Force would go on to receive some assistance from the international community. As an organization that engages with armed non-state actors and which offers consulting in matters pertaining to international humanitarian norms and conduct with civilians in settings of armed conflict, Geneva Call had previously assisted the PLO's military branches in Lebanon when these were in the process of replacing the Armed Struggle Command with the current National Security Forces (PNSF) in 2011/12.[33] After an intensive period of training the PLO's mid- and high-ranking personnel in humanitarian norms, the Switzerland-based organization assisted the former in setting up a Legal Training Center and a Legal Support Unit in ʿAyn al-Hilwe, allowing the PLO to coach its own cadres in international legal standards including the use of force in civilian settings.[34] The Legal Support Unit had been operating independently since its inauguration in October 2014, but the deployment of the JPSF provided an impetus for Geneva Call to engage with the Palestinian factions on a deeper level. According to the organization's Middle East program manager, Armin Köhli, Geneva Call had asked to take part in the training process because the situation in ʿAyn al-Hilwe was deemed more delicate than in the other camps. "In the [Joint Palestinian Security] Force, you had opposing factions like Fatah and ʿUsbat al-Ansar," he said, speaking from his offices in Geneva. "So we proposed to do the training along with the Legal Support Unit, and this was accepted by the Higher Palestinian Security Committee," he explained.[35]

In March 2015, a local trainer from Geneva Call led a session on policing and human rights for fifteen members of the JPSF of ʿAyn al-Hilwe.[36] Specifically, the courses dealt with the use of force and firearms in human rights law. Although all parties reported that they had made significant progress, they were faced with many obstacles. "The main challenge was that, with the lack of resources in the camp, the joint security force did not have access to adequate non-lethal weapons that could be used instead of firearms," Geneva Call's trainer in ʿAyn al-Hilwe reported.[37] Indeed, leading up to the Joint Force's formation, officers from the PNSF had flown in from the West Bank to offer their colleagues in Lebanon exercices in military discipline and training in weapons such as Kalashnikovs, American M16 assault rifles, and Russian B7 rocket launchers.[38] It was not only the JPSF's military division that carried wartime weapons, but from what I could tell during my visits to ʿAyn al-Hilwe', all divisions of the force, including the civilian one, were heavily armed. In the Upper Street, I met a DFLP commander who was in charge of overseeing the flow of traffic. He was giving signals to cars passing by with one arm, while carrying an anti-tank rocket launcher with his other. Abu Wisam spoke passionately about his work, and explained how he recently had negotiated with a group of inhabitants who had blocked off one of the main streets during a protest against the factions (Chapter 7). He was a friendly man, and in lieu of his diplomatic skills, one might wonder why he needed his weapon, or how it would even be possible to use it in the busy street where he was standing. But Abu Wisam begged to differ. "First and foremost, I am a fida'i (guerilla)," he said. "We, the Palestinians, are at war with the Zionist enemy and we refuse to put our weapons down, even when we are conducting traffic! Our people support us in this matter."[39]

Legal Mandate

Cases of crime and violence would be passed on to the JPSF's investigative division (*qism al-tahqiq*), headed by a Fatah official called Abu Tawfiq. Greeting me at the joint force's headquarters in the Bustan al-Yahudi street, the colonel explained that his cadres' ambitions pertaining to solving serious crime, in all honesty, were quite modest. Unlike their colleagues in the Palestinian Territories, members of the JPSF were not left with the responsibility of crafting or interpreting a new legal system. Rather, the joint force was mandated to abide by the Lebanese law.[40] For this reason, it did not have its own prisons or courts, but depended on coordinating its investigations with the Lebanese authorities. On occasion, the latter would task its Palestinian counterparts with looking into the files of certain camp dwellers, Abu Tawfiq explained, but more often than not, they would simply request that suspects were handed over to be investigated (or tried) in Lebanese institutions.

The JPSF's headquarters featured something resembling a jail cell, where suspects could be held overnight before their handover could be coordinated with external parties. For his part, Colonel Abu Tawfiq hoped the cell would remain empty, he told, because the logistics of apprehending and holding suspects was a sensitive issue. Surely, influential families or powerful militias could create upheaval if their next of kin were arrested, or even physically attempt to break them out, if not avenge themselves against the police. The mere notion of keeping a suspect in a "Fatah district" like Bustan al-Yahudi was sensitive in its own regard, Abu Tawfiq explained in a matter-of-fact tone, especially if the former was from an "opposing neighborhood," as he put it, thereby offering a reminder of how fluid the boundaries between faction, territory and kinship are in a place like the Capital of the Diaspora. "In this camp, there are many authorities (*marja'iyyat*)," Abu Tawfiq went on. "People are not used to the fact that there now is an authority called the Joint Security Force where the factions are unified. We are still working to find a balance, and to communicate our role to our people."[41] As we will see next, it would appear that the JPSF leadership, however, had a ways to go in communicating the same idea to its own party fellows.

Leadership and Funding

The third and largest branch of the JPSF was a military division called the Executive Force (*al-quwwa al-tanfidhiyya*), which was to intervene in cases of factional infighting and, if necessary, provide a source of muscle behind the decisions made by its leadership. That being said, determining who constituted the JPSF's leadership was not necessarily an effortless endeavor. On the one hand, the joint force's command in Lebanon was led by Munir al-Maqdah and his deputies Khalid al-Shayib (Fatah) and Khalid 'Ali Isma'il (Hamas), with each actor communicating closely with their respective party hierarchies. On the other hand, their decisions also had to go through the aforementioned Higher Palestinian Security Committee (*al-lajna al-amniyya al-filastiniyya al-'uliya*). This was an upgraded version of the camp's former Follow-up Committee; a mediation council from the early 2000s made up of the camp's main guerilla commanders, some of whom were not involved in the joint force at all (Chapter 4). Rather than having been dissolved and replaced by the new police authority, this institution was deemed necessary to ensure that the new camp police could carry out its mandate without leading to any unfortunate misunderstandings among the cobweb of pre-existing armed forces. Curiously, the militia leaders gathered in this council all headed armed groups that by far outnumbered the cadres of the joint military police, let alone its executive force which with its meager ninety armed members could not even rival the strength of any of the camp's Fatah battalions. These arrangements begged the question, had anything changed in 'Ayn al-Hilwe? Did the faction leaders who had so warmly endorsed the joint force actually believe in the project at all?

At the Palestinian embassy in Beirut, the PLO leadership was well aware of this paradox, and went on to explain to me that the JPSF's meager size came down to issues of funding. The Palestinian Authority in the West Bank had taken upon itself to underwrite 70 percent of the joint force's budget, I was told—a sum which certain sources put at a monthly $250,000 being transferred to the account of its leader, Munir al-Maqdah.[42] The other factions, with Hamas at the helm, were to cover the remaining 30 percent of the costs. However, this was only on paper, head of the PLO/Fatah in Lebanon, Fathi Abu al-'Aradat explained, during our talk. At the time when I met him, in late 2015, PIJ had incurred a financial crisis, presumably due to its falling out with its Iranian main sponsors over the Yemen crisis, and was unable to pay its own cadres. In addition, 'Usbat al-Ansar was also facing financial difficulties. Thus, the PLO found itself forced to cover the salaries of both groups' members in the joint force. "As you can see, there is something that is not right," Abu al-'Aradat said begrudgingly, citing that Fatah could not simply go at it alone and keep recruiting its own cadres for the project as it would create an imbalance between the factions.[43]

In ʿAyn al-Hilwe, however, leaders of the Higher Palestinian Security Committee had a slightly different take on the situation. In our conversations, many of them, especially those belonging to the pro-Syrian bloc and the Islamic Forces, expressed reservations about the joint force, and what they, in the end, considered to be a Fatah project. This is the part where we come back to the point raised earlier about the dilemmas of inter-rebel alliance building.

Inter-Factional Trials

The German sociologist Max Weber famously argued that a state is a "human community that (successfully) claims the monopoly of the legitimate use of physical force within a given territory."[44] Among Palestinian leaders in Lebanon, establishing a monopoly of force in ʿAyn al-Hilwe was deemed pivotal. The JPSF embodied the renewed trust between them and their host nation's authorities, and for all they were concerned, the joint force's success and prosperity were the only thing keeping the Lebanese army from reclaiming its non-state territories. As for the factions outside of the PLO framework, however, supporting a police force which was largely funded and composed by political rivals did not come without a cost. What guarantee did they have, after all, that the PLO was not simply using the joint framework as an excuse to widen its territories within the camp and was merely looking for the right moment to, in the words of political scientist Fotini, "turn on its weaker partner(s) and capture complete control."[45] On this subject, these actors received no assurances from the leader of the PLO's militia branches in Lebanon.

"We view that the National Security Forces are the only legitimate armed forces in the Palestinian camps," the Fatah veteran Subhi Abu ʿArab shared during a meeting at his compound in the Baraksat area. "The joint force is a preliminary measure, and an urgent response to a difficult situation," he contended while around thirty of his combatants were gathered in the room with us. "In the long-term, we wish to see the camps be placed solely under our control."[46] Back at his house, Munir al-Maqdah, the JPSF's leader, did not disapprove of these sentiments. Assuming a slightly more diplomatic tone, nonetheless, he explained that the project was going through a test period, and that the joint force would be able to expand significantly once it gained the trust of the factions involved. He was already in the process of adding new recruits, he told.[47] In the interim, however, he had been left with the responsibility of figuring out how to implement the mandate of ʿAyn al-Hilwe's new military police without the luxury of enjoying any semblance of monopoly of force.

The Maqdisi-affair

It took a year for the JPSF to embark on its stated mission of spreading to all corners of ʿAyn al-Hilwe. The process was not without risk, because as we remember from the last chapter, the radical al-Shabab al-Muslim network had strong opinions regarding which streets and districts it was permissible for the mainstream factions to move, and would continuously release statements regarding the matter. Places like Tawari', Hittin, Tiri, 'Arab al-Zubayd, and Taytaba were regarded as off limits for the JPSF.

Some progress was made when al-Shabab al-Muslim—after lengthy negotiations involving the Islamic Forces and the local neighborhood committee—had agreed to let the joint force set up a checkpoint (the Jalul Station) in the Tawari' street.[48] Whereas JPSF leader Munir al-Maqdah confidently relayed that Tawari' was only the first of many neighborhoods he would reclaim, and that the Palestinian leaders were capable of safely dismantling any mine thrown in front of them,[49] he would have to reconsider this phrasing when the JPSF made plans to move into the Taytaba district. In this area, the joint force would curiously face strong opposition from UNRWA's local field officer Fadi al-Salih.

Al-Salih and his family had for less than a decade been running a religious foundation called the Maqdisi Group (*majmu'at al-Maqdisi*) and had, in late 2014, set up a prayer room (*musalla*) opposite a Fatah checkpoint near Taytaba. Tensions surfaced between local Fatah patron 'Abd al-Sultan and the Maqdisi group, when the latter took measures to equip its building with security cameras that al-Sultan suspected were surveilling his cadres. In response, he set up his own security cameras to surveil the Maqdisi prayer room, and claimed to have made a number of suspicious observations. Fatah, with 'Abd al-Sultan at the helm, went on to accuse Fadi al-Salih, the director of the Maqdisi Group of embezzling UNRWA funds and for using these to support clandestine jihadi cells.[50] In the end, the parts came to blows, and Fatah found itself facing off against the UNRWA field officer's personal militia force, which was promptly defeated. When the JPSF later moved in to secure the area, it claimed to have found large quantities of weapons in possession of the al-Maqdisi Group. Al-Salih for his part was suspended from his position in UNRWA and put under an internal investigation.[51] After the prayer room had been handed over to the Islamic Forces—a symbolic gesture meant to assure neighbors that there was no bad blood between the secularist and Islamist factions—the Higher Palestinian Security Committee announced that the JPSF would continue to expand its presence and put an end to these "[in]security zones" (*murabba'at amniyya*) once and for all.[52]

The next district on the agenda was the southern Hittin neighborhood. However, signs were that al-Shabab al-Muslim, which enjoyed a substantial presence in this area, had gotten cold feet after the Maqdisi-affair. In June, the network released a statement saying that although cadres of the JPSF would be allowed to pass through Hittin, they were under no circumstances allowed to set up a checkpoint there. There was no need for any police force, the statement argued, "because we, al-Shabab al-Muslim, are capable of solving any problem in the Hittin neighborhood."[53] Obviously provoked by these communiques, Munir al-Maqdah went on to make a number of appearances on Sidon-based TV stations, where he was seen preparing his rank and file for deploying in Hittin. "Arrest everyone you see … with force if you have to," he is seen relaying in one of these videos, peering at the camera as much as his own cadres. "Arrest everyone who go by the name al-Shabab al-Muslim, they don't even fast or pray!"[54] Off-camera, things were more complex. Al-Maqdah had not gotten the green light from the Higher Palestinian Security Committee, which went on to postpone the Hittin offensive indefinitely, while contacts were being established with local mediators.

As the process dragged on, ʿAzzam al-Ahmad, President Mahmoud Abbas' envoy to Lebanon, flew in from Ramallah in order to review the efficiency of the joint force. Acknowledging that the JPSF's mandate was hindered by a lack of manpower, al-Ahmad announced that the force would be strengthened by adding new recruits and stripping away inefficient subdivisions.[55] Meanwhile, the animosity between members of Fatah and affiliates of al-Shabab al-Muslim kept growing, with each party measuring the opponent's strength. When the leader of one of Fatah's largest militias in ʿAyn al-Hilwe was gunned down in broad daylight, the situation went from tense to directly confrontational.

War Breaks Out

Talal al-Balawne, better known as Talal the Jordanian, had narrowly escaped an assassination attempt a year earlier. As leader of The Shatila Martyrs' Brigade (*Katibat Shuhada' Shatila)*, one of Fatah's largest military units in the camp counting some 500 combatants, al-Balawne had made many enemies throughout the years—not at least due to his partial closeness to Muhammad Dahlan, the Palestinian president's bitter rival. In July, he was gunned down and killed alongside his two nephews outside the UNRWA health clinic in the Jabal al-Halib neighborhood.[56] Reportedly, surveillance cameras had shown that the killer was Bilal Badr, a young man reputed for being a cold-blooded assassin, and an affiliate of al-Shabab al-Muslim.[57] A month later, on August 22, another violent incident rocked the camp. Colonel Abu Ashraf al-ʿArmushi, the head of Fatah's Abu Hassan Salame Brigade, barely escaped an assassination attempt while he was attending a funeral in the Hittin district. His brigade responded by storming the positions of al-Shabab al-Muslim, triggering a neighborhood war which claimed the lives of three and injured eighteen.[58]

The events were revealing of new dynamics emerging in ʿAyn al-Hilwe. While episodes of factional violence in the past had typically been swift affairs that tended to end quickly with Palestinian officials hurrying to establish a truce between the warring parties, the clashes that were now erupting would drag on for days, if not weeks, before they came to a halt. In ʿAyn al-Hilwe, rumor had it that Fatah officials had turned off their mobile phones during the August clashes, presumably in order to prevent any negotiations about an armistice, while the movement's militia wings attempted to physically eliminate prominent fighters within al-Shabab al-Muslim.[59] Meanwhile, the JPSF found itself paralyzed, unable to prevent the violence from escalating. After more than a week of fighting, Fatah called off its offensive. Its military forces had not produced any victory. Rather the fighting had spread to several other areas in the camp, with more and more actors becoming entangled. In the midst of the chaos, Fatah militants had accidentally fired at the headquarters of HIM, a fellow participant in the JPSF.

In the end, the number of injured civilians rose to seventy, while the damage to the camp's infrastructure was vast. Apartment complexes had been shelled by mortars, and mosques were perforated by bullet holes. During the battles, as many as 3,000 inhabitants were thought to have fled the camp and sought refuge in Sidon, where many found themselves sleeping on the floors of the city's mosques.[60] When I made my first visit to ʿAyn al-Hilwe about a month later, there were still skeletons of burnt-out cars in the Safsaf neighborhood, children were eagerly collecting bullet shells in the Tawari' street, while the entrances of the nearby UNRWA school were damaged badly.[61] "They have destroyed our homes, just like the Jews did in '48," an older camp dweller lamented. She had slept in a nearby mosque while waiting for the fighting to subside—a humiliating experience for a woman at her age. "If Israel wants to exterminate the Palestinian people, it should come to ʿAyn al-Hilwe and learn from the factions," she said bitterly.[62] It was not only civilians who complained. At a press conference, leader of PIJ in Lebanon, Abu ʿImad al-Rifaʿi blamed Fatah for acting recklessly, insisting that "groups outside of the law must be treated with rationality," not through military campaigns.[63] "Is the goal to destroy the ʿAyn al-Hilwe camp with Palestinian instruments?" he asked sardonically.

The events had revealed an inherent weakness in the JPSF framework. How would members of the military police force's dominant faction, Fatah, be able to stop episodes of violence if they were simultaneously receiving orders from the PNSF to engage in them? Where did the mandate of a neutral military police force end, and Fatah's own military ambitions begin? Jamal Khattab, leader of the Islamic Forces, was one of those who had taken issue with the unclear division of roles. "Let's say a problem takes place between people beholden to Fatah on the one hand, and Hamas on the other," the shaykh, whose own militia group also participated in the project, said: "The [joint] security force contains members of both these factions, and will in most instances be unwilling to deploy and resolve the conflict [...] There is a continuing paralysis."[64]

Resorting to Negotiations

Struggling to implement a rule of law in ʿAyn al-Hilwe, and thus, failing to live up to the ambitions of asserting itself as a rational-legal authority in the Weberian sense of the expression, leaders of the JPSF would time and time again fall back on brokered solutions and traditional methods for conflict mitigation. Following the August clashes, Munir al-Maqdah arranged a series of meetings with notables and clan elders from the camp with a hope that they would help him apprehend the militants who killed or wounded Fatah cadres during recent bouts of violence. In a video recorded during his meeting with a committee of neighbors of the Safsaf district, al-Maqdah is seen making the following appeal:

> People of all families of the camp have been slaughtered. But where does the killer go? Where is he sheltered? There is a group of assassins (*qatala*) in Safsaf, why don't you name them by name? If we don't help each other, we won't get anywhere. If you say there is a killer from Fatah, we will take him to prison. If the killer is from ʿUsbat al-Ansar, al-Haraka al-Islamiyya [al-Mujahida] or Ansar Allah—you have my guarantee—he will be tried too. But the killers from "these groups," who will bring them forth? [...] There might come a day when we say "people of Safsaf, hear us out, leave Safsaf for twenty-four hours so we can treat the problem." Can we reach such an agreement?[65]

In the video, the mood is tense, and participants lash out against al-Maqdah, demanding that he clarify who he has in mind. Is the neighborhood to blame for his inability to resolve the security problems of the camp—or are the residents themselves, perhaps, also on his wanted list? Evidently, after decades of tension between the Safsaf neighborhood and Fatah, the former had little trust in faction officials such as al-Maqdah, even though he now fronted an ostensibly neutral military police force.

Once again, the Islamist affiliates of the JPSF had more luck in establishing a dialogue with residents of these neighborhoods. Allegedly, the leader of al-Shabab al-Muslim, Usama al-Shihabi, refused to negotiate with the secularist factions. Therefore, it fell upon the Islamic Forces to find a solution. "We leave the responsibility [of negotiation] with the moderate Islamic forces," explained Abu Iyad Ramiz Mustafa, leader of the PLFP-General Command in Lebanon. "We rely on these to communicate the idea that violence and threats will lead to the destruction of the camp. The Islamists speak a common language. They listen to one another."[66] The fact that the Islamic factions were running these dialogues in absence of the "secularists," was not unproblematic. Some of the PLO groups lamented that they had been left completely in the dark pertaining to the conditions raised in the talks.[67] When Jamal Khattab, leader of the Islamic Forces, in early December announced that the parts had agreed to sign a "charter of honor" (*mithaq sharaf*), which included a binding "obligation to prevent clashes or assassinations in the camp," this wasn't exactly what his colleagues had in mind.[68] Wasn't the point to agree on how to apprehend and hand over those who had killed Palestinian cadres? "This charter is illegal!" a high-ranking Fatah official in Beirut said, speaking on the condition of anonymity. "This is tantamount to saying that violence has no consequences." He also reported that Palestinian leaders had been summoned to a meeting with the Lebanese army to explain the meaning of said charter.[69] "The charter has nothing to do with us," the PLO's Fathi Abu al-ʿAradat weighed in from his office at the Palestinian embassy. "This is an arrangement the Islamists have made with each other. For our part, we remain obliged to hand over every outlaw to the [Lebanese] authorities."[70]

These vows notwithstanding, Fatah would follow suit a few months later. In March 2016, the movement accepted a peace offering made by Usama al-Shihabi on behalf of al-Shabab al-Muslim. During a widely attended reconciliation meeting at the al-Asidi Hall in the Manshiyye district of the camp, some of the public faces of al-Shabab al-Muslim, including Jamal Hamad and the Islamist agitator Rami Ward, lined up in a row and shook hands with the Fatah leadership.[71] Nonetheless, there were also important people missing from the meeting. Rumors in the camp were that al-Shihabi and his allies had made themselves unpopular due to their tendency to speak on behalf of the camp's jihadis, and their new arrangements with Fatah did little to restore their reputation. By the time of the reconciliation ceremony, al-Shabab al-Muslim were already split, and it was not clear whom the arrangement included. Allegedly, militants like Bilal Badr, Bilal al-ʿArqub, and the brothers Muhammad and Haytham al-Shaʿbi were against this approach and had turned their backs on al-Shihabi. It soon transpired that the peace offering had produced few changes in the reality on ground.

The following month, the camp plunged backed into another week of clashes, with militants from Safsaf and the Fatah dominated Baraksat neighborhoods fighting fiercely.[72]

The fact of the matter was that even when the JPSF was able to apprehend outlaws and wanted militants, its leadership was often unsure of how to conduct the handovers to the Lebanese army. In August 2016, members of ʿUsbat al-Ansar stopped a prominent militant called ʿAbd Fadda, one of the killers Munir al-Maqdah had requested during the meeting with the Safsaf committee. Allegedly, he had been provoked when he was implicated in a recent murder of a Fatah official, and had left his hideout in Safsaf to burn al-Maqdah's house to the ground, but was intercepted by ʿUsbat al-Ansar. Having taken the militant into its custody, the movement went on to release a statement saying that "the investigation committee of the [joint] force can now exercise its task and question Fadda or whomever it might want, so that the truth may prevail."[73] Investigations aside, the Lebanese authorities had already requested Fadda, and was eagerly awaiting his handover. The Higher Palestinian Security Committee, however, was not convinced that surrendering him to the Lebanese state was a good idea.

The JPSF had handed over thieves and petty criminals before, but ʿAbd Fadda was a seasoned militant from a powerful family, and his allies were already threatening to retaliate. In the end, the parts decided that Fadda was to be released. Although no one should go unpunished for their crimes, handovers to the state needed to happen gradually JPSF leader Munir al-Maqdah stressed.[74] While local camp media lamented that the "law of the jungle" still prevailed in ʿAyn al-Hilwe,[75] several Palestinian leaders were also beginning to lose faith in the joint force. One of them was its main funder, Palestinian President Mahmoud Abbas.

The Joint Framework Unravels

From the outset, Munir al-Maqdah had intended for the JPSF to spread to the remaining camps of Lebanon. After another chapter of the force was set up in the neighboring al-Miyye wo-Miyye camp in the spring of 2015, the commander announced that the Beirut camps were next.[76] However, not everyone shared his enthusiasm. Leaders of pro-Syrian groups like Fatah al-Intifada and the PLFP-General Command—both managing camp security in the Beirut area—were evidently hesitant to turn their turf over to al-Maqdah. "We consider The Joint Security Force in ʿAyn al-Hilwe a failed project," leader of Fatah al-Intifada in Lebanon, Hassan Zaydan said, during our meeting in the Mar Elias camp. "Munir cannot hold his force together, and now he wants to come to Shatila and create the same mess here? Beirut is already secure and calm, we don't need his assistance," Zaydan chuckled.[77]

Meanwhile the Lebanese authorities were growing impatient with the lack of progress, and appeared to be taking matters into their own hands. In September 2016, Lebanese elite soldiers stormed the Tawari' neighborhood of ʿAyn al-Hilwe, and apprehended the former Jund al-Sham commander ʿImad Yasin. The authorities claimed that Yasin had obtained funding from Raqqa in order to establish an Islamic State-cell within the camp, and that he was already in the process of planning a number of attacks against Lebanese targets, ranging from fast food restaurants and casinos to political leaders.[78] The arrest caused a public outcry in the neighborhood where Yasin lived. By locals, he was not seen as a terrorist, but as a respectable shaykh living in modest conditions with his family in Tawari'. He had also become a symbol of injustice, as his health was failing due to injuries sustained during battles against Fatah's military wings over the years. After his days in Jund al-Sham, he had abandoned his militant exterior in favor of an image of asceticism and piety, and was known for walking around in the streets of his neighborhood unarmed, while teaching the occasional class in religion. Following the dramatic arrest of an aging and ill shaykh like Yasin, the neighborhood was on the verge of revolt, and the Islamic Forces deployed their armed wings in the area, urging residents to keep calm, announcing that "no one has any intention of, or stands anything to gain from provoking the army."[79] As both 'Usbat al-Ansar and HIM were faced with a barrage of criticism from locals, their officials quickly toned down the public support for the Lebanese authorities, and instead went on to announce that they had suspended their participation in the meetings of the Unified Political Leadership in Beirut.[80] Public pressure aside, 'Usbat al-Ansar appeared to have ulterior motives for boycotting the meetings at the Palestinian Embassy. As we remember from previous chapters, 'Imad Yasin had been a member of the group (before defecting to Jund al-Sham), and leaked transcripts from his interrogations had revealed that it was Abu Muhjin, the movement's leader in occultation, who had plotted the controversial killing of the four judges in Sidon in 1999—a hitherto unsolved case.[81] It is very likely that 'Usbat al-Ansar feared that its arrangement with the Lebanese authorities, which permitted its leaders to exit the camp, would suddenly and unexpectedly find itself revoked.

At this point, the Ansar Allah movement had also withdrawn from the Higher Palestinian Security Committee, due to its discontent with the group repeatedly coming under criticism for its behavior during recent clashes, whereas, "other parties", presumably Fatah, were exempt from any blame.[82] The joint framework of the Palestinian factions was coming apart, and Munir al-Maqdah himself turned many heads when he in September went on to recommend the dissolution of the JPSF, instead calling for the reinstatement of the Palestinian Armed Struggle Command, the revolutionary security branch he had once been in charge of.[83]

Despite its substantial budget, the courses and training of its cadres, and the promises of a new era of Palestinian unity, the JPSF had few achievements to its name. Although the project's main funder, President Mahmoud Abbas, shared al-Maqdah's disappointment with the joint force, he viewed that the Fatah commander himself was to blame for its failure. Upon his visit to Lebanon in February 2017, President Abbas removed al-Maqdah from his position, while ordering Fatah to withdraw from the Higher Security Committee altogether.[84] Two and a half years into its existence, the future of Lebanon's Palestinian police was hanging in the balance.

As we have seen so far, the JPSF suffered from a lack of political backing from the faction leaderships, rendering it incapable of transcending the pre-existing faction, kin, and territorial loyalties found in the camp it was set to govern. Nevertheless, there were also external challenges that seemed to hamper its progress. As we in the last part of this chapter move on to explore the joint force's resurrection under a new leadership in the spring of 2017, we will center the discussion around the asymmetrical relations of power between the JPSF and the Lebanese host state authorities.

Lebanese-Palestinian Deliberations

In late 2016, it was revealed that the Lebanese authorities had ordered the building of a cement wall around ʿAyn al-Hilwe.[85] Whereas the wall primarily intended to stop "terrorists" from slipping in and out of the camp unnoticed, a source within Lebanon's General Security bureau said, it was also a matter of sending a message to the Palestinian factions. If they were unwilling to deal with the terror suspects holed up in the camp, then the state was ready to implement harsh measures.[86]

The wall itself was to be five meters tall, cover all sides of the camp, and include several military watchtowers where army personnel could surveil the narrow alleyways of ʿAyn al-Hilwe. Needless to say, the project was controversial. The building of the watchtowers meant that adjacent homes would have to be demolished and their inhabitants moved, while others would find themselves cut off from their natural environment. As was the case in the Hittin district, where neighbors cultivating large fruit gardens just south of the camp pleaded with Lebanese soldiers to halt the construction of the wall when the project commenced.[87] On social media, enraged Palestinians compared it to Israel's "wall of apartheid" in the West Bank, while inhabitants of the Gaza Strip posted pictures of themselves carrying banners with slogans condemning the wall in Lebanon. "I never thought it would get to this point," a PLO official noted. "But apparently our brothers in Rafah [in southern parts of the Gaza Strip] feel that our 'occupation' by the Lebanese state, is worse than the Israeli occupation they live under."[88]

While Palestinian leaders in Lebanon lashed out against "the wall of shame" as it was dubbed locally, politicians and notables in Sidon also weighed in, complaining that they had been not consulted in the matter.[89] Both the Future Movement's Bahiya al-Hariri and her political rival, Usama Saʿd of the Popular Nasserite Organization engaged in dialogues with the army Intelligence, urging it to reconsider the project.[90] After rounds of negotiations, it was announced that the Lebanese authorities would halt the process, and sit down with Palestinian leaders in order to discuss thoroughly the security situation in the camp.[91] This was what had brought Mahmoud Abbas' to Lebanon in February 2017. The Palestinian president had reportedly informed the authorities that he was ready to deploy his National Security Force's in all quarters of the camp, to singlehandedly take the reins on the security situation. Lebanon's General Security bureau objected to this proposition, as did a number of other Palestinian groups.[92] In the end, the parts agreed that the Joint Palestinian Security Force was to be given a second chance. President Abbas, nonetheless, had placed the condition that the inefficient and quarrelsome Higher Palestinian Security Committee would be resolved, and that the joint force's own leadership, now headed by Fatah colonel Bassam Saʿd, was provided with a stronger mandate.

When a 120-strong force was announced in March 2017, it was without fanfares or resounding speeches. The stakes were clear. Either the JPSF was to carry out its mission and hand over every outlaw it came across, or the construction of the wall would commence. While Palestinian leaders had always maintained that the safety of ʿAyn al-Hilwe was equal to the stability of Lebanon, it was becoming obvious that this was not necessarily the case. The situation raised questions about whose security the joint force was meant to provide.

Was the JPSF supposed to serve the Palestinians by bringing a sense of law and order to the camp, or was the priority to protect a state which evidently had no reservations about fencing in its refugee populations between cement walls and watchtowers? Could the camp police realistically pursue terror suspects without triggering new camp wars? Was the JPSF, ultimately, a means of protecting Lebanon from the Palestinians? These questions became acutely relevant when the joint force came under attack by a group of militants the very second it redeployed in April.

Mafiosos in Jihadi Clothing

When the JPSF resurfaced in ʿAyn al-Hilwe on April 7, it was to deploy along three checkpoints: one near the offices of al-Saʿiqa in the Upper Street, another on the Lower Street, and a third one at the entrance of the vegetable market. However, the cadres who deployed in the Upper Street were immediately forced to pull back when they were fired upon by machine guns. The gunfire came from the nearby Tiri neighborhood, more precisely from the stronghold of the young militant Bilal Badr. When one of the joint force's members fell dead to the ground, Fatah battalions stationed in the neighboring Suhun district responded by firing rockets in the direction of Badr's family home in Tiri. Before Colonel Bassam Saʿd could release his planned press statement of the JPSF having successfully assumed its positions in the camp, the media was already reporting of clashes having claimed two lives and injuring twenty-one, while clouds of black smoke were billowing from the rooftops of Tiri.[93]

The Lebanese media had been infatuated with the shadowy figure known as Bilal Badr for a few years. Who was the longhaired man in his early thirties whose ruthless violence and reckless behavior had earned him the nickname "the Rambo of ʿAyn al-Hilwe", but who never revealed his face to the public?[94] Was he funded by Jabhat al-Nusra, or had he switched sides to the Islamic State? Was it true that he had been radicalized after his best friend was gunned down by Fatah militiamen in 2008, or had he been a member of Fatah al-Islam and fought in Nahr al-Barid the year before? Had he, as a relative of his told me, mistakenly ended up on a wanted list in order to cover for his younger brother, and was it true that he, despite this heroic deed, had refused to turn himself in when he learned that the prison authorities likely would cut his long hair?[95] The stories were many. The Lebanese public feared Badr, but loved the mystique that surrounded him. In ʿAyn al-Hilwe, however, the young Palestinian and his armed entourage of roughly fifty heads were viewed as little more than Mafiosos in jihadi clothing who, depending on the request, were willing to rattle their Kalashnikovs or put them down for a little bit of cash. It was widely believed that both Hamas and Fatah regularly paid him money to keep him from creating trouble. Moreover, it was speculated that the JPSF's leadership had done the same upon the redeployment of the force in April. Allegedly, it was a disagreement about the sum that had caused him to attack. In one of his Friday sermons, leader of the Islamic Forces, Jamal Khattab, went so far as to propose that Fatah chieftains had requested Badr to embark on his trail of destruction in order to collect additional funding from the West Bank intended for anti-terrorist purposes.[96]

Regardless of the mechanisms at play, Badr had become a primary symbol of Palestinian terrorism, and the Lebanese authorities continued to pressure the factions to sustain their military campaign against his group. As Fatah combatants were inching closer to Badr's stronghold in Tiri, with the number of casualties increasing accordingly, PLO leader Fathi Abu al-ʿAradat announced to the media that there was a Palestinian consensus to "end Badr's deviant reign and to hand over every person to the authorities who had fired upon the joint force."[97] Faction officials told me that the Lebanese army had opened the heavily guarded gates of ʿAyn al-Hilwe, to allow busloads of Fatah fighters from the southern al-Rashidiyeh camp, to join the offensive. Even combatants from the PLFP-General Command, a group whose participation in the joint Palestinian framework up until this point had been mostly cosmetic, now also threw themselves into the battle. It later turned out that the pro-Syrian group was in the process of bolstering its presence in the southern camps, and publicly announcing its participation in the war against the takfiris (religious extremists) was certainly convenient to this end.[98]

The victims of this "war against terrorism" were the residents of Tiri, whose houses were turned to rubble in the battle. For this reason, the alleged Palestinian consensus also started to show cracks. Anynomous sources from Fatah were complaining to the press that not all of the factions were equally committed to the offensive against Badr.[99] Reportedly, Hamas and the Islamic Forces, all enjoying substantial bases of support in these neighborhoods, were lobbying for a cease-fire behind the curtains, making it near impossible for the PLO and Fatah to sustain their armed campaign. When rumors of Hamas having handed Badr an olive branch were starting to surface, the movement's representative in Lebanon, ʿAli Barake, felt compelled to announce that Hamas was as committed as the other factions to end the "security zone" of Tiri.[100] After four days of fighting, nevertheless, the Palestinian factions found themselves forced to halt the offensive. Badr's cell of militants was largely dispersed, but the man himself had escaped and was thought to be hiding somewhere in the area—a source of much embarrassment for all parties. Meanwhile, an entire neighborhood had been turned into a ghost town.

Ghost Towns of Tiri

In early May, an official from the PLF took me on a tour of the area where the clashes had taken place a month earlier. A crooked sign saying "The village of Tiri salutes you!" was ridden with bullet holes and foreshadowed what was awaiting us inside.[101]

We passed by a purple apartment complex which allegedly was owned by Bilal Badr's father, and climbed up the staircase of an adjacent building, which provided us with a view of the entire neighborhood. The destruction was immense.

In the apartment where we were standing, children's toys and clothing were scattered along the floor, while someone—obviously having scurried to get out in a hurry—had dropped a half-open briefcase displaying a family's belongings. In the kitchen, entire walls were missing, ripped out by bombshells. Through these holes, we could see the Tiri district unfolding alongside the eastern hillside of the camp. Some buildings were entirely blackened and burnt out, while shops and restaurants where penetrated so densely with bullet holes it was a wonder they were still standing. It was a scene reminiscent of the destruction seen in photos from the war-torn Yarmouk-district of the Syrian capital. All of the area's inhabitants, said to be close to 5,000 in total, had sought refuge in other neighborhoods.

Further down the street I was greeted by a group of five cadres from the JPSF who had been tasked with guarding one of the joint force's newly erected checkpoints in the area. They were mainly from the Islamist factions, and one was from the leftist bloc within the PLO. They were proof that the JPSF, for the first time, in one way or another, had managed to stay together during a crisis. Despite having taken these streets from Badr's militants, the men were not optimistic about the future, nor the prospects of their joint force—after all, they were sitting in the rubble of their own neighborhood. To say the least, these cadres were not reassured by the many announcements and press reports claiming that a new era of security-coordination was underway in the Palestinian camps. One of them, an Islamist faction member, complained that his brother, who also was a member of the force, had recently been arrested at the entrance of the camp. He had not been heard from for days. "Where is the security coordination?" he asked. "The [Lebanese] authorities view that any Palestinian who has grown a beard is a terrorist, and they put him on their wanted list." "This is not to say that there aren't *takfiris* in this neighborhood," a member from one of the leftist factions weighed in:

> Everything you have heard is correct. Let's not hide from the truth. But in the latest clash, I didn't fire a single bullet. Why? Have you seen the companions of Bilal Badr? They are all teenagers, sixteen years of age. [This would be like] pointing a rifle at my own children. Would you shoot your neighbor's sons? The Lebanese state is asking us to kill our own people, while it offers us absolutely nothing in return. If they want stability, then at least give our children the right to work!

Possibly, a part of the reason why a force of some 120 grown fighters had struggled to crack down on a group of fifty or so "teenage jihadis" was found in these bonds of solidarity between the Palestinian refugees. That being said, when the JPSF finally moved in to set up its checkpoints in Tiri, its members were not univocally welcomed. With hundreds of families being unable to return to their homes, harsh discussions were raging over who should pay for the damages, estimated at a staggering five million dollars.[102]

Questions of Accountability

After the clashes, Palestinian officials from Sidon released a statement where they urged both their own Unified Political Leadership in Beirut and the international society to heed the calls of Tiri residents who were pleading for help in rebuilding their war-torn neighborhood, and to compensate them for their losses.[103] Among the Palestinian leaderships, no party was eager to assume responsibility for the damages, and the factions continued to pressure UNRWA to pay up, which they figured was in charge of the camp's infrastructure. However, having suffered substantial cutbacks and being stricken by financial crises, the UN agency was not eager to embark on a costly project of this caliber—particularly as none of the Palestinian factions were able to guarantee that the clashes would not erupt anew and bury the neighborhood in rubble once again.[104]

For once, UNRWA seemed to have the backing of the camp's civilian population. In May, frustrated residents of Tiri blocked off the Upper Street with a large tent and a pile of garbage, in protest of the inaction of their leadership. "Let's be very clear," a young woman who lost her family home in April's clashes told me. "It was not UNRWA that fired shells at our house. I call on Fatah, I call on Hamas. I hold them responsible. I won't back down before they repay every *lira*. They have the means."[105] The rage directed against the political groups was understandable. However, in ʿAyn al-Hilwe the boundaries separating armed factions from civilians, and aggressors from victims, did not seem clear-cut and obvious to everyone. During our tour of the Tiri neighborhood, the aforementioned PLF official took a pause as we passed his family home which he had begun rebuilding with his own hands. "The only thing I want, is to move back here with my children," he shared with equal measures hopefulness and despair in his voice. "We just want to live in our house. That's the only thing that matters now."[106]

Small Victories

On the last day of May, I found myself sitting in the office of Fatah commander Bassam Saʿd in the Bustan al-Yahudi district. He was juggling three telephones—two mobile phones and one landline—while he was working hard to figure out the logistics of redeploying the JPSF in the Tiri district after April's clashes.

While Badr had gone underground and was not expected to obstruct the process this time around, the factions had received threats from Bilal al-ʿArqub, another dangerous militant. Palestinian stakeholders had for weeks debated on how to retake the Qaʿet al-Yusef checkpoint, which was found on the ledge of Tiri and was deemed a particularly sensitive spot due to its vicinity to an apartment complex owned by al-ʿArqub. Fearing that an overrepresentation of Fatah militiamen would provoke new acts of aggression, Colonel Saʿd made sure to fill up the checkpoint with members of other political factions. "I need one from Hamas, one from Islamic Jihad, and give me three from [Fatah] al-Intifada," he instructed his affiliates over the phone. At one point, too many Fatah members had deployed, and were immediately and firmly

Figure 6.2 A pile of garbage was used to block off the Upper Street, with bullet-ridden buildings in the background. Author's photo, May 16, 2017.

asked to pull back by the colonel. "Finding a sense of balance between the factions is essential," Saʿd explained while commenting on the process which looked almost as complicated as that of forming a Lebanese cabinet.[107]

The JPSF retook Qaʿet al-Yusef without a hitch, and when we later passed by the checkpoint, the joint force was in place. For a conflict-ridden society like ʿAyn al-

Hilwe, small victories like these mattered. For the time being, the responsibility of the Joint Force seemed to rest safely in the hands of its leader Bassam Saʿd, although the colonel's optimism could only be described as restrained. Any drills in human rights or civilian policing had been put on hold, while Fatah's leadership in the West Bank was reviewing whether or not the JPSF was a project worthy of funding, he relayed. In the meantime, Saʿd had no illusions of what this body of approximately 120 cadres could accomplish. They were up against powerful enemies, and were hardly a cure for the underlying socio-economic circumstances that continue to drive tensions in the camp.

Perhaps this was the reason why the Lebanese authorities had decided to go ahead and reinitiate the construction of their cement wall, which by late May, was nearly complete. In ʿAyn al-Hilwe, people laughed with resignation when peering at their new fence. There appeared to be a shared sentiment among inhabitants that it was poverty, hopelessness, and ultimately, social isolation that were fostering radicalism among youth, and they were quick to point out that the last thing they needed now was more walls. Unlike the Lebanese media, none of my interlocutors and friends in the camp seemed interested in knowing what had happened to Bilal Badr or where he was hiding. Rather, they were asking who would be the next to fill his shoes.

A Precarious Future

In the early 1990s, the formation of a robust Palestinian police force was deemed pivotal in consolidating the rule of the Palestinian Authority in the Gaza Strip and the West Bank. Established twenty years later, the Joint Palestinian Security Force in ʿAyn al-Hilwe is in its own right indicative of the national movement's aspirations to retain modes of statehood in exile. Advertised as a revolutionary vehicle for safeguarding the autonomy of the Palestinian diaspora, their right to return to the homeland, and being the rock that would "break the Zionist enemy," the joint force was soaked in revolutionary symbolism from its inception, which was also mirrored in its organizational structure. As many obstacles as these guerillas have faced, the JPSF's most substantial challenges have not lied in the patrol officers conducting traffic with rocket launchers in hand, but in the lack of trust, backing, and ultimately, belief in the project by the actors funding it.

Lacking both the vision and the manpower to carry out its mandate of bringing a centralized law and order agency to ʿAyn al-Hilwe, the joint force has—along with the Palestinian leaderships—time after time found itself submerged into, rather than transcending the pre-existing systems of loyalty, ranging from faction, to kin and neighborhood. Meanwhile, its cadres have been left navigating disorienting leadership structures and precarious inter-factional alliances, while striving to implement the law of a host nation that regard the Palestinian refugees first and foremost as a security threat.

We should not rule out that the joint force, as well as the unified leadership in Beirut, might emerge as important arenas for cooperation in the future. As it stands, the JPSF does not appear as much of a symbol of unity, as it is emblematic of the lack of progress made between Lebanon and the Palestinian leaderships since the creation of the Lebanese-Palestinian dialogue committee in 2005. Most of all, it resembles a preliminary measure that has allowed both parts to conveniently postpone any substantial dialogue regarding the most fundamental obstacles for progress: a host state that refuses to grant the refugees a modicum of civil rights, and faction leaders who view that arming impoverished camp populations is a viable strategy in their quest for hegemony.

Whereas the Palestinian camp dwellers find themselves between a rock and a hard place, we have seen that they are seldom afraid to speak their minds when frustrated with their leaderships. This is something we will explore in detail, as we move on to the final case of this book, which deals with a form of political activity we have only witnessed in passing so far: civilian protest movements.

7

You Sink Too: Protest Movements and Voices of Dissent

In July 2015, a social media campaign managed to mobilize mass demonstrations in downtown Beirut. The campaign called "You stink"[1] was triggered by the political elite's inability to deal with a mounting garbage crisis. For the protestors, who gathered by the hundreds in Martyr's Square in the Lebanese capital, the "stench" was merely a symptom of a lasting political paralysis. For nearly a year and a half, the country had lacked a president, and had gone on with a resigned caretaker government and a parliament that had extended its own term twice.[2] As the protests spread to other cities, voices of dissent were also heard among the country's Palestinian refugees. The latter, however, were directing their anger against their own political elites in the refugee camps.

On August 5, 2015, scores of protesters filled the main streets of Burj al-Barajne, the largest of three Palestinian refugee camps in the Lebanese capital. The demonstration was a reaction to the death of a young Palestinian named Ahmad Kassab who had been electrocuted by a defunct power line. While deteriorating infrastructure and unhealthy living conditions are recurring problems in all camps, Burj al-Barajne is in particular known for its bewildering jungle of powerlines dwindling down from its rooftops. Inhabitants had complained about a lack of maintenance of the electric system for a longer period of time, as broken cables had led to tens of deaths over the past few years.[3] This time, they had had enough. People gathered around the offices of the Palestinian factions in Burj al-Barajne, asking their leaders to come down to the street. "We, the people of this camp, are no longer able to go on like this," one of the protestors told the TV channel Palestine Today:

> Come down to the people and hear them out, because this movement and this people's revolution will continue. If these political authorities are not able to bring the people their rights through their dialogue with the state, go on, resign, leave this camp, because the people will not leave the streets.[4]

The protestors were, in fact, demanding the resignation of the Popular Committees, the camp's internal political administrations. The protest in Burj al-Barajne was not an isolated incident, but rather the beginning of a phenomenon. In months to follow, demonstrations and strikes against camp leaderships persisted, activist magazines were printed, and campaigns for democratically elected camp committees were initiated. "This is our way of saying *you stink too*," a young Palestinian activist noted.[5]

While the former chapters of this book have sought to understand the Palestinian national movement's perseverance in Lebanon and the role of the faction leaderships in exile, this final chapter explores how these actors are challenged from below. What makes camp dwellers revolt? How do they do it? And what are they able to achieve? Based on interviews with activist collectives, social media activists, and young faction members, this chapter offers a preliminary analysis of the grievances, networks, and strategies of a nascent protest movement among Palestinians in Lebanon echoing the youthful and creative protest tactics of the Arab uprisings. My intention here is not to embark on a comparative study of youth movements in the Arab world. This chapter primarily deals with internal Palestinian politics, where the main takeaway is that the refugee camps have become an arena for a broader clash of generations, where younger opposition forces challenge the hegemony of the older generation within the national movement. In order for us to grasp the full extent of these tensions, I will begin by providing a brief analysis of the political marginalization that Palestinian youth are subject to in Lebanon.

No Camp for the Young

In December 2015, I attended a conference in Sidon called The Problems of Youth in the Camp (*Mushkilat al-shabab fi-l-mukhayyam*). An NGO had invited both youth and political leaders from ʿAyn al-Hilwe, intending to bring the parties together to discuss strategies for tackling some of the problems young Palestinians face in the camps, such as unemployment, the lack of education, and drug abuse. However, during the conference it became clear that the camp youth and their political leaders were not used to hearing each other out.

A controversy arose when a young Lebanese researcher entered the stage and presented statistics of unemployment among Lebanese youth, intending to show the Palestinians that their Lebanese counterparts often face many similar challenges. Provoked by the assessment, enraged delegates from the DFLP interrupted the talk and demanded that the presenter should revise his findings. They felt that he had neglected the structural repression keeping Palestinian youth out of the job market. While the younger camp dwellers were all too aware of the legal oppression they face in Lebanese society, they did not seem to like the idea of anyone speaking on their behalf. The interruption was countered by university students belonging to *Fatah Youth (Shabibat Harakat Fath)*, who took the stage and hurled accusations at the senior leaders. "What do you know about the youth of the camp? When did you start caring about our perspective? You don't see us nor do you hear us!" one participant shouted. The seminar erupted into bouts of harsh verbal altercations, where the organizers had to ask the participants to find their seats.[6] Where did these sentiments come from?

Scholarly literature dealing with Palestinian youth in the West Bank has documented how these are doubly oppressed.[7] As Jacob Høigilt notes, they are not only faced with systematical discrimination by the Israeli occupation, but they have also become alienated from the Palestinian political scene.[8] In Lebanon, Palestinian youth might be said to face a similar type of double repression. They are marginalized not only by the Lebanese state but also by the internal camp authorities. Overall, the situation is emblematic of the present-day national movement's failure to include and cater to the younger generations.

From Mobilization to Decay

In the initial parts of this book, I described how the militarization that the refugee camps of the diaspora witnessed following the Six-Day War (1967) turned the social order of these societies on their heads. When the guerilla groups challenged the PLO from below and took control of the organization from within, it was a process that let young, politically aware refugees living in the margins claim ownership over the national struggle, while turning their backs to the Arab leaders who had attempted to use them as pawns for their own geopolitical gains. The armed struggle demanded the participation of the masses, and no one could remain passive. In the camps and elsewhere, the younger generation was called upon to lead the resistance, as guerilla fighters, the heads of unions, doctors, teachers, or other functions. This also pertained to the women, who seized the opportunity to step beyond the narrow confines of their traditional roles. As Julie Peteet notes, some of the Palestinian militia groups became promotors of an egalitarian form of participation, because the broader national struggle was given priority over traditional customs. Symbols like "the gun, the flag, militancy and steadfastness" emphasized national rather than kin and village loyalties, while the idea of family honor ('ird) was deemed backwards and counterproductive to the revolution.[9]

These egalitarian ideals were at the same time challenged by growing discords and disunity within and between the faction leaderships. In the latter half of the 1970s, the military setbacks incurred in Lebanon, and the PLO's adaption of the controversial Ten Point Program, resulted in a growing dissatisfaction with the leadership of Yasser Arafat (Chapter 2). With tensions brewing in Fatah, the imperative of maintaining political control, Rex Brynen reminds us, was what encouraged Arafat to resort to neopatrimonial rule.[10] As the leader of the PLO and its Fatah movement, he maintained a strategy of distributing funds, jobs, and favors to loyalists in order to secure their allegiance. As a result, patronage and factional loyalty came to trump any bid for bottom-up participation, and corruption and incompetence were overlooked in the interest of maintaining unity and cohesion.[11]

As we have seen throughout this book, the PLO and Fatah leadership's imperative to remain in control of the refugee camps of Lebanon is no less prevalent today. When the PLO resurfaced as a factional framework in the camps toward the turn of the millennium, it was initially in a last-ditch effort exerted by the homeland leadership to strengthen its standings in the final status negotiations. The impromptu resurrection of Fatah's militias and the reopening of former guerilla offices were a pressed response to a critical situation, and these institutions were not intended to remain put for decades. On the surface, the faction structures presently found within 'Ayn al-Hilwe and other camps display what political scientist Francis Fukuyama has referred to as institutional decay. They were a response to a former crisis, but have, due to rapid political changes, become ill-equipped in terms of dealing with the current reality,[12] such as catering to the needs of a burgeoning civilian population. That is not to say they no longer serve a function. While the factional administrations and the funds they receive from their respective patrons are all indicative of the Palestinian leaderships' imperative to retain political control over their contingents in exile, the decay lies in these institution's ineptness to govern civilian lives. In Lebanon, the guerilla groups have remained in charge, but without the participation of the masses. In this picture, the youth of the camps in particular find themselves sidelined.

"They Remain in Their Seats until They Die"

The average age of the Palestinian camp dwellers in Lebanon is 30.3 years, where roughly half are under twenty-four.[13] These age groups hardly have a say in how their societies are run. Take for example Fatah, the most substantial political faction within the camps today. The movement's internal structures are organized in strict hierarchies, where participation is in essence based on the principle of seniority.[14] Moreover, because its officials are either appointed or elected by the movement's central leadership in the West Bank, the local camp populations are kept far away from any decision process, and those filling the lower ranks are expected to follow orders without question. More often than not, getting a job with the movement means being stationed at a checkpoint and carrying a rifle for one of the militia branches, where cult worship of the senior commander often abounds.

Although Fatah also keeps a number of non-military personnel on its payrolls to front various unions, youth branches, and relief organizations, these initiatives typically lack the funding or the necessary infrastructure to carry out their tasks, and often appear to play a symbolic role rather than a functional one. As a member of the General Union for Palestinian Women in Lebanon lamented:

> We were a part of the resistance. We fought alongside the men, and we built this camp [ʿAyn al-Hilwe] with our own hands while they were in prison. But things changed. [The leadership has] neglected our role, and viewed our union merely as something for show and appearances. Have they forgotten how the women fought twice as bravely as the men!?[15]

Pertaining to its youth branches, Fatah pays young members between 30,000 and 60,000 Lebanese Lira a month (depending on their age and education) to represent the movement at various youth arrangements, and feature opinionated university or college students who eagerly engage in campus politics at Lebanese academic institutions.[16] But their experience or skills are rarely consulted by the senior leaderships back in the camps. It is worth noting that Hamas and other Islamist factions seem to differ from the PLO in this regard, and to larger degree draw upon younger members for positions of responsibility. In May 2017, a young member of Fatah spoke with envy when the news broke that Hamas had elected a 26-year-old as the political representative of the three camps found in the city of Tyre.[17] "This is an embarrassment," he said. "Look at us by comparison. Our leaders remain in their seats until they die!"[18]

These words weren't far from the truth. During a visit to the Popular Committee of the Beddawi camp in North Lebanon, I found that its leader—a Fatah official—had remained in his position since 1974. Abu Khalid had sided with the pro-Syrian Palestinian movements following the aforementioned revolt within Fatah in 1983, but had returned to the ranks of his old movement when Arafat initiated his campaign to reclaim the camps of Lebanon in 1999. Through clever maneuvering, Abu Khalid had never had to leave his chair as the Popular Committee's leader. Nonetheless, his ability to serve the camp community was questionable, as old age had caught up with him. Suffering from hearing loss and a failing memory, Abu Khalid fell asleep a number of times during our conversation, and his colleagues had to keep reminding him who I was. The other members of the committee were young by comparison, although they all appeared to be in their early sixties.

The situation in the Beddawi camp was an extreme expression of what seemed to constitute the norm, and was indicative of how the revolutionaries who once had reshaped the camps and mobilized their inhabitants for war over the years had turned into an aging leadership, struggling to adapt to the changing realities. In this situation, it was not only Fatah's young and female partisans who found themselves sidelined, but the camp populations at large had come to question the guerilla factions' ability to provide for civilians on a day-to-day basis. Not surprisingly, the Popular Committees found themselves at the center of controversy.

The Popular Committees

Formed in the early 1970s, the Popular Committees were once the revolutionary councils of the camps, and gathered representatives from each guerilla group. In addition to managing the bureaucratic side of the armed struggle, these councils functioned as a liaison between the Palestinian guerillas, the Lebanese state, NGOs, and the camp populations. To date, the factional representatives of these institutions are tasked with overseeing sub-committees that manage the daily administration of the camps, ranging from waste collection, provision of water and electricity, to keeping tabs on the health situation. It is not unfitting when members of the Popular Committees refer to their institutions as *baladiyyat*, meaning municipalities.[19] Nonetheless, there are important differences that distinguish these revolutionary councils from the municipalities of Lebanon, for example. For one, they are not elected, but appointed by the faction leaderships. Second, we are hard pressed to find any city that features two or several municipalities openly working in parallel. Because of decades of factional rivalry, this is the reality in the Palestinian camps.

Many of the present-day Popular Committees go back to the early to mid-1980s, and were established by the pro-Syrian bloc and other rejectionist factions within the first few years to follow the PLO's evacuation from Lebanon.[20] However, the camps were ravaged by war, and the committees lacked the proper funding or efficiency to carry out their tasks. In Beirut, for example, the Syrian military intelligence refused to deal with camp leaderships who were not deemed servile to Syrian interests, and as a result, finding people with the right connections, rather than the proper vocational or organizational skills, became the priority for the factions.[21] Fatah's return as a social and political force to Lebanon at the turn of the millennium, however, hardly improved the administration of the refugee camps. In the early 2000s, the organization tried to wrestle the power out of the hand of the pro-Syrian movements by resurrecting the former PLO Popular Committees in the Sidon and Beirut regions. Provoked by this move, the APF (Alliance of Palestinian Forces), with Hamas at its helm, responded by launching a number of *People's Committees (lijan ahliyya)* in the PLO's heartland in the al-Rashidiyye, Burj al-Shemali, and al-Buss camps in the South. "The People's Committees don't really have a function," Muhammad Yasin, the leader of the pro-Syrian branch of the PLF explained. "It was more about sending a message to Fatah: if you're going to exclude *us*, we're going to exclude *you*."[22] As a result, nearly every camp in the country ended up with a parallel set of Popular Committees beholden to the PLO and the APF, respectively. Only in the northern camps did the factions form joint committees, as the PLO did not have the means or leverage to overrun the pro-Syrian forces.[23]

While the PLO committees in general have better funding and "larger capabilities"[24] than the APF committees do, the phenomenon of dual camp administrations is a source of much confusion for inhabitants. Some, in fact, are not aware that their camp has two Popular Committees, while others suspect that both committees are corrupt, and that they are only willing to assist their own political affiliates. For example, in the fall of 2013, the PLO's Popular Committee in the Shatila camp in Beirut launched an investigation into a crime allegedly committed by a person associated with the PFLP (the second largest PLO-faction). When the accused's name in the end was cleared, supporters of Hamas complained that the wrong popular committee had carried out the investigation—they didn't consider the PLO to be neutral in the matter. In the end, the conflict was solved the "traditional way" when a *Hajj*, a respectable elder, was asked to intervene and mediate, thereby underscoring the Popular Committees' inability to function as a neutral party.[25]

Often, camp dwellers blame the Popular Committees for appropriating resources for clientelistic purposes, and their leaders for making tacit arrangements with private owners of electric generators or wells, rather than ensuring that their services are distributed at a fair price. It is in particular those who lack social connections who find themselves challenged by these dynamics. In Shatila, a young Palestinian mother who recently had fled the Syrian war found herself struggling to navigate the networks of power in her new shelter. She was frustrated because she had come up empty in her attempts to connect to a generator owned by one of the camp's influential families, who reportedly had close ties to a pro-Syrian faction. Moreover, she and other newcomers lambasted the PLO's Popular Committee for having appropriated and rebranded cartons of food that had originaly been donated to displaced refugees from Syria by Hizballah, and for alerting its own family members about the handout first. "I used to think the factions were supposed to be here for our benefit," she said:

> Now I realize they are only here for their own interests. They should rename their Popular Committees "The committees for corruption and stealing (*lijan al-fasad wal-sirqa*)," because that's the only thing they do right![26]

The demonstrations in Burj al-Barajne, as we remember from this chapter's introduction, were a result of similar frustrations. They were an expression of rage and disappointment triggered by the political leaderships' perceived inability to protect and provide for camp populations living in a dire situation. It is time we took a closer look at the actors who were behind the protests.

Networks of Activists Take Shape

Although it is common to hear inhabitants of the camps complain about the faction leaderships, this discontent rarely results in organized resistance. In order to understand the recent surge of activist networks, we will have to consider three important factors.

Factor 1: The Syrian Refugee Crisis

The networks of activists which we will meet soon trace their roots back to youth initiatives that emerged at a time when the Palestinian camps of Lebanon were rapidly filling up with new refugees fleeing from the Syrian war. In 2012, a group of youth from ʿAyn al-Hilwe embarked on a highly publicized solidarity campaign where they would collect donations for displaced families from Syria, and otherwise played an active role in defusing tensions between the newcomers and the Lebanese army, the latter having ordered the destruction of improvised shelters set up around the camp's ledges. The efforts inspired others to follow suit, and after some time, several youth initiatives from different camps joined forces under the banner of *The Palestinian Youth Network*, whose online forum became an important space for exchanging views on the situation.[27] Viewing with concern the intensifying struggle for scarce resources, the failing infrastructure, but also the radical networks that were recruiting paperless refugees in ʿAyn al-Hilwe, the more vocal affiliates of the Youth Network were convinced that the camp leaderships were ill prepared for countering the mounting crisis. Not surprisingly, the forum rapidly emerged as a place for voicing discontent with the faction authorities and, not at least, for meeting likeminded youth aspiring for change.

"There was a feeling that we need to play a role. We need to have a place in the Palestinian political map, as *shabab*," Badiʿ said.[28] As an educated journalist in his early thirties, and a member of Fatah in Burj al-Barajne, his background was typical and yet distinct among the activists. Typical in the sense that he was well-educated, from a middle class family, and shared with his contemporaries a technocratic vision for camp politics, insisting that skill and experience, not military rank or seniority, should be prerequisites for governing these societies. Distinct in the sense that he worked with one of the militia factions, rather than being employed by an NGO, which mostly seemed to be the case with his colleagues. Despite being an avid supporter of Fatah, he could hardly be accused of being a blind partisan. In fact, it was he and his cousins, all members of the movement, who had rallied friends and family in Burj al-Barajne to demonstrate against the Popular Committees in August 2015 following the death of their friend Ahmad Kassab. For Badiʿ, his complaint with the factions was not their presence, but rather that their incompetence, indifference, and culture of nepotism were putting the camp population at risk.

One would be hard-pressed to trace a clear ideological tendency among Badiʿ's contemporaries from the Youth Network. Some supported the Marxist-Leninist groups, one identified himself as a Hamas supporter, while others expressed a distinct detest of factional politics altogether. Some of the female activists bore the veil, others did not. They were Palestinians in their twenties and thirties from all areas of Lebanon, as well as newcomers from Syria. Rather than being a fixed group of people with a shared ideology, the network seemed to be dominated by one or two key persons in each camp able to rally their respective friends, families, and allies for substantial collective action. Sometimes their opposition was clear and antagonistic, as had been the case in Burj al-Barajne. Other times, it was more concealed. For example, in October 2016, Hassan Othman in Shatila was successful in organizing a huge demonstration against drug trafficking in the camp. As opposition toward drugs is a popular cause and is shared by anyone from concerned families and youngsters to Islamist groups, his anti-drug march was quickly joined by hundreds of inhabitants.[29] However, the protests also conveyed a thinly veiled criticism of the factions. The events came after three major drug barons had "escaped" from the headquarters of the pro-Syrian group Fatah al-Intifada, before they were supposed to be handed over to the Lebanese authorities.[30] As protestors marched through the streets of the camp, their anti-drug slogans could be interpreted as accusations against the factions, hinting that a corrupt camp leadership was implicit in the drug trade. In the words of James Scott, the *hidden transcript*—the dominated group's concealed resentment toward their dominators—had "storm[ed] the stage" and become a public affair.[31]

Despite the informal nature of these nascent networks of activists, a few important circumstances had allowed them to expand and improve their structures. This brings us to the second factor which deals with funding.

Factor 2: New Opportunities for Funding

The international community's humanitarian response to the refugee crisis appeared to give the youth activists some momentum. In 2013, the British government and a number of other Western governments allocated substantial funds intended to strengthen civil society organizations among Lebanon's refugee populations. In the Palestinian camps, the money was spent on a number of initiatives ranging from setting up youth centers, training employees from camp-based NGOs, providing street vendors with tents for the winter season, to—most notably— establishing a Palestinian Civil Defense division in ʿAyn al-Hilwe, which would later be set up in five additional camps.[32] At the time, an array of local and international NGOs begun hiring skilled Palestinian youth with organizational training, many of whom had close ties to the young activists in the camps. This dynamic provided the latter with ample opportunities to apply and seek funding for projects. In the fall of 2015, Badiʿ and his friends from the Youth Network obtained funding for a two-year period to publish a magazine for Palestinian youth, named *Qalam Rasas*, which quickly asserted itself as a mouthpiece for the emerging activist networks.[33]

In addition to featuring interviews with young camp dwellers and educational reportages, including a detailed story on the internal organizational make-up of UNRWA, the first edition of Qalam Rasas reads much like a mission statement for a new generation of Palestinians.[34] Particularly the editorial, resembling a manifesto of sorts, provides us with an idea about how these youths view their place in the Arab world and the camp space alike. Beginning with a comparison between the Arab uprisings and the student revolts of Europe in the late 1960s, it highlights the *double oppression* Palestinian youth are subjected to in the Occupied Palestinian Territories. Not only do they suffer from the "arrogance and monstrosity" of the "Zionist Settler occupation," the editorial says, but they are also facing

> the Palestinian Authority's suppression of freedom of opinion and expression, as well as the increase in political arrests both in the West Bank and Gaza of activists who merely expressed their opinions on social media. This road of force that the PA has embarked on, mimicking the tactics of the Arab regimes, will only lead to a tightening of the chokehold on Palestinian youth—the consequences of which cannot yet be fully grasped.[35]

It then goes on to explain how this injustice reverberates within the camps of Lebanon, stating, "These camps have suffered, and continue to suffer, from a neglect in the administration of the lives of their inhabitants, and the failure of the internal authorities to safeguard their integrity."[36] Encouraging readers to draw inspiration from past student revolts in Europe as well as the current uprisings in the Arab world, not to mention those taking place in the streets of Beirut, the editorial ends by inviting young Palestinians in Lebanon to "resist corruption and demand reform."[37]

In terms of "demanding reform," the activists had more efficient ways of spreading their ideas than a printed magazine. This brings us to our third, and likely, most important factor regarding the formation of the activist networks.

Factor 3: The Role of Social Media

Whereas the Qalam Rasas magazine was only circulated at a few hundred copies per issue, the collective's main output was a Facebook profile followed by thousands, where they would frequently share content such as video reports from the camps.[38] "The leaders have their committees and their means, but we command the mobile phone and the internet," Badiʿ said back in the Burj al-Barajne camp. "For us, Social media is like a weapon."[39]

Scholars have noted how the Arab uprisings of 2010/2011 were preceded by an exceptional growth of social media users in the Middle East, particularly on Facebook.[40] Although research has warned against the assumption that social media leads to more democracy, there is little doubt that online platforms have created new avenues for public dissent and political mobilization for people in the region.[41] In Lebanon, the rapid increase in internet penetration, a relatively unregulated online sphere (at the time), and a number of the established media houses having been dissolved due to bankruptcy are all factors that have rendered social media a powerful tool for actors eager to challenge the narratives of the partisan media outlets. Next, we will see how this also has been the case in the Palestinian camps.

New Platforms, Old Grievances

Because of the centrality of Lebanon in the early days of the Palestinian revolution, many of the factions retain their respective media branches in Beirut. In all camps, publications such as newspapers, pamphlets, and member's magazines are passed around on a routine basis. Not seldom, the political groups will also deliver statements, messages, or news from Palestine through crackling speakers from their compounds. For the Islamist factions, the Friday sermon, which is similarly broadcasted through speakerphones, is often the main avenue for relaying the party line.

While the factions have traditionally made few efforts to address anyone outside of their own circle of partisans, some have in recent years set up social media profiles intending to reach a broader audience, and perhaps, a younger demographic. In Lebanon, Fatah runs its own social media-based news channel (Fateh TV), which airs neatly edited reportages relayed by professional news anchors. In ʿAyn al-Hilwe, many of Fatah's different militia branches have also launched their own Facebook profiles,[42] while al-Haraka al-Islamiyya al-Mujahida's media channel, al-Risala, regularly posts video recordings of the Friday sermons of the movement's leaders on YouTube.[43] While some factional social media platforms enjoy a substantial amount of traction, especially Fateh TV, most are not able to compete with the popularity of the many nonpartisan sites. For example, it has become commonplace for civilian inhabitants to set up Facebook profiles bearing the names of the neighborhoods where they reside, and where they avidly share content from their local environments. Whereas the Facebook profile of an influential Islamist leader like Jamal Khattab is followed by a meager 4,000, it is, by contrast, not uncommon for "neighborhood sites" or other nonpartisan initiatives to have followers in the tens of thousands. If we want to understand why these forums have become so popular, there is no better place to start than with the most successful and controversial of them all, which with over 150,000 followers is run by a collective of friends based in ʿAyn al-Hilwe, and is aptly titled *ʿAsimat al-Shattat*, the Capital of the Diaspora.[44]

The Case of ʿAsimat al-Shattat

The creation of the ʿAsimat al-Shattat Facebook group dates back to May 2011, and was originally intended to be a place for sharing pictures of traditional Palestinian clothing and customs, along with jokes and poems (*ghazal*) between acquaintances hailing from the neighborhood of al-Zib in ʿAyn al-Hilwe. As it represented something new at the time, the site experienced a lot of traction, and by the end of the year, it was, much to the surprise of its creators, followed by 5,000 participants—a number which has increased manifold every year since then. These participants, as it turned out, were not so much interested in Palestinian folklore, but used the site for other purposes. People would continuously inquire about incidents of gunfire in ʿAyn al-Hilwe, and would ask the admins for updates. Had a neighborhood war broken out, or were the sounds merely rounds of celebratory gunfire from a wedding? If clashes were taking place, which neighborhoods should one stay away from? People in the vast diaspora would also tap in for updates, inquiring about the situation of their relatives in Lebanon during times of upheaval. Not surprisingly, the Facebook group also became a resource for Lebanese and Palestinian journalists covering news from the camp.[45]

Because of this rapid growth of followers and the site's nascent public role, the friends in ʿAyn al-Hilwe gathered in early 2013 in order to discuss the future of ʿAsimat al-Shattat. After having been granted external funds, the group was able to shape it into a semi-professional news organization, where a Palestinian in his mid-thirties called Mahmoud ʿAtaya assumed the role as the site's director (*mudir*). He would along with his colleagues continue to publish news stories covering anything from the business of street vendors and UNRWA's policies, to clashes and violence occurring between Fatah's militia wings and Islamists, sometimes complete with commentary or statements from the warring parties. The funds allowed the collective to also set up a complimentary website where most of the content would be archived with permanent links.[46]

Interestingly, the political authorities of the camp would increasingly reach out to ʿAtaya when making public statements. For example, in the summer of 2014, the militant Salafis of ʿUsbat al-Ansar offered ʿAtaya a scoop when they asked him to post a new picture of the movement's emir in occultation, Abu Muhjin, promising his immanent return to ʿAyn al-Hilwe in order to "scare the ISIS supporters in the camp."[47] Although the factions certainly have sought to utilize the potential of these nonpartisan platforms to their benefit, sites like ʿAsimat al-Shattat seem to have removed the one-way dimension of the communication between the camp populations and their leaderships. The aforementioned site has continuously taken upon itself to relay messages from civilians wishing to address the authorities. For example, in September 2015, ʿAtaya and his colleagues gave considerable coverage to a strike held by street vendors in ʿAyn al-Hilwe who protested the inability of the camp's security providers in bringing stability to the community. The renowned vegetable market had for years been the camp's most stable source of income, but now, shop owners claimed the deteriorating security situation was killing commercial life, making it impossible for them to turn a profit. Through social media, a committee of the vendors directed the following statement to the Palestinian political leadership:

> Today's strike is a message to all leaders in order to [remind] them of their responsibility to improve the security of the camp. We are no longer able to handle the recession and the losses. We are now facing bankruptcy.[48]

As the story gained significant traction online and was a source of bad publicity for the camp's Joint Palestinian Security Force, the PLO's leadership in Lebanon went on to invite the committee of street vendors to its headquarters in Beirut, and offered a donation of $1,000 to cover some of their losses.[49] Of course, cameras were brought and pictures from the meeting were spread online as to underscore how eager the PLO was to provide for the camp populations.

Naturally, not all were convinced by such publicity stunts. In June 2017, inhabitants from the Hittin neighborhood of ʿAyn al-Hilwe posted a comedic video on their Facebook site (Hittin is our Neighborhood) which was shared widely online.[50] In the video, two men are seen sarcastically praising the efforts of the Joint Palestinian Security Force in securing the camp, and contend that the only reason why people keep dying and getting injured must be because they simply are not prepared for "civilian life." They go on to introduce a package for "civilian living" in ʿAyn al-Hilwe, consisting of a shield against gunfire, a helmet for protection against stray bullets, and three plastic bags of blood in case one, despite all precautions, is still shot.[51] Although the video was a far cry from the slick high-budget productions of Fateh TV, these antics were one of many indicators that the factional authorities no longer enjoyed a monopoly of the truth, and were struggling to control the narrative.

Between Local News and Online Activism

The ʿAsimat al-Shattat site had in the course of a few years inadvertently become a leading yet informal news provider in Lebanon's Palestinian camps, paving the way for an array of other social media networks covering local news with their smart phones. Although the group of friends behind the project had more or less stumbled into the role as pioneers of a growing trend, they were well aware of their potential influence, and had made a conscious decision to let virtually anyone, ranging from militia factions, to NGOs or begrudged civilians use their platform to express their opinions. "ʿAsimat al-Shattat is not my personal news channel, nor does it belong to a specific group of people," Mahmud ʿAtaya said during a conversation in an office he was in the process of setting up for himself on his street in the western part of ʿAyn al-Hilwe.

> Every Palestinian that feels like writing something can do so. Anyone who wants to upload a piece of news, an article, or inform about activities ... we don't block anyone. [...] It's not enough for us to write news that is welcomed only by a few. No, that's what *they* do, the media offices of the *tanzimat* [factions]. We, on the other hand, write about things the way they are. The fact that someone can go on the site and respond to my view, saying "Mahmud you're not correct," this is something that didn't exist before. This is something new.[52]

ʿAtaya and his friends viewed their work—the act of inviting people to speak their minds—as a form of protest in and of itself. Their stories didn't necessarily have to be critical against the ruling authorities, but the mere act of speaking words not bound by any party program was deemed tantamount to a revolutionary act. Thus, they tended to depict themselves as activists (*nashitin*) rather than media people (*iʿlamiyin*). Moreover, their office seemed to function as a meeting place for activists and dissidents in the ʿAyn al-Hilwe camp who had a connection, in one form or another, to the ongoing surge of protests. Keeping a stack of the Qalam Rasas magazine on their office table, Mahmoud ʿAtaya and a few of his affiliates had recently decided to take their activism offline, and had joined the youth activists behind said magazine in an elaborate campaign for democratic elections of the camp's political bodies. Next, we will see how the momentum gained in the online sphere has played out physically in the camp space.

Calls for Camp Elections

As early as 2014, affiliates of the Youth Network and other activists (before the launch of Qalam Rasas) embarked on an online campaign called *Tabbiq Nizamak*, meaning "Apply your system." The name of the campaign referred to a list of amended by-laws for the Popular Committees issued by the PLO's Department of Refugee Affairs in the West Bank in April 2010.[53]

The activists did in particular highlight article 16 of said document, which stipulates that the Popular Committees should be democratically elected by the camp populations, something that for all practical purposes never has been the case in Lebanon. Equating the inefficiency of the Popular Committees with their inherent nepotism, the online campaign would target individual members of the camp committees, and expose them to public ridicule for lacking the experience or qualifications for carrying out their

Figure 7.1 A Photograph from the Tabbiq Nizamak campaign which was offered to the author by one of the participants.

work, or outing them for their opposition to democratic processes.[54] Under the hashtag #مين_المسؤول؟ (Who is responsible?), users were asked to share pictures of broken down camp infrastructure, while tagging the profiles of camp authorities in the post.[55] To accompany the online campaign, activists would paste mock posters seemingly issued by the Popular Committees, or *graffiti* political slogans in the camp space. The walls of the camps, from the North to the South, found themselves displaying messages like "It is your right to have an elected Popular Committee" or "to prevent favoritism, you need an elected Popular Committee," always followed by the campaign's hashtag #طبق_نظامك (Tabbiq Nizamak).[56]

Factional Views on Camp Democracy

Both Fatah and Hamas, the two major parties likely to gain popular support and thus benefit the most from elections, report that they are not principally against the notion of camp democracy. In some instances, their officials even expressed their unequivocal support for the idea.[57] In reality, neither party has taken any steps to implement elections in the camps, and typically blames the other side for opposing them. As do the Marxist-Leninist bloc within the PLO, whose officials are quick to criticize their peers for having become frightened by the prospects of democracy.[58] On this note, a spokesperson for the PFLP argued that the tendency for leftist and independent lists to do well in the internal elections held every three years for UNRWA's staff and unions had convinced Fatah that it would lose in the election of any Popular Committee and refused to budge.[59] Whatever the case, this did not change the fact that a member of his own party had led the PLO's Popular Committee in Shatila since its creation in the early 2000s, and had no ambitions of stepping down from his position.[60] The smaller Damascus-based or pro-Iranian factions are perhaps the groups that most vehemently oppose the idea of camp elections. Having a strong military presence in the camps found in the northern half of Lebanon, and enjoying little public support, they seemingly have little to gain from a democratic process and are not shy about it. "The people don't want elections," a leader of the pro-Syrian PFLP-General Command, claimed during a conversation in the Shatila camp in 2013. "It would create chaos. The people trust the factions to deal with politics."[61] "We are at war with Israel," an official from the Iranian-backed Palestinian Islamic Jihad in Burj al-Barajne contended. "Since when do armies elect their internal institutions? When we return to our homeland, we can talk about democracy."[62]

While the camp leaderships either ignore or reject the calls for elected bodies, this has not prevented civilians from taking matters into their own hands. Researcher and activist Manal Kortam has covered what to date remains the most elaborate attempt at organizing democratic elections, which took place in the Shatila camp in 2005.[63] Following the death of the chairperson of the APF-dominated Popular Committee, a number of inhabitants, along with notables and shaykhs, used this opportunity to hold an election of a civilian camp leadership. The project, however, collapsed when candidates started to withdraw due to pressure from the factions.[64] Drawing on past experiences with the Popular Committees, my activist interlocutors revealed that they instead had begun working with the so-called Neighborhood Committees in order to circumvent the factions' top-down refusal of camp democracy.

Neighborhood Politics

The Neighborhood Committees (*lijan al-ahya'*) were formed in earnest following the Israeli invasion of Sidon in 1982. Mimicking village and kinship structures from historical Palestine, these civilian cooperatives are said to have emerged as a reaction to the expulsion of the Palestinian leadership, but were in some cases likely also aided materially by the local Israeli military administration as an incentive to keep the PLO from resettling in 'Ayn al-Hilwe. After the IDF abandoned the city in 1985, however, Fatah began funding several of these indigenous institutions to coopt village notables and influential families, and otherwise bolster the influence of Arafat in the Capital of the Diaspora. Having been re-shaped many times in the intervening years, the Neighborhood Committees continue wield considerable influence. Upon my visits, I was told that the PLO's Popular Committee had appointed 25 leaders tasked with representing inhabitants of their respective neighborhoods in matters regarding conflict resolution and service provision.[65] These efforts notwithstanding, there was little to suggest that any political group fully controlled them.

The fragmentation of the camp's governing institutions appeared to have given way to novel expressions of civilian infrastructure existing outside of the faction framework. In 'Ayn al-Hilwe, I was introduced to an array of neighborhood organizations, from smaller village-like councils to larger clan constellations, some of which worked diligently to provide neighbors and relatives with basic services such as water and electricity, and even engaged in restoration of streets and houses. Some of these had clear ties to political factions and reported back to their respective Popular Committee, but there were also those who did not seem to have a clear factional profile. For example, the Hittin Committee, representing a lush and green neighborhood on the southern edge of the camp, was funded and organized by the local leader of the Islamist group Hizb al-Tahrir, while its daily manager belonged to Fatah. What bound them and the rest of the members of the committee together were their shared roots harkening back to the village of Hittin, formerly found west of lake Tiberias in historical Palestine. The arrangement was one of many examples of how familial or geographical ties with time have come to trump factional loyalties. For the same reasons, members of the committee, which was said to be one of the most resourceful and well-functioning civilian institutions in the camp, explained that they repeatedly had been ordered to shut down or scale back their operations by parties that had been left feeling nervous about such blatant inter-factional comingling.[66]

As became clear in my interviews with the factional authorities, the rival political frameworks (the PLO, the APF, and the Islamic Forces) were keeping a careful account of which neighborhoods they perceived to be loyal to them, and any uncertainty to this end tended to result in a lot of friction. Not surprisingly, activists rallying for camp elections had begun mapping out allies among nonpartisan committees. On this note, we will see how an election in one of 'Ayn al-Hilwe's western neighborhoods created a controversy in 2015.

The Zib Elections

In 2015, a group of activists in al-Zib, a neighborhood covering a patch of the western ledge of ʿAyn al-Hilwe, obtained a grant from an international organization in order to improve the livelihood of this area. They went on to gather their neighbors to paint the walls of the district, to decorate its streets with flowers, and to set up a billiard club for the youth, among other things. Dusty streets now came to life with bright yellow colors, and the efforts were followed closely by fellow camp dwellers, and the political factions alike. Inspired by the Tabbiq Nizamak campaign and based on advice given by affiliates of Qalam Rasas, these activists had also began addressing members of Zib's Neighborhood Committee in terms of pushing for elections, arguing that inhabitants had recently "done more for the neighborhood than the factions ever had".[67]

It should be mentioned that quite a few of the Neighborhood Committees have internalized the act of choosing their leaders through casting votes. Neighborhood elections are in and of themselves by no means a foreign idea. That being said, the impact of such "electoral processes" is usually very limited, as it is understood that neighbors should not step on the toes of well-respected village elders or upset established factional balances. The Zib elections, however, transcended these unwritten conventions. Following a short period of campaigning and a blind vote in late 2015, the Zib neighborhood had elected a committee where activists had gained significant ground, among them Mahmoud ʿAtaya, the social media star behind the ʿAsimat al-Shattat site. On the other hand, the election had sidelined the PLO's appointed leader of the neighborhood. The latter had been deeply provoked by and refused to comply with the electoral committee's insistence that he would have to sign up as a candidate if he wanted to participate governing al-Zib. The fact that the neighborhood had more or less announced its independence from factional rule did not sit well with the established authorities. "The PLO is the sole representative of the Palestinian people," a member of the camp's Popular Committee commented about the events. "Any Neighborhood Committee that doesn't have a representative from the PLO is therefore not legitimate."[68] "We are the ones who *are* legitimate," members of the Zib Committee responded rhetorically to these allegations during our conversation: "Who elected you?"[69]

The Zib election was celebrated as a victory among my interlocutors in other camps, and pictures of the flowery streets of the neighborhood were spread widely on social media, as a symbol of freedom and progress. In the months to follow, activists in the Burj al-Barajne camp followed suit and persuaded three more Neighborhood Committees to go through with open elections, while plans were made to embark on a similar effort in al-Beddawi. In all cases, activists stressed that the elections were unique in that neighbors were in agreement that both women and young men were encouraged to both vote and run as candidates. Although these committees were for the most part still run by older men, as far as I could see, this push for neighborhood democracy was hailed as the beginning of a new era among the young activists.

However, when I met with members of the new Zib committee in April 2016, the electoral victory appeared to have left a bitter taste in the mouths of the neighborhood's residents. The more outspoken members of the committee were receiving anonymous death threats on their mobile phones. Moreover, residents lamented that the Joint

Security Forces of the camp had chosen not to deploy during a recent episode of violence in the neighborhood, speculating that the PLO had decided to neglect this part of the camp as a type of collective punishment. As a result, the leader of the Neighborhood Committee had gone to the step of hiring a heavily armed bodyguard who followed him a few feet behind wherever he moved. He no longer dared to leave the neighborhood in fear of repercussions. For the residents of al-Zib, declaring independence had come at a price.[70]

In the last section of this chapter, we will explore in detail how the political authorities in all camps have attempted to discredit the young activists and crack down on their campaigns.

Counter Strikes

At the peak of the Tabbiq Nizamak campaign, the camps of Lebanon witnessed another form of popular uprising that ended up stealing much of the momentum that the protest in Burj al-Barajne had created. In January 2016, a new UNRWA health reform now required Palestinian refugees to pay between 5 and 20 percent of their hospital bills, ending a longstanding arrangement of free secondary healthcare.[71] UNRWA's continued presence is by camp dwellers understood to be a guarantee for the international society's commitment to their right of return. Hence, any cutback or reform of the agency's services is often interpreted as a political act. Frustration turned to outrage when the 23-year-old Omar Khudayr, who no longer could pay the bills for his treatment, self-immolated in front of an UNRWA clinic in the southern Burj al-Shemali camp, an event which triggered mass protests against the UN agency.[72] Five months into the knife Intifada in the Jerusalem area, the Palestinian camps in Lebanon saw an "Intifada against UNRWA" take place, as one Hamas official put it.[73]

The Palestinian factions would proceed to routinely lock UNRWA employees out of their offices, while arranging for busloads of camp dwellers to stage sit-ins in front of the agency's main offices in the southern suburbs of Beirut. Although the youth activists in general seemed to support the protests and went on to cover them extensively in their magazines and on their social media sites, the demands of national unity in face of the international society seemed to have reduced the space for internal criticism of the Palestinian governing bodies. During my visit to Tripoli, an UNRWA employee who found himself locked out of his office in the Beddawi camp begrudgingly noted that the act of rallying camp dwellers against the agency surely was a strategy meant to divert the attention away from the criticism the political factions recently had come under.[74] Whatever the reasons, in this atmosphere, voices of dissent were increasingly treated as treason.

Dahlan's Agents?

It was not only members of the Zib committee who were dealing with threats. Most activists whom I had encountered would eagerly show me text messages displaying anonymous threats to their lives or their families, demanding their silence. However, what seemed to sting the most was the fact that the camp populations often doubted their intent. The idea of young Palestinians from various political orientations or family backgrounds coming together in order to raise their voice simply as youth, while rallying support for causes rather than factions, seemed alien to many. Exploiting this doubt, affiliates of Fatah had gone to great lengths in trying to discredit the calls for reform and camp elections by insisting that the youths had been hired as agents by the Palestinian president's bitter political rival, Muhammad Dahlan.

Although none of my interlocutors seemed to have anything positive to say about Dahlan, and for the most part insisted that his ways were not much different from the leaderships they were already protesting against, they struggled to distance themselves from him. It did not help their case that affiliates of Dahlan's Democratic Reform Current in Lebanon tended to view themselves as a part of the same youthful opposition movement. Moreover, because of Dahlan's habit of funding various charitable projects in the refugee camps,[75] any project having received funding from international NGOs or foreign governments immediately came under suspicion of being an orchestrated effort to usurp the power of Fatah's mainstream. This pertained to not only initiatives such as the Qalam Rasas group but even schools and centers for children were accused of acting as the excommunicated Fatah leader's propaganda machine.[76] In May 2017, a couple of young activists lamented with worry that the dynamics seemed to have pushed some of their colleagues over to Dahlan's side, if nothing else, for the sake of seeking protection against the threats they were receiving.[77] Paradoxically, claiming allegiance to a controversial faction seemed easier than raising one's voice as an independent actor.

Getting the People Talking

Not unlike their Lebanese contemporaries of the You Stink campaign, the Palestinian activists were starting to feel the implications of having picked a battle against an authoritarian system with little tolerance for dissent. Battered but not broken, they were still in the process of learning the art of balancing flashy and antagonistic online campaigns with pragmatic long-term initiatives among Neighborhood Committees and other grassroots activities. Speaking from his flat nearly two years after the initial protests in Burj al-Barajne, Badiʿ maintained that Qalam Rasas' biggest achievement had so far been the former. "We got the people talking," he said. "Any activist will realize that changing the reality around him is tantamount to impossible. But he also knows that once you have got the people talking, once you give them new ideas, there is no turning back."[78]

Perhaps it was this scenario that the political authorities feared. As it turned out, the online campaigns from the camps of Lebanon had also caught the attention of the PA apparatus in Ramallah. In October 2016, the newspaper *Railyoum* published a leaked report from the Palestinian Foreign Ministry, claiming that President Mahmoud Abbas had requested Foreign Minister Riyad al-Maliki to urgently pursue, through diplomatic contacts, a dozen Palestinian networks who stood accused of "targeting the president and the Palestinian leadership."[79] On the list was Mahmud ʿAtaya, the social media star from ʿAyn al-Hilwe. On the same day, P.N. News posted an audio recording of a high-ranking security officer who could be heard revealing that the PA was pursuing the "Facebook activist" ʿAtaya on behalf of the Palestinian President, believing him to be an agent for Hamas.[80] ʿAtaya himself was quick to respond, and set up a live stream on his Facebook site when the news broke out, directing a message back to the Palestinian president in person: "Hi, how are you Abu Mazin? *Habibi*, I've missed you!" he joked. "I'm glad I have your attention," he continued, before his tone grew more serious:

"As Palestinians of the diaspora, we don't elect [our] president, there is no minister for us, no political influence. You don't represent us, and you don't scare anyone," ʿAtaya said while new followers were joining the stream by the second.

> I'm a free man living in the heart of ʿAyn al-Hilwe. If you want to get to me, you'll have to send your private jet to come collect me ... VIP! Take me to the West Bank, take me to your fortress in Ramallah and try me in your court. Whether the judge will be your brother or your cousin, I don't care.[81]

Larger than the Camp

During a conversation in the Shatila camp, a former PFLP leader reminisced about the days of armed struggle in Beirut. "I am not much of a religious man," he said. "But back in the day, when you entered a Popular Committee you felt like you had come to a sacred place, as if you had entered the heart of the revolution."[82] The activists we have met in this chapter, by contrast, will be quick to claim that these very institutions today are a symbol and an extension of the nepotism, clientelism, and autocratic leadership they perceive to be inherent in the dominant Palestinian national elite, particularly within the PLO/PA infrastructure.

The protest groups we have explored in this chapter are still at an embryonic stage and prone to change. There are, nonetheless, a few conclusions we can draw from this preliminary reading. In contrast to their Lebanese contemporaries, who have made it a part of their agenda to topple their own sectarian regime, the Palestinian activists, have not necessarily called for removing or evicting the militia factions from their camps. Some of the young activists are avid supporters of the political groups, and do not differ much from the older generation's ideology in terms of national liberation through armed struggle. What they predominantly are demanding is participation and a thorough reform of the existing systems. Regardless of political orientation, they tend to agree that the never-ending scramble for positions of influence, the institutionalization of corruption, and endemic political splits are among the factors that have rendered the national movement unable to stand up against Israel, or speak for the Palestinian refugees for that matter. Ultimately, their campaigns are not only about improving the administration of Palestinian communities in exile, as we have seen, these actors remain acutely attuned to the plight of youth in the Palestinian Territories, and view themselves as a part of a larger revolt against the gerontocratic tendencies and anti-democratic forces in the homeland. In this way, the struggle over a few small neighborhoods in a refugee camp in South Lebanon becomes events of great symbolic ramifications, that, evidently, even the PA apparatus in Ramallah has found difficult to ignore.

The Palestinian activists in Lebanon have not only struck a nerve among their leaderships, they are also challenging scholars to reconsider a number of axioms concerning the study of political life in exile. As I have tried to illustrate throughout this book, the refugee camps in Lebanon do not constitute "islands" or "spaces of exception," where the everyday order of life is suspended and put on hold, but are intrinsically tied to broader political currents in the Palestinian world and in the Arab street. As follows, researchers interested in Palestinian youth activism are well advised to take the diaspora into account.

8

Conclusion

In May 2017, a friend found himself in a quandary. After the clashes that had torn through the Tiri neighborhood of ʿAyn al-Hilwe a month earlier, he was debating whether or not to leave the camp behind and relocate to a nearby Palestinian gathering in Sidon called Mashariʿ al-Hibba. As a teacher living and working in ʿAyn al-Hilwe, he was used to the turbulent state of the camp, but because he recently had become a father, he was reconsidering the family's future there. The way he saw it, the Hibba neighborhood was calm and secure; there were no warring factions. It was a part of Lebanon. However, the camp offered protection in other ways. In ʿAyn al-Hilwe, he would have social networks to rely on in times of crises. Moreover, there were health services provided by UNRWA, and he had a lucrative deal with his local electricity provider. Most importantly, he owned his own house, something he as a Palestinian would be prevented from doing in Sidon proper. In the camp, he lived among his neighbors of the Safsaf district, the "same" village that his family had fled from following the massacre that the Israel Defense Forces (IDF) had committed in 1948 during *Operation Hiram.* Although the original Safsaf in Galilee no longer existed, it continued to live on in ʿAyn al-Hilwe. Abandoning it seemed tantamount to impossible, he said.

My friend's hesitance to leave the refugee camp the media has dubbed an "Island of insecurity" would perhaps be lost on those who have not visited the place in person, or are unaware of how important of a symbol it is among Palestinians. Back in the camps of Beirut, friends and interlocutors would speak of ʿAyn al-Hilwe with a sense of awe when inquiring about my field visits. On occasion, some would mimic aiming rifles and jokingly ask if I had been recruited by one of the armed groups yet. For their part, faction leaders and Palestinian politicians based at their headquarters in the Lebanese capital would describe the place as the last bastion of Palestinian autonomy and self-determination outside of the homeland. At the same time, it was understood that they could not set a foot there unless accompanied by a squadron of armed bodyguards. ʿAyn al-Hilwe was a paradigm in and of itself, needing no further explanation. Everyday life in the Capital of the Diaspora, as well as the discourse about it, was surrounded by a set of paradoxical dichotomies such as deprivation but autonomy, instability but security, rightlessness but agency, marginality but centrality, legal repression but the freedom to organize and speak one's mind.

Recent scholarly research on Palestinian camps has tended to dwell on notions such as deprivation, rightlessness, or instability, while the other aspects have so often been left out of the equation. In this book, I have attempted to move beyond the typical conceptualizations of the camp space and hopefully offer a more complete picture of present-day Palestinian politics in Lebanon, while I have strived to understand why a refugee camp existing in the margins of the state seemingly has retained importance for so many regional forces, how an impoverished urban slum hardly exceeding one square kilometer hosting some of the most "unwanted" people in the country finds itself the most contested space in the post-war republic, and why the same place has seen a gradual return of the Palestinian political groups in an era where it has been assumed that the Palestinian national movement has played out its purpose in the countries of exile.

The Centrality of the Margins

The signing of the Oslo accords in 1993, which allowed the old guard within the PLO to return to the Palestinian Territories and lay the groundwork for the Palestinian National Authority (PA), was supposed to mark the end of an era for the Palestinian national movement's existence in exile. At least in its former iteration as a collection of revolutionary factions and guerilla leaders poised for armed struggle in the Arab "confrontation states." For some, however, the revolution was not over.

The sheer density of faction offices, paramilitary forces, and guerilla groups found within a place like ʿAyn al-Hilwe reflects the existence of a PLO that did not put down its weapons, as if the fall of the "Fakhani Republic" in 1982 never took place, nor the signing of the Declaration of Principles on the White House lawn more than a decade later. It might perhaps be tempting to say that the camp, on the surface, appears like a cemetery of past revolutions, nationalist or Islamist, where guerilla commanders fronting increasingly obscure political factions have continued to mobilize for wars that in reality were lost years ago. Others will claim that these actors are merely a gang of crooks, scavenging for resources under the guise of national liberation. In this book, I have argued that these exiles play a far larger role in Palestinian politics than what has been accounted for in the literature. They take part in broader, ongoing conflicts over representation, resources, and self-determination that continue to shape the national movement while the question of Palestinian statehood hangs in the balance.

Despite the plentiful arsenals of weapons (within or outside of the camps), the national movement's post-Oslo legacy in Lebanon has to little degree revolved around reinitiating armed struggle against Israel. Rather, it has revolved around meticulous *alliance-building*, in which Lebanon and its refugee camps offer greater freedom to organize and make new connections than what has been the case with the other Arab countries that host substantial Palestinian refugee populations, including Syria, Jordan, and the Occupied Palestinian Territories. Initially, in the early 1990s, this particularly pertained to the actors found along the anti-Oslo rejectionist axis, who fiercely rejected the establishment of a Palestinian quasi-state under Israeli domination, and did everything in their power to latch on to resourceful allies with a shared interest in challenging Israel militarily and thwarting the peace process. In exile, members of Hamas and Palestinian Islamic Jihad were able to acquire funding, support, and military know-how after coming into contact with the Syrian government and the

Iranian-backed Hizballah, which significantly enabled them to strengthen their organizations in the homeland (Chapter 4). Alliance-building was also important for the vast majority of exiles who had no chance of returning, but who continued to challenge the Palestinian leadership from afar. In Lebanon, some of the stiffest resistance to the peace process came from actors within the framework of PA/PLO leader Yasser Arafat's own Fatah movement, who went on to align themselves with the anti-Oslo opposition, take control of the refugee camps, and train militia groups with Syrian and Iranian funding. Operating with measures of territorial autonomy within the camps, these dissidents were able to recruit supporters, connect to a wide array of sympathizers, while they did their utmost to create confusion as to who was in charge of Fatah, and thus potentially undermine its leadership as a credible partner in peace talks with Israel (Chapter 3).

In the end, this was more than the new homeland leadership could bear. Near the end of the millennium, when the long-awaited final-status talks with Israel appeared to be imminent, and the fate of the refugees and Palestinian statehood were to be settled, Arafat initiated a campaign to reclaim the camps of Lebanon by resurrecting Fatah's militia branches, and reviving the PLO as a political framework. As before, he did not attempt to crack down on rivals by using force; he sought to win them over by reenlisting them in his ranks, and the new security branches emerged as his main vehicle for patronage. These measures were more than any simple strategy of clientelism. Redirecting state funds to build personalized (militia) bureaucracies and governance structures to either sideline or reel in political competitors was a well-traveled path for Arafat and the crux of his neopatrimonial rule. As a result, the Palestinian camps of Lebanon became umbilically tied to the PA leadership's state-building ambitions in the Palestinian Territories, and deeply enmeshed into its internal power struggles over hegemony and representation. In the process, ʿAyn al-Hilwe and other refugee camps in Lebanon became cluttered with new militia battalions led by guerilla commanders only partially loyal to their superiors in the Territories, but who played an important role in terms of assuring the PLO's comeback through conferring with a host of other regional and local forces having grown wary of Arafat's expansion. As we have seen, the events coincided with Hamas' efforts to establish a robust network of factional and social institutions in Lebanon (and Syria), where the movement sought to garner the support of Islamist networks and pro-Syrian groups as a means to counter the PLO and Fatah's influence. With funds coming in from an array of different actors, some camp commanders asserted themselves as vital intermediaries between all sides, whether these were jostling for a position at the peace negotiation table or hoping for the peace talks to crumble all together.

Like Arafat, Mahmoud Abbas has continued to treat the camps of Lebanon as auxiliary Palestinian states in exile; however, his rationale for retaining a significant political and military presence in these spaces differs from that of his predecessor. He does not appear to think that the camps and their arms play a "political role," or that imposing his control of them is important in terms of making headway in negotiations regarding the "refugee question." After all, this is an issue that the Palestinians and the Israelis have not seriously attempted to discuss since the failed Camp David Summit and Taba Talks of 2000 and 2001. For Abbas, having a strong presence in the camps has chiefly been a matter of managing power balances within the Fatah movement. More precisely, this has meant maintaining robust channels of funding and political influence as to discourage fractious elements within the faction framework from breaking away, siding with oppositional forces and rival Palestinian leaders, or otherwise hamper his diplomatic ties with an important ally such as Lebanon.

On this note, there appear to be interesting parallels to explore between the processes we have witnessed take place in Lebanon, and the political landscape to emerge in the Palestinian Territories following the Second Intifada. In the late 2000s, substantial funds came into the West Bank from the United States, the EU, and Arab parties to rebuild the post-Second Intifada security sector, and the PA was rewarded significantly for committing to the main pillar of the Oslo accords, namely, maintaining security coordination with the IDF. Unofficially, keeping law and order also entailed pursuing and arresting affiliates of Hamas and other undesired factions regarded by the West and Israel as terrorists, and by Abbas as political rivals. As a token of trust, a few hundred former Fatah-affiliated militants from the al-Aqsa Martyr's Brigades (AMB) were released from Israeli prisons on amnesty deals, and were elusively integrated into informal Fatah militias within various townships and refugee camps to keep rival armed groups from exploiting the prevailing security vacuum.[1] As we have seen up-close in this book, Abbas made good use of the incoming donor money to simultaneously appease troublesome Fatah commanders in Lebanon by integrating them into the broader structure of his new Palestinian National Security Forces (PNSF), mirroring his efforts in the homeland.

In neither case have these actors remained particularly loyal to the PA and its leader. In October and November 2020, the PNSF conducted a series of violent raids against militants affiliated with the deposed UAE-based Fatah leader Muhammad Dahlan in the al-Amʿari and Balata camps in the West Bank. Although the Palestinian Constitutional Court decided to revoke the parliamentary immunity of Dahlan in 2017, presumably in an attempt to put an end to his ambitions for the presidency of the PA, he remains a strong card in the refugee camps. He is far from the only Palestinian leader to view these spaces to be important in terms of controlling, curtailing, or forging alliances with the (militant) grassroots of the Fatah faction. In a camp like Balata, which is the largest in the West Bank, Dahlan's allies are locked in conflict with Fatah forces close to head of the PNSF, Nidal Abu Dukhan, on the one hand, and head of the General Intelligence Service, Majid Faraj, on the other. All of the above are said to have their eyes on the presidency of the PA. As is the case with ʿAyn al-Hilwe, these power plays have created a dynamic in which local camp-based militants—some of them with a prominent past in the AMB, others with a past in criminal networks—assert themselves as crucial intermediaries between all parties eager to dominate the Fatah faction. Curiously, in the West Bank, Palestinian camp youth fed up with the PNSF's frequent security raids, which are coordinated with the IDF, have shown a tendency to idolize these militants as symbols of resistance—not necessarily against Israel, but against the PA and what remains of the Oslo accords.[2]

With illegal Jewish settlements growing exponentially every year, and with Israel's colonization of Palestinian lands persisting whether or not the government might feel compelled to officially "annex" the West Bank, the PLO/PA's hopes of providing its people with any semblance of statehood grow dimmer by the day. Western leaders have yet to acknowledge that their model for peace—that is, complete Palestinian obedience and security coordination in return for foreign aid and economic investments—cannot offer the weaker party any hopes for self-determination, without addressing Israel's fundamental grip on borders, movement, and resources. Instead of a state, the PA has created a robust, donor-sponsored security apparatus as a placeholder for the Israeli occupation, which in contrast to its other governing institutions seems to work with a ruthless efficiency. Indeed, robust and repressive security forces or intelligence institutions are a prevalent feature among neopatrimonial administrations, despite the otherwise seemingly faltering, inefficient, or inaccessible nature of their rule. The PA's security forces have emerged as the most "efficient, visible, and functional arm of Palestinian governance," Hussein Agha and Ahmad Samih Khalidi wrote in 2017, and there might therefore be a strong temptation for these "forces to fill the vacuum of a frail national leadership," the two authors warned.[3] This is something of which the leader of the PA is acutely aware. As a former advisor of Mahmoud Abbas claimed during a meeting in Nablus, staking one's claim to the security branches is necessary for any leader eager to credibly declare themselves the future head of the PA. This means controlling "every township, every village, and every refugee camp," he shared.[4] Especially because the United States and Israel, he went on, are promoting a Bantustan version of Palestine where there soon will not be any self-rule areas left to talk about. Perhaps, he chuckled, there might come a time when every district of the West Bank and the Gaza strip, will find itself negotiating its "separate peace deal with The Occupation."[5] In this book, we have seen how the struggle to maintain control of Palestinian security forces stretches across national borders. Sending his envoys to Lebanon on near annual basis to rearrange or bolster the ranks of the multiplicity of PNSF battalions in ʿAyn al-Hilwe is a price Abbas is willing to pay in order to keep the house of Fatah together. While he has marginalized the refugees politically, these dynamics have created pathways for fringe actors to retain degrees of political influence that far exceed their official role. It would be impossible to begin to understand the chaotic state of Lebanon's most important Palestinian camp, if not in light of these decade-long frictions within the PA and its leading Fatah movement, which will likely only intensify as the succession race to replace Abbas gains momentum. Ultimately, the events described in this book are indicative of a broader trend where the periphery of the national movement—politically, ideologically, and geographically speaking—has since the early 2000s slowly and steadily moved closer to the center of decision-making. To the extent that the Palestinian camps illustrate a "new centrality of the margins,"[6] to reiterate the claim made by anthropologist Michel Agier from an earlier chapter, they do so also in a political sense.

How long will the PA remain? Amidst substantial U.S. aid cuts, Mahmoud Abbas announced in June 2020 that he would no longer accept taxes collected by Israel that account for more than 60 percent of the authority's budget.[7] The measures came as a response to Israeli Prime Minister Benjamin Netanyahu's ambitions of annexing substantial parts of the West Bank, causing painful salary cuts for tens of thousands of civil servants. Meanwhile, the gap continues to grow between a small national elite, who continues to accumulate substantial personal wealth due to their positions in the

PA, and the Palestinian populations, who accuse Abbas and his unwavering support for the dying two-state solution for being out of touch with reality.[8] The dissatisfaction in part also extends to the Hamas leadership and its governance of the Gaza Strip, which has also been marred by charges of corruption, incompetence, political arrests, with the additional burden of operating under a harshly imposed Israeli-Egyptian blockade.[9] As it stands, the Islamist movement does not present much of an alternative to Fatah. Similar to its arch-rival, it has been left stranded with no other way forward than relying on the support provided by its respective foreign backers, hoping for the international and regional climate to change in its favor.

As we have seen in this book, existential crises tend to bring the political leaderships closer (Chapter 6). Following meetings held in Beirut and Ramallah, a collection of Palestinian secretaries-general announced in September 2020 the formation of a United Leadership of Popular Resistance, aiming to develop a comprehensive strategy for the struggle against the challenges facing Palestine today.[10] Most notably, these talks and others appeared to have paved the way for a preliminary agreement made between Hamas and Fatah to hold national elections, which would be the first time since 2006.[11] While some express with measures of relief that such a process would be a necessary prelude to reform Palestinian politics, there is no doubt that there are many obstacles on the road there. The parties would have to overcome decade-long, fundamental disagreements pertaining to questions relating to the feasibility of coordinating security measures with Israel, the viability of co-managing a Palestinian Authority under occupation or, alternatively, shutting it down, and thus removing the largest employer in the Palestinian Territories. If Hamas came to rule the West Bank, the movement would likely face the challenge of revitalizing a tattered Palestinian economy while being countered by harsh international sanctions, something that would lead to substantial domestic tensions. Most importantly, without the presence of a credible third party to guarantee a fair electoral process, there is little to prevent Israel from interfering, annulling the elections, or clamping down on the victor. Whatever the outcome, many Palestinians share a justified fear that the Western world powers, and most prominently the United States, would only accept a Palestinian leader completely servile to Israel. In the time to come, Fatah, Hamas, and the Palestinian populations at large will have to consider to what extent settling for governing separate enclaves with limited territorial control is a viable way forward for the national movement. In this light, the view from ʿAyn al-Hilwe—far from constituting an anomaly or exception to the rule—paints a worryingly accurate picture of where the Palestinian national movement finds itself: stuck in limbo as a collection of guerilla groups without a war to fight and governing bodies without a state to govern, where every leader governs their own neighborhood.

A Mirror Image of Lebanon

The conflicts that ʿAyn al-Hilwe has lived through in the post-Oslo era cannot solely be reduced to a Palestinian problem. In the Capital of the Diaspora, internal strife is exacerbated by the domestic conflicts of a dysfunctional Lebanese state, which after decades of overlapping political deadlocks and endemic splits remains so weak that it is unable to reclaim its own territories. Sources within Lebanon's security agencies reveal that there, in principle, is little in the way of continuing the process that began at Nahr al-Barid in 2007, and place the remaining camps under the rule of the military. These stakeholders do not expect that major Palestinian factions like Fatah or Hamas would resist any such measure, although they also acknowledge that these actors do not necessarily fully control a camp like ʿAyn al-Hilwe. Moreover, the same sources concede that an army takeover would be complicated due to the lack of consensus among the Lebanese governing parties, none of whom are particularly eager to put themselves in a situation where they inadvertently would have to assume the responsibility of or provide for 200,000 Palestinian refugees. Presently, Lebanon's most vocal supporters of the Palestinian national cause, such as the Future Movement, Hizballah, Amal, and the Progressive Socialist Party, do not stand much to gain from rallying for placing the camps under Lebanese control. After all, who would want to be seen committing a cardinal sin like promoting *tawin* (resettlement), especially at a time when other Arab nations are coming under criticism for normalizing their relations with Israel.

Meanwhile, the Lebanese public remains infatuated with its Palestinian "zones of unlaw." The country's media continues to portray the refugee camps as a violent and chaotic *other*, and as an antithesis to everything that is good and sound about Lebanon. The Palestinian refugees must be fenced in, secured, and curtailed, as to make sure their factions and political strife don't jeopardize the stability of the host nation. What the media neglects is that the often chaotic state of a place like ʿAyn al-Hilwe is very similar to the political order of its host state. In all actuality, the Lebanese political class treats the Palestinian camps much like it does its own municipalities—as tools for extracting public resources, where foreign donors are expected to chip in and subsidize the systematic brokenness.[12] Should we consider the notion that the Palestinian camps, as some researchers have argued, are "spaces of exception," where chaos ensues because all law and order is suspended by a powerful sovereign, we cannot reasonably do so without acknowledging that Lebanon in its entirety lives in a "state of exception." This is due to the destructive power plays of a discordant alliance of political leaders who for decades have built their political careers on rendering the central state dysfunctional, so that they can take its place, and gain leverage by weaving constituents into their networks of patronage.

Lebanon's ruling class insists that it must stay out of the Palestinian camps and dictates that these are separate spheres. Nonetheless, as we have seen throughout this book, the same actors have become deeply entrenched in the political economy of the camps, where they extract resources, build alliances, and partner up with Palestinian militia groups to act as their proxies and support their campaigns to dominate local politics in urban Lebanon. In this way, the Palestinian camps have also become an integral part in *Lebanon's* search for a state. Within these spaces, the fault lines of a region in crisis are absorbed and reconstructed according to a uniquely local logic. It is where outlaws and petty criminals cross paths with seasoned jihadi militants, and where the paperless, hopeless, and persecuted are trapped in the quarrels of feuding elites, it is where the militia economy booms while its residents live in abject poverty. The struggle for the control over ʿAyn al-Hilwe and its urban Lebanese surroundings takes on a symbolic dimension that goes far beyond the immediate strategic gains of ruling impoverished urban slum landscapes. Essentially, these spaces find themselves a scene of the most central struggles of the Arab world, where concepts such as autonomy, self-determination, and sovereignty—features which both the Palestinian and Lebanese peoples lack in different ways—are negotiated, contested, and rearranged by actors who build fiefdoms instead of states. In the meeting with its Palestinian other, Lebanon finds a mirror image of its own turbulent political history. "You see, the politicians need the camps," an interlocutor in Sidon noted during a conversation. "ʿAyn al-Hilwe is like a magician's hat," he lamented sardonically. "You can pull anything you want out of it. If you want stateless refugees for cheap labor, you will find them. If you want terrorism (*irhab*,) you can find that too."[13]

The Troublesome Intermediary

Sometimes, however, the "magician's hat" simply refuses to comply. In early 2018, the *New York Times* published a story claiming that Saudi Arabia—at a time when Lebanon's prime minister, Saad al-Hariri, appeared to find himself in the captivity of crown prince Mohammed bin Salman in Riyadh—had tasked a "Lebanese politician" with relaying an unexpected proposal to "splinter jihadists" in ʿAyn al-Hilwe.[14] Allegedly, the proposal was to "help foment a 'Sunni resistance' against Hezbollah." But, a local source was quoted saying, even the most hotheaded jihadists refused.[15] If true, the scenario seems to be yet another example of a point that I've attempted to illustrate in this book; that we would be at fault if we assumed that the Palestinian camps have become mere laboratories for governments and regional forces to play out their conflicts. Coming back to the question I posed in the opening pages of this study, of *who rules the camp*, I have argued in favor of acknowledging the agency of the intermediaries in these exchanges of power. By this, I mean the middle-rank faction officials, the gray bureaucrats, and the informal militia commanders, who have clung on to relevance—not by asserting themselves as willing subordinates of their patrons—but through decades of strategic insubordination and non-compliance. This not only goes for the renegade Fatah officials that the PA simply has been unable to fire from its payrolls but also extends to the camp's veteran militant Islamists, who, despite being marginal in size and popular support, have made themselves indispensable in any decision-process regarding security provision in Lebanon's most significant non-state space. Because of their knack of building alliances with a host of incongruous actors, by placing themselves at the center of every process and in the middle of every road, these groups have expertly honed the craft of exploiting any potential patron's anxiety of losing face and being cut of out the loop, be it Hizballah or the Future Movement, Fatah, or Hamas. Rather than "fighting for the patron's ear," these actors have made careers out of having patrons instead fight for *their* loyalty, and they have gone on to use funds coming in from multiple and often opposing fronts, to carve out their own pockets of influence, and build their own micro-constituencies. As alluded to before, this does not necessarily mean that the protagonists of this book are stone-cold cynics or diluted warlords without tangible political projects. They have used these acts of contention as a viable strategy to force their way onto the negotiation table at critical junctures in Palestinian and Lebanese history, with a view to alter the course of politics. Although this book is primarily a work of history and it has not been my primary goal to refine theories regarding the politics of patronage, I hope these observations could be valuable for other scholars eager to dig into the subject matter from a comparative angle. The findings of this book seem to suggest that invisible, yet difficult cogs in the neopatrimonial machine are able to accumulate political strength by challenging their superiors in fundamental ways, and this is something to keep in mind as both Lebanon and the Palestinian Territories appear to be in the foothills of regime change.

A Future Suspended, Glimmers of Hope

During an interview in Beirut, a Fatah leader scoffed at me when I told him that I was planning to write a book about Lebanon's most important Palestinian camp. "In ʿAyn al-Hilwe, there is a new reality every day," he said. "By the time you write down these words, it will have changed again."[16] Naturally, he was right. Although the fundamental underlying factors and dynamics that drive tensions within the camp are, unfortunately, not likely to change in the foreseeable future, the roster of actors to take part in them is ever-revolving.

Since I concluded my fieldwork, a number of smaller and larger events involving actors from this book have transpired, which might be worth mentioning.

In November 2018, tensions ran high in the al-Miyye wo-Miyye camp, when a longstanding conflict between local Fatah cadres and the leader of the Hizballah-linked Ansar Allah movement, Jamal Sulayman, erupted into violent clashes. Eventually, Sulayman escaped the camp along with a small group of supporters and family, who were able to resettle in Damascus.[17] Following the events, his next in command, Maher ʿUwayd, took charge of the Ansar Allah movement, and looks to have been able to work out an arrangement with Fatah, as to remain present in the Sidon camps.

Islamist agitator Usama al-Shihabi lost much of his momentum after his reconciliation with Fatah in 2016 (Chapter 6), and his support base in ʿAyn al-Hilwe dwindled significantly as the jihadi-funding coming in from Syria near dried up the year after. In a final stunt to regain relevance, al-Shihabi relayed public appeals to Lebanon's General Security bureau to include him in an evacuation deal with Syria-bound militants who were to be escorted across the border and placed in Idlib—the Syrian uprising's last significant stronghold.[18] His plan failed. Al-Shihabi has since disbanded al-Shabab al-Muslim, claiming, much like his Islamist peers in the camp, that he is now "directing all his attention to Palestine."[19] Although he keeps a low profile, the jihadi networks of ʿAyn al-Hilwe have proven to survive years of dormancy before, and no one knows what role al-Shihabi and his likes will assume the next time the region erupts in war.

Having become abandoned by his closest jihadi allies, the former Jund al-Sham operative Bilal al-ʿArqub's militant career came to a tragic end, when he was killed by members of ʿUsbat al-Ansar and Fatah during a joint raid in the summer of 2019. The killing came in the wake of a familial conflict that had manifested itself across factional lines, and for the first time in years, local sources reported that the camp appeared somewhat calm.

Lebanon, however, has remained anything but. The economy has been in a steady state of collapse since the fall of 2019. At the time, the banks responded to a growing liquidity crisis by restricting withdrawals of US dollars and by closing their doors for weeks, which caused the value of the Lebanese pound to plummet on the black market and people's savings to disappear before their eyes. The events coincided with mass protests erupting across all regions of the country, calling for the downfall of the political class in its entirety.

There should be no doubt that the economic collapse has impacted the country's refugee communities greatly. In the summer of 2020, many street vendors and shop owners in the Palestinian camps lamented that they were forced to close their businesses, due to the inflated prices of imported goods. Moreover, detrimental health conditions and overcrowding have rendered the refugees particularly vulnerable to the Covid-19 pandemic.

Although it is no substitute for political solutions, the need for refugee aid remains as dire as ever. Even after being stricken by one of the largest economic crises in its history, UNRWA's secondary schools in Lebanon, of which there are nine in total, continue to outperform and have higher exam pass rates than Lebanese government schools.[20] After the breakout of the Covid-19 pandemic, three-quarters of Palestinian children are said to be continuing their classes through electronic means, seeing as convening in classrooms is not possible.[21] As a part of its Covid-19 response, UNRWA was, in the fall of 2020, able to turn some of its offices and school buildings within ʿAyn al-Hilwe into shelters for people having tested positive for the Corona virus, while it has worked closely with other NGOs to distribute food packages to self-isolating families. The "irredeemably flawed" agency, to paraphrase a past North-American administration, remains operational. Yet, its perseverance should by no means be taken for granted. The United Nations General Assembly voted, as expected, overwhelmingly to renew UNRWA's mandate for another three years in late 2019, but the donor countries, that shouldered the agency's financial crisis the previous year (Chapter 2), have gradually decreased their emergency funding. In November 2020, UNRWA announced that it had run out of money once again, and was unable to pay its staff of 28,000 their full salaries, with no apparent solution in sight.

Contrary to what has been suggested in some of the scholarly literature, the marginalization and suppression of the refugees by the Lebanese state, and their integration into top-down "humanitarian regimes," have not restrained them warehoused in a state of "bare life," deprived of a voice or unable to organize themselves. In this book, we have seen how the humanitarian response to the Syrian crisis strengthened civil society initiatives within the camps, where youth took a leading role. Following its inception in 2015, the Qalam Rasas magazine has since morphed into a semi-professional audiovisual media provider called Nastopia, which under the slogan "*min kull zaruba qissa*—there is a story in every alleyway" continues to relay unbiased reportages from the lives of young Palestinians in the camps of Lebanon, albeit with a less antagonistic angle than before. Meanwhile, the ʿAsimat al-Shattat collective in ʿAyn al-Hilwe has stayed true to its policy of letting virtually anyone use its online platforms, ranging from merchants, disgruntled activists, to faction authorities, to relay their messages to the public. In this regard, the site has expanded its repertoire by launching, in cooperation with local NGOs, a weekly online talk show called *Fishat Khulq* (Letting off steam), where the host Hala Ibriq engages young Palestinians, typically women, as well as senior community leaders, in discussions about the situation in the refugee camps. Lebanon has also seen new Palestinian voices throw themselves into debates about their standing as rightless refugees in the country. In conjunction with the 2018 parliamentary elections, activist Manal Kortam caused much controversy and managed to garnered significant international attention when she ran a faux electoral campaign for a Palestinian seat in the Lebanese parliament.[22] Moreover, the Palestinian Civil Defense in Lebanon, which was spearheaded by some of the aforementioned youth activists, were for a brief moment hailed as national heroes in the Lebanese media due to their life-saving efforts in the wake of the explosion in Beirut in 2020.[23]

If there is a glimmer of hope in this story about the Palestinian national movement and the camps of Lebanon, it lies in the young refugees who remain adamant to educate themselves, evolve and inspire, and who—regardless of political affiliation or ideology—vehemently reject the narrow and neglectful role the older generation has assigned to them. The Palestinian national leaderships and the host state authorities would be wise to recognize some of the creativity and talent found within the country's non-state spaces.

Selection of On-Record Elite Interviews

Fathi Abu al-ʿAradat,
Leader of the **PLO** and **Fatah** in Lebanon,
The Palestinian embassy in Beirut, December 4, 2015.

Abu Iyad al-Shaʿlan,
Fatah official and leader of the PLO's Popular Committees in Lebanon,
I Mar Elias camp, Beirut, January 10, 2014,
II Mar Elias, Beirut, December 14, 2015.

ʿAbd al-Rahman Abu Salah,
Fatah official and leader of the PLO's Popular Committees in Sidon
ʿAyn al-Hilwe, October 13, 2015.

Munir al-Maqdah,
Fatah military commander
ʿAyn al-Hilwe, September 21, 2015.

Subhi Abu ʿArab,
Fatah military commander and leader of the Palestinian National Security Forces (PNSF) in Lebanon,
ʿAyn al-Hilwe, February 24, 2016.

Khalid al-Shayib,
Fatah military commander, and previous leader of the JPSF in ʿAyn al-Hilwe,
ʿAyn al-Hilwe, February 24, 2016.

Bassam Saʿd
Fatah official and leader of the JPSF in ʿAyn al-Hilwe,
ʿAyn al-Hilwe, May 31, 2017.

Abu Tawfiq,
Fatah official and leader of the JPSF's investigative committee in ʿAyn al-Hilwe,
October 15, 2015.

Abu Jihad al-Fiyad,
Leader of **Fatah** in the al-Beddawi camp,
al-Beddawi, Tripoli, April 22, 2016.

Abu Ali al-Sarsawi,
Fatah communication officer in Shatila,
Shatila camp, May 20, 2017.

Abu al-ʿAbd Mahmud "al-Lino" ʿIssa,
Previously in Charge of the PASC Branch, currently one of the leaders of **Fatah's** Democratic Reform Current in Lebanon.
I By phone, January 11, 2014.
II ʿAyn al-Hilwe, October 13, 2015

Edward Kattoura,
Political analyst and affiliate of **Fatah's** Democratic Reform Current
I Beirut, September 29, 2013,
II Beirut, January 7, 2014,
III Beirut, September 8, 2015,
IV Beirut, December 11, 2015.

ʿAli Hamdan,
Leader of political affairs for the **PFLP** in the Sidon region,
ʿAyn al-Hilwe, October 13, 2015

Muhammad ʿAbdu
PFLP official in ʿAyn al-Hilwe,
ʿAyn al-Hilwe, October 13, 2015

Ziad Hammu,
PFLP official, and leader of the PLO's Popular Committee in the Shatila camp,
Shatila, Beirut, October 21, 2013. (RIP).

Abu Mujahid Mahmud ʿAbbas,
Community leader and former **PFLP** leader in Shatila (1984–2004),
Shatila camp, Beirut, November 24, 2015.

Soheil al-Natour,
Spokesperson for the **DFLP** in Lebanon,
I Mar Elias camp, Beirut, November 20, 2013
II Mar Elias camp, November 23, 2015.

Abu al-Muʿtasim,
Leader of the **DFLP** in ʿAyn al-Hilwe,
ʿAyn al-Hilwe, October 13, 2015

Abu Wisam al-ʿUthman,
Military commander for the **DFLP** in ʿAyn al-Hilwe,
ʿAyn al-Hilwe, May 31, 2017.

Ahmad Mustafa,
DFLP official in Burj al-Barajne,
Burj al-Barajne, Beirut, October 21, 2013

Abu Rabiʿ Hassan Sirhan
Leader of the **Palestinian People's Party (PPP)** in ʿAyn al-Hilwe, and leader of the PLO's Popular Committee in the camp from June 2015 to January 2016,
I ʿAyn al-Hilwe, October 13, 2015,
II ʿAyn al-Hilwe, February 2, 2016.

Kamal al-Hajj
Leader of the **Palestinian Arab Front** in ʿAyn al-Hilwe, and leader of the PLO's Popular Committee in the camp from January 2016 to June 2016.
I ʿAyn al-Hilwe, October 13, 2015,
II ʿAyn al-Hilwe, February 2, 2016.

Ali Barake,
The leader of **Hamas** in Lebanon from 2010 to 2017,
I Beirut, November 28, 2013,
II Beirut, October 26, 2015,
III Beirut, May 29, 2017.

Ra'fat Fahd Morra,
The official spokesperson for **Hamas** in Lebanon, and a published author on Islamism in the Palestinian camps of Lebanon,
Beirut, December 12, 2013.

Abu Ahmad Fadl al-Taha,
Leader of **Hamas** in ʿAyn al-Hilwe from 2001 to 2017, and previous leader of the Palestinian branch of al-Jamaʿa al-Islamiyya in said camp.
ʿAyn al-Hilwe, October 15, 2015

Abu Khalil,
Leader of **Hamas** in the Burj al-Barajne camp,
Burj al-Barajen, Beirut, December 10, 2013

Abu Tafish,
Leader of **Hamas** in the Shatila camp,
Shatila, Beirut, November 14, 2013

Abu Ashraf Muhammad,
Leader of **Palestinian Islamic Jihad** in the Burj al-Barajne camp,
Burj al-Barajne, Beirut, December 16, 2013.

Abu Iyad Ramiz Mustafa,
Leader of the **PFLP-GC** in Lebanon, Mar Elias camp,
October 26, 2015.

Abu Musa Sabir,
Leader of the **PFLP-GC** in the Beirut region, Shatila camp, Beirut, November 10, 2013.

Abu Sulayman ʿAbd al-Hadi
Member of the **PFLP-GC** and leader of the APF's Popular Committee of the Shatila camp,
Shatila, Beirut, November 10, 2013

Hassan Zaydan,
Leader of **Fatah al-Intifada** in Lebanon,
Mar Elias camp, October 26, 2015.

Abu Wasim Ahmad Hazine,
Security leader for **Fatah al-Intifada** in Shatila (RIP).
Shatila camp, Beirut, November 10, 2013.

Abu Bassam ʿAbd al-Maqdah
Leader of **al-Saʿiqa** in South Lebanon, and head of the Alliance of Palestinian Forces in Sidon. ʿAyn al-Hilwe, February 4, 2016.

Muhammad Yasin,
Leader of the **PLF** (Talʿat Yʿaqub wing) in Lebanon,
Mar Elias camp, October 24, 2015.

Jamal Khattab,
Secretary for the **Islamic Forces** and leader of **al-Haraka al-Islamiyya al-Mujahida,**
I ʿAyn al-Hilwe, September 21, 2015
II ʿAyn al-Hilwe, October 13, 2015

Abu Sharif ʿAqal,
Spokesperson for, and second-in-command in ʿ**Usbat al-Ansar,**
I ʿAyn al-Hilwe, September 22, 2015
II ʿAyn al-Hilwe, October 15, 2015

Ibrahim Hurani,
Mid-ranking official of '**Usbat al-Ansar**, and member of the Safsaf neighborhood committee,
'Ayn al-Hilwe, October 15, 2015.

'Ali Aslan,
Leader of Hizb al-Tahrir and secretary general of the Hittin Neighborhood Committeee in 'Ayn al-Hilwe, May 19, 2017.

Usama al-Shihabi,
Founder of **al-Shabab al-Muslim.**
'Ayn al-Hilwe, February 24, 2016.

Jamal Hamad,
Salafi Shaykh and affiliate of **al-Shabab al-Muslim**,
'Ayn al-Hilwe, September 21, 2015.

Abu Khalaf,
Former combatant of the Al-Aqsa Martyr's Brigades,
the Balata camp in the West Bank, September 26, 2019.

Jamal al-Tirawi,
Member of the Palestinian Legislative Council, and former combatant of the Al-Aqsa Martyr's Brigades.
Nablus, the West Bank, September 20, 2019.

Hassan 'Uthman,
Activist and community leader.
Shatila camp, May 26, 2017.

Badi' al-Habit,
Activist and member of **Fatah**,
Burj al-Barajne, May 28, 2017.

Mahmud 'Ataya,
Activist, director of the 'Asimat al-Shattat social media site, member of the Zib Committee in 'Ayn al-Hilwe, April 29, 2016.

Abu al-Hind,
Leader of an activist group called The Palestinian Initiative in 'Ayn al-Hilwe,
'Ayn al-Hilwe, May 31, 2017.

Haytham Mi'amari,
Leader of the 'Abkara Neighborhood Committee in 'Ayn al-Hilwe,
'Ayn al-Hilwe, May 19, 2017.

ʿAdnan al-Rifaʿi,
Leader of the Taytaba Neighborhood Committee and **Hamas** official in ʿAyn al-Hilwe, May 19, 2017.

Walif ʿIssa,
Leader of the Vegetable Market Trade Union in ʿAyn al-Hilwe,
May 31, 2017.

Salam Abu Kharroub,
Former leader for the **PLO**'s Cultural Division in Lebanon,
The Hibba district, Saida, May 11, 2017.

Haytham al-Zuʿaytar,
Palestinian author and journalist for the Lebanese al-Liwa' newspaper,
Beirut, April 4, 2016

Khalil al-ʿAli
Palestinian author and journalist for the online publications Saida Online,
Saida, March 4, 2016.

Mahir Hammud,
Imam of of the al-Quds mosque in Sidon. Saida, December 2, 2015

Bassam Hammud,
MP for the March 14th alliance, the leader of **al-Jamaʿa al-Islamiyya** in Sidon, and in charge of the party's "Palestinian affairs."
Saida, April 9, 2016.

Mohsen Saleh,
Palestinian author and director of the Zaytouna Centre for Studies & Consulting,
Beirut, March 23, 2016.

Armin Köhli,
Program manager for Geneva Call's Near- and Middle East division, By Phone, July 25, 2017.

Group interview with APF factions in the Mar Elias camp,
October 26, 2015.

Group interview with joint Popular Committee of the al-Baddawi camp,
April, 22, 2016

Group interview with members of the Hittin Neighborhood Committee,
ʿAyn al-Hilwe, May 19, 2017.

Group interview members of the National Security Forces in ʿAyn al-Hilwe,
ʿAyn al-Hilwe, February 24, 2016.

Group interview with members of the Joint Palestinian Security Force in ʿAyn al-Hilwe,
ʿAyn al-Hilwe, the JPSF's headquarters, October 15, 2015.

Overview of the Palestinian Factions in Lebanon

The Palestine Liberation Organization (PLO)

Fatah (The Palestinian National Liberation Movement)
The Popular Front for the Liberation of Palestine (PFLP)
The Democratic Front for the Liberation of Palestine (DFLP)
The Palestinian People's Party (PPP)
The Palestinian Democratic Union (Fida')
The Palestinian Liberation Front (PLF, Abu al-ʿAbbas wing)
The Palestinian Popular Struggle Front (PPSF, Samir Ghawshe wing)
The Palestinian Arab Front (PAF)
The Arab Liberation Front (ALF)

The Alliance of Palestinian Forces (APF)

Hamas
Palestinian Islamic Jihad (PIJ)
The Popular Front for the Liberation of Palestine – General Command (PFLP-GC)
Fatah al-Intifada
al-Saʿiqa (Vanguard for the Popular Liberation War – The thunderbolt Forces)
The Palestinian Liberation Front (PLF, Talʿat Yaʿqub wing)
The Palestinian Popular Struggle Front (PPSF, Khalid ʿAbd al-Majid wing)
The Palestinian Revolutionary Communist Party (PRCP)

The Islamic Forces

ʿUsbat al-Ansar al-Islamiyya (The Islamic League of Partisans)
al-Haraka al-Islamiyya al-Mujahida (HIM, The Islamic Combatant Movement)

Non-affiliated

Ansar Allah (God's Partisans)
Fatah – Revolutionary Council

Figure 9.1 Scene from ʿAyn al-Hilwe's Lower Street with the Nur Mosque in the background. (Author's photograph, October 13, 2015)

Figure 9.2 A Hamas official speaks at an event arranged by the Democratic Front for the Liberation of Palestine. (Author's photograph, October 13, 2015)

Figure 9.3 Scene from a junction between the ʿArab al-Zubayd and Safsaf neighborhoods. (Author's photograph, February 24, 2016)

Notes

Chapter 1

1 Ali Dawoud, "Tadrībāt ʿaskariyya li Fatḥ ḥatta awākhir Ḥuzayrān [Fatah military drills until the end of June]," *al-Jumhuriyya*, May 25, 2014.

2 Ibid.

3 Amal Khalil, "A New Security Plan for Ain al-Hilweh," *al-Akhbar*, April 29, 2014.

4 I have not been able to locate any written sources that indicate when the camp's nickname as the Capital of the Diaspora was adopted in local Palestinian jargon. Some of my interlocutors claimed the expression was coined by guerilla fighters belonging to Yasser Arafat's Fatah movement when they sought to fortify their bases in South Lebanon in the mid-1980s. Interestingly, Palestinians from the Yarmouk district in the Syrian capital have also been known to refer to their "camp" as the Capital of the Diaspora. The Palestinians do not constitute a homogenous group, and as others have pointed out, their collective designation as a diaspora is not unproblematic. This is particularly due to the ongoing nature of their displacement, and the potential finite and depoliticized connotations of the term itself—at least how it is used in the English language. When I write "diaspora" in this study, I do so exclusively as a self-ascribed term which I have translated from its Arabic equivalent *Shattat,* which also means dispersal. For a thorough discussion regarding the use of the term "diaspora" in the Palestinian context, see Julie Peteet, "Problematizing a Palestinian Diaspora," *International Journal of Middle East Studies* 39, no. 4 (2007). www.jstor.org/stable/30069491.

5 This number also includes the populations of informal gatherings that by and large are indistinguishable from the camp itself. For more information, see Lebanese Palestinian Dialogue Committee, Central Administration of statistics, and Palestinian Central Bureau of Statistics, "Key Findings of the National Population and Housing Census of Palestinian Camps and Gatherings in Lebanon 2017" (Beirut: The Lebanese Palestinian Dialogue Committee, 2017), http://lpdc.gov.lb/statements/key-findings-of-the-national-population-and-housin/398/en.

6 Julie Peteet, *Landscape of Hope and Despair: Palestinian Refugee Camps* (Pennsylvania: University of Pennsylvania Press, 2005), 3.

7 Ibid.

8 For a thorough investigation of the Lebanese discourse surrounding the concept of tawtin, see Daniel Meier, "Lebanon: The Refugee Issue and the Threat of a Sectarian Confrontation," *Oriente Moderno* 94, no. 2 (2014); Maja Janmyr, "No Country of Asylum: 'Legitimizing' Lebanon's Rejection of the 1951 Refugee Convention," *International Journal of Refugee Law* 29, no. 3 (2017). http://dx.doi.org/10.1093/ijrl/eex026.

9 It is hard to give an accurate estimate of the refugees' numbers after more than seventy years in Lebanon. UNRWA has long claimed that roughly 450,000 Palestinians are registered with the agency, but has never shied away from the fact that this does not necessarily reflect the actual number of refugees residing in the

country. In late 2017, a first-ever consensus of Lebanon's Palestinians was carried out by the Central Administration of Statistics, the Lebanese Palestinian Dialogue Committee, and the Palestinian Central Bureau of Statistics. The survey set the number at 174,422. This number excludes displaced Palestinian refugees from Syria, and Palestinians scattered in the cities living far from the camps or informal gatherings.

10 As the political taboo of tawtin persists, the legal situation of the Palestinians has become progressively worse. In 2001, the Lebanese parliament introduced an amendment of the Right to Real Estate Acquisition for Foreigners (1969) which stated that no non-Lebanese person can acquire "real property rights," including inheritance, except through a special permit issued by the Council of Ministers. The amendment seemed to specifically target Palestinians, as the law now excluded foreigners not holding citizenships of a "recognized state." It should be mentioned that the Lebanese parliament introduced amendments to the refugee's labor rights in 2005 and 2010, in which the latter revoked bans on tens of previously unavailable professions while exempting Palestinians from having to pay for work permits. However, for many, obtaining a work permit remains a possibility only in theory. The Ministry of Labor asks that businesses with Palestinian employees (or other foreigners) must renew their employees' permits annually and provide a statement guaranteeing that no Lebanese national could carry out their work. Many employers tend to skip these formal processes, and resort to informal arrangements. Some Palestinians report that they prefer informal work, because they enjoy limited benefits from the Social Security Fund that they are required to pay a part of their salary to. In 2015, the unemployment rate for Palestinians in Lebanon was 23.2 percent (and 31 percent for women), where roughly half of the workforce were paid on daily basis. Meanwhile, half of the Palestinian refugees from Syria were unemployed. Cf. Norwegian Refugee Council, "Palestinian Refugees' Right to Inherit under the 2001 Amendment Law—Beirut Test Case" (2016), https://www.nrc.no/globalassets/pdf/reports/palestinian-refugees-right-to-inherit-under-the-2001-amendment-law.pdf; Ahmed Moor, "Lebanon's Law on Palestinian Workers Does Not Go Far Enough," *The Guardian*, August 27, 2010; UNRWA, "Protection Brief Palestine Refugees Living in Lebanon" (Beirut: UNRWA, 2017), https://www.unrwa.org/sites/default/files/lebanon_protection_brief_october_2017.pdf.

11 The full text of the Cairo agreement is available through the Institute for Palestine Studies: http://www.palestine-studies.org/sites/default/files/Text_of_the_Cairo_Agreement.pdf (Accessed September 17, 2020).

12 Rosemary Sayigh, *Palestinians: From Peasants to Revolutionaries: A People's History* (London: Zed Press, 1979).

13 Nadia Latif, "Fallahin, Fida'iyyin, Laji'in: Palestinian Camp Refugees as Autochtons," *The Arab Studies Journal* 19, no. 1 (2011). http://www.jstor.org/stable/23265811.

14 Ghada Hashem Talhami, *Palestinian Refugees: Pawns to Political Actors* (New York: Nova Publishers, 2003).

15 Aaron David Miller, *The PLO and the Politics of Survival* (Westport, CT: Praeger, 1983); Cheryl A. Rubenberg, "The Civilian Infrastructure of the Palestine Liberation Organization: An Analysis of the PLO in Lebanon Until June 1982," *Journal of Palestine Studies* 12, no. 3 (1983); Rashid Khalidi, *Under Siege: PLO Decisionmaking during the 1982 War* (New York: Columbia University Press, 1986); Emile F. Sahliyeh, *The PLO after the Lebanon War* (London: Westview Press/Boulder, 1986); Alain Gresh, *The PLO: The Struggle Within: Towards and Independent State*, trans. Maxime

Rodinson, 2nd ed. (London & New Jersey: Zed Books, 1988 [1986]); Rex Brynen, "The Politics of Exile: The Palestinians in Lebanon," *Journal of Refugee Studies* 3, no. 3 (1990). http://dx.doi.org/10.1093/jrs/3.3.204; Rex Brynen, *Sanctuary And Survival: The PLO in Lebanon* (Boulder, CO: Westview Press, 1990); Yezid Sayigh, *Armed Struggle and the Search for State: The Palestinian National Movement, 1949–1993*, 2004 reprint, digitalized ed. (New York: Oxford University Press, 1997).

16 Sayigh, *Armed Struggle and the Search for State*, 676.

17 Farid El Khazen, *The Breakdown of the State in Lebanon, 1967–1976* (Cambridge: Harvard University Press, 2000), 387.

18 Rex Brynen, "The Neopatrimonial Dimension of Palestinian Politics," *Journal of Palestine Studies* 25, no. 1 (1995). http://www.jstor.org/stable/2538102.

19 Max Weber, *Economy and Society: A New Translation*, trans. Keith Tribe (Cambridge, MA: Harvard University Press, 2019), 366.

20 Shmuel N. Eisenstadt, *Traditional Patrimonialism and Modern Neopatrimonialism* (Beverly Hills, CA: Sage Publishing, 1973).

21 Frances Fukuyama, *Political Order and Political Decay: From the Industrial Revolution to the Globalization of Democracy* (London: Profile Books, 2014), 26.

22 Brynen, "The Neopatrimonial Dimension of Palestinian Politics," 1995.

23 Menachem Klein, *Arafat and Abbas: Portraits of Leadership in a State Postponed* (London: Hurst, 2020), 8.

24 Ibid., 24–5.

25 Amal Jamal, *The Palestinian National Movement: Politics of Contention 1967–2005* (Bloomington & Indianapolis: Indiana University Press, 2005), 132.

26 Ibid.

27 Khalil Shikaki, "Palestinians Divided," *Foreign Affairs* 81, no. 1 (2002). http://www.jstor.org/stable/20033005.

28 Hillel Frisch, "Modern Absolutist or Neopatriarchal State Building? Customary Law, Extended Families, and the Palestinian Authority," *International Journal of Middle East Studies* 29, no. 3 (1997). www.jstor.org/stable/164584; Jacob Høigilt, "Fatah from Below: The Clash of Generations in Palestine," *British Journal of Middle Eastern Studies* 43, no. 4 (2016). https://doi.org/10.1080/13530194.2015.1116375.

29 Toufic Haddad, *Palestine Ltd: Neoliberalism and Nationalism in the Occupied Territory*, SOAS Palestine Studies (London: I.B. Tauris, 2016); Philip Leech, *The State of Palestine: A Critical Analysis* (Oxfordshire: Routledge, 2016).

30 Jeroen Gunning, *Hamas in Politics: Democracy, Religion, Violence* (New York: Colombia University Press, 2008); Bjorn Brenner, *Gaza Under Hamas: From Islamic Democracy to Islamist Governance* (London: I.B. Tauris, 2016).

31 Adib Nehme, *The Neopatrimonial State and the Arab Spring* (Beirut: AUB Policy Institute, 2016).

32 Bernard Rougier, *Everyday Jihad: The Rise of Militant Islam among Palestinians in Lebanon*, trans. Pascale Ghazaleh (Cambridge: Harvard University Press, 2007 [2004]), 20.

Chapter 2

1 This observation is based on my experience as a foreigner visiting the camp. Palestinians are rarely asked to identify themselves.

2 Michel Foucault, "Space, Knowledge, Power," in *The Foucault Reader*, ed. P. Rabinow (London: Penguin, 1984), 252.
3 Dag Tuastad, "'State of Exception' or 'State in Exile'? The Fallacy of Appropriating Agamben on Palestinian Refugee Camps," *Third World Quarterly* (2016). http://dx.doi.org/10.1080/01436597.2016.1256765.
4 Hannah Arendt, *Totalitarianism: Part Three of the Origins of Totalitarianism* (New York: Harcourt Brace Jovanovich, 1985), 145.
5 Giorgio Agamben, *State of Exception*, trans. Kevin Attell (Chicago: University of Chicago Press, 2005), 2, 87.
6 Giorgio Agamben, *Homo Sacer: Sovereign Power and Bare Life*, trans. Daniel Heller-Roazen (California: Stanford University Press, 1998), 196.
7 Ibid., 8.
8 Sari Hanafi, "Palestinian Refugee Camps in Lebanon as a Space of Exception," *REVUE Asylon(s)* 5 (2008). http://www.reseau-terra.eu/article798.html.
9 Sari Hanafi and Taylor Long, "Governance, Governmentalities, and the State of Exception in the Palestinian Refugee Camps of Lebanon," *Journal of Refugee Studies* 23, no. 2 (2010). http://dx.doi.org/10.1093/jrs/feq014.
10 Are Knudsen, "Camp, Ghetto, Zinco, Slum: Lebanon's Transitional Zones of Emplacement," *Humanity: An International Journal of Human Rights, Humanitarianism, and Development* 7, no. 3, Winter (2016): 443.
11 Adam Ramadan, "Spatialising the Refugee Camp," *Transactions of the Institute of British Geographers* 38, no. 1 (2012): 74–6.
12 Bülent Diken and Carsten B. Laustsen, *The Culture of Exception: Sociology Facing the Camp* (Abingdon, Oxfordshire: Routledge, 2005), 192.
13 Dahna Abourahme, "Kingdom of Women: Ein el Hilweh [Mamlakat al-nisā': ʿAyn al-Ḥilwe]" (Beirut: Protraction Film, 2010)
14 Rosemary Sayigh, *Too Many Enemies: The Palestinian Experience in Lebanon*, 2nd ed. (Beirut: al-Mashriq, 2015 [1994]), 68.
15 Ibid.
16 This in contrast to the Palestinian camps found in Beirut for instance, which host far greater numbers of non-Palestinian populations, and where extended families and kinship groups, according to local residents, are more evenly distributed between the various neighborhoods.
17 Julie Peteet, *Landscape of Hope and Despair: Palestinian Refugee Camps*, 101.
18 The Jewish Orchard is said to have been a piece of land owned by a Lebanese Jewish family. Most of Lebanon's Jewish population was sadly forced to relocate to Israel or other places following the 1967 six-day war due to the mounting pressure for them to leave.
19 Knudsen, "Camp, Ghetto, Zinco, Slum," 444.
20 Michel Agier, "Afterword: What Contemporary Camps Tell Us about the World to Come," *Humanity: An International Journal of Human Rights, Humanitarianism, and Development* 7, no. 3 (2016): 465.
21 Fawwaz Traboulsi, *A History of Modern Lebanon*, 2nd ed. (Beirut: Pluto Press, 2012 [2007]), 114.
22 Ismael Sheikh Hassan and Lyne Jabri, "The Urban-history of a Camp & the Camp-history of a City: The Case of Sidon, Ein El Hilweh and MiyoMiye—Part 1" (Unpublished manuscript last modified July 24, 2017).
23 Ibid., 14–15.
24 Ibid.

25 Ibid.
26 Traboulsi, *A History of Modern Lebanon*, 113.
27 Marwan Ghandour, "Who Is 'Ain al-Hilweh?," *Jadaliyya*, September 30, 2013, https://www.jadaliyya.com/Details/29579
28 This expressing is borrowed from a reported issued by the United Nations-Habitat and United Nations Development Programme, cf. "Investigating Grey Areas: Access to Basic Urban Services in the Adjacent Areas of Palestinian Refugee Camps in Lebanon" (Beirut: UN Habitat / UN Development Programme, 2010), https://unhabitat.org/investigating-grey-areas-access-to-basic-urban-services-in-the-adjacent-areas-of-palestinian-refugee-camps-in-lebanon/.
29 Leading up to Lebanon's untangling from the French mandate power, Sunni Muslim notables gradually abandoned their ambitions of seeking a union with Syria and threw their weight behind the Christian-led state-building project, based on promises that they would be made partners in governing the new state. The national pact was an informal supplement to the 1926 constitution, which sought to amend the power-sharing formula by implying better representation for the Muslims.
30 Jon Nordenson, Magnus Dølerud, and Erling Lorentzen Sogge, "A New Course for Lebanon? (in Norwegian)," *Babylon—Nordic Journal for Middle East Studies*, no. 2 (2019). https://journals.uio.no/babylon/article/view/7773.
31 Joanne Randa Nucho, *Everyday Sectarianism in Urban Lebanon: Infrastructures, Public Services, and Power* (New Jersey: Princeton University Press, 2016), 6.
32 Ibid.
33 Nicholas Blanford, *Warriors of God: Inside Hezbollah's Thirty-Years Struggle against Israel* (New York: Random House Publishing, 2011), xiv.
34 Hannes Baumann, *Citizen Hariri: Lebanon's Neoliberal Reconstruction* (London: Hurst & Company, 2016).
35 Are Knudsen, "Sheikhs and the City," *Conflict and Society* 6, no. 1 (2020). https://www.berghahnjournals.com/view/journals/conflict-and-society/6/1/arcs060103.xml.
36 Khalid Al-Gharbi, "B'us al-Taʿmīr fī Saydā yas'al: al-mustaqbal kayfa? [The misery of Taʿmir begs the question: The future, how?]," al-Modon, February 15, 2018.
37 Cited in Valerie Nader Kassem, "Upgrading Informal Settlements: The Case of Taamir," MA diss. (American University of Beirut, 2018), 58.
38 Author's interview with the leader of a Sidon-based NGO, August 24, 2020.
39 "Lubnān sayuṭālib UNRWA bi dafaʿ 163 milyūn dūlār fī mu'atamar al-daʿm fī-l-Rūm [Lebanon will ask UNRWA to pay 163 million dollars at the donor conference in Rome]," *Wikalat al-Quds lil-anba'*, March 13, 2018.
40 Janoubia, "Fī mukhayyam ʿAyn al-Ḥilwe: qīmat ishtirāk al-kahrabā' 20% aghlā min Ṣaydā [In the ʿAyn al-Hilwe camp: the generator electricity is 20% more expensive than in Sidon]," *Janoubia*, July 3, 2019.
41 Author's interview with one of four of the most substantial generator owners in ʿAyn al-Hilwe, May 31, 2017.
42 Anne E. Irfan, "Educating Palestinian Refugees: The Origins of UNRWA's Unique Schooling System," *Journal of Refugee Studies* (2019): 12. https://doi.org/10.1093/jrs/fez051.
43 Terry Rempel, "From Beneficiary to Stakeholder: An Overview of UNRWA's Approach to Refugee Participation," in *UNRWA and Palestinian Refugees: From Relief and Works to Human Development*, ed. Leila Hilal, Sari Hanafi, and Lex Takkenberg (Oxfordshire: Routledge, 2014).

44 United Nations General Assembly, "Report of the Working Group on the Financing of the United Nations Relief and Works Agency for Palestine Refugees in the Near East" (2019), https://undocs.org/pdf?symbol=en/A/74/337.
45 In an internal communique from 1969, UNRWA defines the camp as "a concentration of refugees and displaced persons which has been recognized by UNRWA as an official camp, which is operated by the Agency, and has in particular a camp leader and environmental sanitation services provided by the Agency." Cited in Kjersti Berg, "From Chaos to Order and Back: The Construction of UNRWA Shelters and Camps, 1950–1970," in *UNRWA and Palestinian Refugees: From Relief and Works to Human Development*, ed. Leila Hilal, Sari Hanafi, and Lex Takkenberg (London: Routledge, 2014), 112.
46 The categories eligible and refugee, however, were not necessarily one and the same. For more on these questions, see Ilana Feldman, "The Challenge of Categories: UNRWA and the Definition of a 'Palestine Refugee,'" *Journal of Refugee Studies* 25, no. 3 (2012): 392–3. https://doi.org/10.1093/jrs/fes004.
47 Ilana Feldman, "Mercy Trains and Ration Rolls: Between Government And Humanitarianism In Gaza (1948–67)," in *Interpreting Welfare and Relief in the Middle East*, ed. Nefissa Naguib and Inger Marie Okkenhaug (Boston: Brill, 2008), 175.
48 Michael Barnett, *Empire of Humanity: A History of Humanitarianism* (Ithaca: Cornell University Press, 2013).
49 Riccardo Bocco, "UNRWA and the Palestinian Refugees: A History within History," *Refugee Survey Quarterly* 28, no. 2–3 (2009): 234. https://doi.org/10.1093/rsq/hdq001.
50 Ibid., 48–9, 61.
51 Berg, "From Chaos to Order and Back," 122.
52 Ibid.
53 Kjersti Berg, "Temporary and Eternal: UNRWA and the Palestinian Refugee Question (in Norwegian)," *Babylon—Nordic Journal for Middle East Studies*, no. 1 (2020). https://jourbergnals.uio.no/babylon/article/view/8148.
54 See for example the following report issued by the Palestinian Authority: State of Palestine, "The Implementation of UNGA Resolution 194/International Support to UNRWA Is a Must" (Negotiation Affairs Department, 2018), https://www.nad.ps/en/publication-resources/special-reports/implementation-unga-resolution-194-international-support-unrwa.
55 Colum Lynch and Gramer Robbie, "Trump and Allies Seek End to Refugee Status for Millions of Palestinians," *Foreign Policy*, August 3, 2018.
56 Aljazeera, "Donors to Increase UNRWA Support and Funding Despite US Cuts," *Aljazeera*, September 2, 2018.
57 Mohammed Zaatari, "Ain al-Hilweh Eases toward Normalcy, Schools Open," *Daily Star*, September 25, 2018.
58 Ibid.
59 The two camps of Sidon, for example, are spread out between the three municipalities of Sidon, Darb al-Sim, and al-Miyye wo-Miyye.
60 Author's interview with a former UNRWA field officer from the Shatila camp, April 12, 2016.
61 Author's interview with Hassan Zaydan, leader of Fatah al-Intifada in Lebanon, October 26, 2015.
62 Author's interview with employees of UNRWA based in the Beddawi camp, April 22, 2016.

63 Author's phone interview with a person close to UNRWA in ʿAyn al-Hilwe, August 27, 2020.
64 Sarah Kenyon Lischer, *Dangerous Sanctuaries: Refugee Camps; Civil War, and the Dilemmas of Humanitarian Aid*, Paperback, 1st ed. (Ithaca: Cornell University Press, 2006).
65 Ibid., 25.
66 Julie Peteet, *Gender in Crisis: Women and the Palestinian Resistance Movement* (New York: Columbia University Press, 1991), 25.
67 Yezid Sayigh, "Reconstructing the Paradox: The Arab Nationalist Movement, Armed Struggle, and Palestine, 1951–1966," *Middle East Journal* 45, no. 4 (1991): 609. http://www.jstor.org/stable/4328352.
68 Fatah, or *Fatḥ*, is the reverse acronym of the movement's full name in Arabic: ḥarakat al-**ta**ḥrīr al-waṭanī al-**fi**lasṭīnī.
69 Yezid Sayigh, *Armed Struggle and the Search for State: The Palestinian National Movement, 1949–1993*, 2004 reprint, digitalized ed. (New York: Oxford University Press, 1997), 608.
70 Ibid., 101–8.
71 Maher al-Charif, *al-Baḥth ʿan kiān: dirāsa fi-l-fikr al-sīāsī al-filasṭīnī 1908–1993 [The search for an entity: A study of Palestinian Political Thought 1908–1993]* (Nicosia: The Center for Socialist Studies and Research in the Arab World (F.K.A.), 1995), 140.
72 For more on the subject, see Nasser Abufarha, *The Making of a Human Bomb: An Ethnography of Palestinian Resistance* (Durha and London: Duke University Press, 2009).
73 For a thorough account of Beidas and his Intra Bank, see Kamal Dib, *Imbrāṭūriyyat Intrā wa ḥītān al-māl fī lubnān 1949–1969: Yūsif Baydas [The Intra empire and money sharks in Lebanon 1949–1969: Yousef Beidas]* (Beirut: Dar al-Nahar, 2014).
74 As early as 1964, Lebanon had introduced a new labor law mandating that all non-Lebanese citizens in the country should obtain a work permit from the Ministry of Labor and Social Affairs.
75 According to a poll from 1969, as many as 46 percent of the public were in full support of the PLO's right to wage a war on Israel from Lebanese soil, and another 40 percent gave their reserved support. For more, see Rex Brynen, "The Politics of Exile: The Palestinians in Lebanon," *Journal of Refugee Studies* 3, no. 3 (1990). http://dx.doi.org/10.1093/jrs/3.3.204.
76 The full text of the Cairo Agreement is available through the Institute for Palestine Studies http://www.palestine-studies.org/sites/default/files/Text_of_the_Cairo_Agreement.pdf (Accessed January 8, 2020).
77 Ihsan Hijazi, A., "Lebanese Scrap P.L.O. Accord, Barring Bases," *The New York Times*, May 22, 1987.
78 Barry Rubin and Judith Colp Rubin, *Yasir Arafat: A Political Biography* (New York: Oxford University Press, 2003), 89.
79 Rex Brynen, *Sanctuary and Survival: The PLO in Lebanon* (Boulder, CO: Westview Press, 1990).
80 Menachem Klein, *Arafat and Abbas: Portraits of Leadership in a State Postponed* (London: Hurst, 2020), 7.
81 Sayigh, *Armed Struggle and the Search for State*, 687.
82 Brynen, "The Politics of Exile," 221.
83 As cited in *Sanctuary and Survival: The PLO In Lebanon*, 174.

84 Sayigh, *Armed Struggle and the Search for State*, 376.
85 For a thorough account of the massacre, see Bayan Nuwayhed al-Hout, *Sabra and Shatila: September 1982* (London: Pluto Press, 2004).
86 Herbert H. Denton, "Arafat and Troops Prepare for Second Exit from Lebanon," *The Washington Post*, December 4, 1983.
87 Anders Strindberg, "From the River to the Sea: Honour, Identity and Politics in Historical and Contemporary Palestinian Rejectionism" (PhD diss., University of St. Andrews, 2001), 150–2.
88 Ibid., 150–2.
89 For a detailed oral account of the notorious War of the Camps, see Sayigh, *Too Many Enemies*.
90 Mamduh Nawfal, *Maghdūshe: qiṣṣat al-ḥarb ʿalā al-mukhayyamāt fī Lubnān [Maghousheh: The Story of the War against the Camps in Lebanon]* (Ramallah: MUWATIN—The Palestinian Institute for the Study of Democracy, 2006).
91 For an interesting insider's account of the events, see the biography of former DFLP military chief Mamduh Nawfal in ibid.
92 Elizabeth Picard, *The Demobilization of the Lebanese Militias* (Oxford: Centre for Lebanese Studies, 1999), 43.
93 Ibid., 5.
94 Suheil al-Natour, spokesperson for the DFLP in Lebanon, author's interview, the Mar Elias camp, Beirut, November 20, 2013.
95 Strindberg, "From the River to the Sea."
96 Thanassis Cambanis, "Rocket Fire From Lebanon Unsettles Israel, but Fears of a Hezbollah Attack Subside," *The New York Times*, January 8, 2009.
97 Ramiz Mustafa, leader of the PFLP-GC in Lebanon, author's interview, the Mar Elias camp, Beirut, October 26, 2015.
98 Cf. Jonathan Schanzer, *Al-Qaeda's Armies: Middle East Affiliate Groups & the Next Generation of Terror* (New York: Specialist Press International, 2005).
99 Bernard Rougier, *Everyday Jihad: The Rise of Militant Islam among Palestinians in Lebanon*, trans. Pascale Ghazaleh (Cambridge: Harvard University Press, 2007 [2004]).
100 Ibid., 20.
101 Bernard Rougier, *The Sunni Tragedy of the Middle East: Northern Lebanon from al-Qaeda to ISIS* (New Jersey: Princeton University Press, 2015).

Chapter 3

1 Mitch Ginsburg, "Why Israel's Retreat from Lebanon Marked the Birth of Today's Middle East," *The Times of Israel*, March 25, 2015.
2 A particularly harrowing event was the 1996 "Operation Grapes of Wrath" in which Israel bombed a UN compound in the southern village of Qana. Shimon Peres, the Israeli minister of defense, deemed the compound to be a base for Hizballah fighters. The massacre claimed the lives of at least 100 civilians. Cf. Robert Fisk, "Shimon Peres Was No Peacemaker. I'll Never Forget the Sight of Pouring Blood and Burning Bodies at Qana," *The Independent*, September 28, 2016.
3 Although Hizballah for the most part preferred Lebanese courts to deal former members of the SLA, the movement was also implicated in several kidnappings.

For more, see Human Rights Watch, "Hizballah Implicated in South Lebanon Kidnappings," Human Rights Watch, 2000. http://pantheon.hrw.org/legacy/english/docs/2000/06/26/lebano556.htm.

4 Mayssun Sukarieh, "Shatila Dispatch: We Are Still Palestinians," *Middle East Research and Information Project (MERIP)* 30 (2000). http://www.merip.org/mer/mer217/shatila-dispatch.

5 "Palestinians in Lebanon Prepare to Resume Armed Struggle," *Middle East Intelligence Bulletin* 2, no. 4 (2000). https://www.meforum.org/meib/articles/0004_l4.htm.

6 Al-Maqdah cited in Middle East Intelligence Bulletin, "Palestinians in Lebanon Prepare to Resume Armed Struggle," 2000.

7 "Abū al-ʿAynayn: mawqif al-Maqdaḥ la yuʿabbir ʿan mawqif al-Munaẓẓama. [Abu al-ʿAynayn: the position of al-Maqdah does not represent the position of the Organization]," *al-Nahar*, April 10, 2000.

8 Ibid.

9 Amal Jamal, *The Palestinian National Movement: Politics of Contention 1967–2005* (Bloomington & Indianapolis: Indiana University Press, 2005), 6.

10 Edward Said, *Reflections on Exile: & Other Literary & Cultural Essays* (London: Granta Publications, 2012 [2000]), 177.

11 Author's field notes, September 21, 2015.

12 His hospital did not appear to be operational at the time of my visit. Rather, it appeared to have been turned into an apartment building.

13 Author's interview with retired Fatah official in Sidon, May 11, 2017.

14 Abu Iyad al-Shaʿlan, the leader of the PLO's Popular Committees in Lebanon, the Mar Elias camp, Beirut, December 14, 2015.

15 Brynjar Lia, *A Police Force without a State: A History of the Palestinian Security Forces in the West Bank and Gaza* (Reading: Ithaca Press, 2006), 207.

16 Jewish Telegraph Agency, "PLO Leadership Seen in Disarray Amid Calls for Arafat's Ouster," *Jewish Telegraph Agency*, August 25, 1993.

17 Reuters cited in Gary C. Gambill, "Dossier: Mounir al-Maqdah Former Fatah Commander," *Middle East Intelligence Bulletin* 5, no. 7 (2003). https://www.meforum.org/meib/articles/0307_pald.htm.

18 "al-Maqdaḥ yusayṭar ʿalā ٣ maqārrin li 'Fatḥ' [al-Maqdah controls 3 Fatah headquarters]," *al-Nahar*, October 10, 1993.

19 "(Without title)," *al-Nahar*, October 15, 1993.

20 Yossi Shain, *The Frontier of Loyalty: Political Exiles in the Age of the Nation-State* (Michigan: University of Michigan Press, 2005 [1989]), 15–16.

21 "al-Mu'assasāt al-Filasṭīniyya fī mukhayyam ʿAyn al-Ḥilwe tantaqil ilā muʿāriḍī ʿArafāt bi tamwīl Īrān [The Palestinian institutions in the ʿAyn al-Hilwe camp are turned over to opponents of Arafat by the means of Iranian funding]," *al-Safir*, June 14, 1994.

22 Ibid.

23 "Ishtibākāt karr wa farr fī ʿAyn al-Ḥilwe bayna anṣār ʿArafāt wa muʿāriḍīhi taḥṣud ١٠ qatlā wa ٢٥ jarḥā wa tuthīr iḥtijājāt wa ittihāmāt [Hit and run-clashes in ʿAyn al-Hilwe between followers of Arafat and his opposition result in 10 deaths and 25 wounded and causes protests and accusations]," *al-Safir*, November 26, 1994.

24 Ibid.

25 "Abū al-ʿAynayn yuḥammil ʿalā al-Dīmūqrāṭiyya wa-l-Shaʿbiyya [Abu al-Aynayn blames the DFLP and the PLFP]," *al-Safir*, June 23, 1995.

26 In mid-November 1993, al-Maqdah's new brigades issued a statement claiming the murder of settler Haim Mizrachi, who was struck by a Katyusha rocket launched across the Israeli border. "Chronology: 16 August–15 November 1993," *Journal of Palestine Studies* 23, no. 2 (1994). http://www.jstor.org/stable/2538249.
27 Ahmad Mantash, "Wilādat al-Jaysh al-Shaʿbī al-Mujāhid fī ʿAyn al-Ḥilwe. Al-Maqdaḥ: narfuḍ ḥiṣāranā fī Filasṭīn wa Lubnān [The birth of the Popular Combatant Army. Al-Maqdah: We reject our besiegement in Palestine and Lebanon]," *al-Nahar*, September 19, 1998.
28 Ibid.
29 Cf. Shaul Bartal, *Jihad in Palestine: Political Islam and the Israeli-Palestinian Conflict* (London: Routledge, 2016).
30 Cf. Robert Baer, *Devil We Know: Dealing with the New Iranian Superpower* (New York: Broadway Books, 2008).
31 Cited in Gambill, "Dossier: Mounir al-Maqdah Former Fatah Commander," 2003.
32 ʿUways, for his part, was expelled to Jordan.
33 This information is gathered from Israeli interrogation reports with members of the AMB. We should not neglect the fact that many of these prisoners were subject to torture during their interrogations and that this might have influenced their statements. For more, see Israel Ministry of Foreign Affairs, "Iran and Syria as Strategic Support for Palestinian Terrorism" (2002), https://mfa.gov.il/mfa/foreignpolicy/iran/supportterror/pages/iran%20and%20syria%20as%20strategic%20support%20for%20palestinia.aspx.
34 Nicholas Blanford, "Al-Aqsa Cells Being Funded and Guided from Ain al-Hilweh," *The Daily Star*, July 4, 2003.
35 As was the case in Balata, where a breakout cell of the AMB calling itself "The Central Command" was headed by local Fatah dissident Jamal al-Tirawi who presumably was funded by his cousin and head of the PA's General Intelligence, Tawfiq al-Tirawi. (Author's interview with former member of the AMB in the Balata refugee camp in Nablus, September 26, 2019).
36 Muhammad Salih, "Al-Maqdaḥ: natāʾij ījābiyya wa sa taẓhar ʿalā ṣaʿīd al-waḍaʿ al-ijtimāʿī li-l-Filasṭīnīīn [Al-Maqdah: Positive results that will be reflected on the social situation of the Palestinians]," *al-Safir*, November 22, 1996.
37 "Al-Maqdaḥ yuaʿrriḍ mutahhiman bi ightiyālihi: yaʿmil li-l-Mussād wa-l-shurṭa fī Ghazza [al-Maqdah exposes the suspect of his assassination (attempt): He works for Mossad and the police in Gaza]," ibid., December 2, 1995.
38 "Abū al-ʿAynayn fī ʿAyn al-Ḥilwe: al-khilāf maʿ al-Maqdaḥ kāna hafwatan [Abu al-ʿAynayn in ʿAyn al-Hilwe: the conflict with al-Maqdah was an error]," *al-Safir*, August 1, 1997.
39 Ahmad Mantash, "Fatḥ tu'akkid faṣl al-Maqdaḥ [Fatah confirms the dismissal of al-Maqdah]," *al-Nahar*, December 24, 1998.
40 Article IV of said document cited in Nigel Parsons, *The Politics of the National Authority: From Oslo to al-Aqsa* (New York and London: Routledge, 2005), 118–20; Graham Usher, "Arafat and the Palestinian Refugees," *Middle East International*, October 15, 1999.
41 Al-Hut cited in *Middle East International*, October 15, 1999, 19.
42 Ibid.
43 al-Nahar, "Abū al-ʿAynayn: Fatḥ amsakat mujaddidan bi ʿAyn al-Ḥilwe [Abu al-ʿAynayn: Fatah has reaffirmed its grip on ʿAyn al-Hilwe]," *al-Nahar*, July 28, 1999.

44 al-Safir, "Naql risālatin min ʿArafāt ilā Ṣfayr. Wafd Filasṭīnī fī-l-Dīmān: rafḍ qāṭiʿ li-l-tawṭīn [A message from Arafat to Sfayr. Palestinian delegation in Dimane: a categorical rejection of tawtin]," *al-Safir*, September 4, 1999.
45 Ibid.
46 For a detailed analysis of the negotiations, see Itamar Rabinovich, *The Brink of Peace: The Israeli-Syrian Negotiations* (New Jersey: Princeton University Press, 1999).
47 On October 29, 1999, Islamic Jihad in Palestine announced what was its first attack against Israel from Lebanese soil since 1994. The press described the events as an anomaly, and connected the incident to the failed Golan Heights talks. Cf. "al-Silāḥ al-Filasṭīnī fī Lubnān: as'ilat al-ʿawda al-thāniyya [Palestinian weapons in Lebanon: Questions upon their second return]," *al-Nahar*, October 29, 1999.
48 "The PFLP is not opposed to Fatah's presence in the camp," a PFLP leader told Middle East International in October 1999. "On the contrary, we are engaged in discussions with Fatah about how to keep the Palestinians in Lebanon focused on the refugee issue and the right to return. Whatever our differences over Oslo, on this issue it is vitally important to speak with one voice and under one umbrella, the PLO" (Hassan cited in *Middle East International*, October 15, 1999).
49 Ahmad Mantash, "Baʿdama talaqqat milyūn dūlār min ʿArafāt Fatḥ taʿīd tanẓīm ṣufūfiha li-l-imsāk mujaddidan bi waraqat al-mukhayyamāt [After receiving a million dollars from ʿArafat, Fatah reorganizes its ranks and reaffirms its grip on the file of the camps]," *al-Safir*, July 26, 1999.
50 *Middle East International*, October 15, 1999.
51 Jim Quilty, "A Taste of the Future," ibid., July 30.
52 Ahmad Mantash, "Fatḥ tastakmil khaṭawātaha al-tanẓīmiyya wa-l-Quwā al-Islāmiyya tarqubuha bi ḥadhr [Fatah completes its organizational plans and the Islamic Forces observe with caution]," *al-Nahar*, October 8, 1999.
53 Yusif al-Hawayk, "Fī ḥiwār khāṣṣ maʿ al-Diyyār nafā ʿilmahu bi qaḍiyyat Abū Muḥjin qabla tawajjah ṣabāḥ al-yawm ilā Lubnān [In an exclusive talk with al-Diyyar he denied his knowledge about the case of Abu Muhjin before his return to Lebanon this morning]," *al-Diyar*, Desember 12, 1999.
54 "al-Ḥūt yuḥāḍir ʿan al-qaḍiyya al-Filasṭīniyya fī Ṣaydā: limādhā takhrīj al-muqātilīn wa-l-ṣulḥ muwaqqaʿ yajib an naʿtrif bi-l-wāqiʿ al-jadīd bi Lubnān [al-Hut lectures on the Palestinian case in Sidon: Why this graduation of fighters when the reconciliation has been signed? We must recognize the new reality in Lebanon]," *al-Safir*, November 11, 1999.
55 Robert Fisk, "Arafat's Power Play Threatens Life of Aide," *Independent*, November 1, 1999.
56 Jim Quilty, "Brothers and Enemies," *Middle East International*, October 26, 1999.
57 Ibid.
58 "ʿArafāt yuṣṣaiʿd li ḥimāyat mas'ūl Fatḥ fī-l-janūb al-Ḥuṣṣ: hadhā amr qaḍā'ī wa lan natadakhkhal fīhi [Arafat steps up his protection of official in the South. Al-Huss: This is a court order and we will not interfere in it]," *al-Safir*, October 30, 1999.
59 The military, however, denied that there was an embargo, and said its measures were a response to the murder of four Lebanese judges who had been shot in a Sidon court during the summer. Cf. Ahmad Mantash, "Maṣdar ʿaskarī nafā ḥiṣār al-mukhayyamāt wa-l-muʿāriḍa al-Filasṭīniyya ittihamat ʿArafāt lāji'ūn qaṭaʿū madākhil ʿAyn al-Ḥilwe wa taẓāharū qubālat ḥawājiz li-l-jaysh [A military source denied the embargo against the camps, and the Palestinian opposition accused Arafat [while]

refugees blocked the entrances of ʿAyn al-Hilwe and demonstrated in front of the army's checkpoints]," *al-Nahar*, November 22, 1999.

60 Ibid.

61 ʿAqil Radawan, "Malāmiḥ ʿawdat Fatḥ ilā mukhayyamāt Bayrūt wa-l-shamāl baʿd al-taqārub al-Sūrī-al-Lubnānī fī ʿAmmān [The prospects of Fatah returning to the camps of Beirut and the North after the Syrian-Lebanese rapprochement in Amman]," ibid., March 31, 2001.

62 Author's conversation with the daughter of a late, prominent Fatah official in Lebanon, among others, Beirut May 5, 2017.

63 Abu Jihad, leader of Fatah in al-Beddawi, author's interview, April 22, 2016.

64 For more on this law, see Chapter 1.

65 Sami Moubayed, "Syria's Romance with Mahmoud Abbas," *al-Ahram*, July 20, 2005.

66 "Maṣādir rasmiyya taqūl inna Laḥūd lam yataṭarraq awḍāʿ al-lāji'īn wafd al-qiyāda al-Filasṭīniyya fī Bayrūt yaltaqī al-ru'asā' al-thalātha: iftitāḥ sifāra wa mawḍūʿ al-silāḥ al-Filasṭīnī fī waqtihi [Official Palestinian sources say that Lahud did not touch upon the situation of the refugees. A delegation of the Palestinian leadership meets three state officials in Beirut: The opening of a Palestinian embassy and the Palestinian weapons will be dealt with in time]," *al-Safir*, December 9, 2004.

67 Are Knudsen, "Nahr el-Bared: The Political Fall-out of a Refugee Disaster," in *Palestinian Refugees; Identity, Space and Place in the Levant*, ed. Sari Hanafi, Knudsen, Are (London: Routledge, 2011), 100–1.

68 Nasir al-Asʿad, "ʿAlā abwāb isti'nāf al-ḥiwār al-Lubnānī al-Filasṭīnī wa fī mā tarbuṭ al-faṣā'il al-muwāliyya li Sūriyā silāḥaha bi-l-tanẓīr li istimrār al-ṣirāʿ maʿ Isrā'il [At the doorstep of a resumption of a Lebanese-Palestinian dialogue, while the Pro-Syrian factions link their weapons to the theoretical continuation of the conflict against Israel]," *al-Mustaqbal*, October 5, 2005.

69 Muhammad Salih, "Ittiṣāl bayna al-Maqdaḥ wa Abū Māzin wafd Filasṭīnī yanqul ajwā' al-tahdi'a ilā ʿAyn al-Ḥilwe [Calls made between al-Maqdah and Abu Mazin. A Palestinian delegation brings the atmosphere of ceasefire to ʿAyn al-Hilwe]," *al-Safir*, February 2, 2005.

70 "Al-Maqdaḥ yastaqīl iḥtijājan ʿalā tajāhul Abū Māzin. [Al-Maqdah resigns in protest of Abu Mazin's neglect]," *al-Safir*, November 7, 2005.

71 "Mā hiya asbāb istiqālat al-ʿaqīd Munīr al-Maqdaḥ? Makhāwif min ḥarb bayna Fatḥ wa Jund al-sham! [What are the reasons behind Colonel Munir al-Maqdah's resignation? Fears of a war between Fatah and Jund al-Sham!]," *al-Safir*, July 31, 2004.

72 "Fatah deserves it," he added: "They are corrupt and have too many cars, too much money that was meant for their people." Cf. Mitchell Prothero, "PLO leadership in power struggle over Lebanese refugee camps," *The National*, March 30, 2010.

73 Author's interview, Sidon, May 11, 2017.

74 Muhammad Salih, "Fatḥ tastashʿir al-khaṭar fī mukhayyam ʿAyn al-Ḥilwe wa tafūḍ Kamāl Madḥat al-marjaʿiyya al-sīāsiyya wa-l-amniyya [Fatah senses the danger in the ʿAyn al-Hilwe camp, and makes Kamal Madhat the political and security authority]," *al-Safir*, September 26, 2008.

75 "Tafāṣīl ṭard al-Līnō min Qiyādat al-Kifāḥ al-Musallaḥ [Details on al-Lino's ousting from the Armed Struggle Command]," *Ra'i al-Yawm*, October 13, 2013.

76 "Abū al-ʿAradāt mas'ūl Fatḥ sāḥat Lubnān, Abū al-ʿAynayn li milaff al-lāji'īn wa-l-Maqdaḥ bilā ḥaqība al-tashkīlāt al-jadīda dākhil Fatḥ: irbāk dākhilī wa alghām khārijiyya [Abu al-ʿAradat is in charge of Fatah on the Lebanese scene, Abu

al-ʿAynayn to assume the refugee file, and al-Maqdah is without a portfolio. New formations within Fatah: internal confusion and external land mines]," *al-Safir*, March 12, 2010.

77 "Abū al-ʿAynayn: al-qarār 1559 Isrā'īlī bi imtīāz [Abu al-ʿAynayn: Resolution 1559 is distinctly Israeli]," ibid., December 12, 2005.

78 Muhammad Salih, "Abū al-ʿAradāt yatasallam mahāmmahu wa Abū al-ʿAynayn intahat ṣalāḥiyātuhu [Abu al-ʿAradat is handed his duties and Abu al-ʿAynayn's powers expire]," ibid., March 3, 2010.

79 "NOW Exclusive: Abbas requested to relieve Abu al-Aynayn from his duties," *NOW Lebanon*, February 23, 2010.

80 Abu al-ʿAradat was the former leader of Fatah's unions in Lebanon, and had been appointed as the organization's leader in the ʿAyn al-Hilwe camp by Arafat at a point when Fatah was targeted by arrests and sanctions by the Lebanese state.

81 One name that in particular would often come up during these conversations was the Lebanon-based Fatah leader Mundhir Hamze, who has strong connections with the general director of the Palestinian National Fund, Ramzi Khoury.

82 "Ḍābit fī Fatḥ yaʿtarif bi qatl murāfiq al-Līnō [Fatah officer confesses to killing companion of Lino]," *al-Jumhuriyya*, December 24, 2011.

83 Author's interview with high-ranking member of General Security, Beirut, June 1, 2017.

84 "Factions to Abbas: Disarming Not an Option," *al-Akhbar*, August 19, 2011.

85 Mohammed Zaatari, "Fatah Groups Unify in Ain alHilweh," *The Daily Star*, March 29, 2012.

86 Hassan Zaydan, leader of Fatah al-Intifada in Lebanon, author's interview, Beirut, October 26, 2015.

87 "Ḍubbāṭ wa kawādir min Fatḥ yuṭālibūn bi saḥb al-safīr Ashraf Dabbūr min Lubnān [Officers and cadres from Fatah demand the withdrawal of Ambassador Ashraf Dabbur from Lebanon]," *Palestine Today*, October 20, 2013.

88 Ibid.

89 Edward Kattoura, author's interview, Beirut, January 7, 2014.

90 Ibid.

91 Asmaa al-Ghoul, "Mohammed Dahlan to Run for Palestinian President," *al-Monitor*, April 14, 2014.

92 *Ra'i al-Yawm*, October 13, 2013.

93 Ibid.

94 Na'ila Khalil, "ʿAbbās: al-mushāraka fī mu'tamar Daḥlān khiyyāna waṭaniyya [Abbas: the participation in Dahlan's conference is national treason]," *al-Araby*, September 29, 2016.

95 Al-Ahmad cited in "Ḥiwār al-sāʿa—khalfiyyāt faṣl al-Līnō min ḥarakat Fatḥ wa-l-khilāfāt al-Filasṭīniyya dākhil al-mukhayyamāt [The talk of the hour—The background of al-Lino's dismissal from the Fatah movement and the Palestinian conflicts inside the camps]." *al-Mayadeen*, October 8, 2013.

96 Author's interview, ʿAyn al-Hilwe, October 13, 2015.

97 Ibid.

98 Nidal al-Mughrabi, "Cracks Deepen in Palestinian Politics as Abbas Clamps Down," *Reuters*, December 19, 2016.

99 Amal Khalil, "Fatḥ Fatḥān fī ʿAyn al-Ḥilwe Daḥlān…Abū Māzin [Fatah is two Fatahs in ʿAyn al-Hilwe. Dahlan…Abu Mazin]," *al-Akhbar*, December 30, 2014.

100 Hussein Agha and Ahmad Samih Khalidi, “The End of This Road: The Decline of the Palestinian National Movement,” *The New Yorker*, August 6, 2017.
101 Although Fatah’s leadership hurried to fire many of the suspected affiliates of the Democratic Reform Current from the movement, it should be noted that far from everyone within the Fatah apparatus perceived Dahlan’s activities in Lebanon as a threat. As a member of the Palestinian embassy put it bluntly: “Marhaba Dahlan! Come out of your Gulf castle and settle down in a bunker in ʿAyn al-Hilwe if that is what you think is best. In fact, send all your men there. I say this because he will never get presidency by going through Lebanon.” (Author’s conversation with officer speaking on the condition of anonymity, May 15, Beirut 2017.)
102 Dov Lieber, “Opening Night of Much-hyped Seventh Fatah Congress a Perplexing Snooze,” *The Times of Israel*, November 30, 2016.
103 Daoud Kuttab, “Lebanese Fatah Delegates Visit Palestine for First Time,” *al-Monitor*, December 15, 2016.
104 Ibid.
105 Rifʿat Shanaʿ, Secretary of the Fatah movement in Lebanon, untitled statement released on social media on October 2, 2016.
106 Videos from the event were shared widely on social media.
107 Indeed, it is an open secret that the PLO appears to have abandoned the right of return as a non-negotiable demand. See Laila al-Arian, “PA Selling Short the Refugees,” *Aljazeera.com*, January 25, 2011.

Chapter 4

1 Cf. Zoltan Pall, *Lebanese Salafis between the Gulf and Europe* (Amsterdam: Amsterdam University Press, 2013); Robert G. Rabil, *Salafism in Lebanon: From Apoliticism to Transnational Jihadism* (Washington, DC: Georgetown University Press, 2014).
2 See for example Amal Khalil, “15 filasṭīnīan min ʿAyn al-Ḥilwe ilā al-Raqqa [15 Palestinians from ʿAyn al-Hilwe to Raqqa],” *al-Akhbar*, February 11, 2016.
3 Rabil, *Salafism in Lebanon*, 148.
4 Sari Hanafi, “Enclaves and Fortressed Archipelago: Violence and Governance in Lebanon’s Palestinian Refugee Camps,” in *Lebanon After the Cedar Revolution*, ed. Are Knudsen, Michael Kerr (London: Hurst & Company, 2012), 117.
5 The term Salafi is a self-appellation commonly used by those who claim to be following in the exact footsteps of the Prophet and his companions, often referred to as *al-salaf al-salih* (the pious ancestors), and who stress that the only way to achieve salvation and retrieve past glory is through the re-assertion of absolute monotheism and the belief in the Oneness of God (*tawhid*) as the basis for the Islamic creed (*ʿaqida*). By attempting to emulate the practices of Islam’s golden era, Salafis view that only *they* constitute the “victorious sect” (*al-ta’ifa al-mansura*) or “saved group” (*al-firqa al-najiha*). As they tend to regard any secular ideology, such as communism, nationalism or socialism as innovation (*bid’a*), many Salafis disapprove of charters of the secular Palestinian groups. Nonetheless, many will still support the struggle to free Jerusalem and its holy Islamic sites, even though they might not think of Palestine in terms of a nation. cf. Roel Meijer, “Introduction,” in *Global Salafism: Islam’s New Religious Movement*, ed. Roel Meijer (London: Hurst & Company,

2009), 4–5. Shiraz Maher, *Salafi-Jihadism: The History of an idea* (London: Hurst & Company, 2016), 7.

6 Thomas Hegghammer refers to this process as a hybridization of rationales. Cf. "The Ideological Hybridization of Jihadi Groups," *Current Trends in Islamist Ideology* 9 (2009). https://www.hudson.org/content/researchattachments/attachment/1298/hegghammer_vol9.pdd

7 G. Scott Morgan, Linda J. Skitka, and Daniel C. Wisneski, "Political Ideology Is Contextually Variable and Flexible Rather than Fixed," *Behavioral and Brain Sciences* 37, no. 3 (2014). https://www.cambridge.org/core/article/political-ideology-is-contextually-variable-and-flexible-rather-than-fixed/FCF22FADEB3B6ACB8E59793ECBAB7069.

8 Author's interview, September 21, 2015.

9 Fidaa Itani, *al-Jihādiyyūn fī Lubnān: min Quwwāt al-Fajr ilā Fatḥ al-Islām [The Jihadis of Lebanon: From Quwwat al-Fajr to Fatah al-Islam]* (Beirut: Dar al-Saqi, 2017), 54–5.

10 The biographical details about Ibrahim Ghunaym in this chapter are taken from a number of eulogies that were posted on the social media site of the Murshid organization following the shaykh's death at ninety-six years old in October 2020. For more on Murshid, see below.

11 Jamal Khattab, author's interview, ʿAyn al-Hilwe, September 21, 2015.

12 "al-Munaẓẓamāt al-islāmiyya (7): al-Ḥaraka al-Islāmiyya al-Mujāhida [The Islamist organizations (7): The Islamic Combatant Movement]," *al-Hayat*, August 1, 2015.

13 Ra'fat Fahd Morra, *al-Ḥarakāt wal-quwā al-islāmiyya fī-l-mujtamʿa al-Filasṭīnī fī Lubnān: al-nishā'—al-ahdāf—al-injāzāt [The Islamic Movements and Forces in the Palestinian Community in Lebanon: Establishment—Objectives—Achievements]* (Beirut: al-Zaytouna Centre for Studies & Consultations, 2010), 164–5.

14 *al-Hayat*, August 1, 2015.

15 HIM's 1975 manifesto cited in Morra, *al-Ḥarakāt wal-quwā al-islāmiyya*, 164.

16 *al-Hayat*, August 1, 2015.

17 Said operation resulted in a witch-hunt for members of HIM carried out by the Lebanese Forces. ʿAbdallah Hallaq himself was forced to make a narrow escape through the backdoor of his house, causing him to resettle in Tripoli and then Beirut before making his return to ʿAyn al-Hilwe Cf. Morra, 167.

18 The militants coordinated with a leader of the Palestinian Armed Struggle Command called Mustafa Khalil, who would go on to spend twenty years in a Syrian prison on charges of having cooperated with what at the time was believed to be the militias of the Muslim Brotherhood (Morra, 167).

19 This was before Jamal Habbal, a prominent official within al-Jamaʿa al-Islamiyya, formed the Quwwat al-Fajr militia and would coordinate with the Palestinian Islamist guerillas in the battle of Eastern Sidon in 1985–6. (Itani, *al-Jihādīūn fī Lubnan*, 33–5.)

20 Yezid Sayigh, *Armed Struggle and the Search for State: The Palestinian National Movement, 1949–1993* (New York: Oxford University Press, 1997): 524–5.

21 Ze'ev Schiff and Ehud Ya'ari, *Israel's Lebanon War* (New York: Touchstone, 1984): 141.

22 See R.D. McLaurin, "The Battle of Sidon" (Maryland: U.S. Army Human Engineering Laboratory, 1989). Ghunaym, however, was not in the country at the time of the Israeli invasion of Lebanon. According to eulogies published in October 2020, it was Ghunaym's sons who led the resistance in the camp. After Israel withdrew from

Sidon in 1985, Ibrahim Ghunaym moved back to the Nahr al-Barid camp, where he continued his religious work, but stayed far away from any militia group or faction.

23 Author's interview, September 21, 2015.
24 James M. Markham, "Arafat, in Teheran, Praises the Victors," *New York Times*, February 19, 1979.
25 Jack Anderson, Dale Van Atta, "Why Arafat Backed Saddam," *The Washington Post*, August 26, 1990.
26 "al-Ḥaraka al-Islāmiyya al-Mujāhida," *al-Mustaqbal*, March 3, 2000.
27 Ibid.
28 Ibid.
29 Anabelle Böttcher, "Sunni and Shi'i Networking in the Middle East," *Mediterranean Politics* 7, 2002 - Issue 3: Shaping the Current Islamic Reformation (2007).
30 Morra, *al-Ḥarakāt wal-quwā al-islāmiyya*, 138.
31 Amal Khalil, "Ain al-Hilweh Islamists: We Are Not al-Nusra Front," *al-Akhbar*, May 4, 2013.
32 Rabil, *Salafism in Lebanon*, 193.
33 HIM's YouTube channel features videos of the majority of Friday sermons held at the Nur Mosque since March 24, 2012: https://www.youtube.com/channel/UCLinvsqCetTjYHm34rV3-xw (Accessed March 15, 2020).
34 "Al-umma fī muwājihat al-ṭāghūt wal-istʿimār wal-istīṭān [The Umma facing tyrants, imperialism and settlerism]," *Minbar al-jihad* 139 (2015).
35 ʿAbdallah Hallaq, "al-Shahāda al-ṭawʿaiyya min manẓūr islāmī (1) [A testimony of volunteerism from an Islamic perspective (1)]," *Minbar al-Jihad* 139 (2015).
36 Abu Hassan Statiyya, "Sibāq fī al-gharb ʿalā ʿitināq al-islām [An increase in the embracement of Islam in the West]," *Minbar al-Jihad* 139 (2015).
37 al-Shaykh Abu Diya', "Allāhu akbar … fataḥat al-khayr," ibid.
38 Al-Haraka al-Islamiyya al-Mujahida, "al-Quwā al-Islāmiyya fī ʿAyn al-Ḥilwe tastaqbil Tayyār al-Mustaqbal [The Islamic Forces of ʿAyn al-Hilwe receive the Future Movement]," ibid.
39 ʿAbdallah al-ʿArid, "al-Quwā al-islāmiyya tataḍāman maʿ Ḥamas [The Islamic Forces in solidarity with Hamas]," ibid.
40 Adnan Abu Amer, "How Hamas Plans to Rebrand Internationally," *al-Monitor*, March 17, 2017.
41 Lizzie Dearden, "Paris Attacks: Hamas Condemns Charlie Hebdo Massacre after Netanyahu Makes Comparison to Gaza Rockets," *The Independent*, January 10, 2015.
42 Retrieved from a video posted on the movement's YouTube channel on January 17, 2015.
43 Ibid.
44 *al-Akhbar*, May 4, 2013.
45 Author's interview, ʿAyn al-Hilwe, September 21, 2015.
46 Author's interview, September 21, 2015.
47 Some accounts claim that Shraydi was also closer to Fatah than the PFLP.
48 Ibrahim Hurani, mid-ranking member of ʿUsbat al-Ansar, ʿAyn al-Hilwe, October 15, 2015.
49 Abu Sharif ʿAqal, spokesperson for ʿUsbat al-Ansar, ʿAyn al-Hilwe, September 22, 2015.
50 Mahir Hammud, author's interview, Sidon, December 2, 2015.
51 Abu Sharif ʿAqal, 'Ayn al-Hilwe, September 22, 2015.
52 Ibid.

53 Author's interview, Sidon, December 2, 2015.
54 "Untitled news report," *al-Nahar*, August 3, 1990.
55 "ʿAwdat Shraydī ilā ʿAyn al-Ḥilwe fī ḍaw' al-nahaj al-siyāsī al-jadīd li ḥarakat Fatḥ [Shraydi returns to ʿAyn al-Hilwe in light of Fatah's new approach]," ibid., December 22.
56 "Taṭwīq al-tawattur bayna Fatḥ wa-l-Majlis al-Thawrī [The besetment of tension between Fatah and the Revolutionary Council]," *al-Nahar*, February 5, 1991.
57 "Ishtibāk fī ʿAyn al-Ḥilwe awqaʿ jarīḥayn ithr ightiyāl mas'ūl ʿUṣbat al-Anṣār [Clash in ʿAyn al-Hilwe leaves two injured in the wake of the assassination of the head of ʿUsbat al-Ansar]," *al-Nahar*, December 16, 1991.
58 "Ḥarakat al-Tawḥīd al-Islāmī [The Islamic Unification Movement]," *al-Nahar*, April 4, 1996.
59 For more details, see A. Nizar Hamzeh and R. Hrair Dekmejian, "A Sufi Response to Political Islamism: Al-Aḥbāsh of Lebanon," *International Journal of Middle East Studies* 28, no. 2 (1996).
60 For more details, see Bernard Rougier, *The Sunni Tragedy of the Middle East: Northern Lebanon from al-Qaeda to ISIS* (New Jersey: Princeton University Press, 2015), 12.
61 Founded in Beirut in 1983, the group was called al-Ahbash because of its Ethiopian founder, the scholar Abdallah al-Harari.
62 Pall, *Lebanese Salafis between the Gulf and Europe*, 47–8.
63 Ibid.
64 Ibid.
65 ʿAqil Radawan, "al-Nahār maʿ amīr min ʿUṣbat al-Anṣār fī manzil Abū Muḥjin fī ʿAyn al-Ḥilwe [al-Nahar with an emir from ʿUsbat al-Ansar in the house of Abu Muhjin in ʿAyn al-Hilwe]," *al-Nahar*, October 26, 1996.
66 Lebanese Republic Judicial Council, "Judgement in the Case of the Homicide of Sheikh Nizar al-Halabi (English translation)" (Beirut: Lebanese Republic Judicial Council, 1997).
67 "Ashar aḥkām al-iʿdām fī Lubnān [The most famous death penalties in Lebanon]," *al-Sharq al-Awsat*, April 26, 2003.
68 Abu Sharif ʿAqal, the movement's official spokesperson, author's interview, ʿAyn al-Hilwe, September 22, 2015.
69 Ibid.
70 Turki al-Suhayl, "Taʿrraf ʿalā ra's al-ḥarba al-Qaṭariyya fī daʿm al-anshiṭa al-irhābiyya [Get to know the Qatari spearhead financing terrorist activities]," *Makka al-Mukarrama*, June 1, 2017.
71 Muhammad Shaqir, "Ijmāʿ rasmī ʿalā taṣnīf al-jarīma bi-l-"munaẓẓama" wa-l-qirā'a al-siyāsiyya tastadʿī iʿdād lā'iḥa bi-l-mustafīdīn [Official consensus of defining the crime as "organized" and the political analysis requires a mapping of possible benifciaries]," *al-Hayat*, July 10, 1999.
72 Elizabeth Picard, "Lebanon in Search of Sovereignty: Post 2005 Security Dilemmas," in *Lebanon: After the Cedar Revolution*, ed. Michael Kerr Are Knudsen (London: Hurst, 2012), 90.
73 Rabil, *Salafism in Lebanon*, 198.
74 Eyal Zisser, "Syria and the United States: Bad Habits Die Hard," *Middle East Quarterly* 10, no. 3 (2003).
75 "ʿAyn al-Ḥilwe … mā zāla muʿskaran lil-muqātilīn alladhīna yatasarrabūn ilā al-ʿIrāq [ʿAyn al-Hilwe … still a stronghold for the fighters infiltrating Iraq]," *al-Sharq al-Awsat*, June 29, 2005.

76 The manifesto can be viewed using archival technology to retrieve the following broken link: http://alqassem.arabblogs.com/nashah/index4.html (Accessed August 1, 2015).
77 Usbat al-Ansar, "Ta'rīf [manifesto]," ibid. (2004).
78 Nicholas Blanford, "Fatah Commander Denies Sending Suicide Bombers to Iraq," *The Daily Star*, March 31, 2003.
79 Al-Arabiya, "Televised Interview with Shahade Jawhar," *Al-Arabiya*, December 7, 2007.
80 "Al-Qaida Leader Zarqawi: Our Eyes Are on Jerusalem," *Haaretz*, April 26, 2006.
81 The group has since 2002 not been involved in any notable incident of violence in Lebanon. For an extensive list of the group's domestic acts of violence between 1994 and 2002, see Morra, *al-Ḥarakāt wal-quwā al-islāmiyya*, 136–8.
82 Radwan 'Aqil, "Jamā'at al-Nūr wulaydat 'Uṣbat al-Anṣār wa qādat al-faṣā'il al-Filasṭīniyya yanfarūna minha [The Nur group is the offspring of 'Usbat al-Ansar and the Palestinian leaders shun it]," *al-Nahar*, November 1, 2001.
83 Among my interlocutors, the Hamade-affair was often seen as a turning point in the group's trajectory, and the renowned Sidon-based Imam Mahir Hammoud who was tasked with bringing his car into the camp in order to smuggle the fugitive out to the authorities was himself surprised by the turn of events: "They called me and said they wanted to take Hamade to a court," the Imam recounted. "I feared they had erected a Shari'a court inside the camp, but was surprised to find they were talking about a Lebanese court" (Author's interview, Sidon, December 2, 2015).
84 Nida' al-Islam, "Bayyān tawḍīḥī min 'Uṣbat al-Anṣār al-Islāmiyya ḥawla qaḍiyyat Badī' Ḥammāde (Abū 'Ubayda) [A clearifying statement from 'Usbat al-Ansar about the case of Badi' Hammade (Abu 'Abayda)]," *Nida' al-Islam* 9, no. 3 (2002): 4.
85 Knudsen, "Islamism in the Diaspora: Palestinian Refugees in Lebanon," 2005, 229.
86 "Qutila 3 min 'Uṣbat al-Nūr wa juriḥa 3 ākharīn fī 'Ayn al-Ḥilwe [Three from 'Usbat al-Nur were killed and three others were injured in 'Ayn al-Hilwe]," *al-Diyar*, April 7, 2005.
87 Abu Bassam al-Maqdah, al-Sai'qa leader in South Lebanon, and in charge of the APF's Popular Committee in 'Ayn al-Hilwe, author's interview, February 4, 2016.
88 These statements were made by a Fatah official in the camp, and largely reflect the attitude of other political leaders in 'Ayn al-Hilwe. (Author's field notes, October 15, 2015.)
89 Rougier, *The Sunni Tragedy of the Middle East*, 48.
90 According to Amnesty International, "dozens of members of the banned Islamist Hizb al-Tahrir (Liberation Party) were detained for days or weeks for the peaceful expression of their political and religious opinions, including organizing a sit-down in July in Tripoli." Cf., "Amnesty International Report 2005—Lebanon" (2005), http://www.refworld.org/docid/429b27ea14.html
91 Rougier, *The Sunni Tragedy of the Middle East*, 48.
92 Ibid.
93 Haytham Zu'aytar, "Ittiṣālāt mutalāḥiqa li taṭwīq dhuyūl aḥdāth minṭaqat Ta'mīr 'Ayn al-Ḥilwe [Successive calls to tie the loose ends of the events of the Ta'mīr area of 'Ayn al-Hilwe]," *al-Liwa*, July 9, 2006.
94 Hazim al-Amin, "Fī 'Ayn al-Ḥilwe ghurabā' yujannidūn intiḥārīīn fi mawsim al-Qā'ida. Al-'ā'idūn min al-'Irāq yaṭruqūn abwāb Lubnān min al-Janūb wa-l-Biqā' [In 'Ayn al-Hilwe strangers enlist suicide bombers in the 'season of al-Qa'ida.' The

returnees from Iraq are knocking on the doors of Lebanon from the South to the Biqaʿ]," *al-Hayat*, January 23, 2006.

95 Knudsen, "Islamism in the Diaspora: Palestinian Refugees in Lebanon," 101.

96 "Awwal iṭlāla li-l-nāṭiq bism Jund al-Shām: ʿumalāʾ al-dawla aṭlaqū al-nār fī-l-Taʿmīr [First appearance of the spokesperson for Jund al-Sham: agents of the state fired shots in Taʿmir]," *al-Mustaqbal*, October 26, 2005.

97 "I wouldn't say that we wouldn't allow the army to enter the camps," Gandhi Sahmarani was cited telling al-Mustaqbal. "Although I would say that the bee, before it stings, it knows it will die, but regardless, she stings. Likewise, I sting, and I die … but I sting. I don't want to make threats by saying I won't allow the army to enter. These words are a precaution." Ibid.

98 Author's field notes from a conversation with leaders of the group, October 15, 2015.

99 Author's interview, June 1, 2017.

100 "al-Jamāʿa: mawqif al-ʿUsba ijābī min intishār al-Jaysh fī-l-Taʿmīr] al-Jamaʿa: al-ʿUsba's position on the deployment of the army in Taʾmīr is positive]," *al-Nahar*, November 1, 2006.

101 "al-Jaysh yuqarrir intishār fī Taʿmīr ʿAyn al-Ḥilwe [The army decides to deploy in Taʿmir, ʿAyn al-Hilwe]," *al-Mustaqbal*, January 16, 2007.

102 Subhi Mundhir Yaghi, "Tanẓīm Jund al-Shām ʿalā ʿalāqa taḥālufiyya wathīqa bi Fatḥ al-Islām [The Jund al-Sham organization has a close alliance with Fatah al-Islam]," *al-Nahar*, June 8, 2007.

103 Charles Lister, *The Syria Jihad: al-Qaeda, the Islamic State and the Evolution of an Insurgency* (London: Hurst, 2015), 39–40.

104 Ibid., 40.

105 Rougier, *The Sunni Tragedy of the Middle East*, 85–9.

106 For a more exhaustive analysis on al- ʿAbsi's background, see Rougier, *The Sunni Tragedy of the Middle East*; Soudad Mekhenet and Michael Moss, "A New Face of Al Qaeda Emerges in Lebanon," *The New York Times*, March 15, 2007; Nir Rosen, *Aftermath: Following the Bloodshed of America's Wars in the Muslim World* (New York: Nation Books, 2010).

107 Rougier, *The Sunni Tragedy of the Middle East*, 85–9.

108 Nir Rosen, "Al-Qaeda in Lebanon: The Iraqi War Spreads," *Boston Review* (2008), http://bostonreview.net/nir-rosen-al-qaeda-in-lebanon-iraq-war.

109 Ibid.

110 *The New York Times*, March 15, 2007.

111 Tine Gade, "Fatah al-Islam in Lebanon: Between Global and Local Jihad," *FFI/Report-2007/02727* (2007): 22.

112 Al-ʿUmle would soon be fired from Fatah al-Intifada for going behind the leadership of his own movement, and he was later detained by the Syrian authorities. Cf. Muhammad Najjar, "Bawādir inshiqāq fī Fatḥ al-Intifāḍa baʿda faṣl al-ʿUmle [Signs of splits within Fatah—al-Intidada after the severance of al-ʿUmle]," *al-Jazira*, December 13, 2006.

113 Mohsen Saleh, *Awḍāʿ al-lāji'īn al-Filasṭīniyyīn fī Lubnān [Conditions of the Palestinian Refugees in Lebanon]* (Beirut: al-Zaytouna Centre for Studies & Consultations, 2012), 172.

114 Rosen, "Al-Qaeda in Lebanon: The Iraqi War Spreads."

115 Abu ʿAbdallah al-Maqdisi, "Liqāʾ muntadā Shumūkh al-Islām maʿ al-Shaykh Abī ʿAbdallāh al-Maqdīsī—al-mas'ūl al-sharʿī li tanẓīm Fataḥ al-Islām [Shumukh al-Islam's meeting with Shaykh Abu ʿAbdallah al-Maqdisi—in charge of religious affairs

in the Fatah al-Islam organization]" (Shumukh al-Islam 2009). This is a manuscript retrieved from the renowned but now closed online discussion forum Shumukh al-Islam, where al-Maqdisi published a widely shared biographical note he had written about the rise and fall of his movement. In addition, he went on to answer the forum users' questions between March 23 and 27, 2009. In these online exchanges, al-Maqdisi is continuously asked about the group's relationship with ʿUsbat al-Ansar, and he shares a longer statement on the matter. Although Shumukh al-Islam has been closed, the transcript of these conversations have been shared widely on the web, and is still available under the title cited above.

116 Jamal Khattab, author's interview, ʿAyn al-Hilwe, September 21, 2015.
117 Abu Sharif ʾAqal, spokesperson for ʾUsbat al-Ansar, ʿAyn al-Hilwe, October 15, 2015.
118 al-Mustaqbal, "Mas'ūl fī ʿUṣbat al-Anṣār yuʿlin ḥall Jund al-shām wa waḍʿ ʿanāṣiriha taḥt imrat al-quwā al-islāmiyya [Usbat al-Ansar officials announces the dissolving of Jund al-Sham, and the placing of its personnel under the command of the Islamic Forces]," *al-Mustaqbal*, July 1, 2007.
119 In the words of a Fatah leader cited in Mohsen Saleh et al., 180.
120 I thank Dr. Marie Kortam for sharing her notes with me on this topic.
121 Edward Kattoura, author's interview, Beirut, December 11, 2015.
122 Ibid.
123 Khalid al-Gharbi, "ʿUsbat al-Anṣār tuḥarrim qitāl al-jaysh al-Lubnānī [ʿUsbat al-Ansar forbids hostility against the Lebanese army]," *al-Akhbar*, December 6, 2008.
124 Ibid.
125 See previous endnote regarding the transcript from the Islamist web forum Sumukh al-Islam.
126 Y. Bilal Saab and Magnus Ranstorp, "Al-Qaeda's Terrorist Threat to UNIFIL" (The Brookings Institution/Center for Asymmetrical Warfare Threat Studies, 2007).
127 Nicholas Blanford, "In Lebanon, the UN and Hizbullah Make Unlikely Bedfellows," *The Christian Science Monitor*, July 24, 2007.
128 Wa'il Najm, "Zaʿīm ʿUṣbat al-Anṣār yataḥaddath ʿan al-ʿalāqa maʿ tanẓīm al-Qāʿida [ʿUsbat al-Ansar chieftain talks about the relations with al-Qaida]," *al-Arabiyya*, June 17, 2007.
129 Tine Gade, "Limiting Violent Spillover in Civil Wars: The Paradoxes of Lebanese Sunni Jihadism, 2011–17," *Contemporary Arab Affairs* 10, no. 2 (2017). http://dx.doi.org/10.1080/17550912.2017.1311601.
130 Author's interview with Ra'fat Morra, December 12, 2013.
131 Morra, *al-Ḥarakāt wal-quwā al-islāmiyya*, 182.
132 Ibid.
133 Jamal Hamad, former member of ʿUsbat al-Ansar, author's interview, ʿAyn al-Hilwe, September 21, 2015. It should be noted he was no longer a member of the movement in 2008. For more on Hamad and other defectors from the group, see the next chapter.
134 Lister, *The Syria Jihad*, 41.
135 Latif, "Fallahin, Fida'iyyin, Laji'in: Palestinian Camp Refugees as Autochtons," 2011.
136 Author's field notes from a trip through the Tawari' street, October 15, 2015.
137 Abu al-Muʿtasim, author's interview, 'Ayn al-Hilwe, October 13, 2015.
138 "Bi-l-sūwar: iftitāḥ markaz Futuwwat al-Anṣār al-Islāmī fī ʿAyn al-Ḥilwe [In pictures: The opening of the center of The Youth of the Islamic Partisans in ʿAyn al-Hilwe," *ʿAsimat al-shattat*, March 24, 2015.

139 Author's conversations with members at the group's headquarters, September 22, 2015.
140 Burhan Yasin, "ʿUṣbat al-Anṣār min ʿiṣāba musallaḥa ilā ʿāmil al-istqrār fī Lubnān [ʾUsbat al-Ansar from armed gang to agent of stability in Lebanon]," *Laji-net—Palestinian Refugees News Network in Lebanon*, April 5, 2013.
141 Author's interview ʿAyn al-Hilwe, September 22, 2015.
142 Ibid.
143 Ibid.
144 Mahir Hammud, author's interview, Sidon, December 2, 2015.
145 Radwan ʿAqil, "ʿUṣbat al-Anṣār maʿ al-infitāḥ ʿalā al-thunāʾī al-Shīʿī [ʿUsbat al-Ansar opens up to the Shia duo]," *al-Nahar*, March 16, 2016.
146 Abu Sharif ʾAqal, spokesperson for ʾUsbat al-Ansar, author's interview, ʿAyn al-Hilwe, October 15, 2015.
147 "ʿUṣbat al-Anṣār tuʿazzī al-rawāfiḍ qātilī ahl al-sunnā fī Sūriā, [Usbat al-Ansar pays tribute to the Shiʿa who are fighting the Sunnis in Syria]" The Sunnis of the Camp, January 25, 2015. Retrieved from http://lebanondebate.com/details.aspx?id=193738 (Accessed January 25, 2015).
148 Jamal Khattab cited in video released on Ahmad al-Asir's YouTube channel: https://www.youtube.com/watch?v=farA4KvvMsY (Accessed March 23, 2020).
149 "Al-faṣāʾil al-filasṭīniyya tarfuḍ zujj mukhayyam ʿAyn al-Ḥilwe fī ishtibākāt ṣaydā [The Palestinian factions prevent the ʿAyn al-Hilwe camp from being dragged in to the Sidon clashes]," *al-Akhbar*, June 19, 2013.
150 Muhammad Dahshe, "Maṭlūbū ʿAyn al-Ḥilwe yusallimūna anfusahum li-l-jaysh: lā ṣafqa … wal-ḥukm li-l-qaḍāʾ [The wanteds of ʿAyn al-Hilwe hand themselves over to the Army: no deal … and court rulings to proceed]," *al-Balad*, August 18, 2016.
151 Radwan Murtada, "ʿUṣbat al-Anṣār wa ḥarakat Ḥamās tusallimān al-maṭlūb Khālid al-Sayyid: ʿAyn al-Ḥilwe yalfiẓ al-irhāb [ʿUsbat al-Ansar and the Hamas movement hand over the wanted Khalid al-Sayyid: ʿAyn al-Hilwe expels terrorism]," *al-Akhbar*, July 3, 2017.
152 "al-Amn al-ʿām yakshif tafāṣīl jaḥīm Ramaḍān [General Security reveals details on the 'Ramadan inferno']," *al-Akhbar*, July 30, 2017.
153 Elnashra, "al-Hanniye yubārik khuṭwat taslīm al-Sayyid wa yuʾakkid ʿalā ḥafẓ al-amn wa-l-istiqrār [al-Hanniye blesses the handing over of al-Sayyid and assures the preservation of security and stability]," *Elnashra*, July 2, 2017.
154 Author's interview, October 15, 2015.
155 Ibid.
156 Ibid.
157 Palestinian Islamic Jihad, "Bayyān ṣādir ʿan Ḥarakat al-Jihād al-Islāmī fī Filasṭīn ḥawla ʿamaliyyat ibʿād arbʿat mujāhidīn min Qiṭāʿ Ghazza [A statement released by the Islamic Jihad Movement in Palestine regarding the deportation of four fighters from the Gaza Strip]," *al-Mujahid*, January 1991.
158 Morra, *al-Ḥarakāt wal-quwā al-islāmiyya*, 127–9.
159 Ann M. Lesch, "Israeli Deportation of Palestinians from the West Bank and the Gaza Strip, 1967–1978," *Journal of Palestine Studies* 8, no. 2 (1979). www.jstor.org/stable/2536512.
160 Erik Skare, "Faith, Awareness, and Revolution: A History of Palestinian Islamic Jihad" (PhD diss., University of Oslo, 2020), 134–43.
161 Deportees such as Fathi al-Shiqaqi (PIJ) and Isma'il Hanniye (Hamas) would go on to become senior officials of their respective organizations.

162 Charbel Ghassan, "zīārat al-dhākira lil-amīn al-ʿām li Ḥarakat al-Jihād al-Islāmī fī Filasṭīn ١ [Revisiting the memoirs of the General Secretary of Islamic Jihad in Palestine 1]," *al-Hayat*, January 7, 2003. I thank Dr. Erik Skare for this reference.
163 William A. Orme Jr, "Jordan Frees Four Jailed Hamas Leaders and Expels Them," *New York Times*, November 22, 1999.
164 See the previous chapter.
165 Author's interview, April 22, 2016.
166 ʿAli Barake, author's interview, Beirut, May 29, 2017.
167 "Cheney yattahim ʿArafāt bi taʿṭīl al-salām wa-l-muqāwama tuʿlin hudna [Cheney accuses Arafat of disrupting the peace process, and the Resistance announces a cease fire]," *Alzazeera*, December 9, 2001.
168 It should be noted that the polls were conducted by Hamas' own think-tank in Beirut. See Mohsen Saleh and al-Hassan Ziyad, *The Political Views of the Palestinian Refugees in Lebanon: As Reflected in May 2006* (Beirut: al-Zaytouna Centre for Studies & Consultations, 2006).
169 In the words of Hamas leader ʿAli Barake, author's interview, Beirut, May 29, 2017.
170 Author's interview, Shatila, Beirut, November 14, 2013.
171 Author's interview, October 15, 2015.
172 Dag Tuastad, "Hamas' Concept of a Long-term Ceasefire: A Viable Alternative to Full Peace?" (Oslo: Peace Research Institute Oslo (PRIO), 2010), https://www.prio.org/Publications/Publication/?x=7277.
173 Video of the speech retrieved through the YouTube profile of al-Islamiyya al-Mujahida, 2015.
174 Author's interview, Beirut, October 26, 2015.

Chapter 5

1 Abu Iyad al-Shaʿlan, the leader of the PLO's Popular Committees in Lebanon, author's interview, Beirut, January 14, 2014.
2 Rifi quoted in Oliver Holmes, Nazih Siddiq, "Bombs Kill 42 Outside Mosques in Lebanon's Tripoli," *Reuters*, August 23, 2013. These attacks, however, were eventually traced back to domestic actors tied to the Tripoli-based and Alwai-oriented Arab Democratic Party, led by Rifaat Eid. For more background, see Human Rights Watch, "Lebanon: Sectarian Attacks in Tripoli: Threats to Alawites Increase as Tensions Mount" (2013), https://www.hrw.org/news/2013/12/19/lebanon-sectarian-attacks-tripoli.
3 "Irhāb ʿalā bāb al-sifāra al-Irāniyya [Terrorism at the gates of the Iranian embassy]," *al-Mustaqbal*, November 20, 2013.
4 Ali Hashem, "Al-Qaeda-Affiliated Emir Arrested in Lebanon," *al-Monitor*, September 9, 2014.
5 Author's interview with Abu Iyad, Beirut, January 14, 2014.
6 US Department of State, "Terrorist Designation of Fatah al-Islam Associate Usamah Amin al-Shihabi" (Bureau of Counterterrorism and Countering Violent Extremism, 2013), https://www.state.gov/j/ct/rls/other/des/266563.htm.
7 "Kushifa anna al-yamanī kāna yuḥāwil al-farār min Lubnān qabla iʿtiqālihi [It was revealed that the Yemeni had attempted to flee from Lebanon before his detention]," *al-Nahar*, December 9, 2003.

8 Subhi Mundhir Yaghi, "ʿUṣbat al-Anṣār tusayṭir ʿalā aḥyā'in bi kāmiliha fī ʿAyn al-Ḥilwe [ʿUsbat al-Ansar controls neighborhoods in their enterity in ʿAyn al-Hilwe]," ibid., May 5, 2007.

9 Fidaa Itani, *al-Jihādiyyūn fī Lubnān: min Quwwāt al-Fajr ilā Fatḥ al-Islām [The Jihadis of Lebanon: From Quwwat al-Fajr to Fatah al-Islam]* (Beirut: Dar al-Saqi, 2017), 267.

10 *al-Nahar*, December 9, 2003.

11 Bernard Rougier, *The Sunni Tragedy of the Middle East: Northern Lebanon from al-Qaeda to ISIS* (New Jersey: Princeton University Press, 2015), 51.

12 Claudette Sarkis, "Yamanī tarājaʿa ʿan iʿtirafātihi al-awwaliyya wa aqarra bi sammāʿhi iqtirāḥan li ḍarb al-sifāra al-amrīkiyya [Yemeni retracts initial confessions and acknowledged overhearing a suggestion to bomb the American embassy]," *al-Nahar*, February 29, 2004.

13 The biographic information provided in this part is taken from an interview with Abu Yusif published in al-Wasat, "al-Amīr Abū Yūsif Sharqiyya: nakhtalif maʿ Ḥizbillāh fī juz'iyyat qatl al-aʿdā' [The Amir Abu Yusif Sharqiyya: We differ with Hizballah regarding minor details on the (permissibility of) killing the enemies]," *al-Wasat*, August 9, 2004.

14 Ibid.

15 Ibid.

16 Ibid.

17 Ibid.

18 Ibid.

19 "We haven't had a chance to fight the Jews yet, we have only just started," Abu Yusif told al-Ra'i al-ʿAm on July 21, 2004.

20 ʿAli Hashishu, "Amīr Jund al-Shām: lā nukaffir ilā al-kāfirīn wa naiʿd Amrīkā wa Isra'īl bi-l-radd ʿalā jarā'imhumā [The Amir of Jund al-Sham: We don't committ takfir except from against infidels, and we promise to respond to the crimes of America and Israel]," *al-Ra'i al-ʿAmm*, July 21, 2004.

21 Statement cited in Ahmad Mantash, "Jund al-Shām tanfī ʿalāqataha bi ightiyāl ʿAwalī [Jund al-Sham denies connections to the assassination of ʿAwali]," *al-Nahar*, July 20, 2004.

22 Ibid.

23 Ibid.

24 *al-Ra'i al-ʿAmm*, July 21, 2004.

25 Ahmad Mantash, "Amīr Jund al-Shām fī ʿAyn al-Ḥilwe yastaqīl wa yaʿtazil al-ʿamal al-tanẓīmī [The emir of Jund al-Sham in ʿAyn al-Hilwe quits and retires from organizational work]," *al-Nahar*, October 6, 2004.

26 Abu Ali, author's interview, Shatila, May 20, 2017.

27 Ahmad Mantash, "Tawattur fi ʿAyn al-Ḥilwe ithr khilāf bayna mas'ūl fī Jund al-Shām wa ʿunṣur min Fatḥ [Tension in ʿAyn al-Hilwe following a conflict between an official from Jund al-Sham and a member of Fatah]," *al-Nahar*, July 4, 2004.

28 Ibid.

29 Kamil Jabir, "Jund al-Shām … dawlat khilāfa min ṭarīq Taʿmīr ʿAyn al-Ḥilwe [Jund al-Sham … a Caliphate State from Taʿmir, ʿAyn al-Hilwe]," *al-Akhbar*, June 6, 2007.

30 Author's interview with former Jund al-Sham affiliate. ʿAyn al-Hilwe, February 24, 2016.

31 Are Knudsen, "Nahr el-Bared: The Political Fall-out of a Refugee Disaster," in *Palestinian Refugees; Identity, Space and Place in the Levant*, ed. Sari Hanafi, and Are Knudsen (London: Routledge, 2011), 101.

32 *al-Nahar*, June 8, 2007.
33 Tine Gade, "Limiting Violent Spillover in Civil Wars: The Paradoxes of Lebanese Sunni Jihadism, 2011–17," *Contemporary Arab Affairs* 10, no. 2 (2017), 193.
34 See for example "Junūd al-sitt Bahiyya al-Ḥarīrī yuṭliqūna tanẓīm Jund al-Shām bi ṭabaʿtihi al-Sūriyya fī madīnati Ḥumṣ wa jiwāriha [The soldiers of madame Bahiyya al-Hariri launch a Syrian version of the Jund al-Sham faction in the city of Homs and its surroundings]," *Syrian Telegraph*, January 5, 2013.
35 Many thanks to Tripoli expert Dr. Tine Gade for sharing her notes on the subject with me.
36 "Maktab al-Ḥarīrī yudaḥḥiḍ al-iddiʿāʾāt al-kādhiba li-l-talifiziūn al-sūrī.. bi sha'n shabakat Fatḥ al-Islām [Hariri's office refutes the false claims made by Syrian television … pertaining to Fatah al-Islam's network]," *al-Sharq al-Awsat*, November 11, 2008.
37 In ʿAbdallah al-Maqdisi's aforementioned statements from March 2009, he claims that the ordeals of Nahr al-Barid had proved that the climate in Lebanon was not ripe for the resurrection of Fatah al-Islam. See the previous chapter.
38 Robert F. Worth, "5 Soldiers Killed in Lebanon Bombing," *The New York Times*, September 29, 2008.
39 "Abū Muḥammad ʿAwaḍ: min ʿUṣbat al-Anṣār ilā al-ʿIrāq fa Fatḥ al-Islām [Abu Muhammad ʿAwad: From ʿUsbat al-Ansar to Iraq, then Fatah al-Islam]," *al-Akhbar*, November 8, 2008.
40 Aljazeera, "ʿAbd al-Raḥmān ʿAwaḍ," December 2, 2010.
41 This included an explosion going off at the ABC Mall in Beirut's Ashrafiyye district the same day that the battles of Nahr al-Barid broke out, on May 20, 2007, killing one person. He was also believed to have been behind a second explosion at mall in Verdun, another residential district in Beirut on May 22, as well as a third bomb going off in the Druze majority village and prominent site for Gulf tourists, ʿAlay, the day after. Cf. "ʿAbd al-Raḥmān Awʿaḍ amīr al-jihād fī ʿAyn al-Ḥilwe [ʿAbd al-Rahman Awʿad, ʿAyn al-Hilwe's emir of jihad]," *al-Hayat*, November 20, 2008.
42 "Rāqabtu al-jaysh wa-l-UNIFIL li istihdāfihumā al-iʿdām li majmūʿatin khaṭṭaṭat li khaṭf suyyāḥ wa mubādalatihim bi mawqūfī Fatḥ al-Islām [I surveilled the army and UNIFIL in order to target them: death sentences for a group that planned the kidnaping of tourists in order to swap them with detainees of Fatah al-Islam]," *al-Mustaqbal*, February 18, 2010.
43 "Iʿtaraf ʿalayhi ibn shaqīqihi bi-annahu kāna yukaffir al-jaysh wa-l-dawla ḥukm jadīd mu'abbid bi ḥaqq Usāma al-Shihābī [His nephew confessed that he was committing takfir against the army and the state. A new life sentence for Usama al-Shihabi]," *al-Mustaqbal*, September 2, 2010.
44 For his part, al-Shihabi always denied having any part in these plots, maintaining that the state merely resorted to blaming Palestinian Islamists because it lacked the resources and ability to confront the real perpetrators. In one of these instances, he seemed to be right. Although his name and ʿAwad's name came up following the car bomb that killed six UNIFIL soldiers in June 2007, there was little evidence that *this* explosion was connected to Palestinian actors. Rather, the bomb had targeted a Spanish UNIFIL battalion that was involved in monitoring the terrain north of the Litani River, where Hizballah was building a new line of defense. For more, see Nicholas Blanford, *Warriors of God: Inside Hezbollah's Thirty-Years Struggle Against Israel* (New York: Random House Publishing, 2011).

45 "Waqā'i' liqā'āt istikhbārāt al-jaysh wa-l-Filasṭīnīīn [Meetings take place between the Army Intelligence and the Palestinians]," *Lebanon Files*, November 11, 2008.

46 For more info on these deliberations, see the previous chapter.

47 Khalid Al-Gharbi, "Mughāmarat Shaḥāde Jawhar al-akhīra [Shahade Jawhar's Last Adventure]," *al-Akhbar*, July 21, 2008.

48 Radwan Murtada, "Laylat maqtal al-amīr: taraqqub wa 'azā' wa 'abwa nāsifa [The night of the killing of the 'emir': Expectations, a funeral, and a roadside bomb," ibid., August 17, 2010.

49 Haytham Zu'aytar, "Maqtal amīr Fatḥ al-Islām Awa'ḍ wa Mubārak khilāl muṭāradat al-jaysh al-lubnānī lahum fī Shtūra [The murder of Fatah al-Islam's emir Awa'd and Mubarak during their ousting by the Lebanese army from Shtura]," *Janobiyat*, August 17, 2010.

50 "Lubnān: al-'uthūr 'alā juththat mas'ūl Jund al-Shām fī mukhayyam 'Ayn al-Ḥilwe [Lebanon: The body of Jund al-Sham leader found in the 'Ayn al-Hilwe Camp]," *al-Iqtisadiyya*, December 26, 2010.

51 Radwan Murtada, "'Ayn al-Ḥilwe: taraqqub wa intiẓār ba'da layla dāmiyya ['Ayn al-Hilwe holds its breath after a violent night]," *al-Akhbar*, August 8, 2011.

52 Ibid.

53 Author's field notes, February 24, 2016.

54 Anne Barnard, "Hezbollah Commits to an All-Out Fight to Save Assad," *The New York Times*, May 25, 2013.

55 Author's interview with Usama Amin al-Shihabi, 'Ayn al-Hilweh, February 24, 2016.

56 Comments made by the movement's official spokesperson Abu Sharif 'Aqal during an interview aired on the al-Jadid channel on December 14, 2014.

57 Abu Sharif 'Aqal, spokesperson for 'Usbat al-Ansar, author's interview, 'Ayn al-Hilwe, October 16, 2015.

58 Jamal Hamed, author's interview, 'Ayn al-Hilwe, September 21, 2015.

59 Ibid.

60 An array of these videos were made public on Facebook and other social media during the clashes in the Tiri neighborhood in April 2017. For more on said clashes, see the next chapter.

61 Author's field notes from February 20, 2016.

62 Based on statements made during a group conversation with Members of Fatah's PNSF militia wings in 'Ayn al-Hilwe, February 24, 2016.

63 Author's field notes, Sidon, September 22, 2015.

64 Author's interview with Usama al-Shihabi, February 24, 2016.

65 Interviewed by Faris Ahmad in "Filasṭīn qalb al-umma: ḥalqa khāṣṣa ma' nā'ib al-amīn al-'āmm li ḥarakat Anṣār Allāh [Palestine is the heart of the Umma: A special episode with deputy general-secretary of the Ansar Allah movement]," *al-Thabat Channel*, January 29, 2016.

66 Ibid.

67 Shadin al-Qays, "Islāmīū mukhayyamāt Bayrūt fī qirā'atin li marḥalat ma ba'da ma'ārik Nahr al-Bārid [Islamists of the Beirut camps evaluate the time to come after the battles of Nahr al-Barid]," *al-Safir*, September 14, 2007.

68 The name appeared in print for the first time in 1987, when two Palestinians in Lebanon released a statement where they threatened to blow up the Italian embassy in Beirut. The threats came as a response to the arrest of Hizballah affiliate Bashir al-Khadur who had been arrested in Milan at a point when European authorities were cracking down on the movement's cells in the European mainland following

the hijacking of the TWA Flight 847 in 1985. This was a joint operation carried out by Hizballah and Palestinian Islamic Jihad, which called for the release of some 700 Shiʿa in Israeli custody, and Ansar Allah's statement urged Italian authorities to "lift your hands from our brothers in prison." Cf. "Anṣār Allāh ḥadhdharat Iṭālīā min tafjīr sifāratiha fī Bayrūt [Ansar Allah threatened Italy with blowing up its embassy in Beirut]," *al-Nahar*, January 27, 1987.

69 Al-Nahar, "Fatḥ andharat al-rāʾid Sulaymān bi-l-khurūj min mukhayyam ʿAyn al-Ḥilwe [Fatah urged Major Sulayman to leave the ʿAyn al-Hilwe camp]," *al-Nahar* January 12, 1991.

70 Ibid.

71 NOW Lebanon, "A Call to Arms: Three Palestinian Militant Groups," *NOW Lebanon*, November 6, 2007.

72 "Anṣār Allāh aʿlanū mas'ūliyyatahum ʿan tafjīr al-markaz al-yahūdī fī-l-Arjantīn [Ansar Allah claimed responsibility of blowing up the Jewish Center in Argentina]," *al-Nahar*, July 20, 1994.

73 "al-Maqdaḥ: bayyān Anṣār Allāh maṣdaruhu Ghazza [Al-Maqdah: Ansar Allah's statement's source is Gaza] " *al-Nahar*, August 3, 1994.

74 Matthew Levitt, *Hezbollah: The Global Footprint of Lebanon's Party of God* (Washington, DC: Georgetown University Press, 2013), 102.

75 Badih Chayban, "Future TV Building Blasted by 'Ansar Allah,'" *The Daily Star*, June 16, 2003.

76 Michael Young, "Future Shock," *Slate Magazine*, June 2003.

77 Curiously, al-Hariri's newspaper al-Mustaqbal (the Future) received two statements signed Ansar Allah, one claiming the attack, the other condemning it.

78 Abu Ashraf, leader of Islamic Jihad in the Burj al-Barajne camp, author's interview, December 16, 2013.

79 Itani, *al-Jihādīūn fī Lubnan*, 128.

80 Ibid.

81 Ibid.

82 Ahmad Mantash, "Anṣār Allāh aḥyū yawm al-quds bi masīra wa ʿaraḍ ʿaskariyya fī ʿAyn al-Ḥilwe [Ansar Allah revives Jerusalem day with a military procession in ʿAyn al-Hilwe]," *al-Nahar*, October 21, 2007.

83 Blanford, *Warriors of God*, 82.

84 Catherine le Thomas, "Socialization Agencies and Party Dynamics: Functions and Uses of Hizballah Schools in Lebanon," in *Returning to Political Parties? Partisan Logic and Political Transformations in the Arab World*, ed. Myriam Catusse & Karam Karam (Beirut: Lebanese Center for Policy Studies & Presses de l'Ifpo, 2010).

85 Interviewed on Thabat Channel, January 29, 2016.

86 Mohammed Zaatari, "Hammoud Mediates for Hezbollah and Ansar Allah," *The Daily Star*, December 7, 2012.

87 Ibid. "Ansar Allah Leader Resigns in 'cry' against Hezbollah," *The Daily Star*, July 20, 2015.

88 Ibid.

89 Elie Lahud, "al-Sarāyā al-Muqāwama li-l-difāʿ am li-ikhtirāq al-sāḥāt wa-l-mujtamaʿāt? [The Resistance Squadrons, for defense or for the penetration of the society?]," *al-Nahar*, October 12, 2013.

90 "Lubnān: ikhbār ḍudd Ḥizballāh wa-l-Sarāyā al-Muqāwama bi maʿrikat ʿAbrā [Lebanon: Information against Hizballah and The Resistance Squadrons in the battle of ʿAbra]," *al-ʿArabi al-Jadid*, January 5, 2016.

91 Author's interview, Sidon, December 12, 2015.

92 Muhammad Salih, "Hākadhā tamm istidrāj wa taʿdhīb al-Lubnānī al-shahīd Marwān ʿīsā qabla taṣfiatihi fī ʿAyn al-Ḥilwe [This is the way in which the Lebanese martyr Marwān ʿIsa was lured before his assassination in ʿAyn al-Hilwe]," *al-Safir*, April 7, 2015.

93 A Palestinian called Mahmud Kaʿsh claimed during an interrogation with the Lebanese army that Shʿabi had paid him to lure ʿIsa further into the camp. Cf. Ibid.

94 Ibid.

95 Statement cited in Arabi Press, "al-Shabāb al-Muslim: Marwān ʿīssa qutila li annahu sabb al-ṣaḥḥāba [al-Shabab al-Muslim: Marwan ʿIsa was killed because he insulted the companions]," *Arabi Press*, April 23, 2015.

96 Ibid.

97 Ra'fat Naʿim, "Bi-l-tawāzī maʿ taslīm 20 maṭlūban min ʿAyn al-Ḥilwe Ḥizballāh yusallim dufaʿtayn min maṭlūbī al-Sarāyā al-Muqāwama [In parallel with the handing over of 20 outlaws from ʿAyn al-Hilwe, Hizballah hands over two batches of outlaws from the Resistance Squadrons]," *al-Mustaqbal*, August 19, 2016.

98 *al-Thabat Channel*, January 29, 2016.

99 Numbers gathered during conversations with local NGOs, Ansar Allah combatants, and members of the Fatah leadership in Lebanon between 2015 and 2016.

100 Conversation with author, Sidon, April 2016.

101 Ibid.

Chapter 6

1 Al-ʿAradat cited in "al-Quwwa al-amniyya al-mushtaraka fī mukhayyam ʿAyn al-Ḥilwe li ḥafẓ al-amn wa-l-istiqrār [The Joint Security Force in the ʿAyn al-Hilwe camp, to preserve security and stability]," *Dunya al-Watan*, July 8, 2014. The rest of the citations in this section are from the same source.

2 Erling Lorentzen Sogge, "The Youth of Balata: A Generation of Hopelessness," *Jadaliyya*, November 18, 2019.

3 Christia Fotini, *Alliance Formation in Civil Wars* (New York: Cambridge University Press, 2012), 31–2.

4 Fares Akram, "Hamas Leader Abandons Longtime Base in Damascus," *The New York Times*, January 27, 2012.

5 Stephen Farrell, "New Winds in Mideast Favor Hamas," *The New York Times*, November 22, 2011.

6 ʿAli Barake, leader of Hamas in Lebanon, author's interview, November 28, 2013, Beirut.

7 Ismail Hanniye cited in Robert M. Danin, "Hamas Breaks from Syria," *Council of Foreign Relations*, February 29, 2012.

8 "Assad: Hamas Has Betrayed Us Repeatedly, but…," *al-Akhbar*, October 14, 2013.

9 Natasha Hall, "Palestinian Refugees and the Siege of Yarmouk," *Sada—Carnigie Endowment for International Peace*, March 13, 2014.

10 Author's field notes from visit to Hamas' local headquarters in Shatila, November 14, 2013.

11 Ibid.

12 Author's interview, November 28, 2013.

13 In the words of Abu Musa Sabir, leader of the PFLP-General Command in the Shatila camp, November 10, 2013.
14 Heather Saul, "Syria Crisis: The Picture That Shows the True Extent of the Humanitarian Crisis Inside Palestinian Refugee Camp Yarmouk," *The Independent*, February 26, 2014.
15 For a detailed discussion on such anxieties, see the next chapter.
16 Much to the dismay of a group of young Palestinians from Syria who, after arranging a commemoration for the "Martyr's of Yarmouk," found themselves kicked out of the camp by the security forces of the pro-Syrian group Fatah al-Intifada (Author's field notes, November 9, 2013).
17 Nathan Thrall and Robert Blecher, "Lebanon's Palestinian Dilemma: The Struggle over Nahr al-Bared" (International Crisis Group, 2012), https://www.crisisgroup.org/middle-east-north-africa/eastern-mediterranean/israelpalestine/next-war-gaza-brewing-heres-how-stop-it.
18 Author's interview, Beirut, December 4, 2015.
19 Abu Sharif ʿAqal, official spokesperson for ʿUsbat al-Ansar, author's interview, ʿAyn al-Hilwe, October 15, 2015.
20 Hassan Zaydan, Leader of Fatah al-Intifada in Lebanon, author's interview, the Mar Elias camp, Beirut, October 26, 2015.
21 Author's interview, the Mar Elias camp, Beirut, October 24, 2015.
22 Abu Sharif ʿAqal cited in Haytham Zuʿaytar, "al-ṭayf al-siyāsī al-Filasṭīnī yujassid khāriṭat Filasṭīn al-siyāsiyya wal-jaghrāfiyya bi daʿwa min al-iʿlāmī Haytham Zuʿaytar [The Palestinian political spectrum embodies Palestine's political and geographical map, at the invitation of journalist Haytham Zuʿaytar] " *Junubiyyat*, October 8, 2013.
23 "Hamas and Islamic Jihad are completely different from the Islamic Forces," Abu Iyad continued. "They have internal conferences and elect their leaders. ʿUsbat al-Ansar, Ansar Allah and Khattab's group are not like this, they don't have bylaws or an internal system. The only two thoughts they are capable of expressing are 'This place is an emirate' and then 'I am the emir.' We don't think of them as organizations (*tanzimat*); these are groups of individuals that are collected under one leader. Tomorrow when Khattab dies, that will be the end of his group. They have no future because they have simplistic organizational structures." (Author's interview, Beirut, the Mar Elias camp, January 10, 2014).
24 Author's interview, Beirut, December 4, 2015.
25 "Tawattur fī mukhayyam ʿAyn al-Ḥilwe baʿda ightiyāl al-qiyādī fī Jamaʿiyyat al-Mashārīʿ al-Islāmiyya al-Aḥbāsh [Tension in the ʿAyn al-Hilwe camp after the assassination of the leader of the Islamic Charitable Assosiacion 'al-Ahbash']," *Ra'i al-Yawm*, April 10, 2014.
26 Amal Khalil, "A New Security Plan for Ain al-Hilweh," *al-Akhbar*, April 29, 2014.
27 Ibid.
28 Brynjar Lia, *A Police Force without a State: A History of the Palestinian Security Forces in the West Bank and Gaza* (Reading: Ithaca, 2006), 429.
29 Author's interview, ʿAyn al-Hilwe, September 21, 2015.
30 Cited in *Dunya al-Watan*, July 8, 2014.
31 Muhammad Dahshe, "Intishār al-quwwa al-amniyya fī ʿAin al-Ḥilwe… bi ijmāʿ Filasṭīnī wa ghiṭā' Lubnānī [The security force deploys in Ain al-Hilwe…under Palestinian consensus and Lebanese cover]," *al-Balad*, July 9, 2014.

32 Abu Sharif ʿAqal, spokesperson for ʿUsbat al-Ansar, author's interview, September 22, 2015.
33 Armin Köhli, program manager for Geneva Call's Near- and Middle East division, author's interview via phone, July 25, 2017.
34 Geneva Call, "Lebanon: Inauguration of the Legal Training Center in Ain al-Hilweh Refugee Camp" (2014).
35 Author's interview, July 25, 2017.
36 Geneva Call, "Palestinian Refugee Camps in Lebanon: An Interview with Wissam Al Saliby, One of Geneva Call's Trainer" (2015).
37 Ibid.
38 Ali Dawoud, "Tadrībāt ʿaskariyya li Fatḥ ḥatta awākhir Ḥuzayrān [Fatah military drills until the end of June]," *al-Jumhuriyya*, May 25, 2014.
39 Author's interview, ʿAyn al-Hilwe, May 31, 2017.
40 Author's interview, ʿAyn al-Hilwe, October 15, 2015.
41 Ibid.
42 Zvi Bar'el, "Palestinian President Abbas Is Not Israel's Partner—or Cairo's," *Haaretz*, March 7, 2017.
43 Author's interview, December 4, 2015.
44 Max Weber, "Politics as Vocation," in *Max Weber: Essays in Sociology*, ed. Hans Heinrich Gerth and C. Wright Mills (New York: Oxford University Press, 1958 [1918]), 77.
45 Fotini, *Alliance Formation in Civil Wars*, 31–2.
46 Author's interview, February 24, 2016.
47 Munir al-Maqdah, initial leader of the JPSF in Lebanon, September 21, 2015.
48 Ra'fat Naʿim, "Ḥayy al-ṭawārī' yʿaūd ilā ʿAyn al-Ḥilwe…amnīan! [The Tawari' neighborhood returns to ʿAyn al-Hilwe…security-wise!]," *al-Mustaqbal*, May 20, 2015.
49 Cited in ibid.
50 Thair Ghandur, "Musalsal damawī mutawāṣil min kābūs ʿAyn al-Ḥilwe fī Lubnān [A series of bloody altercations from the nightmare of ʿAyn al-Hilwe in Lebanon]," *Alaraby*, July 30, 2015.
51 Author's interview with UNRWA's press officer, Beirut, September 29, 2015.
52 "Abū ʿArab li al-Quds li-l-Anbā': sa yurāfiq taslīm al-Maqdisī intishār al-amniyya fī aḥyā' ʿAyn al-Ḥilwe [Abu ʿArab to al-Quds li-l-Anba': The handing over of [the] Maqdisi [prayer room] will be followed by the deployment of the security [force] in the neighborhoods of ʿAyn al-Hilwe]," *Wikalat al-Quds li-l-Anba'*, July 5, 2015.
53 Statement cited in "al-Amniyya tu'ajjil intishāraha fī ḥayy Ḥiṭṭīn bi ʿAyn al-Ḥilwe [The Security (Force) postpones its deployment in the Hittin neighborhood in ʿAyn al-Hilwe]," *Wikalat al-Quds li-l-Anba'*, July 8, 2015.
54 "al-Ḥarāk al-Shaʿbī yaqūm bi jawla fī mukhayyam ʿAyn al-Ḥilwe wa yaltaqī al-Līnō wa-l-Maqdaḥ [The Popular Movement does a tour of the ʿAyn al-Hilwe camp and visits Lino and al-Maqdah]," *Saida TV*, July 29, 2015.
55 "al-Ṣaḥāfa al-Lubnāniyya: al-amniyya amām imtiḥān faʿliyyātiha fī ʿAyn al-Ḥilwe… wa-l-dirāsa tatajjihu naḥwā ta'jīl [The Lebanese Press: The Security [Force] is before an examination of its efficiency in ʿAyn al-Hilwe…and the study is moving towards postponement]," *Wikalat al-Quds li-l-Anba'*, August 13, 2015.
56 Amal Khalil, "Kayfa sayathār al-Līnō li ightiyāl Ṭalāl al-Urdunī [How will Lino avenge the assassination of Talal The Jordanian?)," *al-Akhbar*, July 27, 2015.

57 Naharnet, "Tension in Ain el-Hilweh Following Assassination of Fatah Official," *Naharnet*, July 25, 2015.
58 Mohammed Zaatari, "3 Dead, 18 Wounded in Clashes following Assassination Attempt in Ain al-Hilweh," *The Daily Star*, August 23, 2015.
59 Author's conversation with social worker in the camp September 22, 2015.
60 Patrick Strickland, "Double Displacement: Palestinians Flee Violence in Syria, Then Lebanon," *Electronic Intifada*, September 3, 2015.
61 Author's field notes September 21, 2015.
62 Ibid.
63 "Al-Rifāʿī: Hal al-maṭlūb tadmīr ʿAyn al-Ḥilwe bi adawāt Filasṭīniyya? [al-Rifaʿi: Is the goal to destroy the ʿAyn al-Hilwe camp with Palestinian instruments?," *Wikalat al-Quds li-l-anba'*, August 25, 2015.
64 Author's interview, ʿAyn al-Hilwe, September 21, 2015.
65 Saida TV, "Bi-l-fīdīū…kalimat al-liwā' Munīr al-Maqdaḥ fī-l-mu'tamar al-shaʿbī fī ʿAyn al-Ḥilwe bi tārīkh 2015-9-6 [In the video…the speech of Major-General Munir al-Maqdah in the People's Conference in ʿAyn al-Hilwe on the date 2015-9-6]," 2015. https://www.youtube.com/watch?v=lp9uAXeWuJ4&t=66s.
66 Author's interview, Beirut, October 26, 2015.
67 Muhammad ʿAbdu, PLFP official in ʿAyn al-Hilwe, author's interview, October 13, 2015.
68 "al- Ṣaḥāfa al-lubnāniyya: mīthāq sharaf bayna al-Shabāb al-Muslim wa-l-Quwā al-Islāmiyya li taḥṣīn ʿAyn al-Ḥilwe [The Lebanese press: A Charter of honor between al-Shabab al-Muslim and the Islamic Forces to improve ʿAyn al-Hilwe]," *Wikalat al-Quds li-l-Anba'*, December 7, 2015.
69 Author's interview with high-ranking Fatah leader, Beirut, December 2015.
70 Author's interview, December 4, 2015.
71 "Liqā' muṣālaḥa bayna Fatḥ wa-l-Shabāb al-Muslim fī ʿAyn al-Ḥilwe [Conciliation meeting between Fatah and al-Shabab al-Muslim in ʿAyn al-Hilwe]," *ʿAsimat al-Shattat*, March 13, 2016.
72 The clashes came in the aftermath of car bomb that killed a Fatah leader in the Miyye wo-Miyye camp upon his exit from ʿAyn al-Hilwe. However, certain Fatah officials had it that the clashes, in fact, had been triggered when fisticuffs between children hailing from Safsaf and Baraksat, respectively, had escalated into a battle of neighborhoods. Once again, camp dwellers fled to the streets of Sidon, the UNRWA schools shut down, while the JPSF was sidelined. After the clashes subsided and I was able to get back into the camp, I was told that the school buses no longer would drive through the Safsaf and Baraksat districts in fear of new clashes erupting.
73 Amal Khalil, "ʿAyn al-Ḥilwe: ʿAbd Faḍḍa khārij ṣafqat al-taslīmāt [ʿAyn al-hilwe: ʿAbd Fadda is outside of an extradition agreement]," *al-Akhbar*, August 25, 2016.
74 Sulayman al-Shaykh, "Hal intahā ʿahd al-tawatturāt al-amniyya fī ʿAyn al-Ḥilwe? [Is the era of security incidents in ʿAyn al-Hilwe over?]," *al-Quds al-Arabi*, September 9, 2016.
75 See the following editorial by the camp's own news provider *ʿAsimat al-Shattat*, "Mukhayyam ʿAyn al-Ḥilwe…bi intiẓār jawlāt jadīda [The ʿAyn al-hilwe camp… awaiting new rounds of violence]," August 28, 2015.
76 "al-Quwwa al-Amniyya fī-l-Miyye wo-Miyye wa qarīban fī mukahyyamāt Bayrūt [The Joint Force in al-Miyye wo-Miyye and soon in Beirut]," *al-Jumhuriyya*, March 15, 2015.
77 Author's interview, October 26, 2015.

78 Leaked reports from interrogations claimed that he had confessed to having formed an organization called the League of Muhajirin and Ansar in the Levant (ʿUsbat al-Muhajirin wa-l-Ansar fi Bilad al-Sham) with funding from IS in Raqqa, and that he had planned attacks against Casino du Liban and KFC in the Christian majority town of Jounieh, as well as the famous Sunday Market in the Shiʿ majority city Nabatiyye. A later leaked report claimed that Yasin denied these claims, and had allegedly laughed out at loud when presented with the allegation that he had plotted the assassination of Walid Jumblatt, the leader of the Progressive Socialist Party in Lebanon. See "Yāsīn yatarājaʿ ʿan iʿtirāfātihi ḥawlā takhṭīṭ li ightiyāl Walīd Junblāṭ bi sayyāra mufakhkhakha kawnuhu min adhkā al-siyāsiyīn [Yasin retracts his confessions of planning the assassination of Walid Jumblatt with a car bomb, as he is among 'the most clever politicians']," *al-Mustaqbal*, October 3, 2017.

79 "Khaṭṭāb: la niyya wa la maṣlaḥa la aḥad bi istifzāz al-jaysh aw al-taṣādum ma'hu [Khattab: No one has any intention, or stands anything to gain from provoking the army or clashing with it]," *Wikalat al-Quds li-l-Anbda'*, September 22, 2016.

80 "ʿUṣbat al-Anṣār al-Islamiyya tuqarrir al-ʿitikfāf fi ʿAyn al-Ḥilwe [ʿUsbat al-Ansar decides to suspend (its participation) in ʿAyn al-Hilwe]," *al-Ra'i*, October 14, 2016.

81 In late October 2017, Abu Muhjin and five others were dealt death sentences in absentia for the murders. No one from ʿUsbat al-Ansar's current leadership was on the list. Cf. "Ittihām ʿUṣbat al-Anṣār bi ightiyāl al-qaḍā al-arbaʿa [ʿUsbat al-Ansar charged with the assassination of the four judges]," *al-Hayat*, October 27, 2017.

82 "ʿUwayd yakshif asbāb insiḥābihi min min al-lajna al-amniyya al-ʿuliyā [ʿUwayd reveals the reasons for his withdrawal from the Higher Security Committee]," *ʿAsimat al-Shattat*, April 4, 2016.

83 "Uwlā ḍaḥāyā ʿitiqāl ʿImād Yāsīn [The first victims of the arrest of ʿImad Yasin]," *al-Akhbar*, September 26, 2016.

84 *Haaretz*, March 7, 2017.

85 Daily Mail, "Lebanon Builds Wall near Palestinian Refugee Camp," *Daily Mail*, November 21, 2016.

86 Author's interview with high-ranking official of the General Security, Beirut, June 1, 2017.

87 Author's field notes from conversations with inhabitants of the camp, May 31, 2017.

88 Author's field notes from visit to ʿAyn al-Hilwe, May 24, 2017.

89 "Lubnān: jidār al-ʿazl li mukhayyam ʿAyn al-Ḥilwe yufajjir jidālan ʿan al-jadwā wa… aṣl al-fikra [Lebanon: the isolation wall of ʿAyn al-Hilwe sparks debates about its feasibility and…the origins of the idea]," *al-Ra'i*, November 28, 2016.

90 "Usāma Saʿd: li muqāraba waṭaniyya shāmila li awḍāʿ mukhayyam ʿAyn al-Ḥilwe [Usama Saʿd: for a comprehensive national approach regarding the situation in the ʿAyn al-Hilwe camp]," *al-Manar*, November 30, 2016.

91 "Nā'iba Lubnāniyya tuṭma'inn ʿalā taṭawwurāt al-awḍāʿ fi mukhayyam ʿAyn al-Ḥilwe [Lebanese MP assures progress in the situation of the ʿAyn al-Hilwe camp]," *al-Bawab News*, December 7, 2016.

92 In the account of ʿAli Barake, leader of Hamas in Lebanon, author's interview, Beirut, May 29, 2017.

93 "Qatīlān wa 21 jarīḥan fi ishtibākāt fi ʿAyn al-Ḥilwe [Two dead and 21 injured in clashes in ʿAyn al-Hilwe]," *Arab 48 News*, April 8, 2017.

94 Cf. Ahmad Mantash, "Man huwwa Bilāl Badr Rāmbū ʿAyn al-Ḥilwe [Who is Bilal Badr, the Rambo of ʿAyn al-Hilwe?]," *al-Nahar*, April 10, 2017.

95 A story told to the author by one of Badr's younger relatives, author's conversation, Sidon, September 22, 2015.
96 Jamal Khattab, "al-Khuṭṭa al-mumnajiha li tadmīr ʿAyn al-Ḥilwe…wa-l-hadaf? [The systematic plan to destroy ʿAyn al-Hilwe…and the goal?] [Friday Sermon]," *Al-Risala*, August 25, 2017.
97 "Istimrār ishtibākāt ʿAyn al-Ḥilwe…wa ittifāq filasṭīnī ʿalā tafkīk Bilāl Badr [The clashes of ʿAyn al-Hilwe persist…Palestinian agreement to disperse Bilal Badr]," *al-Sharq al-Awsat*, April 10, 2017.
98 In September 2017, the PLFP-GC announced that it was bolstering its position in ʿAyn al-Hilwe by adding sixty elements to its Elite Forces in the camp. ʿAli Dawoud, "Quwwāt al-Nakhba ilā ʿAyn al-Ḥilwe li ijtithāt al-jamāʿt al-irhābiyya [The Elite Forces head to ʿAyn al-Hilwe…in order to root out the terrorist groups]," *al-Jumhuriyya*, September 17, 2017.
99 "al-Faṣā'il al-Filasṭīniyya tubalwir ṣīgha li waqf iṭlāq al-nār fī ʿAyn al-Ḥilwe ʿaqiba firār Bilāl Badr [the Palestinian factions crystalize a formula for a ceasefire in ʿAyn al-Hillwe following the escape of Bilal Badr]," *Erem News*, April 11, 2017.
100 Barake cited in ibid.
101 This section is based on the author's field notes from May 16, 2017.
102 Radwan Murtada, "Mutaḍarrarū ʿAyn al-Ḥilwe yantaẓirūn taʿwīdahum: al-kull yataharrab! [The victims of ʿAyn al-Hilwe await their compensation: everyone evades the question!]," *al-Akhbar*, May 18, 2017.
103 Cited in Ahmad Mantash, "Iʿādat fatḥ al-ṭarīq ʿand muftaraq sūq al-khuḍḍār fī ʿAyn al-Ḥilwe [The reopening of the road at the vegetable market junction in ʿAyn al-Hilwe]," *al-Nahar*, June 10, 2017.
104 Author's conversation with UNRWA official, Beirut, May 18, 2017.
105 Author's field notes May 16, 2017.
106 Ibid.
107 Author's interview, Ayn al-Hilweh, May 31, 2017.

Chapter 7

1 In colloquial Arabic: Ṭilʿit rīhətkun. Literally: "Your Stench Has Come Out"
2 Samia Nakhoul, "Lebanon's Rubbish Crisis Exposes Political Rot," *Reuters*, September 7, 2015.
3 As noted earlier, UNRWA does no longer profess to be in charge of camp infrastructure. In Lebanon the agency contends that the public utility service Elerctricité Du Liban (EDL) is responsible for maintaining electricity within the country's refugee camps. Cf. Annie Slemrod, "No Accountability for Deadly Burj al-Barajneh Electrocutions," *The Daily Star*, February 18, 2012.
4 Palestine Today, reportage from Burj al-Barajne aired on August 5, 2015.
5 Author's conversation with Palestinian activist, September 8, 2015.
6 Author's field notes December 17, 2015.
7 Jacob Høigilt, "Nonviolent Mobilization between a Rock and a Hard Place: Popular Resistance and Double Repression in the West Bank," *Journal of Peace Research* 52, no. 5 (2015). http://dx.doi.org/10.1177/0022343315572497.
8 Jacob Høigilt, "Fatah from Below: The Clash of Generations in Palestine," *British Journal of Middle Eastern Studies* 43, no. 4 (2016). https://doi.org/10.1080/13530194.2015.1116375.

9 Julie Peteet, *Gender in Crisis: Women and the Palestinian Resistance Movement* (New York: Columbia University Press, 1991), 187.
10 Rex Brynen, "The Neopatrimonial Dimension of Palestinian Politics," *Journal of Palestine Studies* 25, no. 1 (1995). http://www.jstor.org/stable/2538102, 24
11 Ibid.
12 Frances Fukuyama, *Political Order and Political Decay: From the Industrial Revolution to the Globalization of Democracy* (London: Profile Books, 2014).
13 Jad Chaaban, Nisreen Salti, Hala Ghattas, Alexandra Irani, Tala Ismail, Lara Batlouni, "Survey of the Socioeconomic Status of Palestine Refugees in Lebanon 2015" (Beirut: The American University of Beirut/UNRWA, 2016).
14 This is the arrangement as it appears on paper. As we have seen in previous chapters, the act of strategically nurturing ties to the organization's headquarters in Beirut or the PA in the West Bank likely trumps years of loyal service in the party.
15 Author's interview February 4, 2016.
16 These numbers reflect the situation as it was before the subsequent devaluation of the Lebanese pound as a result of the economic crisis that began in the fall of 2019.
17 Cf. "Intikhāb ʿAbd al-Majīd al-ʿAwaḍ al-mas'ūl al-siyāsī li ḥarakat Ḥamās fī minṭaqat Ṣūr [The election of ʿAbd al-Majid al-Awʿas Hamas' political official in Tyre]," *Albuss.net*, May 14, 2017.
18 Field notes from visit to the Burj al-Barajne camp, May 28, 2017.
19 Abu Sulayman ʿAbd al-Hadi, member of the PFLP-GC and leader of the APF's Popular Committee in Shatila, author's interview, November 10, 2013.
20 Mahmoud Abu Mujahid Abbas, leader of the Popular Committee of Shatila from 1984–2004, author's interview, November 24, 2015.
21 Ibid.
22 Muhammad Yasin, the leader of PLF in Lebanon, author's interview, Beirut, October 24, 2015.
23 Abu Jihad al-Fiyad, leader of Fatah in the Beddawi camp, author's interview, April 22, 2016.
24 In the words of Abu Bassam al-Maqdah, leader of the APF's Popular Committee in ʿAyn al-Hilwe. Author's interview, February 4, 2016.
25 Author's field notes from the Shatila camp, October 15–30, 2013.
26 Ibid.
27 I refrain from sharing the link due to the semi-private nature of the forum, which in Arabic is called al-Shabaka al-Filasṭīniyya al-Shabābiyya.
28 Author's interview, Burj al-Barajne, May 28, 2017.
29 Hassan Othman, activist and organizer, author's interview, Shatila, May 26, 2017.
30 "Kayfa 'haraba' tujjār al-mukhaddirāt min mukhayyam Shātīlā? [How did the drug dealers in the Shatila camp 'escape'?]," *Wikalat al-Quds lil-anba'*, September 30, 2016.
31 James Scott, *Domination and the Arts of Resistance: Hidden Transcripts* (Connecticut: Yale University Press, 1990), 16.
32 Six years later, the Palestinian Civil Defense in Lebanon (PCDL) remains one of the most robust non-factional institutions to have emerged in the Palestinian camps in recent years, due in no small part to the efforts exherted by some of the youth activists mentioned in this book. I do not go into the PCDL in this chapter, because it was still in its infancy at the time of my fieldwork, and was seldom brought up by my interlocutors in the context of camp democracy and protest movements, which is the main topic here. For an exhaustive background of the PCDL, see Erling Lorentzen Sogge, "Palestinian Refugee First Responders Rush to Aid Beirut," *Middle East Report Online*, October 13, 2020.

33 Qalam rasas, literally “pen of lead,” is the Arabic name for pencil. The title has a double meaning because rasas (lead) is used synonymously with gunfire or bullets, the implication being that the written word is mightier than the sword, or in this case, the rifle.
34 “Iftitāḥat al-ʿadad al-awwal: limādha kānat Qalam Raṣāṣ [The opening of the first edition: Why Qalam Rasas?],” *Qalam Rasas*, September 2015.
35 Ibid., 3.
36 Ibid.
37 Ibid., 4.
38 At its peak, the Qalam Rasas Facebook site reached close to 33,000 followers, but has since been replaced by another site called Nastopia, which is more journalistic in its scope, and has roughly the same amount of followers: https://www.facebook.com/Naastopia/ (Accessed February 25, 2020).
39 Author’s interview, Burj al-Barajne, May 28, 2017.
40 Albrecht Hofheinz, “Nextopia? Beyond Revolution 2.0,” *Oriente Moderno* 91, no. 1 (2011): 30. http://www.jstor.org/stable/23253704.
41 For an interesting discussion on the topic in the context of the Middle East, see Jon Nordenson, *Online Activism in the Middle East: Political Power and Authoritarian Governments from Egypt to Kuwait* (London and New York: I.B. Tauris, 2017).
42 See for instance the Facebook profile of the ʿAyn al-Ḥilwe Martyr Brigades: https://www.facebook.com/174521926238602/?fref=ts-كتيبة-شهداء-عين-الحلوة-للمهام-الخاصة-لبنان (Accessed August 14, 2019).
43 Cf. The YouTube channel of al-Haraka al-Islamiyya al-Mujahida: https://www.youtube.com/channel/UCLinvsqCetTjYHm34rV3-xw (Accessed August 14, 2019).
44 On August 12, 2019, ʿAsimat al-Shattat had 150,825 followers. The site was shut down by the Facebook administration directly after, and has since resurfaced under slightly different names. For archival purposes, the original Facebook profile can be found under the following cache: https://www.facebook.com/AismatShatatAinAlHelwe/?hc_ref=NEWSFEED&fref=nf
45 Khalil al-ʿAli, a Palestinian journalist based in Sidon, author’s interview, March 4, 2016.
46 Cf. http://www.asematalshatat.com/ (Accessed August 14, 2019).
47 “Mawqiʿ ʿāṣimat al-shattāt yukassir ṣamt al-Shaykh Abū Muḥjin [The Asimat al-Shattat site breaks the silence of the Shaykh Abu Muhjin],” *ʿAsimat al-Shattat*, August 9, 2014.
48 “Iḍrāb fī ʿAyn al-Ḥilwe iḥtijājan ʿalā taraddī al-awḍāʿ al-amniyya wa rukūd al-ḥaraka al-iqtiṣādiyya [Strike in ʿAyn al-Hilwe in protest of the deteriation of the security situation and the recession of the economy],” *ʿAsimat al-Shattat* September 18, 2015.
49 Author’s interview with Walif ʿIssa, leader of the Vegetable Market Trade Union in ʿAyn al-Hilwe, May 31, 2017.
50 Video posted on the Facebook site Hittin Haretna [Hittin is our neighborhood] on June 22, 2017: https://www.facebook.com/mahyobalaa/?fref=ts (Accessed June 22, 2017).
51 Ibid.
52 Mahmoud ʿAtaya, author’s interview, ʿAyn al-Hilwe, April 29, 2016.
53 PLO, “al-Niẓām al-dākhilī al-muʿaddal lil-lijān al-shaʿbiyya lil-khadamāt fī mukhayyamāt lil-lāji’īn al-filasṭīnīyyin [The revised rules of procedure for the Popular Committees for services in camps of Palestinian refugees],” ed. PLO—the Administration for Refugee Affairs (Ramallah: PLO, 2010).
54 Author’s conversation with a young Palestinian activist participating in the campaign, Beirut, August 8, 2015.

55 Cf. The Facebook site of the campaign: https://www.facebook.com/Tabeq.Nizamak/?fref=ts (Accessed July 12, 2017).
56 Ibid.
57 In a conversation with Hamas' spokesperson in Lebanon, Ra'fat Morra underlined Hamas' support for elected Popular Committees, saying that elections would be an efficient way of preventing certain parties from "stealing and plundering the camp population." However, he also felt that the political situation in the camps was "too sensitive and complex" to go ahead with such an experiment, largely echoing the sentiments of his contemporaries of the Fatah movement. (Author's interview, Beirut, December 12, 2013).
58 Soheil al-Natour, spokesperson for the DFLP in Lebanon, author's interview, the Mar Elias camp, November 23, 2015.
59 ʿAli Hamdan, Leader of political affairs for the PFLP in the Sidon region, author's interview, ʿAyn al-Hilwe, October 13, 2015.
60 Ziad Hammu, leader of the PLO's Popular Committee in the Shatila camp, author's interview, October 21, 2013.
61 Abu Musa Sabir, the former leader of the PFLP-GC in Shatila, author's interview, November 10, 2013.
62 Abu Ashraf, leader of Islamic Jihad in the Burj al-Barajne camp, December 16, 2014.
63 Manal Kortam, "Politics, patronage and Popular Committees in the Shatila refugee camp, Lebanon," in *Palestinian refugees: Idenity, Space and Place in the Levant*, ed. Are Knudsen, Sari Hanafi (New York: Routledge, 2011), 193–204.
64 Ibid.
65 Assertions based on the author's interviews with the Taytaba, Akbara, Hittin, Zib, and Baraksat Neighborhood Committtees of ʿAyn al-Hilwe during May 2017.
66 Author's interview with ʿAli Aslan, leader of the local branch of Hizb al-Tahrir and General Secretary of the Hittin Committee in ʿAyn al-Hilwe, May 19, 2017.
67 In the words of a member of the Zib Neighborhood Committee, author's field notes, April 29, 2016.
68 Hassan Sirhan, leader of the PPP in ʿAyn al-Hilwe, and member of the PLO's Popular Committee, author's interview, February 2, 2016.
69 Field notes from author's visit to the Zib neighborhood and a group conversation held at the offices of Mahmud ʿAtaya, April 29, 2016.
70 Ibid.
71 Martin Armstrong "Palestinians Protest against UNRWA Cuts in Lebanon," *Aljazeera.com*, February 29, 2016.
72 "Palestinian, 23, Self-immolates over UNRWA Aid Cuts," *The Daily Star*, January 12, 2016.
73 Author's field notes from 'Ayn al-Hilwe, February 20, 2016.
74 Author's field notes from al-Beddawi, April 22, 2016.
75 See Chapter 3 of this book for more details.
76 For example, in the Shatila camp, a Fatah official spoke to lengths about the danger of the youth development NGO *Ahlam Laji*, which at the time was funded by a Western government. In his mind, the institution had been "created by Dahlan in order to brainwash the youth of the camp" (Author's field notes, May 26, 2017).
77 Author's field notes from visit to the Beirut camps, May 17, 2017.
78 Author's interview May 28, 2017.
79 Mahmud Kʿawush, "Ḥadhār, ḥadhār, yā nushaṭāʾ fi-l-shattāt min ghaḍbat ʿAbbās!! Ḥadhār, ḥadhār!! [Beware, beware of the fury of 'Abbas oh activists in the diaspora!! Beware, beware!!]," *Railyoum*, October 14, 2016.

80 "Bi-l-wathā'iq: tasjīl ma' mas'ūl amnī yu'akkid anna al-ra'īs 'Abbās huwwa man ṭalab al-taḥqīq bi asmā' nāshiṭī-l-facebook [Documented: Recording of security official confirming that 'Abbas was the one who ordered the investigation into the names of Facebook activists]," *P.N. News*, October 14, 2016.
81 Facebook live stream, October 10, 2016, viewed online by the author at the time of streaming.
82 Abu Mujahid Mahmoud 'Abbas, author's interview, November 24, 2015.

Chapter 8

1 In the accounts of Jamal al-Tirawi, Member of the Palestinian Legislative Council, and former militia leader of the Al-Aqsa Martyr's Brigades in Nablus, the West Bank. Author's interview, Nablus, September 20, 2019.
2 For more on these dynamics, see the following piece on the rise to prominence of the militant known as "al-Za'bour," one of Dahlan's local strongmen in the Balata camp who died at the hands of the PNSF in 2018: Erling Lorentzen Sogge, "The Youth of Balata: A Generation of Hopelessness," *Jadaliyya*, November 18, 2019.
3 Hussein Agha and Ahmad Samih Khalidi, "The End of This Road: The Decline of the Palestinian National Movement," *The New Yorker*, August 6, 2017.
4 Author's conversation, September 2019.
5 Ibid.
6 Michel Agier, "Afterword: What Contemporary Camps Tell Us about the World to Come," *Humanity: An International Journal of Human Rights, Humanitarianism, and Development* 7, no. 3 (2016): 465.
7 Adam Rasgon and Najib Mohammed, "Palestinians Rejected Tax Money to Slap Israel. It's Not Israel That's Hurting," *The New York Times*, September 11, 2020.
8 A poll from September 2020 showed that 62 percent of the Palestinian public (in the West Bank and the Gaza Strip) want President Abbas to resign. A majority of 62 percent believed that the two-state solution was no longer practical or feasible due to the expansion of Israeli settlements. Cf. Palestinian Center for Policy and Survey Research (PSR), "Press Release: Public Opinion Poll No (77)" (Ramallah, 2020), http://pcpsr.org/en/node/817.
9 Agha and Khalidi, "The End of This Road," *The New Yorker*, August 6, 2017.
10 Shatha Hammad, "Palestine Politics: Could a Unified Leadership and Elections Herald a New Era?," *Middle East Eye*, September 28, 2020.
11 "Hamas, Fatah Agree to Hold Palestinian Elections within Six Months," *al-Monitor*, September 24, 2020.
12 Christiania Parreira, "The Art of Not Governing: How Lebanon's Rulers Got Away with Doing so Little for so Long," *Synaps Network*, October 23, 2019.
13 Author's interview with the leader of a local NGO by phone, August 17, 2020.
14 Anne Barnard, "On the Trail of a Story in Lebanon, Stumbling on a Scoop," *The New York Times*, January 1, 2018.
15 Ibid.
16 Author's field notes, December 7, 2015.
17 "Palestinian Leader of Hezbollah-linked Ansar Allah leaves Lebanon to Syria," *Al Arabiya*, November 7, 2018.

18 ʿAli Aghalif, "Khurūj maṭlūbī ʿAyn al-Ḥilwe: hal tahdur al-dawla 'furṣatan thamina' [The exit of ʿAyn al-Hilwe's outlaws: is the state wasting a 'valuable opportunity'?," *al-Akhbar*, July 31, 2017.

19 Author's interview by phone with a person close to al-Shihabi in August 2020.

20 Sunniva Rose, "Palestinian Students Show Dedication to e-Learning in Lebanon," *The National*, April 21, 2020.

21 Ibid.

22 Asma Ajourdi, "A Palestinian Seat in Lebanon's Parliament?," *Aljazeera*, March 19, 2018.

23 Erling Lorentzen Sogge, "Palestinian Refugee First Responders Rush to Aid Beirut," *Middle East Report Online*, October 13, 2020.

Bibliography

Books, Chapters, and Journal Articles

Abufarha, Nasser. *The Making of a Human Bomb: An Ethnography of Palestinian Resistance*. Durha and London: Duke University Press, 2009.

Agamben, Giorgio. *Homo Sacer: Sovereign Power and Bare Life*. Translated by Daniel Heller-Roazen. Stanford, California: Stanford University Press, 1998.

———. *State of Exception*. Translated by Kevin Attell. Chicago: University of Chicago Press, 2005.

Agier, Michel. "Afterword: What Contemporary Camps Tell Us about the World to Come." *Humanity: An International Journal of Human Rights, Humanitarianism, and Development* 7, no. 3 (2016): 459–68.

al-Hout, Bayan Nuwayhed. *Sabra and Shatila: September 1982*. London: Pluto Press, 2004.

Arendt, Hannah. *Totalitarianism: Part Three of the Origins of Totalitarianism*. New York: Harcourt Brace Jovanovich, 1985.

Baer, Robert. *Devil We Know: Dealing with the New Iranian Superpower*. New York: Broadway Books, 2008.

Barnett, Michael. *Empire of Humanity: A History of Humanitarianism*. Ithaca: Cornell University Press, 2013.

Bartal, Shaul. *Jihad in Palestine: Political Islam and the Israeli-Palestinian Conflict*. London: Routledge, 2016.

Baumann, Hannes. *Citizen Hariri: Lebanon's Neoliberal Reconstruction*. London: Hurst & Company, 2016.

Berg, Kjersti. "From Chaos to Order and Back: The Construction of UNRWA Shelters and Cmps, 1950–1970." In *UNRWA and Palestinian Refugees: From Relief and Works to Human Development*, edited by Leila Hilal, Sari Hanafi, and Lex Takkenberg, 109–28. London: Routledge, 2014.

———. "Temporary and Eternal: UNRWA and the Palestinian Refugee Question." [In Norwegian]. *Babylon – Nordic Journal for Middle East Studies*, no. 1 (2020): 34–49. https://journals.uio.no/babylon/article/view/8148.

Blanford, Nicholas. *Warriors of God: Inside Hezbollah's Thirty-Years Struggle against Israel*. New York: Random House Publishing, 2011.

Bocco, Riccardo. "UNRWA and the Palestinian Refugees: A History within History." *Refugee Survey Quarterly* 28, no. 2–3 (2009): 229–52. https://doi.org/10.1093/rsq/hdq001.

Böttcher, Anabelle. "Sunni and Shi'i Networking in the Middle East." *Mediterranean Politics* 7, 2002 – Issue 3: Shaping the Current Islamic Reformation (September 2007): 42–63.

Brenner, Bjorn. *Gaza under Hamas: From Islamic Democracy to Islamist Governance*. London: I.B. Tauris, 2016.

Brynen, Rex. "The Neopatrimonial Dimension of Palestinian Politics." *Journal of Palestine Studies* 25, no. 1 (Autumn 1995): 23–36. http://www.jstor.org/stable/2538102.

———. "The Politics of Exile: The Palestinians in Lebanon." *Journal of Refugee Studies* 3, no. 3 (1990): 204–27. http://dx.doi.org/10.1093/jrs/3.3.204.

———. *Sanctuary and Survival: The PLO in Lebanon*. Boulder, CO: Westview Press, 1990.

al-Charif, Maher. *al-Baḥth ʿan kīān: dirāsa fī-l-fikr al-sīāsī al-filasṭīnī 1908–1993 [The search for an entity: A study of Palestinian Political Thought 1908–1993]*. Nicosia: The Center for Socialist Studies and Research in the Arab World (F.K.A.), 1995.

"Chronology: 16 August–15November 1993." *Journal of Palestine Studies* 23, no. 2 (1994): 160–79. https://www.jstor.org/stable/2538249?seq=1.

Dib, Kamal. *Imbrāṭūriyyat Intrā wa ḥītān al-māl fī lubnān 1949–1969: Yūsif Baydas [The Intra empire and money sharks in Lebanon 1949–1969: Yousef Beidas]*. Beirut: Dar al-Nahar, 2014.

Diken, Bülent and Carsten B. Laustsen. *The Culture of Exception: Sociology Facing the Camp*. Abingdon, Oxfordshire: Routledge, 2005.

Eisenstadt, Shmuel N. *Traditional Patrimonialism and Modern Neopatrimonialism*. Beverly Hills, CA: Sage Publishing, 1973.

el Khazen, Farid. *The Breakdown of the State in Lebanon, 1967–1976*. Cambridge: Harvard University Press, 2000.

Feldman, Ilana. "Mercy Trains and Ration Rolls: Between Government and Humanitarianism in Gaza (1948–67)." In *Interpreting Welfare and Relief in the Middle East*, edited by Nefissa Naguib, Inger Marie Okkenhaug, 175–94. Boston: Brill, 2008.

———. "The Challenge of Categories: UNRWA and the Definition of a 'Palestine Refugee.'" *Journal of Refugee Studies* 25, no. 3 (2012): 387–406. https://doi.org/10.1093/jrs/fes004Frisch.

Fotini, Christia. *Alliance Formation in Civil Wars*. New York: Cambridge University Press, 2012.

Foucault, Michel. "Space, Knowledge, Power." In *The Foucault Reader*, edited by P. Rabinow, 239–56. London: Penguin, 1984.

Fukuyama, Frances. *Political Order and Political Decay: From the Industrial Revolution to the Globalization of Democracy*. London: Profile Books, 2014.

Gade, Tine. "Fatah al-Islam in Lebanon: Between Global and Local Jihad." *FFI/Report-2007/02727* (2007): 18–20.

———. "Limiting Violent Spillover in Civil Wars: The Paradoxes of Lebanese Sunni jihadism, 2011–17." *Contemporary Arab Affairs* 10, no. 2 (2017/04/03 2017): 187–206. http://dx.doi.org/10.1080/17550912.2017.1311601.

Ghandour, Marwan. "Who Is 'Ain al-Hilweh?" *Jadaliyya*, September 30, 2013. Accessed October 7, 2020. https://www.jadaliyya.com/Details/29579

Giorgio, Agamben. *State of Exception*. Chicago: University of Chicago Press, 2005.

Gresh, Alain. *The PLO: The Struggle Within: Towards and Independent State*. Translated by Maxime Rodinson. 2nd ed. London and New Jersey: Zed Books, 1988 [1986].

Gunning, Jeroen. *Hamas in Politics: Democracy, Religion, Violence*. New York: Colombia University Press, 2008.

Haddad, Toufic. *Palestine Ltd: Neoliberalism and Nationalism in the Occupied Territory*. SOAS Palestine Studies. London: I.B. Tauris, 2016.

Hamzeh, A. Nizar, and R. Hrair Dekmejian. "A Sufi Response to Political Islamism: Al-Aḥbāsh of Lebanon." *International Journal of Middle East Studies* 28, no. 2 (1996): 217–29.

Hanafi, Sari. "Enclaves and Fortressed Archipelago: Violence and Governance in Lebanon's Palestinian Refugee Camps." In *Lebanon after the Cedar Revolution*, edited by Are Knudsen, Michael Kerr, 105–22. London: Hurst & Company 2012.

———. "Palestinian Refugee Camps in Lebanon as a Space of Exception." *REVUE Asylon(s)* 5 (September 2008). http://www.reseau-terra.eu/article798.html.

Hanafi, Sari and Taylor Long. "Governance, Governmentalities, and the State of Exception in the Palestinian Refugee Camps of Lebanon." *Journal of Refugee Studies* 23, no. 2 (2010): 134–59. http://dx.doi.org/10.1093/jrs/feq014.

Hassan, Ismael Sheikh, and Lyne Jabri. "The Urban-history of a Camp & the Camp-history of a City: The Case of Sidon, Ein El Hilweh and MiyoMiye – Part 1." Unpublished manuscript last modified July 24, 2017.

Hegghammer, Thomas. "The Ideological Hybridization of Jihadi Groups." *Current Trends in Islamist Ideology* 9 (2009): 26–45. https://www.hudson.org/content/researchattachments/attachment/1298/hegghammer_vol9.pdf.

Hillel. "Modern Absolutist or Neopatriarchal State Building? Customary Law, Extended Families, and the Palestinian Authority." *International Journal of Middle East Studies* 29, no. 3 (1997): 341–58. www.jstor.org/stable/164584.

Hofheinz, Albrecht. "Nextopia? Beyond Revolution 2.0." *Oriente Moderno* 91, no. 1 (2011): 23–39. http://www.jstor.org/stable/23253704.

Høigilt, Jacob. "Fatah from Below: The Clash of Generations in Palestine." *British Journal of Middle Eastern Studies* 43, no. 4 (October 1, 2016): 456–71. https://doi.org/10.1080/13530194.2015.1116375.

———. "Nonviolent Mobilization between a Rock and a Hard Place: Popular Resistance and Double Repression in the West Bank." *Journal of Peace Research* 52, no. 5 (September 1, 2015): 636–48. http://dx.doi.org/10.1177/0022343315572497.

Irfan, Anne E. "Educating Palestinian Refugees: The Origins of UNRWA's Unique Schooling System." *Journal of Refugee Studies* (2019). https://doi.org/10.1093/jrs/fez051.

Itani, Fidaa. *al-Jihādiyyūn fī Lubnān: min Quwwāt al-Fajr ilā Fatḥ al-Islām [The Jihadis of Lebanon: From Quwwat al-Fajr to Fatah al-Islam]*. Beirut: Dar al-Saqi, 2017.

Jamal, Amal. *The Palestinian National Movement: Politics of Contention 1967–2005*. Bloomington & Indianapolis: Indiana University Press, 2005.

Janmyr, Maja. "No Country of Asylum: 'Legitimizing' Lebanon's Rejection of the 1951 Refugee Convention." *International Journal of Refugee Law* 29, no. 3 (2017): 438–65. http://dx.doi.org/10.1093/ijrl/eex026.

Khalidi, Rashid. *Under Siege: PLO Decisionmaking during the 1982 War*. New York: Columbia University Press, 1986.

Klein, Menachem. *Arafat and Abbas: Portraits of Leadership in a State Postponed*. London: Hurst, 2020.

Knudsen, Are. "Islamism in the Diaspora: Palestinian Refugees in Lebanon." *Journal of Refugee Studies* 18, no. 2 (2005): 216–34. http://dx.doi.org/10.1093/refuge/fei022.

Knudsen, Are. "Camp, Ghetto, Zinco, Slum: Lebanon's Transitional Zones of Emplacement." *Humanity: An International Journal of Human Rights, Humanitarianism, and Development* 7, no. 3 (2016): 443–57.

———. "Nahr el-Bared: The Political Fall-out of a Refugee Disaster." In *Palestinian Refugees; Identity, Space and Place in the Levant*, edited by Sari Hanafi, Knudsen, Are, 97–110. London: Routledge, 2011.

———. "Sheikhs and the City." *Conflict and Society* 6, no. 1 (2020): 34–51. https://www.berghahnjournals.com/view/journals/conflict-and-society/6/1/arcs060103.xml.

Kortam, Manal. "Politics, Patronage and Popular Committees in the Shatila Refugee Camp, Lebanon." In *Palestinian Refugees: Idenity, Space and Place in the Levant*, edited by Are Knudsen, Sari Hanafi, 193–204. New York: Routledge, 2011.

Latif, Nadia. "Fallahin, Fida'iyyin, Laji'in: Palestinian Camp Refugees as Autochtons." *The Arab Studies Journal* 19, no. 1 (2011): 42–64. http://www.jstor.org/stable/23265811.
le Thomas, Catherine. "Socialization Agencies and Party Dynamics: Functions and Uses of Hizballah Schools in Lebanon." In *Returning to Political Parties? Partisan Logic and Political Transformations in the Arab World*, edited by Myriam Catusse & Karam Karam, 217–49. Beirut: Lebanese Center for Policy Studies & Presses de l'Ifpo, 2010.
Leech, Philip. *The State of Palestine: A Critical Analysis*. Oxfordshire: Routledge, 2016.
Lesch, Ann M. "Israeli Deportation of Palestinians from the West Bank and the Gaza Strip, 1967–1978." *Journal of Palestine Studies* 8, no. 2 (1979): 101–31. www.jstor.org/stable/2536512.
Levitt, Matthew. *Hezbollah: The Global Footprint of Lebanon's Party of God*. Washington DC: Georgetown University Press, 2013.
Lia, Brynjar. *A Police Force without a State: A History of the Palestinian Security Forces in the West Bank and Gaza*. Reading: Ithaca, 2006.
Lischer, Sarah Kenyon. *Dangerous Sanctuaries: Refugee Camps; Civil War, and the Dilemmas of Humanitarian Aid*. Paperback, 1st ed. Ithaca: Cornell University Press, 2006.
Lister, Charles. *The Syria Jihad: al-Qaeda, the Islamic State and the Evolution of an Insurgency*. London: Hurst, 2015.
Maher, Shiraz. *Salafi-Jihadism: The History of an Idea*. London: Hurst & Company, 2016.
Meier, Daniel. "Lebanon: The Refugee Issue and the Threat of a Sectarian Confrontation." *Oriente Moderno* 94, no. 2 (2014): 382–401.
Meijer, Roel. "Introduction." In *Global Salafism: Islam's New Religious Movement*, edited by Roel Meijer, 1–32. London: Hurst & Company, 2009.
Miller, Aaron David. *The PLO and the Politics of Survival*. Westport, CT: Praeger 1983.
Morgan, G. Scott, Linda J. Skitka, and Daniel C. Wisneski. "Political Ideology Is Contextually Variable and Flexible Rather than Fixed." *Behavioral and Brain Sciences* 37, no. 3 (2014): 321–2. https://www.cambridge.org/core/article/political-ideology-is-contextually-variable-and-flexible-rather-than-fixed/FCF22FADEB3B6ACB8E59793ECBAB7069.
Morra, Ra'fat Fahd. *al-Ḥarakāt wal-quwā al-islāmiyya fī-l-mujtam ʿa al-Filasṭīnī fī Lubnān: al-nishā' - al-ahdāf - al-injāzāt [The Islamic Movements and Forces in the Palestinian Community in Lebanon: Establishment—Objectives—Achievements]*. Beirut: al-Zaytouna Centre for Studies & Consultations, 2010.
Nawfal, Mamduh. *Maghdūshe: qiṣṣat al-Ḥarb ʿalā al-mukhayyamāt fī Lubnān [Maghousheh: The Story of the War against the Camps in Lebanon]*. Ramallah: MUWATIN—The Palestinian Institute for the Study of Democracy, 2006.
Nehme, Adib. *The Neopatrimonial State and the Arab Spring*. Beirut: AUB Policy Institute, 2016.
Nordenson, Jon. *Online Activism in the Middle East: Political Power and Authoritarian Governments from Egypt to Kuwait*. London and New York: I.B. Tauris, 2017.
Nordenson, Jon, Magnus Dølerud and Erling Lorentzen Sogge. "A New Course for Lebanon?" [In Norwegian]. *Babylon—Nordic Journal for Middle East Studies,* no. 2 (2019). https://journals.uio.no/babylon/article/view/7773.
Nucho, Joanne Randa. *Everyday Sectarianism in Urban Lebanon: Infrastructures, Public Services, and Power*. New Jersey: Princeton University Press, 2016.
Pall, Zoltan. *Lebanese Salafis between the Gulf and Europe*. Amsterdam: Amsterdam University Press, 2013.

Parsons, Nigel. *The Politics of the National Authority: From Oslo to al-Aqsa*. New York and London: Routledge, 2005.

Peteet, Julie. *Gender in Crisis: Women and the Palestinian Resistance Movement*. New York: Columbia University Press, 1991.

———. *Landscape of Hope and Despair: Palestinian Refugee Camps*. Pennsylvania: University of Pennsylvania Press, 2005.

———. "Problematizing a Palestinian Diaspora." *International Journal of Middle East Studies* 39, no. 4 (2007): 627–46. www.jstor.org/stable/30069491.

Picard, Elizabeth. *The Demobilization of the Lebanese Militias*. Oxford: Centre for Lebanese Studies, 1999.

———. "Lebanon in Search of Sovereignty: Post 2005 Security Dilemmas." In *Lebanon: After the Cedar Revolution*, edited by Michael Kerr Are Knudsen, 156_83. London: Hurst, 2012.

Rabil, Robert G. *Salafism in Lebanon: From Apoliticism to Transnational Jihadism*. Washington, DC: Georgetown University Press, 2014.

Rabinovich, Itamar. *The Brink of Peace: The Israeli-Syrian Negotiations*. New Jersey: Princeton University Press, 1999.

Ramadan, Adam. "Spatialising the Refugee Camp." *Transactions of the Institute of British Geographers* 38, no. 1 (2012): 65–77.

Rempel, Terry. "From Beneficiary to Stakeholder: An Overview of UNRWA's Approach to Refugee Participation." In *UNRWA and Palestinian Refugees: From Relief and Works to Human Development*, edited by Leila Hilal, Sari Hanafi, and Lex Takkenberg, 145–63. Oxfordshire: Routledge, 2014.

Rosen, Nir. *Aftermath: Following the Bloodshed of America's Wars in the Muslim World*. New York: Nation Books, 2010.

———. "Al-Qaeda in Lebanon: The Iraqi War Spreads." *Boston Review* (2008). Published electronically January 1, 2008. http://bostonreview.net/nir-rosen-al-qaeda-in-lebanon-iraq-war.

Rougier, Bernard. *Everyday Jihad: The Rise of Militant Islam among Palestinians in Lebanon*. Translated by Pascale Ghazaleh. Cambridge: Harvard University Press, 2007 [2004].

———. *The Sunni Tragedy of the Middle East: Northern Lebanon from al-Qaeda to ISIS* New Jersey: Princeton University Press, 2015.

Rubenberg, Cheryl A. "The Civilian Infrastructure of the Palestine Liberation Organization: An Analysis of the PLO in Lebanon until June 1982." *Journal of Palestine Studies* 12, no. 3 (Spring 1983): 54–78.

Rubin, Barry, Judith Colp Rubin. *Yasir Arafat: A Political Biography*. New York: Oxford University Press, 2003.

Sahliyeh, Emile F. *The PLO after the Lebanon War*. London: Westview Press/Boulder, 1986.

Said, Edward. *Reflections on Exile: & Other Literary & Cultural Essays*. London: Granta Publications, 2012 [2000].

Saleh, Mohsen. *Awḍāʿ al-lājiʾīn al-Filasṭīniyyīn fī Lubnān [Conditions of the Palestinian Refugees in Lebanon]*. Beirut: al-Zaytouna Centre for Studies & Consultations, 2012.

Sayigh, Rosemary. *Palestinians: From Peasants to Revolutionaries: A People's History*. London: Zed Press, 1979.

———. *Too Many Enemies: The Palestinian Experience in Lebanon*. 2nd ed. Beirut: al-Mashriq, 2015 [1994].

Sayigh, Yezid. *Armed Struggle and the Search for State: The Palestinian National Movement, 1949–1993*. 2004 reprint, digitalized ed. New York: Oxford University Press, 1997.
———. "Reconstructing the Paradox: The Arab Nationalist Movement, Armed Struggle, and Palestine, 1951–1966." *Middle East Journal* 45, no. 4 (1991): 608–29. http://www.jstor.org/stable/4328352.
Schanzer, Jonathan. *Al-Qaeda's Armies: Middle East Affiliate Groups & the Next Generation of Terror*. New York: Specialist Press International, 2005.
Schiff, Ze'ev and Ehud Ya'ari. *Israel's Lebanon War*. New York: Touchstone, 1984.
Shikaki, Khalil. "Palestinians Divided." *Foreign Affairs* 81, no. 1 (2002): 89–105. http://www.jstor.org/stable/20033005.
Scott, James. *Domination and the Arts of Resistance: Hidden Transcripts*. Connecticut: Yale University Press, 1990.
Shain, Yossi. *The Frontier of Loyalty: Political Exiles in the Age of the Nation-State*. Michigan: University of Michigan Press, 2005 [1989]. doi:10.3998/mpub.93349.
Sukarieh, Mayssun. "Shatila Dispatch: We Are Still Palestinians." *Middle East Research and Information Project (MERIP)* 30 (2000). http://www.merip.org/mer/mer217/shatila-dispatch.
Talhami, Ghada Hashem. *Palestinian Refugees: Pawns to Politcal Actors*. New York: Nova Publishers, 2003.
Traboulsi, Fawwaz. *A History of Modern Lebanon*. 2nd ed. Beirut: Pluto Press, 2012 [2007].
Tuastad, Dag. "'State of Exception' or 'State in Exile'? The Fallacy of Appropriating Agamben on Palestinian Refugee Camps." *Third World Quarterly* (2016): 1–12. http://dx.doi.org/10.1080/01436597.2016.1256765.
Weber, Max. *Economy and Society: A New Translation*. Translated by Keith Tribe. Cambridge, MA: Harvard University Press, 2019.
———. "Politics as Vocation." In *Max Weber: Essays in Sociology*, edited by Hans Heinrich Gerth and C. Wright Mills, 77–128. New York: Oxford University Press, 1958 [1918].
Zisser, Eyal. "Syria and the United States: Bad Habits Die Hard." *Middle East Quarterly* 10, no. 3 (Summer 2003): 29–37.

Newspapers, Magazines, and Pamphlets

"ʿAbd al-Raḥmān Awʿaḍ amīr al-jihād fī ʿAyn al-Ḥilwe [ʿAbd al-Rahman Awʿad, ʿAyn al-Hilwe's emir of jihad]." *al-Hayat*, November 20, 2008.
Abu Amer, Adnan. "How Hamas Plans to Rebrand Internationally." *al-Monitor*, March 17, 2017. Accessed August 28, 2017. http://www.al-monitor.com/pulse/originals/2017/03/hamas-to-release-soon-new-policy-document-expressing-stances.html.
Abu Diya', al-Shaykh. "Allāhu akbar … fataḥat al-khayr." *Minbar al-Jihad* 139 (April 2015): 19–22.
Agha, Hussein and Ahmad Samih Khalidi. "The End of This Road: The Decline of the Palestinian National Movement." *The New Yorker*, August 6, 2017. Accessed March 25, 2018. https://www.newyorker.com/news/news-desk/the-end-of-this-road-the-decline-of-the-palestinian-national-movement.

Aghalif, ʿAli. "Khurūj maṭlūbī ʿAyn al-Ḥilwe: hal tahdur al-dawla 'furṣatan thamina' [The exit of ʿAyn al-hilwe's outlaws: is the state wasting a 'valuable opportunity'?"] al-Akhbar, July 31, 2017.

Ajourdi, Asma. "A Palestinian Seat in Lebanon's Parliament?" *Aljazeera*, March 19, 2018. Accessed October 23, 2020. https://www.aljazeera.com/news/2018/3/19/a-palestinian-seat-in-lebanons-parliament.

Akram, Fares. "Hamas Leader Abandons Longtime Base in Damascus." *The New York Times*, January 27, 2012. Accessed October 11, 2017. http://www.nytimes.com/2012/01/28/world/middleeast/khaled-meshal-the-leader-of-hamas-vacates-damascus.html.

al-Akhbar. "Abū Muḥammad ʿAwaḍ: min ʿUṣbat al-Anṣār ilā al-ʿIrāq fa Fatḥ al-Islām [Abu Muhammad ʿAwad: from ʿUsbat al-Ansar to Iraq, then Fatah al-Islam]." *al-Akhbar*, November 8, 2008.

———. "Al-faṣā'il al-filasṭīniyya tarfuḍ zujj mukhayyam ʿAyn al-Ḥilwe fī ishtibākāt ṣaydā [The Palestinian factions prevent the ʿAyn al-Hilwe camp from being dragged in to the Sidon clashes]." *al-Akhbar*, June 19, 2013.

———. "Assad: Hamas Has Betrayed Us Repeatedly, but …." *al-Akhbar*, October 14, 2013. Accessed October 11, 2017. http://english.al-akhbar.com/node/17324.

———. "Factions to Abbas: Disarming Not an Option." *al-Akhbar*, August 19, 2011. Accessed October 15, 2017. http://english.al-akhbar.com/node/150.

———. "Uwlā ḍaḥāyā ʿitiqāl ʿImād Yāsīn [The first victims of the arrest of ʿImad Yasin]." *al-Akhbar*, September 26, 2016. Accessed October 26, 2017. http://www.al-akhbar.com/node/265442.

al-Amin, Hazim. "Fī ʿAyn al-Ḥilwe ghurabā' yujannidūn intiḥāriīn fī mawsim al-Qāʿida. Al-ʿā'idūn min al-ʿIrāq yaṭruqūn abwāb Lubnān min al-Janūb wa-l-Biqāʿ [In ʿAyn al-Hilwe strangers enlist suicide bombers in the 'season of al-Qaʿida'. The returnees from Iraq are knocking on the doors of Lebanon from the South to the Biqaʿ]." *al-Hayat*, January 23, 2006.

al-ʿArabi al-Jadid. "Lubnān: ikhbār ḍudd Ḥizballāh wa-l-Sarāyā al-Muqāwama bi maʿrikat ʿAbrā [Lebanon: Information against Hizballah and The Resistance Squadrons in the battle of ʿAbra]." *al-ʿArabi al-Jadid*, January 5, 2016. Accessed September 25, 2017. https://www.alaraby.co.uk/politics/2016/1/5/
لبنان-إخبار-ضد-حزب-الله-و-سرايا-المقاومة-بمعركة-عبرا.

Al Arabiya. "Palestinian Leader of Hezbollah-linked Ansar Allah Leaves Lebanon to Syria." *Al Arabiya*, November 7, 2018. Accessed October 23, 2020. https://english.alarabiya.net/en/News/middle-east/2018/11/07/Leader-of-Hezbollah-linked-Ansar-Allah-leaves-Lebanon-to-Syria.

al-Arian, Laila. "PA Selling Short the Refugees." *Aljazeera.com*, January 25, 2011. Accessed November 9, 2017. http://www.aljazeera.com/palestinepapers/2011/01/201112412332488 7267.html.

al-ʿArid, ʿAbdallah. "al-Quwā al-islāmiyya tataḍāman maʿ Ḥamas [The Islamic Forces in solidarity with Hamas]." *Minbar al-Jihad* 139 (April 2015): 30–1.

al-Asʿad, Nasir. "ʿAlā abwāb isti'nāf al-ḥiwār al-Lubnānī al-Filasṭīnī wa fī mā tarbuṭ al-faṣā'il al-muwāliyya li Sūriyā silāḥaha bi-l-tanẓīr li istimrār al-ṣirāʿ maʿ Isrā'il [At the doorstep of a resumption of a Lebanese-Palestinian dialogue, while the Pro-Syrian factions link their weapons to the theoretical continuation of the conflict against Israel]." *al-Mustaqbal*, October 2005. Accessed October 15, 2017. http://www.almustaqbal.com/v4/Article.aspx?Type=np&Articleid=149296.

al-Bawab News. "Nā'iba Lubnāniyya tuṭma'inn ʿalā taṭawwurāt al-awḍāʿ fī mukhayyam ʿAyn al-Ḥilwe [Lebanese MP assures progress in the situation of the ʿAyn al-Hilwe camp].” *al-Bawab News*, December 7, 2016. Accessed October 27, 2017. http://www.albawabhnews.com/2257691.

al-Diyar. “Qutila 3 min ʿuṣbat al-nūr wa juriḥa 3 ākharīn fī ʿAyn al-Ḥilwe [Three from ʿUsbat al-Nur were killed and three others were injured in ʿAyn al-Hilwe].” *al-Diyar*, April 7, 2005.

Al-Gharbi, Khalid. “Mughāmarat Shaḥāde Jawhar al-akhīra [Shahade Jawhar's last adventure].” *al-Akhbar*, July 21, 2008. Accessed September 3, 2017. http://www.al-akhbar.com/node/114336.

———. “B'us al-Taʿmīr fī Saydā yas'al: al-mustaqbal kayfa? [The misery of Taʿmir begs the question: The future, how?].” *al-Modon*, February 15, 2018. Accessed October 4, 2020. https://www.almodon.com/politics/2018/2/15/بؤس-التعمير-في-صيدا-يسأل-المستقبل-كيف.

———. “ʿUsbat al-Anṣār tuḥarrim qitāl al-jaysh al-Lubnānī [ʿUsbat al-Ansar forbids hostility against the Lebanese army].” *al-Akhbar*, December 6, 2008. Accessed April 25, 2017. http://www.al-akhbar.com/node/100456.

al-Ghoul, Asmaa. “Mohammed Dahlan to Run for Palestinian President.” *al-Monitor*, April 14, 2014. Accessed November 29, 2017. https://www.al-monitor.com/pulse/originals/2014/04/mohammed-dahlan-wife-interview-presidency-gaza.html.

Al-Haraka al-Islamiyya al-Mujahida. “al-Quwā al-Islāmiyya fī ʿAyn al-Ḥilwe tastaqbil Tayyār al-Mustaqbal [The Islamic Forces of ʿAyn al-Hilwe receive the Future Movement].” *Minbar al-Jihad* 139 (April 2015): 27–9.

al-Hawayk, Yusif. “Fī ḥiwār khāṣṣ maʿ al-Diyyār nafā ʿilmahu bi qaḍiyyat Abū Muḥjin qabla tawajjah ṣabāḥ al-yawm ilā Lubnān [In an exclusive talk with al-Diyyar he denied his knowledge about the case of Abu Muhjin before his return to Lebanon this morning].” *al-Diyar*, Desember 12, 1999.

al-Hayat. “al-Munaẓẓamāt al-islāmiyya (7): al-Ḥaraka al-Islāmiyya al-Mujāhida [The Islamist organizations (7): The Islamic Combatant Movement].” *al-Hayat*, August 1, 2015.

———. “Ittihām ʿUṣbat al-Anṣār bi ightiyāl al-qaḍā al-arbaʿa [ʿUsbat al-Ansar charged with the assassination of the four judges].” *al-Hayat*, October 27, 2017. Accessed October 28, 2017. http://www.alhayat.com/Edition/Print/24922367/اتهام--عصبة-الأنصار-باغتيال-القضاة-الأربعة.

al-Iqtisadiyya. “Lubnān: al-ʿuthūr ʿalā juththat mas'ūl Jund al-Shām fī mukhayyam ʿAyn al-Ḥilwe [Lebanon: The body of Jund al-Sham leader found in the ʿAyn al-Hilwe camp].” *al-Iqtisadiyya*, December 26, 2010. Accessed September 16, 2017. http://www.aleqt.com/2010/12/26/article_483183.html.

al-Islam, Nida'. “Bayyān tawḍīḥī min ʿUṣbat al-Anṣār al-Islāmiyya ḥawla qaḍiyyat Badīʿ Ḥammāde (Abū ʿUbayda) [A clearifying statement from ʿUsbat al-Ansar about the case of Badiʿ Hammade (Abu ʿAbayda)].” *Nida' al-Islam* 9, no. 3 (October - November 2002): 4.

Aljazeera. “ʿAbd al-Raḥmān ʿAwaḍ.” December 2, 2010. Accessed September 17, 2017. http://www.aljazeera.net/encyclopedia/icons/2010/12/2/عبد-الرحمن-عوض.

———. “Baʿda tẓāhurāt munāwi'a lahu ....Quwwāt al-Amn al-Filasṭiniyya taʿtaqil 7 min anṣār Daḥlān [Following demonstrations opposing him ... The Palestinian Security Forces arrest 7 supporters of Dahlan].” *Aljazeera*, September 22, 2020. Accessed October 23, 2020. https://www.aljazeera.net/news/politics/2020/9/22/بعد-تظاهرات-مناوئة-له-قوات-الأمن.

———. “Cheney yattahim ʿArafāt bi taʿṭīl al-salām wa-l-muqāwama tuʿlin hudna [Cheney accuses Arafat of disrupting the peace process, and the Resistance announces a cease fire].” *al-Jazeera*, December 9, 2001. Accessed October 1, 2017. http://www.aljazeera.

net/home/print/f6451603-4dff-4ca1-9c10-122741d17432/c31b4245-dcb1-4ba4-8425-e7b83dd30296.

———. "Donors to Increase UNRWA Support and Funding despite US Cuts." *Aljazeera*, September 2, 2018. Accessed September 27, 2019. https://www.aljazeera.com/news/2018/9/2/donors-to-increase-unrwa-support-and-funding-despite-us-cuts.

al-Jumhuriyya. "al-Quwwa al-Amniyya fī-l-Miyye wo-Miyye wa qarīban fī mukahyyamāt Bayrūt [The Joint Force in al-Miyye wo-Miyye and soon in Beirut]." *al-Jumhuriyya*, March 15, 2015. Accessed October 26, 2017. http://www.aljoumhouria.com/news/index/222450.

———. "Ḍābit fī Fatḥ ya'tarif bi qatl murāfiq al-Līnō [Fatah officer confsses to killing companion of Lino]." *al-Jumhuriyya*, December 24, 2011.

al-Manar. "Usāma Sa'd: li muqāraba waṭaniyya shāmila li awḍā' mukhayyam 'Ayn al-Ḥilwe [Usama Sa'd: for a comprehensive national approach regarding the situation in the 'Ayn al-Hilwe camp]." *al-Manar*, November 30, 2016. Accessed October 27, 2017. http://www.almanar.com.lb/1109491.

al-Monitor. "Hamas, Fatah Agree to Hold Palestinian Elections within Six Months." *al-Monitor*, September 24, 2020. Accessed October 23, 2020. https://www.al-monitor.com/pulse/originals/2020/09/fatah-hamas-elections-palestinian-rivals-israel-deals-trump.html.

al-Mughrabi, Nidal. "Cracks Deepen in Palestinian Politics as Abbas Clamps Down." *Reuters*, December 19, 2016. Accessed December 7, 2017. https://www.reuters.com/article/us-palestinians-fatah-abbas/cracks-deepen-in-palestinian-politics-as-abbas-clamps-down-idUSKBN1481H6.

al-Mustaqbal. "al-Ḥaraka al-Islāmiyya al-Mujāhida." *al-Mustaqbal*, March 3, 2000.

———. "al-Jaysh yuqarrir intishār fī Ta'mīr 'Ayn al-Ḥilwe [The Army decides to deploy in Ta'mir, 'Ayn al-Hilwe]." *al-Mustaqbal*, January 16, 2007. Accessed January 26, 2018. http://almustaqbal.com/article/212320/.

———. "Awwal iṭlāla li-l-nāṭiq bism Jund al-Shām: 'umalā' al-dawla aṭlaqū al-nār fī-l-Ta'mīr [First appearance of the spokesperson for Jund al-Sham: agents of the state fired shots in Ta'mir]." *al-Mustaqbal*, October 26, 2005.

———. "Irhāb 'alā bāb al-sifāra al-Irāniyya [Terrorism at the gates of the Iranian embassy]." *al-Mustaqbal*, November 20, 2013. Accessed September 9, 2017. http://www.almustaqbal.com/v4/Article.aspx?Type=np&Articleid=595604.

———. "I'taraf 'alayhi ibn shaqīqihi bi-annahu kāna yukaffir al-jaysh wa-l-dawla ḥukm jadīd mu'abbid bi ḥaqq Usāma al-Shihābī [His nephew confessed that he was committing takfir against the army and the state. A new life sentence for Usama al-Shihabi]." *al-Mustaqbal*, September 2, 2010. Accessed September 17, 2017. http://www.almustaqbal.com/v4/Article.aspx?Type=np&Articleid=427252.

———. "Mas'ūl fī 'Uṣbat al-Anṣār yu'lin ḥall Jund al-shām wa waḍ' 'anāṣiriha taḥt imrat al-quwā al-islāmiyya [Usbat al-Ansar officials announces the dissolving of Jund al-Sham, and the placing of its personnel under the command of the Islamic Forces]." *al-Mustaqbal*, July 1, 2007. Accessed September 3, 2017. http://www.almustaqbal.com/v4/Article.aspx?Type=np&Articleid=239480.

———. "Rāqabtu al-Jaysh wa-l-UNIFIL li istihdāfihumā al-i'dām li majmū'atin khaṭṭaṭat li khaṭf suyyāḥ wa mubādalatihim bi mawqūfī Fatḥ al-Islām [I surveilled the army and UNIFIL in order to target them: death sentences for a group that planned the kidnaping of tourists in order to swap them with detainees of Fatah al-Islam]." *al-Mustaqbal*, February 18, 2010. Accessed September 17. http://www.almustaqbal.com/v4/Article.aspx?Type=np&Articleid=393929.

———. “Yāsīn yatarājaʿ ʿan iʿtirāfātihi ḥawlā takhṭīṭ li ightiyāl Walīd Junblāṭ bi sayyāra mufakhkhakha kawnuhu min adhkā al-siyāsiyīn [Yasin retracts his confessions of planning the assassination of Walid Jumblatt with a car bomb, as he is among ‘the most clever politicians’].” *al-Mustaqbal*, October 3, 2017.

al-Nahar. “Abū al-ʿAynayn: Fatḥ amsakat mujaddidan bi ʿAyn al-Ḥilwe [Abu al-ʿAynayn: Fatah has reaffirmed its grip on ʿAyn al-Hilwe].” *al-Nahar*, July 28, 1999.

———. “Abū al-ʿAynayn: mawqif al-Maqdaḥ la yuʿabbir ʿan mawqif al-Munaẓẓama. [Abu al-ʿAynayn: the position of al-Maqdah does not represent the position of the Organization].” *al-Nahar*, April 10, 2000.

———. “al-Jamāʿa: mawqif al-ʿUsba ijābī min intishār al-Jaysh fī-l-Taʿmīr] al-Jamaʿa: al-ʿUsba’s position on the deployment of the army in Taʾmīr is positive].” *al-Nahar*, November 1, 2006.

———. “al-Maqdaḥ yusayṭar ʿalā ٣ maqārrin li ‘Fatḥ’ [al-Maqdah controls 3 Fatah headquarters].” *al-Nahar*, October 10, 1993.

———. “al-Maqdaḥ: bayyān Anṣār Allāh maṣdaruhu Ghazza [Al-Maqdah: Ansar Allah’s statement’s source is Gaza] “ *al-Nahar*, August 3, 1994a.

———. “al-Silāḥ al-Filasṭīnī fī Lubnān: as’ilat al-ʿawda al-thāniyya [Palestinian weapons in Lebanon: Questions upon their second return].” *al-Nahar*, October 29, 1999b.

———. “Anṣār Allāh aʿlanū mas’ūliyyatahum ʿan tafjīr al-markaz al-yahūdī fī-l-Arjantīn [Ansar Allah claimed responsibility of blowing up the Jewish Center in Argentina].” *al-Nahar*, July 20, 1994b.

———. “Anṣār Allāh ḥadhdharat Iṭālīā min tafjīr sifāratiha fī Bayrūt [Ansar Allah threatened Italy with blowing up its embassy in Beirut].” *al-Nahar*, January 27, 1987.

———. “ʿAwdat Shraydī ilā ʿAyn al-Ḥilwe fī ḍaw’ al-nahaj al-siyāsī al-jadīd li ḥarakat Fatḥ [Shraydi returns to ʿAyn al-Hilwe in light of Fatah’s new approach].” *al-Nahar*, December 22, 1990.

———. “Fatḥ andharat al-rā’id Sulaymān bi-l-khurūj min mukhayyam ʿAyn al-Ḥilwe [Fatah urged Major Sulayman to leave the ʿAyn al-Hilwe camp].” *al-Nahar*, January 12, 1991a.

———. “Ḥarakat al-Tawḥīd al-Islāmī [The Islamic Unification Movement].” *al-Nahar*, April 4, 1996.

———. “Ishtibāk fī ʿAyn al-Ḥilwe awqaʿ jarīḥayn ithr ightiyāl mas’ūl ʿUṣbat al-Anṣār [Clash in ʿAyn al-Hilwe leaves two injured in the wake of the assassination of the head of ʿUsbat al-Ansar].” *al-Nahar*, December 16, 1991.

———. “Kushifa anna al-yamanī kāna yuḥāwil al-farār min Lubnān qabla iʿtiqālihi [It was revealed that the Yemeni had attempted to flee from Lebanon before his detention].” *al-Nahar*, December 9, 2003.

———. “Taṭwīq al-tawattur bayna Fatḥ wa-l-Majlis al-Thawrī [The besetment of tension between Fatah and The Revolutionary Council].” *al-Nahar*, February 5, 1991.

———. “Untitled News Report.” *al-Nahar*, August 3, 1990.

———. “(Without title).” *al-Nahar*, October 15, 1993.

al-Qays, Shadin. “Islāmīū mukhayyamāt Bayrūt fī qirā’atin li marḥalat ma baʿda maʿārik Nahr al-Bārid [Islamists of the Beirut camps evaluate the time to come after the battles of Nahr al-Barid].” *al-Safir*, September 14, 2007.

al-Ra’i. “Lubnān: jidār al-ʿazl li mukhayyam ʿAyn al-Ḥilwe yufajjir jidālan ʿan al-jadwā wa … aṣl al-fikra [Lebanon: the isolation wall of ʿAyn al-Hilwe sparks debates about its feasibility and …. the origins of the idea].” *al-Ra’i*, November 28, 2016. Accessed

October 27, 2017. http://www.alraimedia.com/ar/article/issues/2016/11/28/726637/nr/lebanon.

———. "ʿUṣbat al-Anṣār al-Islamiyya tuqarrir al-ʿitikfāf fī ʿAyn al-Ḥilwe [ʿUsbat al-Ansar decides to suspend (its participation) in ʿAyn al-hilwe]." *al-Ra'i*, October 14, 2016. Accessed October 26, 2017. http://www.alraimedia.com/ar/article/foreigns/2016/10/14/714979/nr/lebanon.

al-Safir. "Abū al-ʿAynayn fī ʿAyn al-Ḥilwe: al-khilāf maʿ al-Maqdaḥ kāna hafwatan [Abu al-ʿAynayn in ʿAyn al-Hilwe: the conflict with al-Maqdah was an error]." *al-Safir*, August 1, 1997.

———. "Abū al-ʿAynayn yuḥammil ʿalā al-Dīmūqrāṭiyya wa-l-Shaʿbiyya [Abu al-Aynayn blames the DFLP and the PLFP]." *al-Safir*, June 23, 1995.

———. "Abū al-ʿAynayn: al-qarār 1559 isrā'īlī bi imtīāz [Abu al-ʿAynayn: Resolution 1559 is distinctly Israeli]." *al-Safir*, December 12, 2005.

———. "al-Ḥūt yuḥāḍir ʿan al-qaḍiyya al-Filasṭīniyya fī Ṣaydā: limādhā takhrīj al-muqātilīn wa-l-ṣulḥ muwaqqaʿ yajib an naʿtrif bi-l-wāqiʿ al-jadīd bi Lubnān [al-Hut lectures on the Palestinian case in Sidon: Why this graduation of fighters when the reconciliation has been signed? We must recognize the new reality in Lebanon]." *al-Safir*, November 11, 1999.

———. "Al-Maqdaḥ yuaʿrriḍ mutahhiman bi ightiyālihi: yaʿmil li-l-Mussād wa-l-shurṭa fī Ghazza [al-Maqdah exposes the suspect of his assassination (attempt): He works for Mossad and the police in Gaza]." *al-Safir*, December 2, 1995.

———. "al-Mu'assasāt al-Filasṭīniyya fī mukhayyam ʿAyn al-Ḥilwe tantaqil ilā muʿāriḍī ʿArafāt bi tamwīl Īrān [The Palestinian institutions in the ʿAyn al-Hilwe camp are turned over to opponents of Arafat by the means of Iranian funding]." *al-Safir*, June 14, 1994.

———. "ʿArafāt yuṣṣaiʿd li ḥimāyat mas'ūl Fatḥ fī-l-janub al-Ḥuṣṣ: hadhā amr qaḍā'ī wa lan natadakhkhal fīhi [Arafat steps up his protection of official in the South. Al-Huss: This is a court order and we will not interfere in it]." *al-Safir*, October 30, 1999.

———. "Ishtibākāt karr wa farr fī ʿAyn al-Ḥilwe bayna anṣār ʿArafāt wa muʿāriḍīhi taḥṣud ١٠ qatlā wa ٢٥ jarḥā wa tuthīr iḥtijājāt wa ittihāmāt [Hit and run-clashes in ʿAyn al-Hilwe between followers of Arafat and his opposition result in 10 deaths and 25 wounded and causes protests and accusations]." *al-Safir*, November 26, 1994.

———. "Maṣādir rasmiyya taqūl inna Laḥūd lam yataṭarraq awḍāʿ al-lāji'īn wafd al-qiyāda al-Filasṭīniyya fī Bayrūt yaltaqī al-ru'asā' al-thalātha: iftitāḥ sifāra wa mawḍūʿ al-silāḥ al-Filasṭīnī fī waqtihi [Official Palestinian sources say that Lahud did not touch upon the situation of the refugees. A delegation of the Palestinian leadership meets three state officials in Beirut: The opening of a Palestinian embassy and the Palestinian weapons will be dealt with in time]." *al-Safir*, December 9, 2004.

———. "Naql risālatin min ʿArafāt ilā Ṣfayr. Wafd Filasṭīnī fī-l-Dīmān: rafḍ qāṭiʿ li-l-tawṭīn [A message from Arafat to Sfayr. Palestinian delegation in Dimane: a categorical rejection of tawtin]." *al-Safir*, September 4, 1999.

al-Sharq al-Awsat. "Ashar aḥkām al-iʿdām fī Lubnān [The most famous death penalties in Lebanon]." *al-Sharq al-Awsat*, April 26, 2003. Accessed August 30, 2017. http://archive.aawsat.com/details.asp?article=167397&issueno=8915#.WabM_8gjFPY

———. "ʿAyn al-Ḥilwe … mā zāla muʿskaran lil-muqātilīn alladhīna yatasarrabūn ilā al-ʿIrāq [ʿAyn al-Hilwe … still a stronghold for the fighters infiltrating Iraq]." *al-Sharq al-Awsat*, June 29, 2005.

———. "Istimrār ishtibākāt ʿAyn al-Ḥilwe … wa ittifāq filasṭīnī ʿalā tafkīk Bilāl Badr [The clashes of ʿAyn al-Hilwe persist ….Palestinian agreement to disperse Bilal Badr]."

al-Sharq al-Awsat, April 10, 2017. Accessed October 29, 2017. https://aawsat.com/home/article/898591/
استمرار-اشتباكات-«عين-الحلوة»-واتفاق-فلسطيني-على-تفكيك-«بلال-بدر».
———. "Maktab al-Ḥarīrī yudaḥḥiḍ al-iddiʿāʾāt al-kādhiba li-l-talifiziūn al-sūrī. bi sha'n shabakat Fatḥ al-Islām [Hariri's office refutes the false claims made by Syrian television … pertaining to Fatah al-Islam's network]." *al-Sharq al-Awsat*, November 11, 2008. Accessed September 16, 2017. http://archive.aawsat.com/details.asp?section=4&article=494439&issueno=10941#.Wb0MJMgjFPY.

al-Shaykh, Sulayman. "Hal intahā ʿahd al-tawatturāt al-amniyya fī ʿAyn al-Ḥilwe? [Is the era of security incidents in ʿAyn al-Hilwe over?]." *al-Quds al-Arabi*, September 9, 2016. Accessed November 23, 2017. http://www.alquds.co.uk/?p=594848.

al-Suhayl, Turki. "Taʿrraf ʿalā ra's al-ḥarba al-Qaṭariyya fī daʿm al-anshiṭa al-irhābiyya [Get to know the Qatari spearhead financing terrorist activities]." *Makka al-Mukarrama*, June 1, 2017. Accessed August 30, 2017. http://makkahnewspaper.com/article/604415/أعمال/تعرف-على-رأس-الحربة-القطرية-في-دعم-الأنشطة-الإرهابية.

al-Wasat. "al-Amīr Abū Yūsif Sharqiyya: nakhtalif maʿ Ḥizbillāh fī juz'iyyat qatl al-aʿdā' [The Amir Abu Yusif Sharqiyya: We differ with Hizballah regarding minor details on the (permissibility of) killing the enemies]." *al-Wasat*, August 9, 2004.

al-Watan, Dunya. "al-Quwwa al-amniyya al-mushtaraka fī mukhayyam ʿAyn al-Ḥilwe li ḥafẓ al-amn wa-l-istiqrār [The Joint Security Force in the ʿAyn al-Hilwe camp, to preserve security and stability]." *Dunya al-Watan*, July 8, 2014. Accessed October 12, 2017. https://www.alwatanvoice.com/arabic/news/2014/07/08/564235.html.

Albuss.net. "Intikhāb ʿAbd al-Majīd al-ʿAwaḍ al-mas'ūl al-siyāsī li ḥarakat Ḥamās fī minṭaqat Ṣūr [The election of ʿAbd al-Majid al-Awʿas Hamas' political official in Tyre]." *Albuss.net*, May 14, 2017. Accessed June 16, 2017. http://www.albuss.net/2017/05/blog-post_669.html.

Anderson, Jack, Dale Van Atta. "Why Arafat Backed Saddam." *The Washington Post*, August 26, 1990. Accessed August 29, 2017. https://www.washingtonpost.com/archive/opinions/1990/08/26/why-arafat-backed-saddam/904a9366-c1e0-4294-ab64-1391b0e3b452/?utm_term=.6b17c86053c9.

ʿAqil, Radwan. "Jamāʿat al-Nūr wulaydat ʿUṣbat al-Anṣār wa qādat al-faṣā'il al-Filasṭīniyya yanfarūna minha [The Nur group is the offspring of ʿUsbat al-Ansar and the Palestinian leaders shun it]." *al-Nahar*, November 1, 2001.
———. "ʿUṣbat al-Anṣār maʿ al-infitāḥ ʿalā al-thunā'ī al-Shīʿī [ʿUsbat al-Ansar opens up to the Shia duo]." *al-Nahar*, March 16, 2016. Accessed July 19, 2017. https://newspaper.annahar.com/article/335182-
عصبة-الأنصار-مع-الانفتاح-على-الثنائي-الشيعي-الجهاد-قرب-المسافات-والمشكلة-في-عين

Arab 48 News. "Qatīlān wa 21 jarīḥan fī ishtibākāt fī ʿAyn al-Ḥilwe [Two dead and 21 injured in clashes in ʿAyn al-Hilwe]." *Arab 48 News*, April 8, 2017. Accessed October 28, 2017. https://www.arab48.com/
فلسطينيات/الشتات/2017/04/08/قتيلان-و-21جريحا-في-اشتباكات-في-عين-الحلوة.

Arabi Press. "al-Shabāb al-Muslim: Marwān ʿīssa qutila li annahu sabb al-ṣaḥḥāba [al-Shabab al-Muslim: Marwan ʿIsa was killed because he insulted the companions]." *Arabi Press*, April 23, 2015. Accessed September 26, 2017. https://www.arabipress.org/144992.

Armstrong, Martin. "Palestinians Protest against UNRWA Cuts in Lebanon." *Aljazeera.com*, February 29, 2016. Accessed July 12, 2017. http://www.aljazeera.com/indepth/features/2016/02/palestinians-protest-unrwa-cuts-lebanon-160223151011960.html.

ʿAsimat al-shattat. "Bi-l-sūwar: iftitāḥ markaz Futuwwat al-Anṣār al-Islāmī fī ʿAyn al-Ḥilwe [In pictures: The opening of the center of the Youth of the Islamic Partisans in

ʿAyn al-Hilwe." *ʿAsimat al-shattat*, March 24, 2015. Accessed March 21, 2015. http://www.asematalshatat.com/?p=8807.

———. "Iḍrāb fī ʿAyn al-Ḥilwe iḥtijājan ʿalā taraddī al-awḍāʿ al-amniyya wa rukūd al-ḥaraka al-iqtiṣādiyya [Strike in ʿAyn al-Hilwe in protest of the deteriation of the security situation and the recession of the economy]." *ʿAsimat al-Shattat*, September 18, 2015. Accessed July 10, 2017S. http://www.asematalshatat.com/?p=11298.

———. "Liqāʾ muṣālaḥa bayna Fatḥ wa-l-Shabāb al-Muslim fī ʿAyn al-Ḥilwe [Conciliation meeting between Fatah and al-Shabab al-Muslim in ʿAyn al-Hilwe]." *ʿAsimat al-Shattat*, March 13, 2016. Accessed October 26, 2017. http://www.asematalshatat.com/?p=12293.

———. "Mawqiʿ ʿāṣimat al-shattāt yukassir ṣamt al-Shaykh Abū Muḥjin [The Asimat al-Shattat site breaks the silence of the Shaykh Abu Muhjin]." *ʿAsimat al-Shattat*, August 9, 2014. Accessed June 20, 2017. http://www.asematalshatat.com/?p=4275.

———. "Mukhayyam ʿAyn al-Ḥilwe ....bi intiẓār jawlāt jadīda [The ʿAyn al-hilwe camp ....awaiting new rounds of violence]." *ʿAsimat al-Shattat*, August 28, 2015. Accessed October 26, 2017. http://www.asematalshatat.com/?p=10986.

———. "ʿUwayd yakshif asbāb insiḥābihi min min al-lajna al-amniyya al-ʿuliyā [ʿUwayd reveals the reasons for his withdrawal from the Higher Security Committee]." *ʿAsimat al-Shattat*, April 4, 2016. Accessed October 27, 2017. http://www.asematalshatat.com/?p=12419.

Bar'el, Zvi. "Palestinian President Abbas Is Not Israel's Partner—or Cairo's." *Haaretz*, March 7, 2017. Accessed March 27, 2017. http://www.haaretz.com/middle-east-news/.premium-1.775495.

Barnard, Anne. "Hezbollah Commits to an All-Out Fight to Save Assad." *The New York Times*, May 25, 2013. Accessed September 13, 2017. http://www.nytimes.com/2013/05/26/world/middleeast/syrian-army-and-hezbollah-step-up-raids-on-rebels.html?mcubz=1.

———. "On the Trail of a Story in Lebanon, Stumbling on a Scoop." *The New York Times*, January 1, 2018. Accessed October 23, 2020. https://www.nytimes.com/2018/01/01/insider/lebanon-palestine-scoop-saad-hariri.html?smid=tw-share&_r=0.

Blanford, Nicholas. "Al-Aqsa Cells Being Funded and Guided from Ain al-Hilweh." *The Daily Star*, July 4, 2003. Accessed http://www.dailystar.com.lb/ArticlePrint.aspx?id=38308&mode=print.

———. "Fatah Commander Denies Sending Suicide Bombers to Iraq." *The Daily Star*, March 31, 2003. Accessed July 29, 2017. https://dailystar.com.lb/News/Lebanon-News/2003/Mar-31/39618-fatah-commander-denies-sending-suicide-bombers-to-iraq.ashx.

———. "In Lebanon, the UN and Hizbullah Make Unlikely Bedfellows." *The Christian Science Monitor*, July 24, 2007. Accessed December 29, 2017. https://www.csmonitor.com/2007/0724/p04s01-wome.html.

Cambanis, Thanassis. "Rocket Fire from Lebanon Unsettles Israel, but Fears of a Hezbollah Attack Subside." *The New York Times*, January 8, 2009. Accessed May 7, 2019. https://www.nytimes.com/2009/01/09/world/middleeast/09lebanon.html.

Chayban, Badih. "Future TV Building Blasted by 'Ansar Allah.'" *The Daily Star*, June 16, 2003. Accessed September 24, 2017. http://www.dailystar.com.lb/News/Lebanon-News/2003/Jun-16/39108-future-tv-building-blasted-by-ansar-allah.ashx.

Dahshe, Muhammad. "Intishār al-quwwa al-amniyya fī ʿAin al-Ḥilwe ... bi ijmāʿ Filasṭīnī wa ghiṭāʾ Lubnānī [The security force deploys in Ain al-Hilwe ... under Palestinian consensus and Lebanese cover]." *al-Balad*, July 9, 2014.

———. "Maṭlūbū ʿAyn al-Ḥilwe yusallimūna anfusahum li-l-jaysh: lā ṣafqa … wal-ḥukm li-l-qaḍā' [The wanteds of ʿAyn al-Hilwe hand themselves over to the Army: no deal … and court rulings to proceed]." *al-Balad*, August 18, 2016.

Danin, Robert M. "Hamas Breaks from Syria." *Council of Foreign Relations*, February 29, 2012. Accessed October 11, 2017. https://www.cfr.org/blog/hamas-breaks-syria.

Dawoud, Ali."Quwwāt al-Nakhba ilā ʿAyn al-Ḥilwe li ijtithāt al-jamāʿt al-irhābiyya [The Elite Forces head to ʿAyn al-Hilwe … in order to root out the terrorist groups]." *al-Jumhuriyya*, September 17, 2017. Accessed October 28, 2017. http://www.aljoumhouria.com/news/index/382191.

———. "Tadrībāt ʿaskariyya li Fataḥ ḥatta awākhir Ḥuzayrān [Fatah military drills until the end of June]." *al-Jumhuriyya*, May 25, 2014.

Dearden, Lizzie. "Paris Attacks: Hamas Condemns Charlie Hebdo Massacre after Netanyahu Makes Comparison to Gaza Rockets." *The Independent*, January 10, 2015. Accessed August 28, 2017. http://www.independent.co.uk/news/world/europe/paris-attacks-hamas-condemns-charlie-hebdo-massacre-after-netanyahu-makes-comparison-to-gaza-rockets-9970096.html.

Denton, Herbert H. "Arafat and Troops Prepare for Second Exit from Lebanon." *The Washington Post*, December 4, 1983.

Elnashra. "al-Hanniye yubārik khuṭwat taslīm al-Sayyid wa yu'akkid ʿalā ḥafẓ al-amn wa-l-istiqrār [al-Hanniye blesses the handing over of al-Sayyid and assures the preservation of security and stability]." *Elnashra*, July 2, 2017. Accessed July 2. 2017. http://www.elnashra.com/news/show/1115643/هنية-يبارك-خطوة-تسليم-السيد.

Erem News. "al-Faṣā'il al-Filasṭīniyya tubalwir ṣīgha li waqf iṭlāq al-nār fī ʿAyn al-Ḥilwe ʿaqiba firār Bilāl Badr [the Palestinian factions crystalize a formula for a ceasefire in ʿAyn al-Hillwe following the escape of Bilal Badr]." *Erem News*, April 11, 2017. Accessed October 29, 2017. https://www.eremnews.com/news/arab-world/795124.

Farrell, Stephen. "New Winds in Mideast Favor Hamas." *The New York Times*, November 22, 2011. Accessed January 1, 2018. http://www.nytimes.com/2011/11/23/world/middleeast/hamas-gains-momentum-in-palestinian-rivalry.html.

Fisk, Robert. "Arafat's Power Play Threatens Life of Aide." *Independent*, November 1, 1999. Accessed November 15, 2017. http://www.independent.co.uk/news/world/arafats-power-play-threatens-life-of-aide-1120272.html.

———. "Shimon Peres Was No Peacemaker. I'll Never Forget the Sight of Pouring Blood and Burning Bodies at Qana." *The Independent*, September 28, 2016. Accessed November 8, 2017. http://www.independent.co.uk/voices/shimon-peres-dies-israel-qana-massacre-never-forget-no-peacemaker-robert-fisk-a7334656.html.

Ghandur, Thair. "Musalsal damawī mutawāṣil min kābūs ʿAyn al-Ḥilwe fī Lubnān [A series of bloody altercations from the nightmare of ʿAyn al-Hilwe in Lebanon]." *Alaraby*, July 30, 2015. Accessed October 20, 2017. https://www.alaraby.co.uk/politics/2015/7/29/مسلسل-دموي-متواصل-من-كابوس-عين-الحلوة-في-لبنان.

Ghassan, Charbel. "zīārat al-dhākira lil-amīn al-ʿām li Ḥarakat al-Jihād al-Islāmī fī Filasṭīn ١ [Revisiting the memoirs of the General Secretary of Islamic Jihad in Palestine 1]." *al-Hayat*, January 7, 2003.

Ginsburg, Mitch. "Why Israel's Retreat from Lebanon Marked the Birth of Today's 'Middle East." *The Times of Israel*, March 25, 2015. Accessed November 7, 2017. https://www.timesofisrael.com/why-israels-retreat-from-lebanon-marked-the-birth-of-todays-middle-east/.

Haaretz. "Al-Qaida Leader Zarqawi: Our Eyes Are on Jerusalem." *Haaretz*, April 26, 2006 http://www.haaretz.com/news/al-qaida-leader-zarqawi-our-eyes-are-on-jerusalem-1.186164.

Hall, Natasha. "Palestinian Refugees and the Siege of Yarmouk." *Sada—Carnigie Endowment for International Peace*, March 13, 2014. Accessed October 12, 2017. http://carnegieendowment.org/sada/54925.

Hallaq, ʿAbdallah. "al-Shahāda al-ṭawʿaiyya min manẓūr islāmī (1) [A testimony of volunteerism from an Islamic perspective (1)]." *Minbar al-Jihad* 139 (April 2015): 6–9.

Hamzeh, A. Nizar and R. Hrair Dekmejian. "A Sufi Response to Political Islamism: Al-Aḥbāsh of Lebanon." *International Journal of Middle East Studies* 28, no. 2 (1996): 217–29.

Hashem, Ali. "Al-Qaeda-affiliated Emir Arrested in Lebanon." *al-Monitor*, September 9, 2014 http://www.al-monitor.com/pulse/originals/2013/12/abdullah-azzam-emir-custody-hashem.html#ixzz2pE3635md.

Hashishu, ʿAli. "Amīr Jund al-Shām: lā nukaffir ilā al-kāfirīn wa naiʿd Amrīkā wa Isra'īl bi-l-radd ʿalā jarā'imhumā [The Amir of Jund al-Sham: We don't committ takfir except from against infidels, and we promise to respond to the crimes of America and Israel]." *al-Ra'i al-ʿAmm*, July 21, 2004.

Hijazi, Ihsan, A. "Lebanese Scrap P.L.O. Accord, Barring Bases." *The New York Times*, May 22, 1987. Accessed December 16, 2017. http://www.nytimes.com/1987/05/22/world/lebanese-scrap-plo-accord-barring-bases.html.

Holmes, Oliver, Nazih Siddiq. "Bombs Kill 42 Outside Mosques in Lebanon's Tripoli." *Reuters*, August 23, 2013. Accessed September 13, 2017. http://www.reuters.com/article/us-lebanon-explosion-deaths/bombs-kill-42-outside-mosques-in-lebanons-tripoli-idUSBRE97M0FL20130823.

Jabir, Kamil. "Jund al-Shām … dawlat khilāfa min ṭarīq Taʿmīr ʿAyn al-Ḥilwe [Jund al-Sham … a caliphate state from Taʿmir, ʿAyn al-Hilwe.]." *al-Akhbar*, June 6, 2007.

Janoubia. "Fī mukhayyam ʿAyn al-Ḥilwe: qīmat ishtirāk al-kahrabā' 20% aghlā min Ṣaydā [In the ʿAyn al-Hilwe camp: the generator electricity is 20% more expensive than in Sidon]." *Janoubia*, July 3, 2019. Accessed September 25, 2020. https://janoubia.com/2019/07/03/في-مخيّم-عين-الحلوة-قيمة-اشتراك-الكهرب.

Jewish Telegraph Agency. "PLO Leadership Seen in Disarray amid Calls for Arafat's Ouster." *Jewish Telegraph Agency*, August 25, 1993. Accessed November 11, 2017. https://www.jta.org/1993/08/25/archive/plo-leadership-seen-in-disarray-amid-calls-for-arafats-ouster.

Kʿawush, Mahmud. "Ḥadhār, ḥadhār, yā nushaṭā' fī-l-shattāt min ghaḍbat ʿAbbās!! Ḥadhār, ḥadhār!! [Beware, beware of the fury of 'Abbas oh activists in the diaspora!! Beware, beware!!]." *Railyoum*, October 14, 2016. Accessed October 20, 2016. http://www.raialyoum.com/?p=541885.

Khalil, Amal. "15 filasṭīnīan min ʿAyn al-Ḥilwe ilā al-Raqqa [15 Palestinians from ʿAyn al-Hilwe to Raqqa]." *al-Akhbar*, February 11, 2016. Accessed July 19, 2017. http://al-akhbar.com/node/251814.

———. "Ain al-Hilweh Islamists: We Are Not al-Nusra Front." *al-Akhbar*, May 4, 2013. Accessed September 28, 2017. http://english.al-akhbar.com/node/15709.

———. "ʿAyn al-Ḥilwe: ʿAbd Faḍḍa khārij ṣafqat al-taslīmāt [ʿAyn al-hilwe: ʿAbd Fadda is outside of an extradition agreement]." *al-Akhbar*, August 25, 2016. Accessed October 26, 2017. http://www.al-akhbar.com/node/263711.

———. "Fatḥ Fatḥān fī ʿAyn al-Ḥilwe Daḥlān.Abū Māzin [Fatah is two Fatahs in ʿAyn al-Hilwe. Dahlan.Abu Mazin]." *al-Akhbar*, December 30, 2014.

———. "Kayfa sayathār al-Līnō li ightiyāl Ṭalāl al-Urdunī [How will Lino avenge the assassination of Talal The Jordanian?)." *al-Akhbar*, July 27, 2015. Accessed October 21, 2017. http://al-akhbar.com/node/238612.

———. "A New Security Plan for Ain al-Hilweh." *al-Akhbar*, April 29, 2014. Accessed March 26, 2017. http://english.alakhbar.com/node/19589

Khalil, Na'ila. "ʿAbbās: al-mushāraka fī mu'tamar Daḥlān khiyyāna waṭaniyya [Abbas: the participation in Dahlan's conference is national treason]." *al-Araby*, September 29, 2016. Accessed November 29, 2017. https://www.alaraby.co.uk/politics/2016/9/29/ عباس-المشاركة-في-مؤتمر-دحلان-خيانة-وطنية.

Kuttab, Daoud. "Lebanese Fatah Delegates Visit Palestine for First Time." *al-Monitor*, December 15, 2016. Accessed December 5, 2017. https://al-monitor.com/pulse/originals/2016/12/palestinian-delegation-lebanon-first-visit-fatah-congress.html.

Lahud, Elie. "al-Sarāyā al-Muqāwama li-l-difāʿ am li-ikhtirāq al-sāḥāt wa-l-mujtamaʿāt? [The Resistance Squadrons, for defense or for the penetration of the society?]." *al-Nahar*, October 12, 2013. Accessed September 25, 2017. https://newspaper.annahar.com/article/188597- سرايا-المقاومة-للدفاع-أم-لاختراق-الساحاتحات-والمجتمعات-القائد-الحاج-يخرج-عن-صمته

Lebanon Files. "Waqā'iʿ liqā'āt istikhbārāt al-jaysh wa-l-Filasṭīniīn [Meetings take place between the Army Intelligence and the Palestinians]." *Lebanon Files*, November 11, 2008. Accessed September 18, 2017. http://www.lebanonfiles.com/print.php?id=19552.

Lebanon, NOW. "NOW Exclusive: Abbas Requested to Relieve Abu al-Aynayn from His Duties." *NOW Lebanon*, February 23, 2010. Accessed November 26, 2017. https://now.mmedia.me/lb/en/nownews/now_exclusive_abbas_requested_to_relieve_abu_al-aynayn_from_his_duties_1.

Lieber, Dov. "Opening Night of Much-hyped Seventh Fatah Congress a Perplexing Snooze." *The Times of Israel*, November 30, 2016. Accessed December 5, 2017. https://www.timesofisrael.com/opening-night-of-much-hyped-seventh-fatah-congress-a-perplexing-snooze/.

Lynch, Colum and Gramer Robbie. "Trump and Allies Seek End to Refugee Status for Millions of Palestinians." *Foreign Policy*, August 3, 2018.

Mail, Daily. "Lebanon Builds Wall Near Palestinian Refugee Camp." *Daily Mail*, November 21, 2016. Accessed October 27, 2017. http://www.dailymail.co.uk/wires/afp/article-3958600/Lebanon-builds-wall-near-Palestinian-refugee-camp.html.

Mantash, Ahmad. "Amīr Jund al-Shām fī ʿAyn al-Ḥilwe yastaqīl wa yaʿtazil al-ʿamal al-tanẓīmī [The emir of Jund al-Sham in ʿAyn al-Hilwe quits and retires from organizational work]." *al-Nahar*, October 6, 2004.

———. "Anṣār Allāh aḥyū yawm al-quds bi masīra wa ʿaraḍ ʿaskariyya fī ʿAyn al-Ḥilwe [Ansar Allah revives Jerusalem day with a military procession in ʿAyn al-Hilwe]." *al-Nahar*, October 21, 2007.

———. "Baʿdama talaqqat milyūn dūlār min ʿArafāt Fatḥ taʿīd tanẓīm ṣufūfiha li-l-imsāk mujaddidan bi waraqat al-mukhayyamāt [After receiving a million dollars from ʿArafat, Fatah reorganizes its ranks and reaffirms its grip on the file of the camps]." *al-Safir*, July 26, 1999.

———. "Fatḥ tastakmil khaṭawātaha al-tanẓīmiyya wa-l-quwā al-islāmiyya tarqubuha bi ḥadhr [Fatah completes its organizational plans and the Islamic Forces observe with caution]." *al-Nahar*, October 8, 1999.

———. "Fatḥ tu'akkid faṣl al-Maqdaḥ [Fatah confirms the dismissal of al-Maqdah]." *al-Nahar*, December 24, 1998.

———. "I'ādat fatḥ al-ṭarīq 'and muftaraq sūq al-khuḍḍār fī 'Ayn al-Ḥilwe [The reopening of the road at the vegetable market junction in 'Ayn al-Hilwe]." *al-Nahar*, June 10, 2017. Accessed October 30, 2017. https://www.annahar.com/article/599261-اعادة-فتح-الطريق-عند-مفترق-سوق-الخضر-في-عين-الحلوة.

———. "Jund al-Shām tanfī 'alāqataha bi ightiyāl 'Awalī [Jund al-Sham denies connections to the assassination of 'Awali]." *al-Nahar*, July 20, 2004.

———. "Man huwwa Bilāl Badr Rāmbū 'Ayn al-Ḥilwe [Who is Bilal Badr, the Rambo of 'Ayn al-Hilwe?]." *al-Nahar*, April 10, 2017. Accessed October 28, 2017. https://www.annahar.com/article/568368-من-هو-بلال-بدر-رامبو-عين-الحلوة.

———. "Maṣdar 'askarī nafā ḥiṣār al-mukhayyamāt wa-l-mu'āriḍa al-Filasṭīniyya ittihamat 'Arafāt lāji'ūn qaṭa'ū madākhil 'Ayn al-Ḥilwe wa taẓāharū qubālat ḥawājiz li-l-jaysh [A military source denied the embargo against the camps, and the Palestinian opposition accused Arafat [while] refugees blocked the entrances of 'Ayn al-Hilwe and demonstrated in front of the army's checkpoints]." *al-Nahar*, November 22, 1999.

———. "Tawattur fi 'Ayn al-Ḥilwe ithr khilāf bayna mas'ūl fī Jund al-Shām wa 'unṣur min Fatḥ [Tension in 'Ayn al-Hilwe following a conflict between an official from Jund al-Sham and a member of Fatah]." *al-Nahar*, July 4, 2004.

———. "Wilādat al-Jaysh al-Sha'bī al-Mujāhid fī 'Ayn al-Ḥilwe. Al-Maqdaḥ: narfuḍ ḥiṣāranā fī Filasṭīn wa Lubnān [The birth of the Popular Combatant Army. Al-Maqdah: We reject our besiegement in Palestine and Lebanon]." *al-Nahar*, September 19, 1998.

al-Maqdisi, Abu 'Abdallah. "Liqā' muntadā Shumūkh al-Islām ma' al-Shaykh Abī 'Abdallāh al-Maqdīsī - al-mas'ūl al-shar'ī li tanẓīm Fataḥ al-Islām [Shumukh al-Islam's meeting with Shaykh Abu 'Abdallah al-Maqdisi—in charge of religious affairs in the Fatah al-Islam organization]." Shumukh al-Islam, 2009.

Markham, James M. "Arafat, in Teheran, Praises the Victors." *New York Times*, February 19, 1979.

Mekhenet, Soudad and Michael Moss. "A New Face of Al Qaeda Emerges in Lebanon." *The New York Times*, March 15, 2007. Accessed August 11, 2017. http://www.nytimes.com/2007/03/15/world/africa/15iht-lebanon.4924895.html.

Minbar al-Jihad. "Al-umma fī muwājihat al-ṭāghūt wal-ist'imār wal-istīṭān [The Umma facing tyrants, imperialism and settlerism]." *Minbar al-jihad* 139 (April 2015): 1–6.

Moor, Ahmed. "Lebanon's law on Palestinian Workers Does Not Go Far Enough." *The Guardian*, August 27, 2010. Accessed December 14, 2017. https://www.theguardian.com/commentisfree/2010/aug/27/lebanon-law-palestinian-workers-refugees.

Moubayed, Sami. "Syria's Romance with Mahmoud Abbas." *al-Ahram*, July 20, 2005. Accessed November 23, 2017. http://weekly.ahram.org.eg/Archive/2005/751/re3.htm.

Murtada, Radwan. "al-Amn al-'ām yakshif tafāṣīl jaḥīm Ramaḍān [General Security reveals details on the 'Ramadan inferno']." *al-Akhbar*, July 30, 2017. Accessed October 1, 2017. http://www.al-akhbar.com/node/278528.

———. "'Ayn al-Ḥilwe: taraqqub wa intiẓār ba'da layla dāmiyya ['Ayn al-Hilwe holds its breath after a violent night]." *al-Akhbar*, August 8, 2011.

———. "Laylat maqtal al-amīr: taraqqub wa 'azā' wa 'abwa nāsifa [The night of the killing of the 'emir': Expectations, a funeral, and a roadside bomb,]." *al-Akhbar*, August 17, 2010. Accessed September 18, 2017. http://www.al-akhbar.com/node/43169.

———. "Mutaḍarrarū 'Ayn al-Ḥilwe yantaẓirūn ta'wīdahum: al-kull yataharrab! [The victims of 'Ayn al-Hilwe await their compensation: everyone evades the question!]." *al-Akhbar*, May 18, 2017. Accessed October 29, 2017. http://www.al-akhbar.com/node/277362.

———. "ʿUṣbat al-Anṣār wa ḥarakat Ḥamās tusallimān al-maṭlūb Khālid al-Sayyid: ʿAyn al-Ḥilwe yalfiẓ al-irhāb [ʿUsbat al-Ansar and the Hamas movement hand over the wanted Khalid al-Sayyid: ʿAyn al-Hilwe expels terrorism]." *al-Akhbar*, July 3, 2017. Accessed September 6, 2017. http://www.al-akhbar.com/node/279577.

Naharnet. "Tension in Ain el-Hilweh Following Assassination of Fatah Official." *Naharnet*, July 25, 2015. Accessed October 21, 2017. http://www.naharnet.com/stories/en/185658.

Naʿim, Ra'fat. "Bi-l-tawāzī maʿ taslīm 20 maṭlūban min ʿAyn al-Ḥilwe Ḥizballāh yusallim duʿfatayn min maṭlūbī al-Sarāyā al-Muqāwama [In parallel with the handing over of 20 outlaws from ʿAyn al-Hilwe, Hizballah hands over two batches of outlaws from the Resistance Squadrons]." *al-Mustaqbal*, August 19, 2016. Accessed September 26, 2017. http://almustaqbal.com/v4/Article.aspx?Type=NP&ArticleID=714141.

———. "Ḥayy al-ṭawārī' yʿaūd ilā ʿAyn al-Ḥilwe … amnīan! [The Tawari' neighborhood returns to ʿAyn al-Hilwe … security-wise!]." *al-Mustaqbal*, May 20, 2015. Accessed October 20, 2015. http://almustaqbal.com/v4/Article.aspx?Type=NP&ArticleID=661542.

Najjar, Muhammad. "Bawādir inshiqāq fī Fatḥ al-Intifāḍa baʿda faṣl al-ʿUmle [Signs of splits within Fatah - al-Intidada after the severence of al-ʿUmle]." *al-Jazira*, December 13, 2006. Accessed September 5, 2017. http://www.aljazeera.net/news/reportsandinterviews/2006/12/13/بوادر-انشقاق-في-فتح-الانتفاضة-بعد-فصل-العملة.

Najm, Wa'il. "Zaʿīm ʿUṣbat al-Anṣār yataḥaddath ʿan al-ʿalāqa maʿ tanẓīm al-Qāʿida [ʿUsbat al-Ansar chieftain talks about the relations with al-Qaida]." *al-Arabiyya*, June 17, 2007. Accessed September 4. http://www.alarabiya.net/articles/2007/06/17/35582.html.

Nakhoul, Samia. "Lebanon's Rubbish Crisis Exposes Political Rot." *Reuters*, September 7, 2015. Accessed June 23, 2017. http://www.reuters.com/article/us-lebanon-protests-crisis-insight-idUSKCN0R70GO20150907.

NOW Lebanon. "A Call to Arms: Three Palestinian Militant Groups." *NOW Lebanon*, November 6, 2007. Accessed September 23, 2017. https://now.mmedia.me/lb/en/commentaryanalysis/a_call_to_arms_three_palestinian_militant_groups_.

NOW Lebanon. "Fī jazīrat ʿAyn al-ḥilwe … baqāyā faṣā'il wa ṭalā'iʿ al-qāʿida [In the island of ʿAin al-Hilwe … the remnants of factions and the vanguards of al-Qaida]." *NOW Lebanon*, January 13, 2014. Accessed March 26, 2017. https://now.mmedia.me/lb/ar/nowspecialar/529999-في-جزيرة-عين-الحلوة-بقايا-فصائل-وطلائع-القاعدة.

Orme Jr, William A. "Jordan Frees Four Jailed Hamas Leaders and Expels Them." *New York Times*, November 22, 1999. Accessed March 16, 2020. https://www.nytimes.com/1999/11/22/world/jordan-frees-four-jailed-hamas-leaders-and-expels-them.html.

Palestine Today. "Ḍubbāṭ wa kawādir min Fatḥ yuṭālibūn bi saḥb al-safīr Ashraf Dabbūr min lubnān [Officers and cadres demand the withdrawal of Ambassador Ashraf Dabbur from Lebanon]." *Palestine Today*, October 20, 2013. Accessed December 4, 2017. https://paltoday.ps/ar/post/178537.

Palestinian Islamic Jihad. "Bayyān ṣādir ʿan Ḥarakat al-Jihād al-Islāmī fī Filasṭīn ḥawla ʿamaliyyat ibʿād arbʿat mujāhidīn min qiṭāʿ ghazza [A statement released by the Islamic Jihad Movement in Palestine regarding the deportation of four fighters from the Gaza Strip]." *al-Mujahid*, January 1991.

PLO. "al-Niẓām al-dākhilī al-muʿaddal lil-lijān al-shaʿbiyya lil-khadamāt fī mukhayyamāt lil-lāji'īn al-filasṭīnīyyin [The revised rules of procedure for the Popular Committees for services in camps of Palestinian refugees]." edited by PLO—the Administration For Refugee Affairs. Ramallah: PLO, 2010.

P.N. News. "Bi-l-wathā'iq: tasjīl ma' mas'ūl amnī yu'akkid anna al-ra'īs 'Abbās huwwa man ṭalab al-taḥqīq bi asmā' nāshiṭī-l-facebook [Documented: Recording of security official confirming that 'Abbas was the one who ordered the investigation into the names of Facebook activists]." *P.N. News*, October 14, 2016. Accessed July 12, 2017. http://www.pn-news.net/news.php?extend.3601.

Prothero, Mitchell. "PLO Leadership in Power Struggle over Lebanese Refugee Camps." *The National*, March 30, 2010. Accessed November 24, 2017. https://www.thenational.ae/world/mena/plo-leadership-in-power-struggle-over-lebanese-refugee-camps-1.508890.

Qalam Rasas. "Iftitāḥat al-'adad al-awwal: limādha kānat Qalam Raṣāṣ [The opening of the first edition: Why Qalam Rasas?]." *Qalam Rasas*, September 2015.

Quilty, Jim. "Ain al-Hilwa—Microcosm of the Palestinian Diaspora." *Middle East International*, October 1, 1999.

———. "Brothers and Enemies." *Middle East International*, October 26, 1999.

———. "A Taste of the Future." *Middle East International*, July 30, 1999.

Ra'i al-Yawm. "Tafāṣīl ṭard al-Līnō min Qiyādat al-Kifāḥ al-Musallaḥ [Details on al-Lino's ousting from the Armed Struggle Command]." *Ra'i al-Yawm*, October 13, 2013. Accessed May 11, 2017. http://www.raialyoum.com/?p=11750.

———. "Tawattur fī mukhayyam 'Ayn al-Ḥilwe ba'da ightiyāl al-qiyādī fī Jama'iyyat al-Mashārī' al-Islāmiyya al-Aḥbāsh [Tension in the 'Ayn al-Hilwe camp after the assassination of the leader of the Islamic Charitable Assosiacion 'al-Ahbash']." *Ra'i al-Yawm*, April 10, 2014. Accessed October 14, 2017. http://www.raialyoum.com/?p=73409.

Radawan, 'Aqil. "al-Nahār ma' amīr min 'Uṣbat al-Anṣār fī manzil Abū Muḥjin fī 'Ayn al-Ḥilwe [al-Nahar with an emir from 'Usbat al-Ansar in the house of Abu Muhjin in 'Ayn al-Hilwe]." *al-Nahar*, October 26, 1996.

———. "Malāmiḥ 'awdat Fatḥ ilā mukhayyamāt Bayrūt wa-l-shamāl ba'd al-taqārub al-Sūrī-al-Lubnānī fī 'Ammān [The prospects of Fatah returning to the camps of Beirut and the North after the Syrian-Lebanese rapprochement in Amman]." *al-Nahar*, March 31, 2001.

Rose, Sunniva. "Palestinian Students Show Dedication to e-learning in Lebanon." *The National*, April 21, 2020. https://www.thenational.ae/world/mena/palestinian-students-show-dedication-to-e-learning-in-lebanon-1.1008909.

Salih, Muhammad. "Abū al-'Aradāt mas'ūl Fatḥ sāḥat Lubnān, Abū al-'Aynayn li milaff al-lāji'īn wa-l-Maqdaḥ bilā ḥaqība al-tashkīlāt al-jadīda dākhil Fatḥ: irbāk dākhilī wa alghām khārijiyya [Abu al-'Aradat is in charge of Fatah on the Lebanese scene, Abu al-'Aynayn to assume the refugee file, and al-Maqdah is without a portfolio. New formations within Fatah: internal confusion and external land mines]." *al-Safir*, March 12, 2010.

———. "Abū al-'Aradāt yatasallam mahāmmahu wa Abū al-'Aynayn intahat ṣalāḥiyātuhu [Abu al-'Aradat is handed his duties and Abu al-'Aynayn's powers expire]." *al-Safir*, March 3, 2010.

———. "Al-Maqdaḥ yastaqīl iḥtijājan 'alā tajāhul Abū Māzin. [Al-Maqdah resigns in protest of Abu Mazin's neglect]." *al-Safir*, November 7, 2005.

———. "Al-Maqdaḥ: natā'ij ījābiyya wa sa taẓhar 'alā ṣa'īd al-waḍa' al-ijtimā'ī li-l-Filasṭīnīīn [Al-Maqdah: Positive results that will be reflected on the social situation of the Palestinians]." *al-Safir*, November 22, 1996.

———. "Fatḥ tastash'ir al-khaṭar fī mukhayyam 'Ayn al-Ḥilwe wa tafūḍ Kamāl Madḥat al-marja'iyya al-sīāsiyya wa-l-amniyya [Fatah senses the danger in the 'Ayn al-Hilwe camp, and makes Kamal Madhat the political and security authority]." *al-Safir*, September 26, 2008.

———. "Hākadhā tamm istidrāj wa ta'dhīb al-Lubnānī al-shahīd Marwān 'īsā qabla taṣfīatihi fī 'Ayn al-Ḥilwe [This is the way in which the Lebanese martyr Marwān 'Isa was lured before his assassination in 'Ayn al-Hilwe]." *al-Safir*, April 7, 2015.

———. "Ittiṣāl bayna al-Maqdaḥ wa Abū Māzin wafd Filasṭīnī yanqul ajwā' al-tahdi'a ilā 'Ayn al-Ḥilwe [Calls made between al-Maqdah and Abu Mazin. A Palestinian delegation brings the atmosphere of ceasefire to 'Ayn al-Hilwe]." *al-Safir*, February 2, 2005.

———. "Mā hiya asbāb istiqālat al-'aqīd Munīr al-Maqdaḥ? Makhāwif min ḥarb bayna Fatḥ wa Jund al-sham! [What are the reasons behind Colonel Munir al-Maqdah's resignation? Fears of a war between Fatah and Jund al-Sham!]." *al-Safir*, July 31, 2004.

Sarkis, Claudette. "Yamanī tarāja'a 'an i'tirafātihi al-awwaliyya wa aqarra bi sammā'hi iqtirāḥan li ḍarb al-sifāra al-amrīkiyya [Yemeni retracts initial confessions and acknowledged overhearing a suggestion to bomb the American embassy]." *al-Nahar*, February 29, 2004.

Saul, Heather. "Syria Crisis: The Picture That Shows the True Extent of the Humanitarian Crisis Inside Palestinian Refugee Camp Yarmouk." *The Independent*, February 26, 2014. Accessed October 15, 2017. http://www.independent.co.uk/news/world/middle-east/syria-crisis-the-picture-that-shows-the-true-extent-of-the-devastation-inside-palestinian-refugee-9154455.html.

Shaqir, Muhammad. "Ijmā' rasmī 'alā taṣnīf al-jarīma bi-l-"munaẓẓama" wa-l-qirā'a al-siyāsiyya tastad'ī i'dād lā'iḥa bi-l-mustafīdīn [Official consensus of defining the crime as "organized" and the political analysis requires a mapping of possible benifciaries]." *al-Hayat*, July 10, 1999.

Slemrod, Annie. "No Accountability for Deadly Burj al-Barajneh Electrocutions." *The Daily Star*, February 18, 2012. Accessed May 27, 2017. http://www.dailystar.com.lb/News/Lebanon-News/2012/Feb-18/163745-no-accountability-for-deadly-burj-al-barajneh-electrocutions.ashx.

Sogge, Erling Lorentzen. "Palestinian Refugee First Responders Rush to Aid Beirut." *Middle East Report Online*, October 13, 2020. Accessed October 13, 2020. https://merip.org/2020/10/palestinian-refugee-first-responders-rush-to-aid-beirut/.

———. "The Youth of Balata: A Generation of Hopelessness." *Jadaliyya*, November 18, 2019. Accessed April 22, 2020. https://www.jadaliyya.com/Details/40236/The-youth-of-Balata-A-generation-of-hopelessness.

Statiyya, Abu Hassan. "Sibāq fī al-gharb 'alā 'itināq al-islām [An increase in the embracement of Islam in the West]." *Minbar al-Jihad* 139 (April 2015): 11–18.

Strickland, Patrick. "Double Displacement: Palestinians Flee Violence in Syria, then Lebanon." *Electronic Intifada*, September 3, 2015. Accessed October 22, 2017. https://electronicintifada.net/content/double-displacement-palestinians-flee-violence-syria-then-lebanon/14821.

Syrian Telegraph. "Junūd al-sitt Bahiyya al-Ḥarīrī yuṭliqūna tanẓīm Jund al-Shām bi ṭaba'tihi al-sūriyya fī madīnati Ḥumṣ wa jiwāriha [The soldiers of madame Bahiyya al-Hariri launch a Syrian version of the Jund al-Sham faction in the city of Homs and its surroundings]." *Syrian Telegraph*, January 5, 2013. Accessed September 15, 2017. http://www.syriantelegraph.com/?p=62479.

The Daily Star. "Palestinian, 23, Self-immolates over UNRWA Aid Cuts." *The Daily Star*, January 12, 2016. Accessed July 12, 2017. http://www.dailystar.com.lb/News/Lebanon-News/2016/Jan-12/331471-palestinian-23-self-immolates-over-unrwa-aid-cuts.ashx.

Times of Israel. "Rallying Masses in Lebanon, Hamas Leader Threatens Rockets on Tel Aviv." *Times of Israel*, September 7, 2020. Accessed September 26, 2020. https://www.timesofisrael.com/rallying-masses-in-lebanon-hamas-leader-threatens-rockets-on-tel-aviv/.

Usher, Graham. "Arafat and the Palestinian Refugees." *Middle East International*, October 15, 1999.

Wikalat al-Quds li-l-Anba'. "Abū ʿArab li al-Quds li-l-Anbā': sa yurāfiq taslīm al-Maqdisī intishār al-amniyya fī aḥyā' ʿAyn al-Ḥilwe [Abu ʿArab to al-Quds li-l-anba': The handing over of [the] Maqdisi [prayer room] will be followed by the deployment of the security [force] in the neighborhoods of ʿAyn al-Hilwe]." *Wikalat al-Quds li-l-Anba'*, July 5, 2015. Accessed October 20, 2017. http://alqudsnews.net/post/76543.

———. "al-Amniyya tu'ajjil intishāraha fī ḥayy Ḥiṭṭīn bi ʿAyn al-Ḥilwe [The Security (Force) postpones its deployment in the Hittin neighborhood in ʿAyn al-Hilwe]." *Wikalat al-Quds li-l-Anba'*, July 8, 2015. Accessed October 20, 2017. http://alqudsnews.net/post/75337.

———. "al-Ṣaḥāfa al-Lubnāniyya: al-amniyya amām imtiḥān faʿliyyātiha fī ʿAyn al-Ḥilwe ... wa-l-dirāsa tatajjih naḥwā ta'jīl [The Lebanese Press: The Security [Force] is before an examination of its efficiency in ʿAyn al-Hilwe ... and the study is moving towards postponement]." *Wikalat al-Quds li-l-Anba'*, August 13, 2015. Accessed October 21, 2017. http://alqudsnews.net/post/78156.

———. "Al-Rifāʿī: Hal al-maṭlūb tadmīr ʿAyn al-Ḥilwe bi adawāt Filasṭīniyya? [al-Rifaʿi: Is the goal to destroy the ʿAyn al-Hilwe camp with Palestinian instruments?" *Wikalat al-Quds li-l-anba'*, August 25, 2015. Accessed October 22, 2017. http://alqudsnews.net/post/78773.

———. "al- Ṣaḥāfa al-lubnāniyya: mīthāq sharaf bayna al-Shabāb al-Muslim wa-l-Quwā al-Islāmiyya li taḥṣīn ʿAyn al-Ḥilwe [The Lebanese press: A Charter of honor between al-Shabab al-Muslim and the Islamic Forces to improve ʿAyn al-Hilwe]." *Wikalat al-Quds li-l-Anba'* December 7, 2015. Accessed October 25, 2017. http://alqudsnews.net/post/83749.

———. "Kayfa 'haraba' tujjār al-mukhaddirāt min mukhayyam Shātīlā? [How did the drug dealers in the Shatila camp 'escape'?]." *Wikalat al-Quds lil-anba'*, September 30, 2016. Accessed December 26, 2017. http://alqudsnews.net/post/98684.

———. "Khaṭṭāb: la niyya wa la maṣlaḥa la aḥad bi istifzāz al-jaysh aw al-taṣādum ma'hu [Khattab: No one has any intention, or stands anything to gain from provoking the army or clashing with it]." *Wikalat al-Quds li-l-Anbda'*, September 22, 2016. Accessed October 26, 2017. http://alqudsnews.net/post/98302.

———. "Lubnān sayuṭālib UNRWA bi dafaʿ 163 milyūn dūlār fī mu'atamar al-daʿm fī-l-Rūm [Lebanon will ask UNRWA to pay 163 million dollars at the donor conference in Rome]." *Wikalat al-Quds lil-anba'*, March 13, 2018. Accessed September 25, 2020. http://alqudsnews.net/post/123347.

Worth, Robert F. "5 Soldiers Killed in Lebanon Bombing." *The New York Times*, September 29, 2008. Accessed April 4, 2020. https://www.nytimes.com/2008/09/30/world/middleeast/30lebanon.html.

Yaghi, Subhi Mundhir. "Tanẓīm Jund al-Shām ʿalā ʿalāqa taḥālufiyya wathīqa bi Fatḥ al-Islām [The Jund al-Sham organization has a close alliance with Fatah al-Islam]." *al-Nahar*, June 8, 2007.

———. "ʿUṣbat al-Anṣār tusayṭir ʿalā aḥyā'in bi kāmiliha fī ʿAyn al-Ḥilwe [ʿUsbat controls neighborhood in their entirety in ʿAyn al-Hilwe]." *al-Nahar*, May 5, 2007.

Yasin, Burhan. "ʿUṣbat al-Anṣār min ʿiṣāba musallaḥa ilā ʿāmil al-istqrār fī Lubnān [ʿUsbat al-Ansar from armed gang to agent of stability in Lebanon]." *Laji-net -*

Palestinian Refugees News Network in Lebanon, April 5, 2013. Accessed August 3, 2017. http://laji-net.net/arabic/default.asp?ContentID=18950&menuID=31.

Young, Michael. "Future Shock." *Slate Magazine*, June 2003. Accessed September 24, 2020. http://www.slate.com/articles/news_and_politics/international_papers/2003/06/future_shock.html.

Zaatari, Mohammed. "3 Dead, 18 Wounded in Clashes Following Assassination Attempt in Ain al-Hilweh." *The Daily Star*, August 23, 2015. Accessed October 21, 2015. https://www.dailystar.com.lb/News/Lebanon-News/2015/Aug-22/312316-1-fatah-member-killed-in-clashes-following-assassination-attempt-in-ain-al-hilweh.ashx#.

———. "Ain al-Hilweh Cases toward Normalcy, Schools Open." *Daily Star*, September 25, 2018. Accessed October 2, 2020. https://www.dailystar.com.lb/News/Lebanon-News/2018/Sep-25/464365-ain-al-hilweh-eases-toward-normalcy-schools-open.ashx

———. "Ansar Allah Leader Resigns in 'Cry' against Hezbollah." *The Daily Star*, July 20, 2015.

———. "Fatah Groups Unify in Ain al-Hilweh." *The Daily Star*, March 29, 2012.

———. "Hammoud Mediates for Hezbollah and Ansar Allah." *The Daily Star*, December 7, 2012. Accessed September 25, 2017. http://www.dailystar.com.lb/News/Lebanon-News/2012/Dec-07/197542-hammoud-mediates-for-hezbollah-and-ansar-allah.ashx.

Zuʿaytar, Haytham. "al-ṭayf al-siyāsī al-Filasṭīnī yujassid khāriṭat Filasṭīn al-siyāsiyya wal-jaghrāfiyya bi daʿwa min al-iʿlāmī Haytham Zuʿaytar [The Palestinian political spectrum embodies Palestine's political and geographical map, at the invitation of journalist Haytham Zuʿaytar] " Janobiyat, October 8, 2013. Accessed December 18, 2016. http://www.janobiyat.com/news1/
الطيف-السياسي-الفلسطيني-يجسد-خارطة-فلسطين-السياسية-والجغرافية-بدعوة-من-الإعلامي-هيثم-عيترز

———. "Ittiṣālāt mutalāḥiqa li taṭwīq dhuyūl aḥdāth minṭaqat Taʿmīr ʿAyn al-Ḥilwe [Successive calls to tie the loose ends of the events of the Taʿmīr area of ʿAyn al-Hilwe]." *al-Liwa*, July 9, 2006.

———. "Maqtal amīr Fatḥ al-Islām Awaʿḍ wa Mubārak khilāl muṭāradat al-jaysh al-lubnānī lahum fī Shtūra [The murder of Fatah al-Islam's emir Awaʿd and Mubarak during their ousting by the Lebanese army from Shtura]." *Janobiyat*, August 17, 2010. Accessed September 15, 2017. http://janobiyat.com/oldsite/index.php?s=news&id=15823.

Reports, Press Releases, and Legal Documents

Abdelnour, Ziad K. "Syria's Proxy Forces in Iraq." *Middle East Intelligence Bulletin* 5, no. 4 (April 2003). https://www.meforum.org/meib/articles/0304_s2.htm.

Chaaban, Jad, Hala Ghattas, Rima Habib, Sari Hanafi, Nadine Sahyoun, Nisreen Salti, Karin Seyfert, and Nadia Naamani. "Socio-Economic Survey of Palestinian Refugees in Lebanon." Beirut: American University of Beirut and UNRWA 2010. Accessed April 20, 2017. https://www.unrwa.org/userfiles/2011012074253.pdf.

Chaaban, Jad, Nisreen Salti, Hala Ghattas, Alexandra Irani, Tala Ismail, Lara Batlouni. "Survey of the Socioeconomic Status of Palestine Refugees in Lebanon 2015." Beirut: The American University of Beirut/UNRWA 2016.

Gambill, Gary C. "Ain al-Hilweh: Lebanon's 'Zone of Unlaw.'" *Middle East Intelligence Bulletin* 5, no. 6 (2003). https://www.meforum.org/meib/articles/0306_l1.htm.

———. "Dossier: Mounir al-Maqdah Former Fatah Commander." *Middle East Intelligence Bulletin* 5, no. 7 (July 2003). https://www.meforum.org/meib/articles/0307_pald.htm.

Geneva Call. "Lebanon: Inauguration of the Legal Training Center in Ain al-Hilweh Refugee Camp." 2014. Accessed October 10, 2020 https://www.genevacall.org/lebanon-inauguration-legal-training-center-ain-al-hilweh-refugee-camp/

———. "Palestinian Refugee Camps in Lebanon: An Interview with Wissam Al Saliby, One of Geneva Call's Trainer." 2015. Accessed October 10, 2020. https://www.genevacall.org/palestinian-refugee-camps-lebanon-training-armed-security-forces-human-rights-interview-wissam-al-saliby-one-geneva-calls-trainer/.

Human Rights Watch. "Hizballah Implicated in South Lebanon Kidnappings." Human Rights Watch, 2000. http://pantheon.hrw.org/legacy/english/docs/2000/06/26/lebano556.htm.

———. "Lebanon: Sectarian Attacks in Tripoli: Threats to Alawites Increase as Tensions Mount." 2013. Accessed October 11, 2020. https://www.hrw.org/news/2013/12/19/lebanon-sectarian-attacks-tripoli.

International Amensty. "Amnesty International Report 2005—Lebanon." 2005. Accessed August 19, 2017. http://www.refworld.org/docid/429b27ea14.html

International Crisis Group. "Nurturing Instability: Lebanon's Palestinian Refugee Camps." International Crisis Group 2009. Accessed July 19, 2017. https://www.crisisgroup.org/middle-east-north-africa/eastern-mediterranean/lebanon/nurturing-instability-lebanon-s-palestinian-refugee-camps.

Israel Ministry of Foreign Affairs. "Iran and Syria as Strategic Support for Palestinian Terrorism." 2002. Accessed February 12, 2020. https://mfa.gov.il/mfa/foreignpolicy/iran/supportterror/pages/iran%20and%20syria%20as%20strategic%20support%20for%20palestinia.aspx.

Lebanese Palestinian Dialogue Committee, Central Administration of statistics, and Palestinian Central Bureau of Statistics. "Key Findings of the National Population and Housing Census of Palestinian Camps and Gatherings in Lebanon 2017." Beirut: The Lebanese Palestinian Dialogue Committee 2017. Accessed December 31, 2017. http://lpdc.gov.lb/statements/key-findings-of-the-national-population-and-housin/398/en.

Lebanese Republic Judicial Council. "Judgement in the Case of the Homicide of Sheikh Nizar al-Halabi (English translation)." Beirut: Lebanese Republic Judicial Council 1997.

McLaurin, R.D. "The Battle of Sidon." Maryland: U.S. Army Human Engineering Laboratory 1989, 76.

Middle East Intelligence Bulletin. "Palestinians in Lebanon Prepare to Resume Armed Struggle." *Middle East Intelligence Bulletin* 2, no. 4 (April 2000). https://www.meforum.org/meib/articles/0004_l4.htm.

Refugee Council, Norwegian. "Palestinian Refugees' Right to Inherit under the 2001 Amendment Law—Beirut Test Case." 2016. Accessed December 13, 2017. https://www.nrc.no/globalassets/pdf/reports/palestinian-refugees-right-to-inherit-under-the-2001-amendment-law.pdf.

Saab, Y. Bilal and Magnus Ranstorp. "Al-Qaeda's Terrorist Threat to UNIFIL." The Brookings Institution/Center for Asymmetrical Warfare Threat Studies 2007. Accessed September 4, 2017. https://www.brookings.edu/wp-content/uploads/2016/06/20070608saab_ranstorp.pdf.

Saleh, Mohsen and al-Hassan Ziyad. *The Political Views of the Palestinian Refugees in Lebanon: As Reflected in May 2006*. Beirut: al-Zaytouna Centre for Studies & Consultations, 2006.

State of Palestine. "The Implementation of UNGA Resolution 194/International Support to UNRWA Is a Must." Negotiation Affairs Department 2018. Accessed January 3,

2019. https://www.nad.ps/en/publication-resources/special-reports/implementation-unga-resolution-194-international-support-unrwa.
Thrall, Nathan and Robert Blecher. "Lebanon's Palestinian Dilemma: The Struggle over Nahr al-Bared." International Crisis Group 2012. Accessed October 12, 2017. https://www.crisisgroup.org/middle-east-north-africa/eastern-mediterranean/israelpalestine/next-war-gaza-brewing-heres-how-stop-it.
Tuastad, Dag. "Hamas' Concept of a Long-Term Ceasefire: A Viable Alternative to Full Peace?" Oslo: Peace Research Institute Oslo (PRIO) 2010. Accessed October 1, 2017. https://www.prio.org/Publications/Publication/?x=7277.
United Nations General Assembly. "Report of the Working Group on the Financing of the United Nations Relief and Works Agency for Palestine Refugees in the Near East." 2019. Accessed January 3, 2019. https://undocs.org/pdf?symbol=en/A/74/337.
UN Habitat/UN Development Programme. "Investigating Grey Areas: Access to Basic Urban Services in the Adjacent Areas of Palestinian Refugee Camps in Lebanon." Beirut: UN Habitat/UN Development Programme 2010. Accessed July 30, 2017. https://unhabitat.org/investigating-grey-areas-access-to-basic-urban-services-in-the-adjacent-areas-of-palestinian-refugee-camps-in-lebanon/.
UNRWA. "Protection Brief Palestine Refugees Living in Lebanon." Beirut: UNRWA 2017. Accessed December 14, 2017. https://www.unrwa.org/sites/default/files/lebanon_protection_brief_october_2017.pdf.
———. "Working at UNRWA." 2017. https://www.unrwa.org/careers/working-unrwa.
U.S. Department of State. "Terrorist Designation of Fatah al-Islam Associate Usamah Amin al-Shihabi." Bureau of Counterterrorism and Countering Violent Extremism 2013. Accessed July 19, 2017. https://www.state.gov/j/ct/rls/other/des/266563.htm.

Films and Videos

Abourahme, Dahna. "Kingdom of Women: Ein el Hilweh [Mamlakat al-nisā': ʿAyn al-Ḥilwe]." Beirut: Protraction Film, 2010.
Ahmad, Faris. "Filasṭīn qalb al-umma: ḥalqa khāṣṣa maʿ nā'ib al-amīn al-ʿāmm li ḥarakat Anṣār Allāh [Palestine is the heart of the Umma: A special episode with deputy general-secreatry of the Ansar Allah movement]." *al-Thabat Channel*, January 29, 2016. Accessed September 22, 2017. https://www.youtube.com/watch?v=tsD8boVty_s&t=2s.
Al-Arabiya. "Televised Interview with Shahade Jawhar." *Al-Arabiya*, December 7, 2007.
Al-Mayadeen. "Ḥiwār al-sāʿa - khalfiyyāt faṣl al-Līnō min ḥarakat Fatḥ wa-l-khilāfāt al-Filasṭīniyya dākhil al-mukhayyamāt [The talk of the hour - The background of al-Lino's dismissal from the Fatah movement and the Palestinian conflicts inside the camps]." *al-Mayadeen*, October 8, 2013. Accessed December 21, 2017. https://www.youtube.com/watch?v=p7hKtAZXa5g&t=1650s.
Khattab, Jamal. "al-Khuṭṭa al-mumnajiha li tadmīr ʿAyn al-Ḥilwe … wa-l-hadaf? [The systematic plan to destroy ʿAyn al-Hilwe … and the goal?] [Friday Sermon]." *Al-Risala*, August 25, 2017. Accessed October 28, 2017. https://www.youtube.com/watch?v=-6PB8WCEG-w&t=877s.
Saida TV. "al-Ḥarāk al-Shaʿbī yaqūm bi jawla fī mukhayyam ʿAyn al-Ḥilwe wa yaltaqī al-Līnō wa-l-Maqdaḥ [The Popular Movement does a tour of the ʿAyn al-Hilwe camp and visits Lino and al-Maqdah]." *Saida TV*, July 29, 2015. Accessed October 20, 2017. https://www.youtube.com/watch?v=6bpjx8rD1PU.

Saida TV. "Bi-l-fīdīū … kalimat al-liwā' Munīr al-Maqdaḥ fī-l-mu'tamar al-sha'bī fī 'Ayn al-Ḥilwe bi tārīkh 2015-9-6 [In the video … the speech of Major-General Munir al-Maqdah in the People's Conference in 'Ayn al-Hilwe on the date 2015–9–6]." 2015. https://www.youtube.com/watch?v=lp9uAXeWuJ4&t=66s.

Dissertations

Kassem, Valerie Nader. "Upgrading Informal Settlements: The Case of Taamir." MA diss., American University of Beirut, 2018.

Skare, Erik. "Faith, Awareness, and Revolution: A History of Palestinian Islamic Jihad." PhD diss., University of Oslo, 2020.

Strindberg, Anders. "From the River to the Sea: Honour, Identity and Politics in Historical and Contemporary Palestinian Rejectionism." PhD diss., University of St. Andrews, 2001.

Index

www.ingramcontent.com/pod-product-compliance
Lightning Source LLC
Chambersburg PA
CBHW071354290326
41932CB00045B/1850